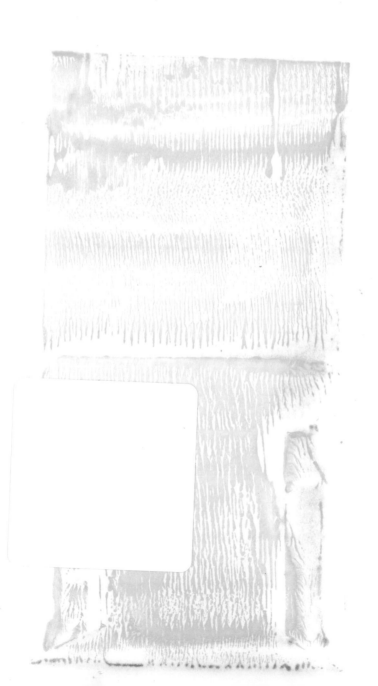

THE
AMERICAN
THEATRE

AS SEEN BY ITS CRITICS

1752-1934

EDITED BY

MONTROSE J. MOSES

AND

JOHN MASON BROWN

COOPER SQUARE PUBLISHERS, INC.
NEW YORK   1967

Copyright 1934 by W. W. Norton & Company, Inc.
Copyright reassigned to John Mason Brown
Published 1967 by Cooper Square Publishers, Inc.
59 Fourth Avenue, New York, N. Y. 10003
Library of Congress Catalog Card No. 66-30782

Printed in the United States of America

TO

MONTROSE J. MOSES

A YOUNG SPIRIT,
A DEVOTED ENTHUSIAST,
A LEARNED AUTHORITY, A WISE CRITIC,
AND A VALUED FRIEND
WHOSE HAND WAS STILLED AS THIS
VOLUME NEARED COMPLETION.

CONTENTS

INTRODUCTION

I N A S M U C H as the writing of history and the writing of criticism have as little in common as an airplane view of the countryside has with the landscape that is seen through one's own window, it seems unnecessary to point out that such a collection of American dramatic criticism as the present volume represents does not pretend to be a history of the American theatre. Its concern is with our native theatre in performance, when its history is still in the process of being made, rather than with the entirely different theatre which survives in the text-books when that history has already been made and time has robbed it of its first night enthusiasms.

The word "theatre" is as loosely used as any word in the language. It is made to cover more kinds of entertainment than the most garrulous of Poloniuses could list. But the intentions of the Brothers Minsky and those of the directors of the Theatre Guild do not differ more markedly from one another than does the theatre behind the footlights from the theatre that is written about by the historians.

The historian of the drama is usually a learned person who, though stage-struck in his way, is compelled to do his playgoing in the library. The past is his province, and he performs an immense service in re-creating it, simplifying it, arranging it according to key men and pivotal tendencies, and giving it a logic it could never boast in its own time. But though he may have pored over every dusty manuscript that has contributed its mite to a nation's dramatic literature; though he may know the prints, the portraits, biographies and newspaper estimates of the thousand and one actors who have quickened the dramas he discusses; be an authority on the demolished playhouses in which notable productions have been made; and write in the sprightliest of sprightly styles, the simple fact remains that it is a librarian rather than an usher who has handed him the playbills he consults.

No audience surrounds him. No curtains are raised on unknown offerings which invite him as a playgoer to embark on an adventure. No houselights lower to reveal a production of which he becomes a part by merely having seen it. Like Tytyl he is forced to play at eating cakes, and presses his nose against the thick windowpanes of time to enjoy vicariously a feast at which he has not been present as a guest.

Even when he deals with productions he has himself witnessed, the historian is not apt to write of them until they have dimmed for him as actual experiences in the theatre; until they have taken their place in a different scheme of things; and the particularizing details which have made them real and vital to playgoers no longer stand in the way of the final judgment that time and perspective make possible. The very trivialities for which he may have been most grateful in the theatre of amusement have been lost sight of in favor of those dramas which, because they were possessed of literary excellence or themes of some importance, are bound to be the ones he must depend upon to justify his annals. Productions for him have ceased to be single evenings or isolated instances (as they always are to those who sit before them) and become against their will connectives in the special paragraphing of events which is known as history. Where they have once counted as complete experiences in the theatre, they now find themselves remembered as related episodes in the scenario of a plot which time has forced upon them.

In other words, the writer who functions as an historian of the theatre is apt to be one who has ceased to feel or think as a playgoer. Yet the history that he writes is the history of productions which have deserved to win their place in his records because of what they have meant to audiences who have seen them in the theatre and judged them there by utterly different standards than the ones he now brings to them. The result of his research is unquestionably a chronicle of the stage, but the theatre that gains admittance to his pages is seldom, if ever, the same theatre which playgoers know, and which succeeds or fails according to the personal responses it awakens in them. It has lost its flesh and blood, its colors and its shadows, its hazards and its expectancy, its first-run meaning, and the men and women on both sides of the footlights who give it its point and its appeal. The theatre's present being in many ways the shortest present known to any of the arts and having a stubborn habit of slipping into the past of each person who has shared it with the lowering of the final curtain on any night's performance of any play, the theatre of the historian is bound to be a different theatre from the one that playgoers know, and to bear the same relationship to it that a half-tone reproduction of a painting does to the original.

For that very reason a collection of American dramatic criticism such as the present volume represents may not be without its value. It neither is, nor pretends to be, a history of the American theatre. But incomplete as it must be when crowded into the space of a single volume, it does perhaps offer an instructive supplement—or shall we say antidote?—to the works of historians. For whatever else may be said against the dramatic critics—and plenty has been said against them since the beginning of time—they have at least done their playgoing in the theatre. Even when it is their recollections upon which they draw, as William Winter does in the critical estimates he writes of Charlotte Cushman and Mary Anderson many years after he has seen them, or as J. Ranken Towse does in his discussions of the acting of Edwin Booth and Ada Rehan, it is clear that these memories are based upon the first-hand impressions of men who have gained them in the presence of the footlights. That matters immensely from the theatre's point of view, and gives to the most ephemeral of journalistic reactions, which have been formed in the same way, a documentary interest that time cannot dim for those who are interested in discovering what the theatre of yesterday, or of last season, or of a hundred and fifty years ago, was like when, in its own ephemeral way, it was attempting to cast its theatrical spell.

It was James Agate's *The English Dramatic Critics—1660-1932* which paved the way for the present collection of American dramatic criticism. But where Mr. Agate's chief, and quite justifiable, concern was the critics whose works he was assembling, we have endeavored to make our selections not only on the basis of what is characteristic of the critics whose writings we have included but also on the basis of what happens to have been typical of the theatre about which they have written. Even when assembled with such an aim in view, this record of first-hand impressions can make no claims to completeness. It can only hope to suggest the story it has been bold enough to tell by touching upon a few of its high-spots. Of necessity it must depend

upon the mercy of the reader. For in seeking to give in one volume a
sense of the emerging American theatre that contemporary playgoers
have seen, it has committed many sins of omission which, though they
may be unpardonable, have in reality been unavoidable. No library
shelf is large enough to hold the books that would be needed to do
proper justice to all of the dramatists and producers, the actors and
playhouses, the productions and designers—yes, and the critics, too—
that in their day have figured prominently in the annals of the American stage.

As New York City has for so long a time been the distributing
agent and the theatrical capital of America, it has seemed both practical and advisable to rely in the majority of cases upon the critics of
New York for the picture of the American stage which is given in
the following pages. To narrow that selection even more it has been
necessary, with a few notable exceptions, to choose only from the
writings of those men who have, for a time at least, attended the
theatre as professional observers.

Naturally enough, these critics have brought many different
standards and many different points of view to their work. Some of
them have been content to write merely as reporters. Many of them
have been faced with the pressure of early dead-lines and come straight
from theatres to their offices to review the night's opening for the
next day's papers. Others have been contributors to weeklies and
monthlies and have had their chance to record their reactions in a
more leisurely fashion. Some of them have undertaken critical estimates or pen portraits of playwrights, actors and producers; others
have had occasion to deplore the miserable state of the stage, to describe the audiences in which they have found themselves, to deal with
the function of dramatic criticism, to tap their memories in their
autumn years, to reconsider their first judgments in Saturday or Sunday articles, to appraise the work of distinguished foreign visitors, to
cover burlesque shows or musical comedies, to discuss the nature of
contemporary tragedy and comedy, to have their say in chapters from
their books, to take the theatre seriously as an art, or to report its
box-office possibilities for the trade journals in the vivid language that
is peculiar to Broadway.

By sampling the work of these reviewers one follows a playgoer's chronicle of the American stage that has the virtue of being recorded by eye-witnesses. The story they tell is the story of a theatre, which though it begins in the eighteenth century as a colonial institution based upon British models, gradually emerges, by the time the nineteenth century has faded into the twentieth, as the indisputably native product we know today. Little by little American types and American themes begin to find their way behind the footlights, and the dramatists who have brought them there become more interested in what they have to say for themselves than in what they may have given others to say. The actor's theatre that flourished in this country from the coming of the Hallams down to the seventies of the last century; the theatre in which audiences gladly assembled to see great performers make their points in famous plays, ceases to be the theatre of the actor and turns into the theatre of the playwright. The theatre of Edwin Forrest and the Booths, of Charlotte Cushman and Mary Anderson, is metamorphosed into the theatre of George S. Kaufman and Eugene O'Neill. Realism and the drama of the idea replaces the robustious romanticism of the earlier stage. The Ibsen controversy is fought here with almost the same bitterness it was fought abroad. And here, too, it marks the closing of one period in dramatic history and the dawning of another.

As tastes in playwriting have changed and the kitchen and the cottage, the drawing-room and the stoop of a brown-stone front have become accepted substitutes for Elsinore and the Roman forum, the actor's approach to his craft has undergone appropriate alterations. What was magniloquent in his style has dwindled to meet the new demands of new playwrights. The actor has also turned realist, and his performances are no longer subjected to those detailed appraisals which were once the common concern of criticism. As he is seldom seen in parts about which playgoers know anything in advance, reviewers are rarely able to judge him by the comparative standards that used to be among their chief delights. The result is, as far as the reviewing is concerned, that the actor has tended to become a last paragraph figure, or at best the subject of portrait sketches which attempt to catch the essence of either his acting or his personality, but which no longer challenge his reading of particular lines or question at any length his contributions as an interpreter.

When the American theatre was in its infancy and Washington Irving, with a bow to Addison and Sir Roger de Coverley, was writing his Jonathan Oldstyle letters for his brother's paper, *The Morning Chronicle,* he came near to stating the critical ideal of his day by inventing a correspondent, known as Andrew Quoz, who challenged the presumptions of the New York reviewers in 1801 in the following terms. "Let me ask them one question," demanded Quoz. "Have they ever been to Europe? Have they ever seen a Garrick, a Kemble, or a Siddons? If they have not, I can assure you, (upon the words of two or three of my friends, *the actors,*) they have no right to the title of critics."

Since that time not only have critical requirements altered but the American critic is no longer obliged to go to London because most of the important figures of the stages of London and the world have come to America. From the early visits of Kean and Kemble to the recent appearances of Moissi and the Moscow Art Theatre, the American stage has been enlivened by the presence of many distinguished foreigners and just as many foreign influences. These have reshaped its course; given it new standards of excellence at which to aim in acting, playwriting, production and stage design; and found it operating as a clearing house for international ideas. So important to the development of our native stage have these outside influences been that some of them must find a place in any volume which attempts to tell the story of the American theatre in performance.

All of them did not meet with hospitable receptions. Some of them caused much hostile ink to flow and, occasionally, as in the case of the famous Astor Place Riot, that ink was reddened by the blood of misguided patriots. Ibsen, in particular, and after him the so-called New Movement, with its revolutionary aims in settings and direction, invited sharp alignments and found the old men defending their memories of the theatre as they had first known it and the younger ones battling for the theatre as they saw it might be. But all of these foreign influences, these distinguished players and troupes, these new tendencies, and innovations in thought and method which have touched these shores from season to season have played a vital part in making the American theatre what it now is.

In following that theatre's development in terms of its contemporary criticism it is interesting to see how many men, who are remembered for other things than their reviewing, have sat in judgment in our playhouses. They, too, have worked as journalists, recording their own first-hand reactions to the plays and players they have seen, and writing—as most of the men represented in this volume have written—when what they had to say still had "news" value for their readers.

The date lines on the copy of these critics are important. They were the *raisons d'être* of many of the pieces which have been taken from the yellow files of old newspapers and reprinted here. Most of the men included in this book have written with no thought of being read when their "stuff" has lost its timeliness. Their concern has been whatever readers they might have on the date of publication and the theatre they were bringing to them. In terms of the truth as they have seen it and been able to express it, they have, without meaning to, preserved in the amber of print the likeness of an art which is fated to leave no other permanent record of itself behind than the impressions of it which have been written down by those who have experienced its performances. For that very reason these critics can help us to recapture a sense of what our theatre of the past has been like when it has still belonged in the theatre. With their different vocabularies, their different standards, their different personalities, their different assignments and their different aims, these men have been as much the product of their times as the theatre has been which they have covered.

JOHN MASON BROWN

THE AMERICAN THEATRE

THE
AMERICAN THEATRE

PROLOGUE

T O this new world, from fam'd Britannia's shore,
Through boist'rous seas where foaming billows roar,
The Muse, who Britons charm'd for many an age,
Now sends her servants forth to tread the stage;
Britain's own race, though far removed, to show
Patterns of every virtue they should know.
Though gloomy minds through ignorance may rail,
Yet bold examples strike where languid precepts fail.

The world's a stage, where mankind act their parts;
The stage a world to show their various arts;
While th' soul, touch'd by Nature's tend'rest laws,
Has all her passions rous'd in Virtue's cause.
Reason we hear, and coolly will approve,
But all's inactive till the passions move.
Such is the human mind, so weak, so frail,
"Reason's her chart, but passion is her gale."
Then raise the gale to waft fair Virtue o'er
The sea of life where Reason points the shore.
But ah! let Reason guide the course along,
Lest Passion, list'ning to some siren's song,

Rush on the rocks of Vice, where all is lost,
And shipwreck'd Virtue renders up the ghost.

Too oft, we own, the stage with dangerous art,
In wanton scenes has played the siren's part.
Yet if the Muse, unfaithful to her trust,
Has sometimes strayed from what is pure and just,
Has she not oft, with awful, virtuous rage,
Struck home at vice and nobly trod the stage—
Made tyrants weep, the conscious murderer stand
And drop the dagger from his trembling hand?
Then, as you treat a favorite fair's mistake,
Pray spare her foibles for her virtue's sake
And while her chastest scenes are made appear—
For none but such will find admittance here—
The Muse's friends, we hope, will join our cause
And crown our best endeavors with applause.

WRITTEN BY JOHN SINGLETON AND
SPOKEN BY MR. RIGBY ON THE EVE-
NING OF SEPTEMBER 5, 1752, AT THE
THEATRE IN WILLIAMSBURG, VIRGINIA.

AN EVENING AT THE JOHN STREET THEATRE

Jane Shore

By *CRITICUS*

MR. CHILDS

Upon Friday evening last, curiosity and a respect for theatrical exhibitions, engaged my attention: The tragedy of Jane Shore was acted—the tears of many of the female part of the audience occasioned by the pictured distresses of Shore and Alicia, are urgent proofs that the actresses understood the parts they performed.

The character of Shore was well supported by Mrs. Harpur: The plaintive tone of voice, the mien, the gesture, the countenance of this lady, were strikingly descriptive of the object she personated. The last tragic scene of affliction and death, were so admirably depicted, that had the *grim tyrant* himself come upon the stage, he would have felt a jealousy lest so formidable a rival should have encroached on his gloomy dominions!—She seems, however, to have been off her guard for a moment, when Gloster tells her "that Hastings stubbornly opposed his aims at royalty." She is not to be supposed to have had any knowledge that the children of Edward had so powerful a friend as Hastings. This intelligence favorable to her intention, coming upon her unexpectedly, and with surprise, should have rendered her answer animated and vigorous; not dull and languid.

Mrs. Kenna in such characters as Alicia, never fails to do them justice. To exhibit the tumultuous and turbulent passions of our nature in a masterly manner, appears to be her forte.—When she expresses anger, rage, indignation, horror, despair, you think you see a real image—you can scarcely suppose you behold a fictitious character. Nature seems to be actually convulsed. We should be pleased to see her oftener come upon the stage in some leading character. The gentleman who played the part of the infamous Richard certainly forgot himself; none of those quick rapid emotions; none of that fawning hypocrisy; none of those bloody and deceitful looks that hung about Gloster, and made him the terror of his age, were to be seen in you— your actions throughout partook of a dull and dispirited sameness— you seemed to present us with a picture of *Antoninus Pius,* or some such grave character.

CRITICUS

From *The Daily Advertiser* (New York),
March 27, 1787.

ROYALL TYLER'S *THE CONTRAST* [1]

By CANDOUR

MR. CHILDS

I was present last evening at the representation of *The Contrast,* and was very much entertained with it. It is certainly the production of a man of genius, and nothing can be more praise-worthy than the sentiments of the play throughout. They are the effusions of an honest patriot heart expressed with energy and eloquence. The characters are drawn with spirit, particularly Charlotte's; the dialogue is easy, sprightly, and often witty, but wants the pruning knife very much. The author has made frequent use of soliloquies, but I must own, I think, injudiciously; Maria's song and her reflections after it, are pretty, but certainly misplaced. Soliloquies are seldom so conducted as not to wound probability. If we ever talk to ourselves, it is when the mind is much engaged in some very interesting subject, and never to make calm reflections on indifferent things. That part of her speech which respects Dimple, might be retained; she may very well be supposed to talk on so material a subject to her own happiness, even when alone, and her feelings, upon a marriage with a man she has every reason to despise and abhor, are very well painted. Col. Manly's advice to America, tho' excellent, is yet liable to the same blame, and perhaps greater. A man can never be supposed in conversation with himself, to point out examples of imitation to his countrymen: at the same time the thoughts are so just, that I should be sorry they were left out entirely, and I think they might be introduced with greater propriety, in the conversation with Dimple.

I cannot help wishing the author had given a scene between Dimple and Maria. The affronting coldness of Dimple's manner might have interested us for Maria, and would in some degree have supplied the greatest defect of the play, the want of interest and plot. We might then have been more easily reconciled to the sudden affection and declaration of love between Manly and Maria, which cannot

---

[1] *The Contrast* was the first comedy written by an American to be produced in this country. It was presented at the John Street Theatre, New York, by the American Company, April 16, 1787.

fail, as the play now is, to hurt our opinion of both. The author's great attention to the unity of time, which he has indeed very well preserved, has in some degree produced this sudden attachment.

Jessamy is a closer imitation of his master than is natural, and his language in general is too good for a servant; the character would have produced a better effect if he had been more awkward in his imitation. The satire of the play is in general just, but the ridicule of Lord Chesterfield's letters, should be well considered. If he is sometimes so attentive to his son's person as to mention too trifling things, let us remember that his letters were certainly never meant for the public eye, and we may forgive a father's tenderness even when he recommends how to cut the nails, and if we must allow that he appears more solicitous to form his son's manners than his heart, (which might arise from thinking him more deficient in the one than the other), let us not overlook his profound knowledge of the world, the excellent sense and most admirable style of his letters.

Jonathan's going to the play, and his account of it, is a very happy thought, and very well drawn. The laughing gamut has much humour, but is dwelt rather too much upon, and sometimes degenerates into farce. To point out the many beauties of the play, tho' an agreeable, would be an unnecessary task, the unceasing plaudits of the audience did them ample justice, and it cannot fail, if judiciously curtailed, being a great favorite. The play was preceded by a good prologue, which was very well spoken by Wignell, but the effect much spoilt by the unskilfulness of the prompter. It was very well acted. Mrs. Morris gave the sprightly lively coquet, with great ease and elegance, and if Wignell had not quite the right pronunciation of Jonathan, he made ample amends by his inimitable humour. Upon the whole the defects of the play are so much overbalanced by its merits, that I have made no scruple of mentioning those which occurred to me, and I have done so the rather, because I think in general they may be easily remedied, and that the piece, particularly when considered as the first performance, does the greatest credit to the author, and must give pleasure to the spectator.

CANDOUR

From *The Daily Advertiser,*
April 18, 1787.

WILLIAM DUNLAP'S *THE FATHER*

T H E principal part of the entertainment at the *Theatre,* on Monday evening, was the new comedy, entitled *The Father, or American Shandyism,* the production of an American, a young gentleman of this city.—This circumstance occasioned a crowded house; and from the reiterated plaudits which followed almost every exhibited incident, it is presumed that the public has very seldom been gratified in a higher degree.

The parts were very judiciously assigned, and supported with great animation and propriety.

The *Prologue* and *Epilogue* were finely adapted, and their delivery received uncommon applause.

A correspondent observes that sentiment, wit and *comique* humour are happily blended in that most ingenious performance *The Father, or American Shandyism,* nor is that due proportion of the pathetic which interests the finest feelings of the human heart, omitted. The happy allusions to characters and events, in which every friend to our country feels interested—and those traits of benevolence which are brought to view in the most favourable circumstances, conspired to engage, amuse, delight, and instruct the audience through five acts of alternate anticipations, and agreeable surprises.—This *Comedy* bids fair to be a favorite entertainment, and a valuable acquisition to the stage.

From *The Gazette of the United States,*
September 9, 1789.

DUNLAP'S *DARBY'S RETURN*

T H E Entertainment at the Theatre [John Street], on Tuesday evening last, appeared, by the repeated plaudits, to give the fullest satisfaction to a very crouded house: The selections for the Evening were made with judgment—and animated by the presence of the illustrious personages, who honored the exhibition, the Players excited their best abilities. The Pieces performed, were the *Toy—The Critic,* and a new Comic Sketch, entitled *Darby's Return.* The latter piece is the production of the same ingenious hand, who hath already contributed so much to the entertainment of the public by *The Father, or American Shandyism. Darby's Return* is replete with the happiest illusions to interesting events, and very delicately turned compliments. On the appearance of *The President;* the audience rose, and received him with the warmest acclamations—the genuine effusions of the hearts of *Freemen.*

From *The Gazette of the United States,*
November 28, 1789.

KOTZEBUE'S *THE STRANGER*

L A S T evening *The Stranger* was introduced to the acquaintance of a crouded audience at our Theater, and received with a most hearty welcome. We think that no piece, since the *School for Scandal,* has made so favorable an impression upon the public as this Comedy. Mrs. Barrett made likewise her first appearance on our boards, and we trust we do not go too far, when we say that she was as well received as the Play—better could not be. Her powers seemed happily adapted to the character of Mrs. Haller; and for elegance of manner, dignity of deportment, and true pathos, there are very few in Europe or America who can surpass this first specimen of Mrs. Barrett's abilities. Mr. Cooper was at home in the Stranger.—But we did not set down to panegyrize the performers, only this we must say, that we have never had a play on our stage so ably supported in *all* its parts as *The Stranger.* The effect of the pathetic scenes was beyond any former example within our remembrance; and the concluding comic scene exceeded anything for the effect produced on the spectators, which we have witnessed for many years. Mrs. Barrett in the Epilogue gave proof of comic powers which prove her to be an invaluable acquisition to our Theatre. The after-piece of the *Adopted Child* seemed to be received with the zest of novelty, and Mr. Barrett's Michael did him great honor. On announcing the Play of *The Stranger* for the next night, the audience testified their approbation by huzzas.

From *The Commercial Advertiser* (New York),
December 11, 1798.

"MOURN, WASHINGTON IS DEAD"

THEATRICAL COMMUNICATION:[1]

Monday evening was presented, for the first
time, to *an overflowing house,*
The Robbery,
Translated from the French of Monvel;
With the after-piece of
The Ship-wreck

A B O U T 6 o'clock the band very improperly struck up "Wash-ington's March"; it was executed in a somewhat slow and lingering manner, but Mr. Hewit should certainly have remembered that no alteration in the mood can ever change a sharp key to a flat one.

In about 20 minutes the increasing impatience of the audience was relieved, by the curtains drawing up; it arose slowly and discov-ered the scenery all in black, with the words

MOURN,
WASHINGTON IS DEAD

in large letters painted on a black background.

A Monody was now spoken by Cooper; he came on, with a bow not the most graceful in the world, but with a countenance that seemed to say, *"If you have tears prepare to shed them now,"* and in truth never was an audience more predisposed to harmonize with *"sorrow's saddest note."* His tongue, however, soon counteracted every such emotion, for he began to speak in the very tones of Mrs. Mel-moth, artificial and declamatory, ending his lines with a full cadence of voice, exactly in the manner of that actress when she repeats her Black-bird Elegy. Still we were in hopes that as he went on, his feel-ings would have got the better of this schoolboy rehearsal and have enabled or rather betrayed him to do the poetry a little more justice; but ah! pitiful to relate, he had hardly exceeded thirty lines when *"Vox faucibus hæsit"* or in plain English, his words stuck in his throat, and he lost all power of recollecting a line further, we do not say *"Steruntque comæ,"* each *"particular hair stood on end,"* for the gentleman has such a decent share of what my Lord Chesterfield

---

[1] Washington died December 14, 1799, at Mount Vernon.

calls, *"modest assurance,"* that when every one in the house blushes
for him, he never blushes for himself. He edged a little nearer the
prompter, caught his cue and went on—stopt again—moved on a
word—stopt again—the ladies cast down their eyes—he caught another word, and went on—stopt again—the Pit groaned aloud, and a
small hiss began to issue from the gallery—when some good honest
fellow got up and clapped his hands, which encouraged our *favorite
Cooper* to start once more, and to go quite thro the piece, consisting
in all, perhaps of 60 or 70 lines, much to our own as well as his relief.
To add that he pronounced it very ill, after the above, is, we presume,
unnecessary, as no man can ever speak with propriety and effect,
whose whole attention is constantly occupied in the sole business of
recollection. If Mr. Cooper's sensibility is hurt at our remarks, his
conscience must at least acquiesce in their justice, for how will he
excuse it to us, that after having had the Monody in his possession
ten days, he has had the unparalleled assurance to present himself on
the stage in such a state of utter deficiency, as to call up the sympathetic emotions of shame in a whole auditory? If what we have now
said, is not sufficient to reclaim him, perhaps he may learn, when it is
too late, that he is not so firmly rooted in the *blind* affections of the
public as he has hitherto persuaded himself to believe.

The Robbery,

Is like several of our late most successful plays, of foreign growth,
but we should be sorry to feel or to express any prejudice against it
on that account. Having only seen it once represented, and not having had an opportunity to peruse either the original or a translation,
we hesitate to pronounce decisively on its merits, especially since we
observed that the principal character was so wretchedly filled, that
we could hardly tell what to make of it. The play has an excellent
moral, and the fourth act has much interesting incident. We hope the
manager will not give it up, because it went off rather coldly, for we
repeat it, we think this was owing in a great measure, if not entirely,
to the want of support in the character of Orlando.

Mr. Cooper *got thro with* the part of Orlando. We do not say that
he played ill from beginning to end, for he was so totally deficient in
point of recollection, that he could not fairly be said to play at all;

he not only mistook the name of his beloved mistress, (for he told Mrs. Melmoth to give his letter to *Julia*), but he was even obliged to look up to Jefferson to know when to set down. He was neither lover, son, or indeed any thing else—such playing is certainly beneath all criticism.

Lest, however, Mr. Cooper should pretend to think himself entitled to complain at the freedom of these remarks, we take this occasion to observe to him, that this asperity, as he may perhaps term it, is not provoked by his negligence of study this night only, but we have long with sincere regret remarked that his indolent indifference to please, has been growing upon him from the days when Mrs. Merry used to complain of his habitual inattention to his study, up to the present hour; we can adduce numerous instances in support of this charge, from the first time he appeared in King John (he will understand this!!) down to his Wieland, when it was absolutely necessary to remind him in the face of the audience, by Erlach and Emmy, that they were waiting for him to wish them joy. We have really been in hopes that Mr. C. would have profited by the hints we have occasionally given several of the performers on this subject; but since he has not chosen to do so, he must consider that he has drawn down our direct censure upon his own head. We have only to add, that if he will bestow a moderate share of industry upon his profession, he will find us as ready to applaud, as he may now think us to censure.

Mr. Hodgkinson played Count Raimond to the entire satisfaction of every person of just taste, and he more than once received the best marks of our sincere applause, that of *mute attention.* How much do actors mistake when they regard the *clapping of hands* as the most unequivocal tribute to their merit? Excepting in comic scenes, silence is ever the real index of the highest approbation. Too much credit cannot be given to Mr. H. for the admirable accuracy of *his* study, which indeed is correct to a degree we have scarcely witnessed in any other; and which certainly gives him a decided advantage in his acting, over those who are less perfect in this respect.

Mr. Hallam supported the Marquis with perfect propriety and effect. He recognizes his son with the sensibility of an affectionate parent, and the audience testified that they here felt his powers.

Mr. Martin, in Lord Edmund, played remarkably well, till somewhere near the close, when he became spiritless—and this too at a very important moment; we did not even hear the conclusion of his moral on the pernicious consequences of gaming. One fault, however, we cannot overlook, as it attended him from beginning to the end of the play—it was, that he spoke in so low a voice, and in such a kind of manner, that we heard little more than simply the emphatic word, in many, if not most of his sentences. Was it because he was imperfect in his role?

Mr. Tyler acquired great credit in Saint Germain, and made us wish the author had enabled him to preserve to the end that character of inflexible integrity, which he supports for so long a time. We will venture to recommend it to the translator that he take the liberty of deviating so far from the plan of the original, as to make St. Germain more consistent, for his honesty seems to give way all at once, without anything like an adequate temptation.

Mrs. Melmoth did very considerable justice to her part; she deserves our gratitude for her ceaseless endeavors to please, and for her very excellent study. The two last lines of her epilogue were particularly well pronounced.

Mrs. Hodgkinson, in the very difficult part of Clementina, is entitled to our unqualified praise. Altho entirely forsaken by her *stage lover* who seemed the only person in the house unmoved by her sorrows, unmelted at her woes, and who even looked upon her piteous state of delirium on his account with a stupid apathy, yet she continued to fill her character with wonderful powers and unusual effect—we certainly have no terms sufficiently warm to express our sentiment of her excellence. Her Clementina is only surpassed by her Ophelia, and in that we have heretofore said, we thot her unrivalled. We must, however, observe that in one speech of some length, in the early part of the play, she uttered her words much too rapidly, too "trippingly enough on the tongue," yet she should never forget "to use all gently," and "in the very tempest and whirlwind of passion to acquire a temperance that may give it smoothness."

The Shipwreck

Is above the common run of Afterpieces, altho it has many faults, and particularly a most lame conclusion. The scene opens with the view of a storm at sea, and soon after appears a ship in distress which is struck with lightning and is supposed to be wrecked.

We think it hardly worth our while to be particular in our remarks on this piece which has been so often played before and is well known to the public.

Mr. Hodgkinson in Harry Hawser afforded us much pleasure, but we think he drank *rather* too much brandy and staggered about a little too much. Martin filled the incongruous character of Goto with much discrimination, but 'tis certainly a motley thing, he is a conscientious thief and a moralizing assassin, notwithstanding which the author has very injudiciously attempted to excite our commiseration for him. Jefferson in Stave gave the part an effect which no other man could: but we should think after swigging his brandy he ought to appear a little more affected by it. We suggest to Mr. J. if it would not be an improvement. Mrs. Seymour was uncommonly successful in Sally Shamrock and sung charmingly. Miss E. Westray makes the prettiest Fanny in boy's cloaths we have ever seen. Angellica was unworthy our favorite Mrs. H. We could not help continually thinking of her father, nor were we much pleased at her having such a lover as Fox.

Crito

From *The Commercial Advertiser* (New York),
January 1, 1800.

CRITICS—CRITIQUES—PLAYS—PLAYERS

By WILLIAM DUNLAP

IN the year 1796, that memorable year in the theatrical history of the New World which gave to New York a band of distinguished actors, at the head of whom stood Mr. and Mrs. Johnson and Mr. Jefferson; and to Philadelphia, Mrs. Merry, and Messrs. Cooper and Warren; a company of critics was organized, who may not unaptly be characterized as sharp-shooters.

These gentlemen were regular frequenters of the New York theatre, enjoyed its productions as men of education and lovers of literature, and wished to correct the abuses existing in the costume, demeanour, and general conduct of the actors *on the stage*.

Messrs. John Wells, Elias Hicks, Samuel Jones, William Cutting, Peter Irving and Charles Adams formed themselves into a species of dramatic censorship, and by turns put down their remarks on the play of the evening, meeting *next* evening to criticise the critique, and give it passport to the press. The last named of these gentlemen was only distinguished as being the son and brother of presidents of the United States; others are known as distinguished by their own talents and attainments. They signed with the initials of their names, the *last* letter being the actual writer. Finding that these initials led to the detection of the offenders against the liberty of murdering plays at will, they inserted other letters to mislead, but still continued the last as the initial of the writer. The letter D is frequently inserted, although no person whose name begins with that letter belonged to, or wrote for, the club; the rogues intended to throw some of the credit on the writer of this work. We will review these effusions of the *box* critics of that day—for the pit had even then ceased to be the centre from which public opinion was to be enlightened on subjects of theatrical taste.

Farquhar's *Inconstant,* judiciously revived by Hodgkinson, they condemn; and do not approve Cumberland's *Wheel of Fortune,* a play which with Cooper's Penruddock, and other alterations of the cast, became a favourite. They speak respectfully of Mr. Hodgkinson's Penruddock, and of Mrs. Johnson's Emily Tempest—of Mr. Jefferson's Daw they say it had "confirmed the favourable impression he had made." Of Prigmore, who played Tempest, they say, "We have desisted from remarking on our old acquaintance, Prigmore, in the hope he might (at least by accident) afford us something to applaud. But that same uniformity of acting, which has ever characterized him, still continues, and we can find in him no other difference than may be found in a 'cocked up hat' and a 'hat cocked up.'" They speak of attempts behind the scenes *to get up* applause, by beginning to knock or clap, "whenever the manager has delivered anything extremely witty or sentimental. Whether it is by direction of him 'whose sole ambition is the lust of praise,' or proceeds from the officiousness of some candidate for managerial favour, we shall not pretend to determine." . . .

It appears by the remarks of this band of scalpers and tomahawkers on the *School for Scandal,* that they truly estimated its beauties and its immoralities, and that they had seen the play played in times past. They remark: "Though Mrs. Hallam in Lady Teazle, and Mr. Hallam in Sir Peter, equalled our expectations, we could not forget that Mr. and Mrs. Henry formerly appeared in those characters: we could not but remember that such things were, and were most precious to us." They praise Dibdin's *Quaker,* but justly remark that play-house representations of Quakers are unnatural, and generally disgusting.

It appears by Critique No. 8, that the body of critics had been called "Liar and assassin," but they say "they are none"—and go on as usual. They talk of Hodgkinson's *bawling,* and of "Poor Vulcan," that it is "insipid, tasteless, and unentertaining"—praising the "modest diffidence" of Miss Broadhurst in all she does.

In remarking on the comedy of *Know Your Own Mind,* and its performance, they ask, "Why was not the part of Miss Neville given to Mrs. Johnson, or Mrs. Hallam?" (It was played by Mrs. Cleveland.) "Where was Mr. Hallam when the part of Captain Bygrove was cast upon Mr. Munto, who, whenever he appears 'in uniform,' perpetually reminds us of a servant in livery." Madame Gardie, the fascinating dancer and pantomime actress, whose story ended so fatally in tragedy, played in this comedy a *speaking part,* Madame Larouge, and was "perfectly natural." They laugh at the manager's apology for the nonappearance of a performer, who he said could not appear, but "at the risk of her life and future health."

Cumberland's *Jew* was performed, March 21st, 1796, and Hodgkinson played Sheva with that versatile excellence which rendered him so remarkable, and after it, his Walter in the *Children in the Wood,* showed even superior powers. Miss Harding and Master Stockwell were the children—the first, Mr. Hodgkinson's ward, a pretty, innocent, black-eyed girl, looking as if she might be destined to a life of purity and happiness. The comedy is deservedly praised by the critics as abounding in "the purest morality, and the most instructive lessons of disinterested virtue."

The principal thing to be noted in the *critique* on the excellent comedy of the *Clandestine Marriage,* is the just reprehension of the manager for putting a poor deformed idiot, of the name of Roberts, into the fine part of Canton. Those who remember Baddely and Wewitzer, in London, and Darley and Harwood, in New York, will think of the murder of poor Canton in the hands of one thus described by the Mohawks, one "whose dress and figure reminds us of the *ponies* in the races at the *circus.*" They lament that they could not express at the time their disapprobation of the manager, without hurting the feelings of the *actor.* Gentle savages!

In their notice of *Jane Shore,* the savages are *really gentle.* They are more—they are complimentary. The ladies, however, have the greater share in their praise, and we know they deserved it. Mrs. Melmoth's Alicia, and Mrs. Johnson's penitent Jane, were, the first full of fiery passion, the second of tender pathos. Mr. Hallam had the merit of being respectable in Hastings, at the same time that he was, as Mercutio, in *high,* and Jabel, Mungo, Clod, and many other *low* comedy parts, far above mediocrity.

The Belle's Stratagem, Mountaineers, Irish Widow, Florizel, and *Pirdetta, Alexander the Great, Maid of the Mill,* etc., pass under review, and are treated fairly; and the performers quite as gently as heretofore. Of the *Archers* we have spoken elsewhere—we may observe here, that the critics treat it with as much favour as it deserves. They take the occasion to recommend a national drama, and an independence in literature, as well as politics. In a second critique on the piece, they express themselves more fully in its favour, both in the serious and comic parts.

As the benefits came on, the critiques became more complimentary and less discriminating. *Charlotte and Werter,* by Reynolds, was *got up,* but received very coldly; and the critics censured both the play and the performance of it.

On the 20th of May, the band of censors were called to an account for all their missayings and misdoings, by *Verax*—who tells them they are *ignorant,* for they have not travelled—they are young— they are malicious—and that they war upon the actors because they are emigrants. The critics made no answer to this attack on them—

probably they thought it *unanswerable*. This curious performance was known to come from Mr. Hodgkinson....

From *A History of the American Theatre,*
Chapter XVI. (1832.)

JONATHAN OLDSTYLE GOES TO THE PLAY

Tilts and Tournaments

By WASHINGTON IRVING

LETTER II

SIR,

THERE is no place of public amusement of which I am so fond as the Theatre. To enjoy this with the greater relish I go but seldom; and I find there is no play, however poor or ridiculous, from which I cannot derive some entertainment.

I was very much taken with a play bill of last week, announcing, in large capitals, *The Battle of Hexham, or, Days of Old*. Here, said I to myself, will be something grand—*Days of old*—my fancy fired at the words. I pictured to myself all the gallantry of chivalry. Here, thought I, will be a display of court manners, and true politeness; the play will, no doubt, be garnished with tilts and tournaments; and as to those *banditti,* whose names make such a formidable appearance on the bills, they will be hung up, every mother's son, for the edification of the gallery.

With such impressions I took my seat in the pit, and was so impatient that I could hardly attend to the music, though I found it very good.

The curtain rose—out walked the Queen with great majesty; she answered my ideas—she was dressed well, she looked well, and she acted well. The Queen was followed by a pretty gentleman, who, from his winking and grinning, I took to be the court fool; I soon found out my mistake. He was a courtier *"high in trust,"* and either general, colonel, or something of *martial* dignity. They talked for some time, though I could not understand the drift of their discourse, so I amused myself with eating pea-nuts.

In one of the scenes I was diverted with the stupidity of a corporal and his men, who sung a dull song, and talked a great deal about nothing: though I found by their laughing, there was a great deal of fun in the corporal's remarks. What this scene had to do with the rest of the piece, I could not comprehend; I suspect it was a part of some other play, thrust in here *by accident.*

I was then introduced to a cavern, where there were several hard looking fellows, sitting around a table carousing. They told the audience they were banditti. They then sung a *gallery song,* of which I could understand nothing but two lines:

> *"The Welshman lik'd to have been chok'd by a mouse,*
> *But he pull'd him out by the tail."*

Just as they had ended this elegant song, their banquet was disturbed by the *melodious sound* of a horn, and in marched a *portly gentleman,* who, I found, was their captain. After this worthy gentleman had fumed his hour out, after he had slapped his breast and drawn his sword half a dozen times, the act ended.

In the course of the play, I learnt that there had been, or was, or would be, a battle; but how, or when, or where, I could not understand. The banditti once more made their appearance, and frightened the wife of the portly gentleman, who was dressed in man's clothes, and was seeking her husband. I could not enough admire the dignity of her deportment, the sweetness of her countenance, and the unaffected gracefulness of her action; but who the captain really was, or why he ran away from his spouse, I could not understand. However, they seemed very glad to find one another again; and so at last the play ended, by the falling of the curtain.

I wish the manager would use a *drop scene* at the close of the acts; we might then always ascertain the termination of the piece by the *green* curtain. On this occasion, I was indebted to the polite bows of the actors for this pleasing information. I cannot say that I was entirely satisfied with the play, but I promised myself ample entertainment in the after-piece, which was called the *Tripolitan Prize.* Now, thought I, we shall have some *sport* for our money; we will, no doubt, see a few of those Tripolitan scoundrels spitted like turkeys, for our amusement. Well, sir, the curtain rose—the trees waved in front of the stage, and the sea rolled in the rear—all things looked very pleasant and smiling. Presently I heard a bustling behind the scenes—here, thought I, comes a band of fierce Tripolitans, with whiskers as long as my arm. No such thing—they were only a party of village masters and misses, taking a walk for exercise, and very pretty behaved young gentry they were, I assure you; but it was cruel in the manager to dress them in *buckram,* as it deprived them entirely of the use of their limbs. They arranged themselves very orderly on each side of the stage, and sung something, doubtless very affecting, for they all looked pitiful enough. By and by came up a most tremendous storm: the lightning flashed, the thunder roared, and the rain fell in torrents: however, our pretty rustics stood gaping quietly at one another, until they must have been wet to the skin. I was surprised at their torpidity, till I found they were each one afraid to move first, for fear of being laughed at for their awkwardness. How they got off I do not recollect: but I advise the manager, in a similar case, to furnish every one with a *trap-door,* through which to make this exit. Yet this would deprive the audience of much amusement; for nothing can be more laughable than to see a body of guards with their spears, or courtiers with their long robes, *get* across the stage at our theatre.

Scene passed after scene. In vain I strained my eyes to catch a glimpse of a Mahometan phiz. I once heard a great bellowing behind the scenes, and expected to see a strapping Mussulman come bouncing in; but was miserably disappointed, on distinguishing his voice, to find out by his *swearing* that he was only a *Christian.* In he came—an American navy officer. Worsted stockings—olive velvet small clothes— scarlet vest—pea-jacket, and *gold-laced hat*—dressed quite *in character.* I soon found out, by his talk, that he was an American prize-master; that, returning through the *Mediterranean* with his Tripolitan prize, he was driven by a storm on the *coast of England.* The honest gentleman seemed, from his actions, to be rather intoxicated: which I could account for in no other way than his having drank a great deal of salt water, as he swam ashore.

Several following scenes were taken up with hallooing and huzzaing, between the captain, his crew, and the gallery, with several amusing tricks of the captain and his son, a very funny, mischievous little fellow. Then came the cream of the joke: the captain wanted to put to sea, and the young fellow, who had fallen desperately in love, to stay ashore. Here was a contest between love and honour—such piping of eyes, such blowing of noses, such slapping of pocket-holes! But *old Junk* was inflexible—What! an American tar desert his duty! (three cheers from the gallery,) impossible! American tars for ever!! True blue will never stain, &c., &c. (a continual thundering among the gods). Here was a scene of distress—here was bathos. The author seemed as much puzzled to know how to dispose of the young tar, as old Junk was. It would not do to leave an American seaman on foreign ground, nor would it do to separate him from his mistress.

Scene the last opened.—It seems that another Tripolitan cruiser had bore down on the prize, as she lay about a mile off shore. How a Barbary corsair had got in this part of the world—whether she had been driven there by the same storm, or whether she was cruising to pick up a few English first rates, I could not learn. However, here she was. Again were we conducted to the sea-shore, where we found all the village gentry, in their buckram suits, ready assembled, to be entertained with the rare show of an American and Tripolitan engaged yard-arm and yard-arm. The battle was conducted with proper decency and decorum, and the Tripolitan very politely gave in —as it would be indecent to conquer in the face of an American audience.

After the engagement the crew came ashore, joined with the captain and gallery in a few more huzzas, and the curtain fell. How old Junk, his son, and his son's sweetheart, settled it, I could not discover.

I was somewhat puzzled to understand the meaning and necessity of this engagement between the ships, till an honest old countryman at my elbow said, he supposed *this* was *the Battle of Hexham,* as he recollected no fighting in the first piece. With this explanation I was perfectly satisfied.

My remarks upon the audience, I shall postpone to another opportunity.

JONATHAN OLDSTYLE.

From *The Morning Chronicle*, 1801; reprinted in "The Letters of Oldstyle."

Audiences

Sir,

My last communication mentioned my visit to the theatre; the remarks it contained were chiefly confined to the play and the actors; I shall now extend them to the audience, who, I assure you, furnish no inconsiderable part of the entertainment.

As I entered the house some time before the curtain rose, I had sufficient leisure to make some observations. I was much amused with the waggery and humour of the gallery, which, by the way, is kept in *excellent* order by the constables who are stationed there. The noise in this part of the house is somewhat similar to that which prevailed in Noah's ark; for we have an imitation of the whistles and yells of every kind of animal. This, in some measure, compensates for the want of music, as the gentlemen of our orchestra are very economic of their favours. Somehow or another, the anger of the gods seemed to be aroused all of a sudden, and they commenced a discharge of apples, nuts, and gingerbread, on the heads of the honest folks in the pit, who had no possibility of retreating from this new kind of thunderbolts. I can't say but I was a little irritated at being saluted aside of my head with a rotten pippin; and was going to shake my cane at them, but was prevented by a decent looking man behind me, who informed me that it was useless to threaten or expostulate. They are only *amusing themselves* a little at our expense, said he; sit down quietly and bend your back to it. My kind neighbour was interrupted by a hard green apple that hit him between the shoulders—he made a wry face, but knowing it was all a joke, bore the blow like a philosopher. I soon saw the wisdom of this determination; a stray thunderbolt happened to light on the head of a little sharp faced Frenchman, dressed in a white coat and small cocked hat, who sat two or three benches ahead of me, and seemed to be an irritable little animal. Monsieur was terribly exasperated; he jumped upon his seat, shook his fist at the gallery, and swore violently in bad English. This was all nuts to his merry persecutors; their attention was wholly turned on him, and he formed their *target* for the rest of the evening.

I found the ladies in the boxes, as usual, studious to please; their charms were set off to the greatest advantage; each box was a little battery in itself, and they all seemed eager to outdo each other in the havoc they spread around. An arch glance in one box was rivalled by a smile in another, that smile by a simper in a third, and in a fourth a most bewitching languish carried all before it.

I was surprised to see some persons reconnoitring the company through spy-glasses; and was in doubt whether these machines were used to remedy deficiencies of vision, or whether this was another of the eccentricities of fashion. Jack Stylish has since informed me, that glasses were lately all *the go;* though hang it, says Jack, it is quite *out* at present; we used to mount our glasses in *great snuff,* but since so many *tough jockies* have followed the lead, the bucks have all *cut* the custom. I give you, Mr. Editor, the account in my dashing cousin's own language. It is from a vocabulary I do not well understand.

I was considerably amused by the queries of the countryman mentioned in my last, who was now making his first visit to the theatre. He kept constantly applying to me for information, and I readily communicated, as far as my own ignorance would permit.

As this honest man was casting his eye round the house, his attention was suddenly arrested. And pray, who are these? said he, pointing to a cluster of young fellows. These, I suppose, are the critics, of whom I have heard so much. They have, no doubt, got together to communicate their remarks, and compare notes; these are the persons through whom the audience exercise their judgments, and by whom they are told when they are to applaud or to hiss. Critics! ha! ha! my dear sir, they trouble themselves as little about the elements of criticism, as they do about other departments of science and belles-lettres. These are the beaux of the present day, who meet here to lounge away an idle hour, and play off their little impertinences for the entertainment of the public. They no more regard the merits of the play, nor of the actors, than my cane. They even *strive* to appear inattentive; and I have seen one of them perched on the front of the box with his back to the stage, sucking the head of his stick, and staring vacantly at the audience, insensible to the most interesting specimens of scenic representation, though the tear of sensibility was trembling in every eye around him. I have heard that some have even gone so far in search of amusement, as to propose a game of cards in the theatre, during the performance. The eyes of my neighbour sparkled at this information—his cane shook in his hand—the word *puppies* burst from his lips. Nay, says I, I don't give this for absolute fact: my cousin Jack was, I believe, *quizzing* me (as he terms it) when he gave me the information. But you seem quite indignant, said I, to the decent looking man in my rear. It was from him the exclamation came: the honest *countryman* was gazing in gaping wonder on some new attraction. Believe me, said I, if you had them daily before your eyes, you would get quite used to them. Used to them, replied he; how is it possible for people of sense to relish such conduct? Bless you, my friend, people of sense have nothing to do with it; they merely endure it in silence. These young gentlemen live in an indulgent age. When I was a young man, such tricks and follies were held in proper contempt. Here I went a little too far; for, upon better recollection, I must own that a lapse of years has produced but little alteration in this department of folly and impertinence. But do the ladies admire these manners! Truly, I am not as conversant in female circles as formerly; but I should think it a poor compliment to my fair country-women, to suppose them pleased with the stupid stare and cant phrases with which these votaries of fashion add affected to real ignorance.

Our conversation was here interrupted by the ringing of a bell. Now for the play, said my companion. No, said I, it is only for the musicians. These worthy gentlemen then came crawling out of their holes, and began, with very solemn and important phizzes, strumming and tuning their instruments in the usual style of discordance, to the great *entertainment* of the audience. What tune is that? asked my neighbour, covering his ears. This, said I, is no tune; it is only a pleasing *symphony,* with which we are regaled, as a preparative. For my part, though I admire the effect of contrast, I think they might as well play it in their cavern under the stage. The bell rung a second time—and then began the tune in reality; but I could not help observing, that the countryman was more diverted with the queer grimaces and contortions of countenance exhibited by the musicians, than their melody. What I heard of the music, I liked very well; (though I was told by one of my neighbours, that the same pieces have been played every night for these three years;) but it was often overpowered by the gentry in the gallery, who vociferated loudly for *Moll in the Wad, Tally ho the Grinders,* and several other *airs* more suited to their tastes.

I observed that every part of the house has its different department. The good folks of the gallery have all the trouble of ordering the music; (their directions, however, are not more frequently followed than they deserve). The mode by which they issue their mandates is stamping, hissing, roaring, whistling; and, when the musicians are refractory, groaning in cadence. They also have the privilege of demanding a *bow* from *John,* (by which name they designate every servant at the theatre, who enters to move a table or snuff a candle); and of detecting those cunning dogs who peep from behind the curtain.

By the by, my honest friend was much puzzled about the curtain itself. He wanted to know why that *carpet* was hung up in the theatre? I assured him it was no carpet, but a very fine curtain. And what, pray, may be the meaning of that gold head, with the nose cut off, that I see in front of it? The meaning—why, really, I can't tell exactly—though my cousin, Jack Stylish, says there is a great deal of meaning in it. But surely you like the *design* of the curtain? The design,—why really I can see no design about it, unless it is to be brought down about our ears by the weight of those gold heads, and that heavy *cornice* with which it is garnished. I began now to be uneasy for the credit of our curtain, and was afraid he would perceive the mistake of the painter, in putting a *harp* in the middle of the curtain, and calling it a *mirror;* but his attention was *happily* called away by the *candle-grease* from the chandelier, over the centre of the pit, dropping on his clothes. This he loudly complained of, and declared his coat was *bran-new.* How, my friend? said I; we must put up with a few trifling inconveniences, when in the pursuit of pleasure. True, said he; but I think I pay pretty dear for it;—first to give six shillings at the door, and then to have my head battered with rotten apples, and my coat spoiled by candle-grease; by and by I shall have my other clothes dirtied by sitting down, as I perceive every body mounted on the benches. I wonder if they could not see as well if they were all to stand upon the floor.

Here I could no longer defend our customs, for I could scarcely breathe while thus surrounded by a host of strapping fellows, standing with their dirty boots on the seats of the benches. The little Frenchman, who thus found a temporary shelter from the missive compliments of his gallery friend, was the only person benefited. At last the bell again rung, and the cry of *down, down—hats off,* was the signal for the commencement of the play.

If, Mr. Editor, the garrulity of an old fellow is not tiresome, and you choose to give this *view of a New-York Theatre* a place in your paper, you may, perhaps, hear further from your friend,

JONATHAN OLDSTYLE.

From The Morning Chronicle, 1801;
reprinted in "The Letters of Oldstyle."

Jonathan Oldstyle Recommends

LETTER IV

SIR,

I shall now conclude my remarks on the Theatre, which I am afraid you will think are spun out to an unreasonable length; for this I can give no other excuse, than that it is the privilege of old folks to be tiresome, and so I shall proceed.

I had chosen a seat in the pit, as least subject to annoyance from a habit of talking loud that has lately crept into our theatres, and which particularly prevails in the boxes. In old times, people went to the theatre for the sake of the play and acting; but I now find that it begins to answer the purpose of a coffee-house, or fashionable lounge, where many indulge in loud conversation, without any regard to the pain it inflicts on their more attentive neighbours. As this conversation is generally of the most trifling kind, it seldom repays the latter for the inconvenience they suffer, of not hearing one half of the play. I found, however, that I had not much bettered my situation; but that every part of the house has its share of evils. Besides those I had already suffered, I was yet to undergo a new kind of torment. I had got in the neighbourhood of a very obliging personage, who had seen the play before, and was kindly anticipating every scene, and informing those that were about him what was to take place;

to prevent, I suppose, any *disagreeable* surprise to which they would otherwise have been liable. Had there been any thing of a plot to the play, this might have been a serious inconvenience; but, as the piece was entirely *innocent* of every thing of the kind, it was not of so much importance. As I generally contrive to extract amusement from every thing that happens, I now entertained myself with remarks on the self-important air with which he delivered his information, and the distressed and impatient looks of his unwilling auditors. I also observed, that he made several mistakes in the course of his communications. "Now you'll see," said he, "the queen in all her glory, surrounded with her courtiers, fine as fiddles, and ranged on each side of the stage, like rows of pewter dishes." On the contrary, we were presented with the portly gentleman and his *ragged regiment* of banditti. Another time he promised us a regale from the fool; but we were presented with a *very fine speech* from the queen's *grinning counsellor.*

My country neighbour was exceedingly delighted with the performance, though he did not half the time understand what was going forward. He sat staring, with open mouth, at the portly gentleman, as he strode across the stage, and in furious rage drew his sword on the *white lion.* "By George, but that's a brave fellow," said he, when the act was over; "that's what you call first-rate acting, I suppose."

Yes, said I, it is what the critics of the present day admire, but it is not altogether what I like; you should have seen an actor of the *old school* do this part; he would have given it to some purpose; you would have had such ranting and roaring, and stamping and storming; to be sure, this honest man gives us a *bounce* now and then in the true old style, but in the main he seems to prefer walking on plain ground to strutting on the *stilts* used by the tragic heroes of my day.

This is the chief of what passed between me and my companion during the play and entertainment, except an observation of his, that it would be well if the manager was to drill his nobility and gentry now and then, to enable them to go through their evolutions with more grace and spirit. This put me in mind of something my cousin Jack said to the same purpose, though he went too far in his zeal for reformation. He declared, "he wished sincerely one of the critics of the day would take all the *slab-shabs* of the theatre, (like *cats in a bag,*) and *twig* the whole bunch." I can't say but I like Jack's idea well enough, though it is rather a severe one.

He might have remarked another fault that prevails among our performers (though I don't know whether it occurred this evening,) of dressing for the same piece in the fashions of different ages and countries, so that while one actor is strutting about the stage in the cuirass and helmet of Alexander, another, dressed up in a gold-laced coat and bag-wig, with a chapeau de bras under his arm, is taking snuff in the fashion of one or two centuries back, and perhaps a third figures in Suwarrow boots, in the true style of modern buckism.

But what, pray, has become of the noble Marquis of Montague, and Earl of Warwick? (said the countryman, after the entertainment was concluded). Their names make a great appearance on the bill, but I do not recollect having seen them in the course of the evening. Very true—I had quite forgot those worthy personages; but I suspect they have been behind the scenes, smoking a pipe with our other friends *incog.,* the Tripolitans. We must not be particular now-a-days, my friend. When we are presented with a battle of Hexham *without fighting,* and a Tripolitan after-piece without even a *Mahometan whisker,* we need not be surprised at having an *invisible* marquis or two thrown into the bargain.—"But what is your opinion of the house?" said I; "don't you think it a very substantial, *solid-looking* building, both inside and out? Observe what a fine effect the dark colouring of the wall has upon the white faces of the audience, which glare like the stars in a dark night. And then, what can be more pretty than the paintings in the front. of the boxes, those little masters and misses sucking their thumbs, and making mouths at the audience?"

"Very fine, upon my word. And what, pray, is the use of that chandelier, as you call it, that is hung up among the clouds, and has showered down its favours upon my coat?"

"Oh, that is to illumine the heavens, and set off to advantage the little periwig'd cupids, tumbling head over heels, with which the painter has decorated the *dome.* You see we have no need of the chandelier below, as here the house is *perfectly well* illuminated; but I think it would have been a great saving of candle-light, if the manager had ordered the painter, among his other pretty designs, to paint a moon up there, or if he was to hang up that sun with whose *intense light* our eyes were greatly annoyed in the beginning of the after-piece?"

"But don't you think, after all, there is rather a—sort of a—kind of a *heavyishness* about the house? Don't you think it has a little of an *under groundish* appearance?"

To this I could make no answer. I must confess I have often thought myself the house had a *dungeon-like* look; so I proposed to him to make our exit, as the candles were gutting out, and we should be left in the dark. Accordingly, groping our way through the dismal *subterraneous* passage that leads from the pit, and passing through the ragged bridewell-looking ante-chamber, we once more emerged into the purer air of the park, when bidding my honest countryman good night, I repaired home, considerably pleased with the amusements of the evening.

Thus, Mr. Editor, have I given you an account of the chief incidents that occurred in my visit to the Theatre. I have shown you a few of its accommodations and its imperfections. Those who visit it more frequently may be able to give you a better statement.

I shall conclude with a few words of advice for the benefit of every department of it. I would recommend—

To the actors—less etiquette, less fustian, less buckram.
To the orchestra—new music, and more of it.
To the pit—patience, clean benches, and umbrellas.
To the boxes—less affectation, less noise, less coxcombs.
To the gallery—less grog, and better constables;—and,
To the whole house, inside and out, a total reformation.

And so much for the Theatre.

JONATHAN OLDSTYLE.

From *The Morning Chronicle,* 1800; reprinted in "The Letters of Oldstyle."

EDMUND KEAN'S *RICHARD III* [1]

By WILLIAM COLEMAN

T H E A T R I C A L .—We had the pleasure last evening, of being one of a crowded audience to greet the entrance of Mr. Kean, on the American boards, and never did we witness a warmer reception, which was returned in the most grateful and graceful manner. No actor, perhaps, has ever appeared in New-York, with such prepossessions in his favor, or such prejudices to encounter, and we candidly confess, we were among the number of those who entertained the latter. We were assured that certain imitations of him were exact likenesses; and that certain actors were good copies; that his excellencies consisted in sudden starts, frequent and unexpected pauses, in short, a complete knowledge of what is called stage trick, which we hold in contempt. But he had not finished his soliloquy before our prejudices gave way, and we saw the most complete actor, in our judgment, that ever appeared on our boards.—The imitations we had seen, were indeed, likenesses, but it was the resemblance of copper to gold; and the copies no more like Kean "than I to Hercules."

It cannot be expected that we should here enter into particulars, nor shall we attempt it.—We will confine ourselves to a few remarks.

As to figure, Mr. Kean appears to be beneath the middle size, (for we have never seen him but on the stage); his features are good, and his eye particularly expressive and commanding; his voice, in which he is most deficient, is, however, in its lower tones, sonorous, and he has the power of throwing it out so as to be heard at the extremity of the house; at least, when the hurry and violence of passion does not choke his utterance. Though we often see this effect in real life, and know, therefore, it is nature herself, yet the actor upon the stage should remember the instruction of Shakespeare to his players: "In the very torrent, tempest, and (as I may say) whirlwind of your passion, you must acquire and beget *a temperance that may give it* [*distinctness*]."

We had been induced to suppose that it was only in the more important scenes that we should see Kean's superiority, and that the

---

[1] Edmund Kean appeared for the first time in America in *Richard III* at the Anthony Street Theatre, New York, on November 29, 1820.

lighter passages would, in theatrical phrase, be *walked over*. Far otherwise: he gave to what has heretofore seemed the most trivial, an interest and effect never by us imagined. The most striking point he made in the whole play, (for we cannot notice the many minor beauties he exhibited,) was his manner of waking and starting from the couch, with the cry of "Give me a horse—Bind up my wounds! Have mercy, heaven! Ha! soft, 'twas but a dream!" &c. "Cold drops of blood hang on my trembling flesh. My blood grows chilly, & I freeze with horror." This with all that followed, was so admirable; bespeaking a soul, so harrowed up by remorse, so loaded with his guilt, as gave such an awful and impressive lesson to youth, that no one who witnessed it can ever forget it. We must not pass over the unnatural love scene with lady Ann; and can say, Kean is the only actor, that we have ever seen, that could ever render it reconcilable with even bare possibility.

We beg pardon, but if we might make a suggestion to so consummate a judge as Mr. Kean, we would hint that he is deficient in manifesting his anger and disappointment, after his failure to bring Buckingham to his guilty purpose and the latter has gone out. "The king seems angry," says Catesby. We did not observe it. Some instances of misplaced emphasis we noticed. "Didst thou see them *dead?*" I think, with submission, *see* is the emphatic word. "Saddle White Surry for the field to-morrow." By placing the stress on the last word, he insinuates that he has no other horse, instead of directing to select his favorite. "But from the eager love I bear another." Why this line is given in a loud and angry voice, instead of a low and taunting tone, we are at a loss to conceive. But those are peccadilloes. We cannot finish without pointing out the extraordinary fine effect with which he gave "Off with his head—so much for Buckingham." The bitter tone of malignant exultation with which he uttered the latter part of this line, can only be conceived by those who heard, saw, and felt it.

We were rejoiced, once more, to behold our Theatre filled to overflowing, from top to bottom, by the most respectable gentlemen; for of ladies there was a *plentiful scarcity,* owing to fears, which had taken possession of the town, that the house was not safe for an overflow, but which we are morally certain were entirely groundless. We are desirous that all should witness the exhibitions of Kean, because we believe he will introduce a new and better taste in acting, as Philipps did in singing, and thus materially improve the judgment of the public.

We hope we shall stand excused this evening for having permitted our attention to be engrossed by the theatrical department of our paper, as it is a sort of truantry, we admit, from our more grave and regular pursuits; but let it be remembered that it is not often that we thus trespass upon the good nature of those readers, who, we are perfectly aware, take but little or indeed no interest in whatever relates to that subject.

From *The New York Evening Post,*
November 30, 1820.

CHARLES KEMBLE'S *HAMLET*

By WILLIAM LEGGETT

P A R K   T H E A T R E.—Mr. Charles Kemble made his first appearance in America last evening. The house was, of course, thronged at an early hour. The reception of Mr. Kemble must have convinced him that we are no strangers to his various titles to our courtesy. He was welcomed, not only as a member of a family which has exalted the character of the stage wherever English literature is understood; but as one who has deserved highly on his own account. To appreciate what the Kembles have done for the drama, requires a recollection of its state when they came into power. All its proprieties were then disregarded. Coriolanus appeared in a snuff colored suit, such as we constantly see worn now by the old men of comedy; the dignity of the Roman head was caricatured in a bag wig; and Garrick said, when it was proposed to substitute the toga and the human head divine in the majestic simplicity of nature, that he had already stood his ground against the pelting of oranges, but he dared not venture to confront flying benches and bottles. Indeed, it was scarcely credited that Othello could gain any thing from oriental magnificence to atone for the loss of the impressive contrast between a white glove and a black hand, which was sure to be hailed with a round of applause, when the Moor, in a British General's red coat, commenced his appeal to such a senate as is now convened around King Arthur in Tom Thumb. The brother of Mr. Charles Kemble reformed all this. Obvious as the necessity for the change now appears to us, Garrick's alarm shows how much Kemble risqued in the revolution. He was the Brougham of his sphere. Mr. Charles Kemble ably followed up the improvement projected by his brother.

During his management of Covent Garden, he endeavored to exhibit in the dresses and the scenery of every play, a picture of the precise era in which the action was supposed to pass. It was not in a mere general idea of the age and nation; but so minute as to mark the very day and spot. Some of the works he brought out afforded the finest studies for the artist. They carried back the imagination to the moment when the characters of history really existed, and the heroes of the theatre became the breathing images of the past. Many, however, regretted that this strict adherence to nature was not carried still further by the Kembles. They were accused of being less real in their style of acting than in their costume; of speaking and of moving like the creatures of an ideal world, while they wore the robes of this. It was thought, (perhaps with some truth) that the fashion of acting had undergone a regular alternation of changes from right to wrong, and from wrong to right, till the side then uppermost had got to be the wrong again; that the style which Shakespeare censures in his directions to the players had been supplanted after him by the realization of his instructions in the acting of Betterton, which presently gave way to the pomp of Quin, whose exaggeration lost its fame in the surpassing truth and nature of Garrick, to whom John Kemble succeeded, restoring the colossal and declamatory school, which has in our days, been overpowered by the return of the Bettertons and the Garricks in Cooke and Kean.

When we heard that Mr. Charles Kemble was expected here, we felt that if he adhered to the school his brother revived, it would be a disadvantage to him in America. Not that we supposed it would not have been felt here, as in England, that Mr. John Kemble was "the noblest *Roman* of them all";—that Shakespeare himself would have thought Coriolanus, as acted by Kemble, more like Coriolanus than it could have been rendered by Garrick;—but still we were apprehensive that the application of the Kemble manner to other characters might not be relished;—(that manner, in which, a critic said, "he endeavours to raise nature to the dignity of his own person and demeanour, and declines, with a graceful smile and a wave of the hand, the ordinary services she might do him")—and fearing that, if Mr. Kemble, like "Pope Quin," considered the Cookes and Keans as guilty of "heresy," the public might, like the public who patronized Quin's successor, look upon it as "not heresy but reformation"—we were not without a doubt that Mr. Kemble's acting might be regarded as something like a reminiscence of Rip Van Winkle coming after a twenty years' slumber, upon altered times and modes of thinking.

We are gratified in having it in our power to say we were, in a great degree, mistaken. Long accustomed, as Mr. Charles Kemble has been, to the gay and the gallant heroes of high comedy, his style seems to have gained a buoyancy which raises it above the mass of his school; and although we sometimes missed the epigrammatic flashes, the searching glance and the intense passion of Kean; and that eloquence of eye and gesture which said all that Shakespeare could not say in words, but without which his intention can never be adequately expressed;—yet there was a grace and a polish about the personation, beyond that of any actor we in America have seen attempting the character. The form of Mr. Kemble is towering and manly; not of the most finished symmetry; but managed with so much unostentatious ease and elegance, that the spectator does not pause to consider whether there *can* be one more nobly moulded.—In his face, there needs no introduction to enable one to recognize a Kemble. The lower part is prominent and Roman; the brow is not lofty,—the eye is not large,—but the stage light falls on the countenance in such a way as to depress the less imposing features while they display the nobler ones in all their masculine beauty. To look upon him and know he has seen so many winters, one can scarce help fancying but that Mr. Kemble must have realized the fiction of St. Leon and tasted the *elixir vitæ*. Perhaps there could be no better qualification for the performance of Hamlet than this exterior of five and twenty, with the accomplishments and experience he can add to it. The only physical point in which his capabilities might be improved, is his voice. This has not the fullness and clearness and alertness we have heard in others, or should have expected from such a presence. But though sometimes languid and husky, it is never guilty of an unconsidered intonation; and Mr. Kemble always speaks as if he understood himself.

With regard to the critical correctness of the picture Mr. Kemble gave us of Hamlet, perhaps there are few who would agree in every particular respecting him or any one else who should attempt the part. Hamlet, unluckily for actors, is a character about which many really have a theory, and all fancy they have one. There is but one way, therefore, of dealing justly with a debutant in such a part. The observer must state his own view of it, and see how nearly that view is approached. This is the course we shall take; and the occasion will, we hope, be some excuse for the prolixity into which we are betrayed by it.

Hamlet appears to us a young Prince of almost miraculous genius and accomplishments, bearing, amid a Court distinguished for all the barbarous profligacies of power five hundred years ago, an intellect and a heart even more than five centuries in advance of his era—a necessity seems imposed upon him to perform deeds of blood against which his gentle nature revolts;—he is perpetually soliciting opportunities for revenge, he is also perpetually evading them by over refinements; he deceives himself into a dread that he may be deceived, and counterfeits madness to create new opportunities for observation, which perplex him into starts of real madness; and when the object for which he has lived is achieved,—it is only achieved by an accident which, at the same time, renders him the victim of his own indecision. In walking through the world, he may be compared with Lady Macbeth in the dream:—"his eyes are open, but their *sense* is shut." ...

Every portion of *Hamlet* but the scene with Ophelia, is, in some degree, plain sailing. There are two established ways of doing the part, and the chief difference between actors consists in the greater or lesser adroitness with which one executes what all undertake. Some regard the Prince as really mad throughout; others as throughout only pretending to be so. But the scene with Ophelia has long been a stumbling block in the way of either view, and those who could not comprehend what the author meant by it, galloped over the difficulty by fancying that he did not know himself.—When, turning, they suddenly discovered Ophelia, they would run mad, roar, and shake their fists; and then swing out at the side wing and slam the door,— and then fling it again, and roar, and slap their foreheads and abuse the poor girl, till, as a critic observes, "the fashionable in the boxes who hate their wives, and the honest simpletons in the pit who are afraid of theirs, seemed to rejoice at this triumph over the daughter of Polonius, as if it had avenged their own particular wrongs." It was reserved for Kean to attempt something better than this nonsense, but even Kean only lighted the way to the truth; he did not find it. One of his describers has said of him in this scene: "He is surprised and vexed to find that his deliberation on suicide has been overheard by Ophelia, but his thoughts are too much elevated for bitterness or paltry pique, and he addresses her as so pure a being *ought* to be addressed: he thinks her, like himself, the destined victim of affliction, and so thinking, expresses for her at once tenderness and severity: he is tender, because he knows her innocence and gentleness; he is severe, because he cannot endure that so exalted a being as his grieving fancy makes her, should have the common foibles and be subject to the common accidents of her sex. In perfect conformity with this only intelligible construction of the part, Mr. Kean treated her with mournful gravity, and not with noisy railing; and, at the end, as he was leaving her, afraid that even this treatment had been unkind, he returns to her with the humility of a man who thinks he has offended a virtuous being, and kisses her hand, at once to reassure her and to vindicate himself. This was better than had been attempted before. It proved that Mr. Kean knew his predecessors had been in error, and from the acclamations with which the new reading was welcomed, it was plain that the public was pleased even with the admission that a fault had been detected, and that genius was on the wing to set it right. But Mr. Kean's silent action at the end of the scene did not explain Hamlet's conduct during the progress of it. It was simply saying—Shakespeare committed an indecorum, and Mr. Kean makes this apology for it to Ophelia. There is, we repeat, no way of justifying it, but the one we mention.

Here Mr. Charles Kemble, too, failed last evening. He seemed to have taken the side of those who imagine Hamlet to be really and permanently mad, and therefore to have thought he might play what pranks he liked. Under this conception (and only the supposition of madness will account for his execution of the scene) his manner of giving most of it was admirable. He began in confusion and ended in raving; but softened throughout by a pitying gentleness towards her he loved, which looked somewhat rational. Still, much as we admire Mr. Kemble's skill in expressing his impression, and his policy in, at the same time, so qualifying it as to take away all it involves of the repulsive, we quarrel with the conception. True, we have heard the conception defended upon this ground: Hamlet, when soliloquizing upon suicide, speaks of "that undiscovered country from whose bourne *no traveller returns,"* although he has so lately seen a "returning traveller" in the person of his own father, upon the most awful of missions. Now, say the vindicators of his permanent real madness, if he were not incurably mad, would he have made this blunder? They might, perhaps, with greater reason ask, if not mad, would he, or would any one, entertain a thought of suicide? Although this debate in his own mind may have arisen in a moment of derangement, there is no necessity for its continuing after the train of thought which called it up had been broken,—and especially after having been broken so abruptly. Whether Shakespeare or Hamlet forgot himself in the line we speak of, appears to us of little consequence to the general argument; for Shakespeare is full of negligences regarding trifles, even in the play before us. The Soliloquy, indeed, might have been conceived before the character or apart from it, and adopted as likely to aid the general effect of the scene, without the author's remembering the disqualifying parenthesis. As well might the argument be sustained upon the Joe Miller notion of Horatio being a spirit-merchant, because Hamlet tells him he "no *revenue* has but *good spirits";* or that he is Hamlet's real father, because the Prince asks him, speaking of Yorick's skull, "and smelt so, Pah?"—or even that Bernardo, the least part in appearance, is in reality the greatest, and plotting an usurpation, because, when Francisco exclaims, "stand and unfold yourself"—it is answered "Long live the king!" on which the question "Bernardo?" is met by the rejoinder "He!" asserting Bernardo to be a pretender to the throne. No, we must look for the key of Hamlet to the context, and that does not seem to us to support the view apparently taken of it by Mr. Charles Kemble, that Hamlet is permanently mad—mad from the moment of parting with the Ghost in the beginning of the play.

We have already expatiated so much at large upon this performance, that we fear our readers will have great cause to wish we had stayed away from the theatre and spared our dollar to ourselves and our criticism to them. But this is the first time a Kemble has visited us, and we feel that it is our duty not to suffer anything to pass unquestioned from an authority whose weight might otherwise convert it into a precedent.—Were the Kembles less famed for their minute and unsparing watchfulness, over even the most trifling accessories to the truth of what they represent, we should not go into such points as now we think it our duty to mention. Remembering that Mr. Young was formerly praised for having changed the style of sword usually worn by Hamlet and upon which he swears his friends, for having introduced the cross-shaped handle, instead of the modern black-hilted dress sword, we looked for the fashion of Mr. Kemble's sword and were gratified to find that he had sanctioned the improvement ascribed to Mr. Young—that he wore a sword of the fashion we had read of. But why did he not use it as we have every reason to fancy it should have been used?—as enjoined by the institutions of chivalry, in which pagan savageness and religious sublimity are so strangely and so wildly mingled? ...

Mr. Kemble imposes the oath more with the flippancy of the robber hero of a melodrama, than the solemnity of a Prince under an injunction direct from another world, to bind those he was deeply interested to impress, by the most terrible responsibility which can be imposed in this. Again: he omits the fine soliloquy, "Why what a wretch and peasant slave am I?"—proceeding at once to the passage, "I have heard that guilty creatures," &c.—uttering it as if in that moment the idea of the play had *first* arisen, although every arrangement about it had been previously made. ... His asking the players sometime before the soliloquy, if they could play the murder of Gonzago, and study the addition he purposed to make, certainly denotes "a foregone conclusion." It therefore appears to us that the mention of his project in the soliloquy afterwards is only a part of the artifice of the poet to explain his view more fully to the audience, and to express the misgiving so characteristic of Hamlet, on which the intended trial is founded. To accomplish this, we look for a different emphasis from that given by Mr. Kemble. His bitter laugh is often good, but perhaps it is too often repeated. Its application, where, in dismissing Rosencrantz and Guildenstern, at the end of Act 3, Scene 2; exclaiming—"Leave me—Friends"—he mixes it with the last word, is new and effective, and takes off the impolicy of forgetting the mask of courtesy he has worn so long and so warily, by the usual expression of contempt and disgust. But may we not ask, is this in perfect keeping with Mr. Kemble's theory that Hamlet is mad?—His sly chuckle in asking his mother "Is it the king" after he had slain Polonius, was a failure.

As it is our business to be critical, we have scarcely left ourselves time and room to expatiate on the particular beauties of this performance, and they were many. Indeed we have seldom seen an audience more delighted—or *better* delighted, for they were louder in their praises after the play had been seen through, than they were disposed to be at first. Mr. Kemble grew upon their liking. He will continue to grow upon it. Many points last evening, not contravening any general theory of the part, were given with a felicity and a power tempered with more elegance than we are accustomed to see upon our stage; which render the exhibition richly deserving the warm applause with which it was welcomed. The obvious situations for effect, the play scene, and especially its close—the scene with the Queen mother, and especially that part of it in which he springs from his chair and stands petrified in the presence of the Ghost—were never more applauded, and perhaps seldom indeed so well acted. Some entire novelties of a more delicate nature in other passages pleased us particularly, though they escaped the clappers and shouters of "bravo." One which we now remember is the courtly deference with which he turns to Polonius, asking him whether it shall be a passionate speech, without consulting the pleasure of any one present but himself. Another of these choice *morceaux* now occurs to us. When Polonius says he was killed in the capitol on his playing Cæsar, by Brutus, the reply—"it was a brute part in him"—is broken, so as to take off its rudeness. Kemble tells Polonius "it was a brute part," and then walks away, chuckling to himself over the remainder of the joke—"to kill so capital a calf there." Affording a trait of character in a lesson of politeness. Other beauties we may enumerate on another performance....

We sometimes doubt whether it would not be better that such plays as Shakespeare's finest, should be kept off the stage. When we see them attempted there, we think less of them. We can generally imagine much beyond what we find. Mr. Simpson, however, in the present instance is entitled to some praise. He has endeavored to recruit his company so as to give us something nearer what a New York audience has a right to look for than he could have done with his meagre regular supplies. Whether he *ought* to be so ill provided that even a play so often required as Hamlet cannot be acted without new engagements, is another affair. In bringing forward Miss Clara Fisher he has done wisely. If she is not exactly what we would wish in Ophelia, she is better than any the stock company could produce. She has not the figure, the face, nor the manner of Ophelia; she is too full of twitchings and tossings in her carriage—of baby-like fingerings of the lip in her naïveté,—and of the tetchy "what do you mean by that, sir?" in her dignity. But she gave one or two touches with consummate genius. We have never seen anything more finished, more full of all the truth and poetry of feeling, than her wild, mute, mournful look of inquiry just brightening into recognition, when she sinks overwhelmed with the agony of confusion upon the bosom of the brother whose face has aroused the struggle between her reason and the delirium which retains the mastery. Barry's voice would qualify him for the Ghost, if he would let it speak for itself. Shakespeare is said to have excelled in the Ghost, because it enabled him to humour the folly he censures in his times respecting acting and to be monotonous, stilted and declamatory without being out of propriety. Barry tries to be conversational and now and then pathetic; he seems tenacious of showing that the other world has not spoiled him for the sensibilities of this; and does his performance the same mischief by tones and tears, that he inflicts on his person in encumbering it with a fine scarlet robe and spangles (which must have been sadly in his way in getting in and out of his coffin;) instead of being satisfied with the *grave* propriety of "complete steel." Placide appears to have no distinct idea of Polonius beyond that of its being better than the buffoon which others often render it; and he who is so adroit in raising a laugh, ought to be praised for this sacrifice of his temptations to his sense. The actor of Osric seemed a sort of Loony McTwoulter in finery; a *smirking* potatoe—and Wilkinson in the Grave Digger gives us the idea of an effigy of old Dr. Franklin playing Nipperkin: but he was deservedly applauded—as was Mrs. Sharpe in the Queen; whose performance, without being over-ambitious, was sensible and stately; and, perhaps, there is no stage on either side of the Atlantic, which could afford characters of this cast an abler representative.

And now, in dismissing Mr. Kemble's performance, we will sum up all "in little." If he did not express *our* conception of Hamlet, he expressed his own with great ability; a rarer quality than, at first blush, it would appear. His school of declamation is not the one we have been most accustomed to admire; but it is polished, critically studied and impressive. We doubt if our stage has ever before witnessed so fine a picture of unaffected courtliness; of the gallant and the finished gentleman. We think Mr. Kemble's appearance in America will do a service to the art; that it will raise and refine its style; and if our predispositions are likely to preserve us from imitating what may seem less estimable in the school of which he is now the head, that portion which is sure to be admired and adopted may correct the abruptness and elevate the homeliness, sometimes almost touching vulgarity, of the intenser manner to which we are wedded, and a system grow out of the two, chastening the fiery outbreakings of Kean, with the grace and ease, and elegance of Kemble.

From The New York Evening Post,
September 18, 1832.

MRS. MOWATT'S *FASHION*

By EDGAR ALLAN POE

...THE day has at length arrived when men demand rationalities in place of conventionalities. It will no longer do to copy, even with absolute accuracy, the whole tone of even so ingenious and really spirited a thing as the *School for Scandal*. It was comparatively good in its day, but it would be positively bad at the present day, and imitations of it are inadmissible at any day.

Bearing in mind the spirit of these observations, we may say that *Fashion* is theatrical but not dramatic. It is a pretty well-arranged selection from the usual *routine* of stage characters, and stage manœuvres, but there is not one particle of any nature beyond green-room nature, about it. No such events ever happened in fact, or ever could happen, as happen in *Fashion*. Nor are we quarrelling, now, with the mere *exaggeration* of character or incident;—were this all, the play, although bad as comedy might be good as farce, of which the exaggeration of possible incongruities is the chief element. Our fault-finding is on the score of deficiency in verisimilitude—in natural art—that is to say, in art based in the natural laws of man's heart and understanding.

When, for example, Mr. Augustus Fogg (whose name by the bye has little application to his character) says, in reply to Mrs. Tiffany's invitation to the conservatory, that he is "indifferent to flowers," and replies in similar terms to every observation addressed to him, neither are we affected by any sentiment of the farcical, nor can we feel any sympathy in the answer on the ground of its being such as any human being would naturally make at all times to all queries—making no other answer to any. Were the thing absurd in itself we should laugh, and a legitimate effect would be produced; but unhappily the only absurdity we perceive is the absurdity of the author in keeping so pointless a phrase in any character's mouth. The shameless importunities of Prudence to Trueman are in the same category—that of a total deficiency in verisimilitude, without any compensating incongruousness—that is to say, farcicalness, or humor. Also in the same category we must include the rectangular crossings and recrossings of the *dramatis personae* on the stage; the coming forward to the foot-lights when any thing of interest is to be told; the reading of private letters in a loud rhetorical tone; the preposterous soliloquising; and the even more preposterous "asides." Will our play-wrights never learn, through the dictates of common sense, that an audience under no circumstances can or will be brought to conceive that what is sonorous in their own ears at a distance of fifty feet from the speaker cannot be heard by an actor at the distance of one or two?

No person of common ingenuity will be willing to admit that even the most intricate dramatic narrative could not be rendered intelligible without these monstrous inartisticalities. They are the relics of a day when men were content with but little of that true Art whose nature they imperfectly understood, and are now retained solely through that supine spirit of imitation which grows out of the drama itself as the chief of the imitative arts, and which has had so much to do in degrading it, in effect, by keeping it stationary while all of its sisters have been making rapid progress. The drama has not declined as many suppose: it has only been left out of sight by every thing else. We must discard all models. The Elizabethan theatre should be abandoned. We need thought of our own—principles of dramatic action drawn not from the "old dramatists" but from the fountain of a Nature that can never grow old.

It must be understood that we are not condemning Mrs. Mowatt's comedy in particular, but the modern drama in general. Comparatively, there is much merit in *Fashion,* and in many respects (and those of a *telling* character) it is superior to any American play. It has, in especial, the very high merit of simplicity in plot. What the Spanish play-wrights mean by dramas of *intrigue* are the worst acting dramas in the world:—the intellect of an audience can never safely be fatigued by complexity. The necessity for verbose explanation on the part of Trueman at the close of *Fashion* is, however, a serious defect. The *dénouement* should in all cases be full of *action* and nothing else. Whatever cannot be explained by such action should be communicated at the opening of the play.

The colloquy in Mrs. Mowatt's comedy is spirited, generally terse, and well seasoned at points with sarcasm of much power. The *management* throughout shows the fair authoress to be thoroughly conversant with our ordinary stage effects, and we might say a good deal in commendation of some of the "sentiments" interspersed:—we are really ashamed, nevertheless, to record our deliberate opinion that if *Fashion* succeed at all (and we think upon the whole that it will) it will owe the greater portion of its success to the very carpets, the very ottomans, the very chandeliers, and the very conservatories that gained so decided a popularity for that most inane and utterly despicable of all modern comedies—the *London Assurance* of Boucicault.

The above remarks were written before the comedy's representation at the Park, and were based on the author's original MS., in which some modifications have been made—and not at all times, we really think, for the better. A good point, for example, has been omitted at the *dénouement*. In the original, Trueman ... pardons the Count, and even establishes him in a *restaurant,* on condition of his carrying around to all his fashionable acquaintances his own advertisement as *restaurateur*. There is a *piquant,* and dashing deviation, here, from the ordinary *routine* of stage "poetic justice," which could not have failed to tell, and which was, perhaps, the one original point of the play. We can conceive no good reason for its omission. A scene, also, has been introduced, to very little purpose. We watched its effect narrowly, and found it null. It narrated nothing; it illustrated nothing; and was absolutely nothing in itself. Nevertheless it *might* have been introduced for the purpose of giving time for some other scenic arrangements going on out of sight....

A well written prologue was well delivered by Mr. Crisp, whose action is far better than his reading—although the latter, with one exception, is good. It is pure irrationality to recite verse, as if it were prose, without distinguishing the lines:—we shall touch this subject again. As the Count, Mr. Crisp did everything that could be done:— his grace of gesture is preëminent. Miss Horne looked charmingly as Seraphina. Trueman and Tiffany were represented with all possible effect by Chippendale and Barry:—and Mrs. Barry as Mrs. Tiffany was the life of the play. Zeke was caricatured. Dyott makes a bad colonel— his figure is too diminutive. Prudence was well exaggerated by Mrs. Knight—and the character in her hands, elicited more applause than any one other of the *dramatis personae*.

Some of the author's intended points were lost through the inevitable inadvertences of a first representation—but upon the whole, every thing went off exceedingly well. To Mrs. Barry we would suggest that the author's intention was, perhaps, to have *élite* pronounced *ee-light,* and *bouquet,* bokett:—the effect would be more certain. To Zeke we would say, bring up the table bodily by all means (as originally designed) when the *fow tool* is called for. The scenery was very good indeed—and the carpet, ottomans, chandelier, etc., were also excellent of their kind. The entire "getting up" was admirable. *Fashion,* upon the whole, was well received by a large, fashionable, and critical audience; and will succeed to the extent we have suggested above. Compared with the generality of modern dramas, it is a good play— compared with most American dramas it is a *very* good one—estimated by the natural principles of dramatic art, it is altogether unworthy of notice.

From *The Broadway Journal,*
March 29, 1845.

MRS. MOWATT'S COMEDY RECONSIDERED

By EDGAR ALLAN POE

S O deeply have we felt interested in the question of *Fashion's* success or failure, that we have been to see it every night since its first production; making careful note of its merits and defects as they were more and more distinctly developed in the gradually perfected representation of the play.

We are enabled, however, to say but little either in contradiction or in amplification of our last week's remarks—which were based it will be remembered, upon the original MS. of the fair authoress, and upon the slightly modified performance of the first night. In what we then said we made all reasonable allowances for inadvertences at the outset—lapses of memory in the actors—embarrassments in scene-shifting—in a word for general hesitation and want of *finish*. The comedy now, however, must be understood as having all its capabilities fairly brought out, and the result of the perfect work is before us.

In one respect, perhaps, we have done Mrs. Mowatt unintentional injustice. We are not quite sure, upon reflection, that her entire thesis is not an original one. We can call to mind no drama, just now, in which the design can be properly stated as the satirizing of fashion *as* fashion. Fashionable follies, indeed, as a class of folly in general, have been frequently made the subject of dramatic ridicule—but the distinction is obvious—although certainly too nice a one to be of any practical avail to the authoress of the new comedy. Abstractly we may admit some pretension to originality of plan—but, in the representation, this shadow of originality vanishes. We cannot, if we would, separate the *dramatis personae* from the moral they illustrate; and the characters overpower the moral. We see before us only personages with whom we have been familiar time out of mind:—when we look at Mrs. Tiffany, for example, and hear her speak, we think of Mrs. Malaprop in spite of ourselves, and in vain endeavour to think of anything else. The whole conduct and language of the comedy, too, have about them the unmistakable flavor of the green-room. We doubt if a single *point* either in the one or the other, is not a household thing with every play-goer. Not a joke is any less old than the hills—but this conventionality is more markedly noticeable in the sentiments, so called. When, for instance, Gertrude in quitting the stage, is made to say, "If she fail in a certain scheme she will be the first woman who was even at a loss for a stratagem," we are affected with a really painful sense of the antique. Such things are only to be ranked with the stage "properties," and are inexpressibly wearisome and distasteful to every one who hears them. And that they are sure to elicit what appears to be applause, demonstrates exactly nothing at all. People at these points put their hands together, and strike their canes against the floor for the reason that they feel these actions to be required of them as a matter of course, and that it would be ill-breeding not to comply with the requisition. All the talk put into the mouth of Mr. Trueman, too, about "when honesty shall be found among lawyers, patriotism among statesmen," etc. etc. must be included in the same category. The error of the dramatist lies in not estimating at its true value the absolutely certain *"approbation"* of the audience in such cases—an approbation which is as pure a conventionality as are the "sentiments" themselves. In general it may be boldly asserted that the clapping of hands and the rattling of canes are no tokens of the *success* of any play—such success as the dramatist should desire:—let him watch the *countenances* of his audience, and remodel his points by these. Better still—let him "look into his own heart and write"—again better still (if he have the capacity) let him work out his purposes *à priori* from the infallible principles of a Natural Art.

We are delighted to find, in the reception of Mrs. Mowatt's comedy, the clearest indications of a revival of the American drama—that is to say of an earnest disposition to see it revived. That the drama, in general, can go down, is the most untenable of all untenable ideas. Dramatic art is, or should be, a concentralization of all that which is entitled to the appellation of Art. When sculpture shall fail, and painting shall fail, and poetry, and music;—when men shall no longer take pleasure in eloquence, and in grace of motion, and in the beauty of woman, and in truthful representation of character, and in the consciousness of sympathy in their enjoyment of each and all, then and not till then, may we look for *that* to sink into insignificance, which, and which alone, affords opportunity for the conglomeration of these infinite and imperishable sources of delight.

There is not the least danger, then, that the drama shall fail. By the spirit of imitation evolved from its own nature and to a certain extent an inevitable consequence of it, it has been kept absolutely stationary for a hundred years, while its sister arts have rapidly flitted by and left it out of sight. Each progressive step of every other art *seems* to drive back the drama to the exact extent of that step—just as, physically, the objects by the way-side seem to be receding from the traveller in a coach. And the practical effect, in both cases, is equivalent:—but yet, in fact, the drama has not receded: on the contrary it has very slightly advanced in one or two of the plays of Sir Edward Lytton Bulwer. The apparent recession or degradation, however, will, in the end, work out its own glorious recompense. The extent—the excess of the seeming declension will put the right intellects upon the serious analysis of its causes. The first noticeable result of this analysis will be a sudden indisposition on the part of all thinking men to commit themselves any farther in the attempt to keep up the present mad —mad because false—enthusiasm about "Shakespeare and the musical glasses." Quite willing, of course, to give this indisputably great man the fullest credit for what he has done—we shall begin to ask our own understandings why it is that there is so very—very much which he has utterly failed to accomplish.

When we arrive at this epoch, we are safe. The next step may be the electrification of all mankind by the representation of *a play* that may be neither tragedy, comedy, farce, opera, pantomime, melodrama, or spectacle, as we now comprehend these terms, but which may retain some portion of the idiosyncratic excellences of each, while it introduces a new class of excellence as yet unnamed because as yet undreamed-of in the world. As an absolutely necessary condition of its existence this play may usher in a thorough remodification of the theatrical *physique.*

This step being fairly taken, the drama will be at once side by side with the more definitive and less comprehensive arts which have outstripped it by a century:—and now not merely will it outstrip them in turn, but devour them altogether. The drama will be all in all.

We cannot conclude these random observations without again recurring to the effective manner in which *Fashion* has been brought forward at the Park. Whatever the management and an excellent company could do for the comedy, has been done. Many obvious improvements have been adopted since the first representation, and a very becoming deference has been manifested, on the part of the fair authoress and of Mr. Simpson, to every thing wearing the aspect of public opinion—in especial to every reasonable hint from the press. We are proud, indeed, to find that many even of our own ill-considered suggestions, have received an attention which was scarcely their due.

In *Fashion* nearly all the Park company have won new laurels. Mr. Chippendale did wonders. Mr. Crisp was, perhaps, a little too gentlemanly in the Count—he has *subdued* the part, we think, a trifle too much:—there is a *true* grace of manner of which he finds it difficult to divest himself, and which occasionally interferes with his conceptions. Miss Ellis did for Gertrude all that any mortal had a right to expect. Millinette could scarcely have been better represented. Mrs. Knight as Prudence is exceedingly comic. Mr. and Mrs. Barry do invariably well—and of Mr. Fisher we forgot to say in our last paper that he was one of the strongest points of the play. As for Miss Horne—it is but rank heresy to imagine that there could be any difference of opinion respecting *her.* She sets at naught all criticism in winning all hearts. There is about her lovely countenance a radiant *earnestness* of expression which is sure to play a Circean trick with the judgment of every person who beholds it.

From *The Broadway Journal,*
April 5, 1845.

A THOUGHT ON SHAKSPERE

By WALT WHITMAN

T H E most distinctive poems—the most permanently rooted and with heartiest reason for being—the copious cycle of Arthurian legends, or the almost equally copious Charlemagne cycle, or the poems of the Cid, or Scandinavian Eddas, or Nibelungen, or Chaucer, or Spenser, or *bona fide* Ossian, or *Inferno*—probably had their rise in the great historic perturbations, which they came in to sum up and confirm, indirectly embodying results to date. Then however precious to "culture," the grandest of those poems, it may be said, preserve and typify results offensive to the modern spirit, and long past away. To state it briefly, and taking the strongest examples, in Homer lives the ruthless military prowess of Greece, and of its special god-descended dynastic houses; in Shakspere the dragon-rancors and stormy feudal splendor of mediæval caste.

Poetry, largely consider'd, is an evolution, sending out improved and ever-expanded types—in one sense, the past, even the best of it, necessarily giving place, and dying out. For our existing world, the bases on which all the grand old poems were built have become vacuums—and even those of many comparatively modern ones are broken and half-gone. For us to-day, not their own intrinsic value, vast as that is, backs and maintains those poems—but a mountain-high growth of associations, the layers of successive ages. Everywhere—their own lands included—(is there not something terrible in the tenacity with which the one book out of millions holds its grip?)—the Homeric and Virgilian works, the interminable ballad-romances of the middle ages, the utterances of Dante, Spenser, and others, are upheld by their cumulus-entrenchment in scholarship, and as precious, always welcome, unspeakably valuable reminiscences.

Even the one who at present reigns unquestion'd—of Shakspere —for all he stands for so much in modern literature, he stands entirely for the mighty esthetic sceptres of the past, not for the spiritual and democratic, the sceptres of the future. The inward and outward characteristics of Shakspere are his vast and rich variety of persons and themes, with his wondrous delineation of each and all—not only

limitless funds of verbal and pictorial resource, but great excess, super-
fœtation—mannerism, like a fine, aristocratic perfume, holding a touch
of musk (Euphues, his mark)—with boundless sumptuousness and
adornment, real velvet and gems, not shoddy nor paste—but a good
deal of bombast and fustian—(certainly some terrific mouthing in
Shakspere)!

Superb and inimitable as it all is, it is mostly an objective and
physiological kind of power and beauty the soul finds in Shakspere
—a style supremely grand of the sort, but in my opinion stopping
short of the grandest sort, at any rate for fulfilling and satisfying
modern and scientific and democratic American purposes. Think, not
of growths as forests primeval, or Yellowstone geysers, or Colorado
ravines, but of costly marble palaces, and palace rooms, and the noblest
fixings and furniture, and noble owners and occupants to correspond
—think of carefully built gardens from the beautiful but sophisticated
gardening art at its best, with walks and bowers and artificial lakes,
and appropriate statue-groups and the finest cultivated roses and lilies
and japonicas in plenty—and you have the tally of Shakspere. The
low characters, mechanics, even the loyal henchmen—all in themselves nothing—serve as capital foils to the aristocracy. The comedies
(exquisite as they certainly are) bringing in admirably portray'd common characters, have the unmistakable hue of plays, portraits, made
for the divertisement only of the élite of the castle, and from its point
of view. The comedies are altogether non-acceptable to America and
Democracy.

But to the deepest soul, it seems a shame to pick and choose from
the riches Shakspere has left us—to criticise his infinitely royal, mul-
tiform quality—to gauge, with optic glasses, the dazzle of his sun-
like beams.

The best poetic utterance, after all, can merely hint, or remind,
often very indirectly, or at distant remove. Aught of real perfection,
or the solution of any deep problem, or any completed statement of
the moral, the true, the beautiful, eludes the greatest, deftest poet—
flies away like an always uncaught bird.

From *November Boughs*

THE GLADIATOR—MR. FORREST—ACTING

By WALT WHITMAN

F R O M footlights to lobby doors—from floor to dome—were packed crowds of people last night at the Park Theatre, New York, to see Mr. [Edwin] Forrest in *The Gladiator.* . . . This play is as full of "Abolitionism" as an egg is of meat. It is founded on that passage of Roman history where the slaves—Gallic, Spanish, Thracian and African—rose against their masters, and formed themselves into a military organization, and for a time successfully resisted the forces sent to quell them. Running o'er with sentiments of liberty—with eloquent disclaimers of the right of the Romans to hold human beings in bondage—it is a play, this *Gladiator,* calculated to make the hearts of the masses swell responsively to all those nobler manlier aspirations in behalf of mortal freedom!—The speech of Spartacus, in which he attributes the grandeur and wealth of Rome, to her devastation of other countries, is fine; and Mr. Forrest delivered it passing well. Indeed, in the first part of the play, this favorite actor, with his herculean proportions, was evidently i' the vein—but the later parts were not so well gone through with. . . . We do not intend the following reflections—which started during the view of Mr. Forrest's performances—to bear directly on that actor. Mr. F. is a deserved favorite with the public—and has high talent in his profession. But the danger is, that as he has to a measure become identified with a sort of American style of acting, the crowd of vapid imitators may spread quite all the faults of that style, with none of its excellencies. Indeed, too, in candor, all persons of thought will confess to no great fondness for acting which particularly seeks to "tickle the ears of the groundlings." We allude to the loud mouthed ranting style—the tearing of every thing to shivers—which is so much the ambition of some of our players, particularly the younger ones. It does in such cases truly seem as if some of Nature's journeymen had made men, and not made them well—they imitate humanity so abominably. They take every occasion, in season and out of season, to try the extremist strength of their lungs. They never let a part of their dialogue which falls in the imperative mood—the mood for exhorting, commanding, or permitting—pass by without the loudest exhibition of sound, and the most distorted gesture. If they have to enact passion, they do so by all kinds of unnatural and violent jerks, swings, screwing of the nerves of the face, rolling of the eyes, and so on. To men of taste, all this is exceedingly ridiculous. And even among the inferior portion of the audience it does not always pass safely. We have frequently seen rough boys in the pit, with an expression of sovereign contempt at performances of this sort.—For there is something in real nature which comes home to the "business and bosoms" of all men.—Who ever saw love made as it is generally made upon the stage? How often have we heard spontaneous bursts of approbation from inferior audiences, toward acting of the most unpretending kind, merely because it was simple, truthful, and natural! ... If we thought these remarks would meet the eye of any young theatrical artist, we would like through him to beg all—for we cannot call to mind any who are not more or less tainted with this vice—to take such hints as the foregoing, to their hearts— aye, to their heart of hearts. It is a common fallacy to think that an exaggerated, noisy, and inflated style of acting—and no other—will produce the desired effect upon a promiscuous audience. But those who have observed things, theatres, and human nature, know better. Where is there a good, truthful player that is not appreciated? Who, during the past season, has dared compare the quiet polish of Mrs. Kean with the lofty pretensions of the general run of tragedy queens?

From *The Brooklyn Eagle,*
December 26, 1846.

MISERABLE STATE OF THE STAGE

Why Can't We Have Something Worth the Name of American Drama!

By WALT WHITMAN

O F all "low" places where vulgarity (not only on the stage, but in front of it) is in the ascendant, and bad-taste carries the day with hardly a pleasant point to mitigate its coarseness, the New York theatres—except the Park may be put down (as an Emeralder might say,) at the top of the heap! We don't like to make these sweeping assertions in general—but the habit of such places as the Bowery, the Chatham, and the Olympic theatres is really beyond all toleration; and if the New York prints who give dramatic notices, were not the slaves of the paid puff system, they surely would sooner or later be "down" on those miserable burlesques of the histrionic art. Yet not one single independent dramatic critic seems to be among the many talented writers for the New York press. Or rather, we should say, not one single upright critic is permitted to utter candidly his opinion of the theatricals of the metropolis; for we would not insult the good taste of the intelligent literary men connected with the press over the river, so much as to suppose that their eyes and ears do not make the same complaint to them as ours make to us in the matter alluded to.

We have excepted the Park theatre in the charge of vulgarity, because the audiences there are always intelligent, and there is a dash of superiority thrown over the performances. But commendation can go not much further. Indeed it is not a little strange that in a great place like New York, acknowledged as the leading city on the Western Hemisphere, there should be no absolutely *good* theatres. The Park, once in a great while, gives a fine play, performed by meritorious actors and actresses. The Park is still very far, however, from being what we might reasonably expect in the principal dramatic establishment of the metropolis. It is but a third-rate imitation of the best London theatres. It gives us the cast off dramas, and the unengaged players of Great Britain; and of these dramas and players, like garments which come second hand from gentleman to valet, everything fits awkwardly. Though now and then there is ground for satisfaction, the average is such as men of refinement cannot applaud at all. A play arranged to suit an English audience, and to jibe with English localities, feelings, and domestic customs, can rarely be represented in America, without considerable alteration. This destroys its uniformity, and generally deprives it of all life and spirit. One of the curses of the Park, and indeed of nearly all theatres now, is the *star* system. Some actor or actress flits about the country, playing a week here and a week there, bringing as his or her greatest recommendation, that of *novelty* —and very often indeed having no other.—In all the intervals between the appearance of these much trumpeted people, the theatre is quite deserted, though the plays and playing are often far better than during some star engagement. We have seen a fine old English drama, with Miss Cushman and her sister—Mrs. Vernon, Placide, Fisher, and several others whose betters in their departments could hardly be found—we have seen such a beautiful piece, well put upon the stage, and played to a forlorn looking audience, thinly scattered here and there through pit and box—while the very next week crowds would crush each other to get a sight of some flippant well-puffed star, of no real merit, and playing a character written (for the play consists of nothing but *one,* in such cases) by nobody knows whom—probably an ephemeral manufacturer of literature, with as little talent as his employer.

If some bold man would take the theatre in hand in this country, and resolutely set his face against the starring system, as a system,— some *American* it must be, and not moulded in the opinions and long established ways of the English stage,—if he should take high ground, revolutionize the drama, and discard much that is not fitted to present tastes and to modern ideas,—engage and encourage American talent, (a term made somewhat nauseous by the use it has served for charlatans, but still a good term,) look above merely the gratification of the vulgar and of those who love glittering scenery—give us American plays too, matter fitted to American opinions and institutions—our belief is he would do the Republic service, and himself too, in the long round.

From *The Brooklyn Eagle,*
February 8, 1847.

UNCLE TOM'S CABIN

M R S. Harriet Beecher Stowe's novel of *Uncle Tom's Cabin* has been dramatized at the National Theatre, and, being something of a novelty, it draws crowded houses nightly.

The practice of dramatizing a popular novel, as soon as it takes a run, has become very common. In many instances, and particularly with regard to the highly dramatic and graphic novels of Dickens, these new plays have been very successful, giving pleasure and satisfaction to the public, and putting money into the pockets of the chuckling manager. But in the presentation of *Uncle Tom's Cabin* upon the boards of a popular theatre, we apprehend the manager has committed a serious and mischievous blunder, the tendencies of which he did not comprehend, or did not care to consider, but in relation to which we have a word or two of friendly counsel to submit.

The novel of *Uncle Tom's Cabin* is at present our nine days' literary wonder. It has sold by thousands, and ten, and hundreds of thousands—not, however, on account of any surpassing or wonderful literary merits which it may be supposed to possess, but because of the widely extended sympathy, in all the North, with the pernicious abolition sympathies and "higher law" moral of this ingenious and cunningly devised abolition fable. The *furore* which it has thus created, has brought out quite a number of catchpenny imitators, *pro* and *con,* desirous of filling their sails while yet the breeze is blowing, though it does appear to us to be the meanest kind of stealing of a lady's thunder. This is, indeed, a new epoch and a new field of abolition authorship—a new field of fiction, humbug and deception, for a more extended agitation of the slavery question—than any that has heretofore imperiled the peace and safety of the Union.

The success of *Uncle Tom's Cabin* as a novel, has naturally suggested its success upon the stage; but the fact has been overlooked, that any such representation must be an insult to the South—an exaggerated mockery of Southern institutions—and calculated, more than any other expedient of agitation, to poison the minds of our youth with the pestilent principles of abolitionism. The play, as performed at the National, is a crude and aggravated affair, following the general plot of the story, except in the closing scene, where, instead of allowing Tom to die under the cruel treatment of his new master in Louisiana, he is brought back to a reunion with Wilmot and his wife —returned runaways—all of whom, with Uncle Tom and Aunt Chloe, are set free, with the privilege of remaining upon the old plantation. The incidents of the piece are thus set forth in the "small bill":—

PROGRAMME.

ACT I—Exterior of Uncle Tom's Cabin on Shelbey's Plantation; Negro Celebration. Chorus, "Nigga in de Cornfield;" Kentucky Breakdown Dance; Innocence Protected; Slave Dealers on hand. Chorus, "Come then to the Feast;" the Mother's Appeal; Capture of Morna;[1] Interior of Uncle Tom's Cabin; Midnight Escape; Tom driven from his Cabin; Search of the Traders; Miraculous Escape of Morna and her Child. Offering Prayer; the Negro's Hope; Affecting Tableau.

ACT 2—Family Excitement; Dark Threatenings; Ohio River Frozen over; Snow Storm; Flight of Morna and her Child; Pursuit of the Traders; Desperate Resolve and Escape of Morna on Flowing Ice; Mountain Torrent and Ravine; Cave of Crazy Mag; Chase of Edward; Maniac's Protection; Desperate Encounter of Edward and Traders on the Bridge; Fall of Springer down the Roaring Torrent; Negro Chorus, "We Darkies Hoe the Corn;" Meeting of Edward and Morna; Escape over Mountain Rocks.

ACT 3—Roadside Inn; Advertisement Extraordinary; the Slave Auctioneer; Rencontre between Edward and Slave Dealers; Interposition of Crazy Mag; Arrival from the West Indies; Singular Discovery. Mountain Dell; Recognition of the Lost Mother; Repentance and Remorse; Return of Tom; the Log Cabin in its Pride; Freedom of Edward and Morna &c.

In the progress of these varied scenes, we have the most extravagant exhibitions of the imaginary horrors of Southern slavery. The negro traders, with their long whips, cut and slash their poor slaves about the stage for mere pastime, and a gang of poor wretches, handcuffed to a chain which holds them all in marching order, two by two, are thrashed like cattle to quicken their pace. Uncle Tom is scourged by the trader, who has bought him, for "whining" at his bad luck. A reward is posted up, offering four hundred dollars for the runaway, Edward Wilmot, (who, as well as his wife, is nearly white,) the reward to be paid upon "his recovery, or upon proof that he has been killed." But Wilmot shoots down his pursuers in real Christian style, as fast as they come, and after many marvellous escapes, and many fine ranting abolition speeches, (generally preceding his dead shots,) he is liberated as we have described.

This play, and these scenes, are nightly received at one of our most popular theatres with repeated rounds of applause. True, the audience appears to be pleased with the novelty, without being troubled about the moral of the story, which is mischievous in the extreme.

The institution of Southern slavery is recognized and protected by the federal constitution, upon which this Union was established, and which holds it together. But for the compromises on the slavery question, we should have no constitution and no Union—and would, per-

[1] Eliza.

haps, have been at this day, in the condition of the South American republics, divided into several military despotisms, constantly warring with each other, and each within itself. The Fugitive Slave law only carries out one of the plain provisions of the constitution. When a Southern slave escapes to us, we are in honor bound to return him to his master. And yet, here in this city—which owes its wealth, population, power, and prosperity, to the Union and the constitution, and this same institution of slavery, to a greater degree than any other city in the Union—here we have nightly represented, at a popular theatre, the most exaggerated enormities of Southern slavery, playing directly into the hands of the abolitionists and abolition kidnappers of slaves, and doing their work for them. What will our Southern friends think of all our professions of respect for their delicate social institution of slavery, when they find that even our amusements are overdrawn caricatures exhibiting our hatred against it and against them? Is this consistent with good faith, or honor, or the every day obligations of hospitality? No, it is not. It is a sad blunder; for when our stage shall become the deliberate agent in the cause of abolitionism, with the sanction of the public, and their approbation, the peace and harmony of this Union will soon be ended.

We would, from all these considerations, advise all concerned to drop the play of *Uncle Tom's Cabin* at once and for ever. The thing is in bad taste—is not according to good faith to the constitution, or consistent with either of the two Baltimore platforms; and is calculated, if persisted in, to become a firebrand of the most dangerous character to the peace of the whole country.

From *The New York Herald,*
September 3, 1852.

JOSEPH JEFFERSON'S RIP

By L. CLARKE DAVIS

...I T is an accepted dogma in dramatic art, that whatever is presented on the stage must necessarily be measurably enlarged and exaggerated, or, as it were, looked at through a mental as well as a material lorgnette; that in no other wise can the fictions of the stage be made real to the senses of the spectator. In consequence of the actor's belief in this theory, he is apt to represent all shades and degrees of passion through the medium of exaggerated tone, stride, and gesture. And indeed it seems without the bounds of reason to suppose, that, should the tragedian speak the words of Hamlet in his ordinary tones of feeling, he would very adequately express the sublimity and weirdness of Hamlet's griefs, doubts, and struggles, or show, as in a mirror, the subtle depths of his nature. And yet, after witnessing the rendition of the character of Rip Van Winkle by Mr. Jefferson, we are disposed to think that, if he who enacted Hamlet possessed the genius of this comedian, he might show us such a portrait of the Dane as no one has seen since Betterton, without exaggeration of tone or robustious action, charmed the town in that part.

In the play of *Rip Van Winkle,* the scant material of Irving, borrowed by him from the German, is eked out by the skill of the dramatist into a play of moderate excellence, but admirably adapted to display Mr. Jefferson's peculiar powers.

From the moment of Rip's entrance upon the scene,—for it is Rip Van Winkle, and not Mr. Jefferson,—the audience has assurance that a worthy descendant of the noblest of the old players is before them. He leans lightly against a table, his disengaged hand holding his gun. Standing there, he is in himself the incarnation of the lazy, good-natured, dissipated, good-for-nothing Dutchman that Irving drew. Preponderance of humor is expressed in every feature, yea, in every limb and motion of the light, supple figure. The kindly, simple, *insouciant* face, ruddy, smiling, lighted by the tender, humorous blue eyes, which look down upon his dress, elaborately copied bit by bit from the etchings of Darley; the lounging, careless grace of the figure; the low, musical voice, whose utterances are "far above singing"; the sweet, rippling laughter,—all combine to produce an effect which is rare in its simplicity and excellence, and altogether satisfying.

The impersonation is full of what are technically known as *points;* but the genius of Mr. Jefferson divests them of all "staginess," and they are only such points as the requirements of his art, its passion, humor, or dignity, suggest. From the rising of the curtain on the first scene, until its fall on the last, nothing is forced, sensational, or unseemly. The remarkable beauty of the performance arises from nothing so much as its entire repose and equality.

The scene, however, in which the real greatness of the player is shown in his "so potent art," is the last scene of the first act. It is marvellously beautiful in its human tenderness and dignity. Here the debauched good-for-nothing, who has squandered life, friends, and fortune, is driven from his home with a scorn pitiless as the storm-filled night without. The scene undoubtedly owes much to the art of the dramatist, who has combined the broadest humor in the beginning with the deepest pathos at the close. Here there is "room and verge enough" for the amplest display of the comedian's power. And the opportunities are nobly used. His utterance of the memorable words, "Would you drive me out like a dog?" is an unsurpassed expression of power and genius. His sitting with his face turned from the audience during his dame's tirade, his stunned, dazed look as he rises, his blind groping from his chair to the table, are all actions conceived in the very noblest spirit of art.

In a moment the lazy drunkard, stung into a new existence by the taunts of his vixenish wife, throws off the shell which has encased his better self, and rises to the full stature of his manhood,—a man sorely stricken, but every inch a man. All tokens of debauchery are gone; vanished all traces of the old careless indolence and humor. His tones, vibrating with the passion that consumes him, are clear and low and sweet,—full of doubt that he has heard aright the words of banishment,—full of an awful pain and pity and dismay. And so, with one parting farewell to his child, full of a nameless agony, he goes out into the storm and darkness.

The theatre does not "rise at him": it does more,—gives finer appreciation of the actor's power; it is deadly silent for minutes after, or would be, but for some sobbing women there. . . .

The versatility of Mr. Jefferson's powers is finely shown in the scene of Rip's awaking from his sleep in the Catskills, and in those scenes which immediately follow. Here he has thrown off his youth, his hair has whitened, his voice is broken to a childish treble, his very limbs are shrunken, tottering, palsied. This maundering, almost imbecile old man, out of whose talk come dimly rays of the old quaint humor, would excite only ridicule and laughter in the hands of an artist less gifted than Mr. Jefferson; but his griefs, his old affections, so rise up through the tones of that marvellous voice, his loneliness and homelessness so plead for him, that old Lear, beaten by the winds, deserted and houseless, is not more wrapped about with honor than poor old Rip, wandering through the streets of his native village.

Exactly wherein lies Mr. Jefferson's chief power it is not easy to show. With the genius inherited from "Old Joe," he possesses a mind richly stored, a refined taste, and that rare knowledge of his art which teaches the force of repression as well as expression. Mr. Jefferson is also a close and conscientious student. The words that flow from his tongue in such liquid resonance seem the very simplest of utterances. And so they are; but it would be interesting to know how many hours of study it cost him to arrive at that simplicity which is the crowning charm and secret of success. Why, in the very speaking of his daughter's name in the last scene,—in that matchless appeal to her for recognition,—"Meenie, Meenie,"—there is a depth of pathos, tenderness, and beauty that charms like music, and attunes the heart to the finest sense of pity....

From *The Atlantic Monthly,*
June, 1867.

LYDIA THOMPSON AT NIBLO'S

By RICHARD GRANT WHITE

... I T was not until *The Forty Thieves* were about sinking into their unsavory oil-jars for the last time that I saw Miss Lydia Thompson and her company, at Niblo's. But going there at a morning's performance, in search of a needed laugh, which I confess I did not get, I was surprised, not only with the merit of the lady herself, and of some of her companions, but with the character of the audience. The latter I expected to find made up of coarse and flashy people; but, on the contrary, it was notable in the main, for simple and almost homely respectability. Comfortable, middle-aged women from the suburbs, and from the remoter country, their daughters, groups of children, a few professional men, bearing their quality in their faces, some sober, farmer-looking folk, a clergyman or two, apparently, the usual proportion of nondescripts, among which were not many very young men, composed an audience less fashionable than that I had seen in Fourteenth street, but at least as respectable. And the Lydia Thompson, in whom I had expected to find a coarse, Anglo-Saxon exaggeration of Mlle. Tostée, I found one of the most charming comic actresses it had been my good fortune to see.

She played burlesque with a daintiness with which few actresses of note are able to flavor their acting, even in high comedy. She was doing hard work, no doubt, but her heart must have been in it, for she was the embodiment of mirth, and moved others to hilarity by being moved herself. It was as if Venus, in her quality of the goddess of laughter, had come upon the stage. And if there was a likeness to Venus in the costume, as well as in manner, I must confess that I saw in it no chance of harm to myself or to any of my fellow spectators, old or young, male or female. Indeed, it seems rather to be desired that the points of a fine woman should be somewhat better known, and more thought of among us than they have been. They seem to me quite as important, and I think they are quite as interesting, as those of a fine horse; and I should be sorry to believe that they are more harmful, either to taste or to morals. Some of the outcry that we hear against the costume of which the burlesque actresses wear, in the way of their profession, has in it such a tone of personal injury, that it might come from mammas and papas who, having a very poor article of young woman lying heavy on their hands, are indignant that there should be so good and so easy an opportunity of trying it by a very high standard. As to any impropriety in this costume, in its place, that is, seriously speaking, a matter of individual opinion; but if there is any, it is far less, both in degree and in kind, than that of the ordinary ballet dancer, with her flying petticoat, alternately concealing and revealing the attractions of her figure, which we have looked at ever since we were children, even in this dear old Niblo's Garden, without a thought of shamefacedness, and very much less than that of the tilting hoops, which lent such peculiar attractions to the "German" in fashionable society only two years ago.

This gayety of heart and overrunning glee, Miss Thompson shows even to a greater degree in *Sinbad* than in its predecessor. What an overflow of mirth and humor breaks from her when she takes the auctioneer's stand, at the wife-market, to set forth her own qualifications as a "Girl of the Period!" With what a radiant outbreak of fun does she announce "we are aware of our own awarishness!" and how thoroughly she seems to enjoy that queer word "thunk," which the author has given her for *thought!* I must confess, with proper contrition, that I liked her performance in this part better than much high tragedy that I have seen—better, for instance, than Mr. Forrest in *Hamlet.* As to *thunk,* I venture to say that her author probably took that word from a passage in an article on "Words and their Uses," where I used it some months ago, whimsically, of course. But probably neither he nor one or two of the prim purists who scoffed at me for it, knew how old a word it is, and how good authority there is for its use. Here it is, in the famous old satirical poem of *The Owl and the Nightingale,* written six hundred years ago, about A. D. 1250:

> *Me* thunch *that thu for-lcost that game*
> *Thu yulpest of thire oye schame;*
> *Me* thunch *that thue me gest an honde*
> *Thus yulpest of thire oyene schonde.*

And this reminds me of one striking excellence in this company of actresses—the beautiful manner in which they speak English. It is noticeable in all, but particularly in two, one of whom is Miss Thompson herself; the other is the second lady of the company, Miss Pauline Markham, she who has found the long lost arms of the *Venus of Milo,* and whose speech is vocal velvet. It is with a recollection of all the public elocution and private conversation that ever impressed me, that I say that Miss Markham, whose voice and style are not of the heroic or high-tragedy order, speaks the most beautiful colloquial English that I ever heard. More reserved in manner, and less sprightly by nature, I should say, than Miss Thompson (whose part, nevertheless, she took with very great success), her voice and her smile give to her presence a rare attraction, that calls to mind the allurements which Horace immortalized in the closing lines of his most famous ode:

> *Dulce ridentem Lalagen amabo,*
> *Dulce loquentem.*

This was apparent in the *School for Scandal,* in which she played "Maria," a part that gives an actress only the opportunity to be quiet, and simple, and lady-like, as she was; but in which her speech was so lovely in manner and in tone, that she made that of all the other women on the stage seem sharp, and rough, and forbidding. If the ladies of our most cultivated society need an excuse for attending the performances at Niblo's, the lack of which they do not seem to feel, they may find it in the benefit which they might derive from listening to Miss Thompson, Miss Markham, and their companions (with one exception, now, however, no longer a member of the company), as they utter the puns and doggerel of their parts, which are almost as significant and as silly as the words of Italian opera.

On one point these burlesques have transgressed, gravely and without excuse—their dances, some of which, although not to be compared, for voluptuous effect or immodesty, with Gérome's superb picture, *L'Almée,* which hung unrebuked and admired for months in one of the most fashionable resorts in the city, are vulgar and gross—being made so by the lack of any element of beauty in form or spirit. *La Grande Duchesse, Genevieve de Brabant,* and *The Forty Thieves,* sinned gravely in this regard, in which *Sinbad* is without reproach. And I will say in passing, that in the last-named play, the dancing of the member of the Clodoche troupe who wears the Normandy head-dress, is really grand. He steps as if he could take in half the earth at a bound, and as if he rose from the ground by volition, rather than by exertion. In this respect he far surpasses any dancer whose performance I remember. The style of his companions is always grotesque and clownish; his is rarely other than severe and simple. The dancing is the most vulnerable part of these burlesque performances, and is worthy of condemnation even more for its silliness than its indecorum. But what can we expect in a day when the Princess Metternich kicks the Emperor's hat off at the Tuileries, and when a Yankee girl I have heard of, who, and whose friends, would be surprised if told that she, or the society in which she moved, was not perfectly respectable, has boasted of her ability to remove papa's hat in the same manner? Were either of these ladies an actress who went through this performance in public, she would be subjected to disparaging remarks of a kind as well as of a degree which she now, in a great measure, escapes. And with some reason; although it must be confessed that, if such an act admits at all of comparison, when done openly and as business, it is less objectionable than when it is private, and must be accepted as an example of the manners of the day.

From "The Age of Burlesque,"
in *The Galaxy,* August, 1869.

WILLIAM WARREN, COMEDIAN

By HENRY AUSTIN CLAPP

B O S T O N was fortunate, indeed, to be the home and workshop of William Warren for the better part of half a century. His career as an actor covered exactly fifty years, extending from 1832 to 1882; and during the entire period between 1847 and 1882, except for a single break of one year, he was the central sun of the stock company of the Boston Museum. Of the modern mode of histrionic vagabondage he had no experience,—no experience, of course, of the mercenary "star" system, which binds the artist to very numerous repetitions of a very few plays. When his seventieth birthday was celebrated, a little while before the close of his professional career, the tale of his work was told: he had given 13,345 performances, and had appeared in 577 characters! What a record is this, and how amazingly it contrasts with the experience of other noted modern players! It may be safely presumed, I think, that no other American actor, even in the early part of the nineteenth century, ever matched Mr. Warren's figures.... As I look back upon Mr. Warren and his playing, the lives of all his rivals seem narrow, monotonous, and unfruitful. His art touched life, as life is presented in the drama, at ten thousand points. His plays were in every mode and mood of the Comic Muse, and ranged in quality from the best of Shakespeare to the worst of Dr. Jones. In old-fashioned farces, with their strong, sometimes vulgar, often noisy, usually vital fun; in tawdry patriotic or emotional melodramas; in standard old English comedies; in cheap local pieces, narrow and petty in their appeal; in delicate French comediettas, whose colors are laid on with a brush like Meissonier's; in English versions of the best Parisian dramas, subtle, sophisticated, exigent of *finesse* and *adresse* in the player,—in each and all of these Mr. Warren was easily chief among many good actors; to the demands of each and all he was amply adequate. The one fault of his style was a slight excess in the use of stentorian tones,—the result, I suspect, of his early immersion in farce,—and his gift of pathetic suggestion, though generally sure, did not always have the deepest penetrative power. Otherwise, it may be said, with sober scruple for the exact truth, that Mr. Warren was nearly faultless. His acting seemed the fine flower of careful culture, as well as the free outcome of large intelligence and native genius. His enunciation and pronunciation of English were beyond criticism. His Latin was perfect, even in its quantities. His French was exquisite in intonation, and its accent was agreeable to Parisian ears. In all details of costume and "make-up" he showed the nicest taste and judgment, and the results of scholarly pains. So Mr. Warren was a School and Conservatory of acting in himself. In him Boston had a Théâtre Français, situated on Tremont Street, as long as he lived and played; and Boston ought to be ashamed of itself that it did not derive more profit from the inspection and enjoyment of his masterly art than the present time gives any proof of.

From *The Reminiscences of a Dramatic Critic,*
(Houghton, Mifflin & Co., 1902.)

EDWIN FORREST

By WILLIAM WINTER

I T has often been said of Forrest that he was a melodramatic actor. He was not; he was a tragedian. His Othello, his Virginius, and, in later years, his King Lear were the sufficient proof of this. He had imagination,—though it was seldom informed by fine intelligence and never by spirituality,—and he had passion and tenderness. Even in Spartacus, the gladiator, though the method was melodramatic, there was a noble assumption of tender and manly attributes, which dwarfed the physical ebullitions. That which marred his acting, to the judicious, was that which marred his character,—his colossal, animal selfishness.

His impulses, aided by physical strength, manly beauty, and natural talent, impelled him,—over many obstacles and much hardship,—to prosperity and precarious eminence, but they did not conduct him to greatness. His nature fulfilled itself, and for that reason his life was a failure. It was this which made him a pathetic object. He was never able, as a matter of destiny, to reach the goal which, nevertheless, he vaguely saw. To a man of susceptive temperament, picturesque attributes, and a heart capable of suffering, that was a sad fate. It resulted not by reason of what he did but by reason of what he was,—a vast animal, bewildered by a grain of genius.

Forrest's physical attributes determined his course. He directly inherited the traditions of Cooke and Cooper, and his method and style were founded on the latter, modified by the influence of Edmund Kean, becoming (as is the case with all actors) distinctive as he matured. As an actor Forrest, at his best, was remarkable for iron repose, perfect precision of method, immense physical force, capacity for leonine banter, fiery ferocity, and occasional felicity of elocution in passages of monotone and colloquy. Strength and definiteness are always comprehensible and generally admirable. Forrest was the union of both. He resembled, in this, a rugged old tower, conspicuous in a landscape. The architecture may not be admired, but the building is distinctly seen and known. You might not like the actor, but you could not help seeing that he was the bold representative of a certain set of ideas in art. But while Forrest illustrated the value of earnestness and of assured skill, he also illustrated the law of classification in art as well as in humanity. Mankind,—artists among the rest,—are distinctly classified. We are what we are. Each man develops along his own grade. Hence the world's continual wrangling over representative men,—wrangling between persons of different classes, who can never become of one mind. Forrest was continually the theme of that sort of controversy. He represented the physical element in art. He was a landmark on the border-line between physical and spiritual power.

Natures kindred with his own admired him, followed him, and reverenced him, as the finest type of artist. That was natural and inevitable. But there is another sort of nature, with which neither Forrest nor his admirers could sympathize,—that asks continually for some great spiritual hero and leader; that has crowned and uncrowned many false monarchs; and that must forever hopelessly pursue its ideal. This nature feels what Shelley felt when he wrote of "the desire of the moth for the star." To persons of this order,—and they are sufficiently numerous to constitute a large minority,—Forrest's peculiar interpretations of character and passion were unsatisfactory. They admired his certainty of touch, his profound assurance, his solid symmetry, but they felt that something was wanting to complete the artist. They did not belong to his audience, and they were as much out of place in listening to him as a congregation of Methodist theologians would have been listening to Emerson. He had nothing to say to them. He was great in his way, they perceived, but, like the Gallic wit, they also perceived that his way was small.

To his natural admirers, on the contrary, he was great in his way, and his way was the greatest of ways. Those two parties long assailed and defended him: fruitlessly,—because this kind of dispute cannot, in nature, come to an end or even to a compromise. The respect wherein Forrest was peculiar, the distinguishing excellence that gave him his victory and made him memorable, was a puissant animal splendor and ground-swell of emotion. He was tremendously real. He could be seen and heard and understood. He had a grand body and a glorious voice, and in moments of simple passion he affected the senses like the blare of trumpets and clash of cymbals, or like the ponderous, slow-moving, crashing, and thundering surges of the sea. In that quality he stood alone. In all others he has been surpassed. That was his charm, and through that he was enabled to render whatever service he did render to the cause of the Drama. That service consisted in a widespread, delightful, and improving interpretation of the art of acting to the lower order of public intelligence. To the higher order of mind Forrest was superfluous, and of this fact he seemed, in a certain blind way, to be aware,—although neither he nor any of his adherents could understand and believe that it was possible for any person, honestly and without hostility or prejudice, to dislike the snorts and grunts, the brays and belches, the gaspings and gurglings, the protracted pauses, the lolling tongue and the stentorian roar, with all of which ornaments it pleased him to overlay his acting,—often remarkably fine and sometimes great. In acting, as in poetry, there are, popularly, two schools. The one is all for spirit; the other is all for body. The eclectic school, which is the right school,—in acting and in every other art,—stands between those extremes and simply asks the harmonious, symmetrical blending of the spiritual and physical. England saw it in Garrick and Kemble; America enjoyed it in Edwin Booth and Henry Irving. Neither of those latter actors equalled Forrest in his distinctive element, but each excelled him in fine mentality, spirituality, and poetry.

From *The Wallet of Time.*
(Moffat, Yard, 1913.)

CHARLOTTE CUSHMAN

By WILLIAM WINTER

...C H A R L O T T E C U S H M A N, like Henry Irving, grandly illustrated the truth of Shakespeare's saying, "In the reproof of chance lies the true proof of men"; for she left nothing to chance, and she made impotent the caprice of all observers. You might resent her dominance, and shrink from it, calling it "masculine"; you could not doubt her massive reality, nor escape the spell of her imperial power. She was a tall woman, of large person and of commanding aspect, and in her demeanor, when she was thoroughly aroused, there was an innate grandeur of authority that no sensitive soul could resist.... She needed great moments on the stage, and when they came she invariably filled them. It is not meant that she acted for points; her performances were always of a uniform fabric, symmetrical, coherent, lucid, distinct; but whenever the occasion arrived for liberated power, passionate feeling, poetic significance, dramatic effect, she rose to that occasion and made it superb. Nothing has been seen, since her time, to surpass her appalling impartment of predestinate evil and sinister force in the scenes that lead up to the murder of the King, in *Macbeth.* When she said, in those deep, thrilling, pitiless tones, "He that's coming must be provided for," and when, with wild, roving, inspired glances, comprehending earth and air, she invoked the angels of crime ("you murdering ministers, *wherever* in your sightless substances you wait on Nature's mischief"), the blood of the listener was chilled with the horror of her infernal purpose, fiend-driven and inspired of hell. There were other great moments in her personation of Lady Macbeth—a personation which, to this day, remains unequaled; among them, her profoundly reverential greeting to King Duncan on his arrival at the Castle of Inverness; her magnificently royal bearing in the interrupted banquet scene; her desolation—the immedicable, hopeless agony of a lost soul—in the pathetic scene of haunted sleep; but throughout her temptation of Macbeth and in her conduct of the murder she diffused, as no other representative of the part in our time has done, the awe-inspiring, preternatural horror which is the spirit of that great tragedy —the most weird, portentous, sinister, afflicting work of poetic imagination that the brain of man has produced.

Miss Cushman was not prone to the critical custom, so common of late years, of refining on Shakespeare's meaning, and thus reading subtle significations into his text. She perceived and imparted the obvious meaning, and her style was strong, definite, bold and free: for that reason some observers described it as "melo-dramatic." She did not make long pauses and stare fixedly at nothing, as Madame Sarah Bernhardt does; nor did she wander to the back drop and whisper to the scenery, after the manner (supposedly inspired) of Madame Eleanora Duse. She had always a distinct purpose, and that purpose she distinctly executed. . . .

Though she insisted on the basis of fact in acting, she was not mindless of the essential spirit of poetry. In each of her supreme performances—which were Lady Macbeth, Queen Katharine and Meg Merrilies—that spirit suffused the impersonation and made it radiant with intrinsic light. The part that she preferred to act was Queen Katharine; for she was of a deeply sympathetic temperament, and the tender human feeling, the pathos, and the woman-like loveliness of that character touched her heart and aroused all the enthusiasm of her moral nature; but, potent as she was in the realm of feeling, she was still more potent in the realm of imagination; and to my remembrance her Meg Merrilies, while not the highest ideal of human nature to which she gave an embodiment, was the one achievement that immediately and wholly revealed her distinctive, unique individualism. She first acted that part in 1837, when she was only twenty-one years old, but she always retained it in her repertory. She was higher, broader, larger, stronger than the part; she descended upon it; she acted it with consummate ease and fluency; she loosed into it a frenzy of the imagination, the nervous system, and the physical energies, blending poetic stress of feeling with a cumulative continuity of action, like the wild sweep of the tempest; and thus she made it magnificent and irresistible. The character, as drawn by Sir Walter Scott, in his novel of *Guy Mannering,* is somewhat fantastic and a little touched with insanity. The actress made it consistently superior and romantic, investing it with the fanatical purpose of his Magdalen Graeme, in *The Abbot,* together with the inspirational emotion and prophetic grandeur of his Norna, in *The Pirate.* The attributes of Miss Cushman's performance were romance, tenderness, pathos, profound knowledge of grief, and the authentic royalty of innate power. It was a creation of wild excitement, wavering reason and physical misery, incident upon frequent famine and years of habitual hardship, the compulsory recollection of a terrible crime committed by others, lonely communing with the haunting mysteries of Nature, and a rooted devotion to one purpose of sacred duty and love. At the moment, in the play, when Meg Merrilies encounters Bertram in the gipsy camp, at night, Miss Cushman made an entrance of felicitous dexterity and startling effect—thrusting back the fold of a tent and suddenly projecting herself from the aperture, but doing this in such a manner that she occupied exactly her right place in the dusky, romantic stage picture, before any except an expert observer could discern whence she came or how she got there; and the figure that she then presented—gaunt, haggard, disheveled, piteous and yet majestic—a veritable incarnation of all that is ominous, fateful and strangely beautiful—was a vision to register itself at once in the memory and there to remain forever. It was in that scene that she crooned the lullaby of the Bertrams of Ellangowan; and human ears have not heard a more touching cadence than when her voice trembled and broke in that simple, tender, fitful melody. . . .

Miss Cushman was not an egotist. She thought of her duty as an intellectual leader and exemplar; and in all that she undertook she wrought for the benefit of society. She not only acted great parts, but, in acting them, she gave something to her auditors. She imparted to them a conception of noble individuality and an incentive to noble behavior. She told them that they also were of an immortal spirit; that it was their duty to live pure lives; to do right; to endure with fortitude;

and to look onward with hope and trust. She did not fill their minds with images of decadence and promptings to degeneracy, recklessness and failure. She was a minister of the beautiful; and therefore she was a benefactor to her time and to all the times that are to follow. It is difficult to convey an adequate sense of the mental, moral and artistic superiority that she exemplified, or the inspiring influence that she exerted. Within the last thirty years many female actors have been distinguished in tragedy on the American stage, many beautiful women have appeared, and many displays have been made of genius and ability in various lines of dramatic art; but of opulent power, in acting, such as was manifested, at certain supreme moments, in the Othello of Forrest, the Lear of Booth, the Virginius of McCullough, the Cassius of Barrett, and the Lady Macbeth of Charlotte Cushman, the audience of the present day has seldom seen a suggestive example. The contemporary American stage is fortunate, as to actresses, in the romantic loveliness of Miss Julia Marlowe, the intellectual force and striking originality of Mrs. Fiske, the gentle beauty and profound devotion of Miss Viola Allen, the abundant passion and exquisite vocalism of Mrs. Carter, and the wild, dashing, picturesque abandonment of Miss Blanche Bates; but no woman in the theatre of this period shows the inspirational fire, the opulent intellect, the dominant character and the abounding genius—rising to great heights and satisfying the utmost demand of great occasions—that were victorious and imperial in Charlotte Cushman.

From *The Saturday Evening Post,*
December 29, 1906; reprinted in
Shadows of the Stage.

IRVING AND TERRY IN *MUCH ADO*

By WILLIAM WINTER

T H E excitement of that cheerful October evening, last year, when Henry Irving made his first appearance in New York, was repeated last night, at the Star Theatre, where *Much Ado About Nothing* was presented, and where Mr. Irving and Miss Terry effected their re-entrance, and were welcomed by a brilliant company, with the heartiest admiration and goodwill. The scene, indeed, was one of unusual brightness and enjoyment, both before the curtain and upon the stage. The applause, upon the entrance of Beatrice,—a rare vision of imperial yet gentle beauty!—broke forth impetuously and continued long; and upon the subsequent entrance of Benedick it rose into a storm of gladness and welcome.

Mr. Irving and Miss Terry—received here, at the outset, six months ago, more as old friends than as strangers—have now firmly established themselves in the admiration and esteem of the American audience; and, whatever difference of opinion may exist as to the aptitude or felicity of either of them, in any specific character, there is neither denial nor doubt of their sterling ability, achievements, and merits. They have become a portion of our pleasant, instructive, and valuable experience; and, since the American stage is cosmopolitan, they doubtless will long retain their place among the forces whence our culture as a people is stimulated and refreshed. The circumstances which attended their reëntrance were confirmatory of their permanent success and auspicious for their future.

Much Ado had not before been given in New York by Mr. Irving, but it had been given by him in other cities, and the rosy accounts of it sent from those cities had inspired a lively anticipation as to its general presentment, and as to the acting of Mr. Irving and Miss Terry in Benedick and Beatrice. This anticipation was fulfilled. The scenic exposition of the piece was elaborate, sufficiently correct, and often beautiful. "The inside of a church," as Shakespeare calls it, with his excellent directness, was one of the most imposing sets that have been displayed. The cast was the same, in many features, with which Mr. Irving revived this comedy at the London Lyceum, on October 11th, 1882, and the acting, throughout, was careful, even, and harmonious, as well in the subsidiary parts as in the principals.

Extended comment on the comedy of *Much Ado* is not requisite here. To traverse that familiar field must necessarily be to walk again in the path that many footsteps have already made. The piece was written at what seems to have been the happiest period of Shakespeare's life—the period when also he produced *A Midsummer Night's Dream* and *The Merchant of Venice*. To the analytic mind *Much Ado* is especially interesting as showing the maturity of Shakespeare's humor, his power to contemplate life in the objective point of view, and to portray it as if seen from above, with all its contrarieties and all its lights and shadows. To such a student the comedy is impressive, also, as showing the transfiguring power of Shakespeare's artistic skill and the fertile wealth of his invention; for in this piece he made an old story new by his treatment of it, and he invented Benedick and Beatrice, Dogberry and Verges, and all that relates to them—a remarkable feat of literary creation.

Upon Mr. Irving's impersonation of Benedick it is not easy to form a precise judgment. The performance is interesting and charming. The actor's personal singularity and the peculiarities of his histrionic method do not detract from its charm: on the contrary, they give it piquancy and make it unique. His way is his own way, and it is richly fraught with high-bred ease, intellectual repose, and demure gravity. He speaks the soliloquies, to be sure, more with the author's appreciation of them than with the air of the impersonator; but he banters and fences nimbly with the provoking Beatrice, and his demeanor in the challenge scene is resolute, dignified, simple, and rightly touched with a tone of dangerous menace. It is a certain moral and mental exaltation in his ideal of the part, combined with a sequent quietude or lack of dash in his execution, that perplex judgment, and make it difficult for an observer to determine whether this is Shakespeare's Benedick or a glorification of it. Whichever it be, it is a rich display of the art which an actor should peculiarly possess—the art to invest a fanciful conception with a natural body—and it is full of pleasure for those who see it. . . .

Mr. Irving's humor may, perhaps, be best defined as subtle playfulness. In Louis XI. it is the grisly playfulness of the sick panther. In Doricourt it is the mocking playfulness of the accomplished and fastidious gentleman. In Richard III. it is the heartless, sardonic, cruel playfulness of the astute, hypocritical villain. In Dubosc it is the cold, depraved, hideous playfulness of the insensate, swaggering ruffian. In each case it is playfulness—which, of course, may be either amiable or baleful—and it is invariably subtle. It is not the humour that laughs and shakes; it is the humour that smiles; and whether the smile shall be pleasant or unpleasant must depend upon the quality of the character out of which the humour is derived. Such humour may surprise and gratify a spectator, but it seldom or never can rejoice him. The word "amusing" seems a strange word to apply to either Dubosc or Louis XI.; but the most amusing moments that have been provided by the acting of Mr. Irving, thus far, in America, have been provided in those characters.

His Benedick, to be sure, amuses, but it is less amusing than charming. In this part his playfulness reappears under still another guise, and is the playfulness of an odd, quaint fellow, eccentric although elegant, and, although volatile and nimble on occasion, mostly observant, quizzical, fond of sagacious rumination, and slightly saturnine. If this is Shakespeare's Benedick, Mr. Irving has exactly reproduced him. If not, he has exalted him, intellectually and by personal traits, to a place among the gentle and sprightly satirical thinkers of the Shakespearean world. And this, perhaps, expresses his real achievement—that he has substituted a complex nature, based on goodness, merrily pretending to cynicism, and having rich reserves, for the dashing, predominant, sonorous, gallant known since Charles Kemble's day as the Benedick of the stage.

There are certain lines of the play which spring into the memory of every reader of *Much Ado,* the moment Beatrice is mentioned; and they help to elucidate her character. "A star danced," she says, "and under that was I born. . . . I thank my heart, poor fool, it keeps on the windy side of care. . . . I was born to speak all mirth and no matter. . . . I have a good eye, uncle, I can see a church by daylight. . . . I had rather hear my dog bark at a crow than a man swear he loves me." And Hero, who knows her best and loves her most, declares that "her spirits are as coy and wild as haggards of the rock. Disdain and scorn ride sparkling in her eyes, misprizing what they look on."

So far as a woman can be understood at all Beatrice has commonly been understood as the image and essence of flippant vivacity, strong, bold, brilliant, exultant, but untender and devoid of woman-like gentleness. She is a female Benedick, but, like Benedick, she is sound and wholesome at heart. If she has not the softness of her sex, neither has she its weakness, its conventionality, its fickleness, nor is there any romantic element in her nature. When once it is touched her heart will glow with generous warmth, but her sense is paramount to her sentiment, and a passionate resentment of injustice, where her family affections are concerned, is the deepest feeling that she displays; for at the very moment when she owns her love for Benedick she pledges him to risk his life in a duel in behalf of another woman.

Miss Terry's art is kindred with that of Mr. Irving, and her success was of the same description. She permeates the raillery of Beatrice with an indescribable charm of mischievous sweetness. The silver arrows of her pungent wit have no barb—for evidently she does not mean that they shall really wound. Her appearance and carriage are beautiful, and her tones melt into music. There is no hint of the virago here, and even the tone of sarcasm is superficial. Archness playing over kindness is the leading characteristic of Miss Terry's ideal of Beatrice. She is nothing harsher than a merry tease, and in the soliloquy after the arbor scene she drops all flippancy and glows into tender and loving womanhood. A more fascinating personality than this Beatrice could not be wished; and Miss Terry's method of expressing it is marked with pliant, effortless power and absolute simplicity.

In these impersonations, Mr. Irving and Miss Terry apparently have chosen—partly with conscious design and partly under the stress of inexorable temperamental conditions—to transfigure rather than literally to interpret the conception of Shakespeare, as to Benedick and Beatrice. Mr. Irving presents a higher and finer character than Benedick is in Shakespeare's page; and Miss Terry presents a more lovely and tender woman than the Beatrice of the comedy.

Much Ado has been several times as well set upon the American stage as it is now set by Mr. Irving, if reference be made to dresses and to construction of scenes. The superiority of Mr. Irving's mounting of it consists in the colouring and tone of the scenery, and in a studiously minute attention to minor detail—nothing being omitted, within reason, that can heighten illusion or deepen the effect of nature. It is difficult to keep the judicious line in these matters, and stage-mounting may easily be carried too far. The acting is more important than the trappings that surround it. Much of the scenery habitually used on the American stage, however, is too obviously "scenery," and it may be said to smell of new paint. In England Stanfield and Telbin, among others, have painted stage scenery, and particular attention has been given there to mellowness of colour and to a due simulation of the effects of time and climate upon architecture. Mr. Irving has lived and laboured where he could have the counsel of such artists as Alma Tadema and such scholars as Planché. He tells nothing that was not known before; but he practically enforces his lesson, pointing out the right way by zealously pursuing it.

And what is true of much American stage scenery is equally true of much American acting—it is too obviously "acting"; the wires are not concealed. Under the instructive influence of Mr. Irving's performances numbers of persons have been made to understand this truth, which yet is not a new truth to the habitual thinker upon this subject. From the completeness of the representation of *Much Ado,* whether viewed as picture or performance, this is the chief deducible lesson.

From *The New York Tribune,* April 1, 1884.
Reprinted in *Henry Irving.* (1885.)

IBSENITES AND IBSENISM

By WILLIAM WINTER

I B S E N has been thrust upon the English-speaking Stage as a Dramatic Messiah, charged with a New Revelation, another Moses emergent from the celestial Presence with a message for mankind, paramount to all other messages that have ever been received. He is, we are assured, the foremost dramatic influence of our age, penetrating all nations and affecting all minds, and society is summoned to bow before this stern and awful Scandinavian person and learn at last the truth. It has come to pass, furthermore, that to disregard that summons, to dissent in any degree from the proposition that Ibsen was a great dramatist and that his dramas ought to be universally acted and admired, is to incur the hideous penalty of denunciation as a reactionist and a fogy. Yet Ibsen is not a dramatist, in the true sense of that word, and Ibsenism, which is rank, deadly pessimism, is a disease, injurious alike to the Stage and to the Public,—in as far as it affects them at all,—and therefore an evil to be deprecated.

The didactic tendency of which, in his group of "sociological plays," Ibsen is a principal exponent is pernicious, for the reason that it is a tendency to represent human nature as radically and universally vile and human society as hopelessly corrupt. "I go down into the sewers," said the Norwegian writer, and "my business is to *ask* ques-tions, not to *answer* them." So be it. But, whatever be the motive, *why* should the product of an exploration of "sewers" be exploited through the medium of the Theatre? Granting to Ibsen and his followers the highest and best motives, they have altogether mistaken the province of the Theatre in choosing it as the fit medium for the expression of sociological views,—views, moreover, which, once adopted, would disrupt society. There are halls to be hired. There is an audience for the lecture,—if lecturing would serve any good purpose. There are societies of learned men who study sociology and are ever ready to accept illumination on the subject, from any one who can provide it. Why inflict the Stage with inquiry as to "original sin," or the conse-quence of ancestral wickedness, or the moral obliquity resultant from hereditary disease, or the various forms of corruption incident to vice and crime? Since when did the Theatre become a proper place for a clinic of horrors and the vivisection of moral ailments?

It is easy to say, as was said by the despondent, hysterical, inflam-matory Jeremiah, in the Bible, that the heart of man is deceitful above all things and desperately wicked. But what good have you done when you have made that statement? As a matter of fact it is only half true. There are in the world many kind, pure hearts and noble minds; not a day passes without its deeds of simple heroism; not an hour passes without some manifestation of beautiful self-sacrifice, splendid patience, celestial fidelity to duty, and sweet manifestation of unselfish love. There must be evil to illustrate good, but in art, and emphatically in dramatic art, it must be wisely selected. The spectacle of virtue in human character and loveliness in human conduct will accomplish far more for the benefit of society than ever can be accomplished by the spectacle of imbecile propensity, vicious conduct, or any form of the aberrancy of mental disease....

As a moral philosopher Ibsen stultifies himself: "My business is to *ask* questions, not to *answer* them!" Did Ibsen seriously suppose,—do his advocates seriously suppose,—that the defects of Society were unknown or unregarded before he noticed them? A moral philosopher, if he is to be of any use to the world, must do something besides "ask questions,"—something more than amble in the streets vociferating "rottenness, sin, and iniquity!" Ibsen's sociological plays neither impart nor enforce helpful significance as to the social themes they present: they suggest no improvement. Their author was not only dreary and dejected himself; he was the cause that dreariness and dejection are in the minds of all clear-brained thinkers who study his writings. His ability, such as it was,—and it was not extraordinary,—entitles him to fair recognition, which he has received, but neither Ibsen's ability nor that of any other individual is of the slightest practical value to the public unless, whatever be the medium of expression, it is used for the public good. The need of the world is direction and assistance, and its honor and reverence are due to those who help it. Ibsen's "philosophic" plays are intolerable,—one reason being that they deal not with characteristics, but with symptoms: in the expressive phrase of Wordsworth, they "murder to dissect." A reformer who calls you to crawl with him into a sewer, merely to see and breathe its feculence, is a pest. As a thinker, as a moral philosopher, as a commentator, as an artist, whether in writing or in life, Ibsen was so far below and so far behind such a man, for example, as the great novelist and true reformer Charles Reade (whose moral enthusiasm was almost unique, and whose perception of moral obliquity and social injustice was only equalled by his wrathful, scorching antagonism of them, in sympathy with human goodness, potential and actual), that it would be an insult to Reade's memory to institute any comparison between them.

It has already been noticed that the accomplished actress Mrs. Fiske has been more influential than any other member of the dramatic profession in America in the encouragement and practical support of the Ibsen movement. It must always be difficult to comprehend why this should be so, because Mrs. Fiske possesses a good repertory of old plays and has shown judgment and taste, when she so pleased, in acquiring new ones. The befogging effect, even on a vigorous intellect, of surrender to Ibsenism is well illustrated by the published remarks on Ibsen made by that actress. Mrs. Fiske observes that "as the principal characters in an Ibsen drama were living many years before the visible presentation, the producer of an Ibsen drama must delve into the childhood of those characters, and discover and comprehend all that has gone before." Since that is true as to the stage treatment of all characters that are worthy of serious consideration in any and every play, the appliance of the principle to Ibsen's colloquial fabrics serves only once more to suggest Dr. Holmes's familiar insect which "says an undisputed thing in such a solemn way." ...

The case for Ibsenism, in as far as there is any case, has not been urged more ardently or insistently than by Harrison Grey Fiske, for many years owner and editor of *The New York Dramatic Mirror,* and advocacy of it by that authority can rightly be accepted as comprehensive and representative.

"Truth will not down," says Mr. Fiske, "and the speaker of it must, sooner or later, be heard. Ibsen is *the apostle of truth,* and his dramas mean something that is human. *Much of his dramatic motivity is aberrant, but aberrancy, unhappily, is a strong characteristic of humanity itself, under the artificial standards that have sought to control impulse....*"

Nothing has been more fully demonstrated by the experience of mankind than that a work which is distinctly moral in its platitudinous precept can be, and frequently is, potently immoral not by reason of what it preaches, but by reason of what it exhibits. This fact, however, is beyond the comprehension of a certain order of mind, and, consequently, those persons who, acting on conviction, have opposed the Ibsen movement, as a movement pernicious alike to morals and to art, are denounced as "abnormal moralists," "prurient purists," and "sentimental back-numbers." The study of Ibsen seems to infect his "all or nothing" admirers with a mental confusion kindred with his own,—or perhaps, it is a mental confusion kindred with his own that makes them his admirers. "Ibsen's men and women," says James Huneker, *"offend those who believe the Theatre to be a place of sentimentality or clowning."* That may be true—or false. Credible testimony on the subject could come only from persons, whosoever they may be, who entertain such a silly belief. But some of the plays of Ibsen and his kind *do* offend persons who respect the Theatre, when maintained as a place for pure drama and fine acting; a place in which, while presenting the widest variety of right subject,—tragedy, comedy, farce, melodrama, burlesque, musical comedy, pantomime, or spectacle,—nothing can be shown or discussed which is outside the legitimate province of art, or offensive to the general sense of decency, refinement, and good taste.

Much encomium has, from time to time, been printed, relative to the alleged supreme "technique" of Ibsen's plays, but particular elucidation of it is not provided. A disquisition is not a play. There is more true *drama* in Wills's *Olivia,* Young's *Jim the Penman,* Thomas's *The Witching Hour,* and McLellan's *Leah Kleschna* (though the latter is overfreighted with didacticism and marred by a weak last act) than there is in a round dozen of the works of Ibsen. The beneficent effect of a work of art can operate as subtly as that of sunlight: it certainly is not less sure. The injurious effect of a perversion of art can operate as subtly as does the infection of disease: often it is not less harmful. All persons who chance to be exposed to disease are not necessarily infected. There is, however, no room to doubt the benefit or to question the need of sunlight. The province of art is the ministry of beauty, and beauty, in art, is inseparable from morality. That is the only ground on which the existence of art can be incontestably justified. . . .

"The immorality of these plays is so well concealed that only abnormal moralists can detect it. These plays are not *sex dramas* at all, in the sense that Sardou's dramas are." Thus Mr. Huneker. Quite true, in as far as the latter proposition is concerned,—though false and impudent in the former. As far as known nobody has described them as "sex dramas." Immorality, in its worst aspects, is not a matter of sexual relation between men and women. Some of Sardou's plays represent not only the great, fundamental attribute of drama,—that of action,— but also they represent the crime, suffering, and lethal catastrophe that frequently, and naturally, proceed from illicit conduct, and often they interest the mind (and therein are hurtful, because vicious), and sometimes, while they interest, they do not offend. Ibsen's dramas, when treating of the relations of sex,—notably in *Hedda Gabler, Rosmersholm* and *Ghosts,*—treat them as affected under the reaction of disease, and thus they fill the mind, whether of the reader or the auditor, with disgust and gloom: they pervert life: they tend to disseminate misinformation, augment ignorance, and mislead weak or ill-educated minds, and therein they are immoral. . . .

The most essential attribute, whether for a dramatist or a philosopher, is clarity of thought and statement. In that respect the writings of Ibsen are conspicuously deficient. Among his most devoted followers there is dissension as to his meanings, one of them, indeed, not hesitating to declare, as a merit, that the bard himself very likely did not always know precisely what he meant. Nevertheless, it is claimed that an author who could not,—and certainly did not,—state his own thoughts clearly ought to be recognized and exalted as a leader of the thought of the world. The commonplace element in literature, as it stands forth in its true colors, can be endured, but when it vaunts itself or is thrust upon thoughtful attention as genius, originality, and power it becomes intolerable. Ibsen, as a writer of a number of variously flaccid, insipid, tainted, obfuscated, and nauseous plays, could be borne, although, even in that aspect, he is an offence to taste and a burden on patience, but Ibsen obtruded as a sound leader of thought is a grotesque absurdity. As a dramatic writer he distorted almost everything he touched. Not since the halcyon days of Tupper, when the reading world was gravely apprized that "a babe in the house is a well-spring of pleasure," and was expected to be thrilled by that announcement, has such a torrent of mingled imbecility and commonplace been poured into print as is found in the writings of that crazy theorist; and not since Tupper's noon of notoriety as the prophet of milk and water have the disciples of any literary exotic ventured to vaunt him as a philosopher, with nothing to sustain the pretension except a mass of crotchets and platitudes.

Strange assertions are made by the Ibsenite. "The form of the Ibsen plays," says Mr. Huneker, "is compact with ideas and emotions. We don't usually go to the Theatre to think or to feel." That assurance may convey the truth as to Ibsenites: there is abundant reason for supposing some of them to be incapable of either feeling or thought; but, in view of the decisive fact that, primarily and essentially, the acted drama always does and always must appeal to the emotions and then to the mind, that is, to the intellectual faculties, what should be thought of the mental condition which makes it possible for such a statement to be made? If it is not *feeling* enforced by *thought* that brings tears to the eyes at a performance of *Lear* or *Becket* or *Sweet Lavender* or *Alabama* or *The Middleman*—what, in the name of common sense, is it?...

A final objection to this author is that, apart from the lack of fitness in his themes, he does not discuss his subjects in a fair manner,

looking at both sides of the question, and without specious special
pleading. "He is determined" (still Mr. Huneker) "to tell the truth
about our microcosmic baseness." If so, why does it happen that his
determination generally eventuates not in truth, but in falsehood? Does
it follow, because a Caligula and a Faustina once existed, and still, perhaps, are possibilities, that all men are monsters and all women bestial
wantons? Are there no unselfish persons? Ibsen, we are assured by
the same authority, "made his report of the human soul *as he saw it.*"
In that, clearly, he was within his right; but, since his report was to be
inflicted on the public through the medium of the Stage, it is greatly to
be regretted that his optics were not in a healthful condition. Mental
astigmatism is an infirmity, not a talent, and the "report" is not the
less misleading and injurious, because inadequate through lack of perception, than it would be if false through deliberate intention to deceive. Furthermore, even in his misrepresentation of human nature,
Ibsen was not original. Cynics have always existed, and Dean Swift's
report of the human soul as *he* saw it,—a report made nearly two
hundred years ago (1727),—far transcends that of Ibsen not only in
every particular of technical expertness of expression, but in melancholy incompleteness, purblind censoriousness, gross falsehood, and
ignominious censure. The excuse, or at least the explanation, for Swift
is—incipient insanity, which terminated in madness. The explanation
of Ibsen, likewise, is, unquestionably, a disordered brain.

One great error of dramatic "reformers" lies in the basic assumption that change necessarily signifies improvement. Often it is recession. Achievement in the future may excel achievement in the past.
It was long ago observed by a wise observer that "we know not what
a day may bring forth." Let us hope that the new day will provide
dramatic writers of greater and finer ability than has ever been manifested and that the art of acting will attain to a loftier height than it
ever yet has reached. Entertainment of that hope and endeavor to
realize it will not retard advancement! There are many adverse influences, but in the strife between good and evil good is destined ultimately to prevail. Great minds will be born, and noble thoughts will
impel to noble endeavor. The movement of the world is onward and
upward, but that movement has never been helped, and it never will
be helped, by any such gospel of disordered mentality, distrust, de-

spondency, bitterness, and gloom as that which proceeded from the diseased mind of Henrik Ibsen. And if the reader is half as sick of the whole subject of his plays as I am, he must be indeed rejoiced to come to the end of this chapter!

From *The Wallet of Time*,
Moffat, Yard & Company, 1913.

THE FIRST IBSEN IN AMERICA

Modjeska's *Thora*[1] in Louisville

A BRILLIANT audience crowded Macauley's Theatre last evening, the occasion being the first performance in America of *Thora,* a Norwegian drama by Henrik Ibsen. Mme. Modjeska, if the *Courier-Journal* is not mistaken, has appeared in this play before, but not in this country. The production last evening was, therefore, a novelty, curiosity to see Modjeska in a new rôle, as well as admiration for the great actress, arousing more than ordinary interest in the performance.

Thora is the young wife of Oswald Helmer, who has just been promoted to the position of "manager of a bank." She is looked on by her husband and the world as scarcely more than a doll and she is loved by Helmer more as a child than a woman; he is content that she should laugh, prattle, sing and dance through life for his delectation. Thora, in consonance with her seemingly frivolous nature, is apparently rather extravagant, as she is constantly appealing to her husband for money. Unknown to him, however, she needs this money in paying off a debt which she has contracted in this way: A year after their marriage Helmer became so broken down from overwork that his physician decreed that unless he should take a holiday in the South he would die, and Thora, to secure the means for defraying the expenses of such a journey, borrowed the money from a man who was not surfeited with conscientious scruples. It being necessary that in addition to her own name the acknowledgment should bear that of her father also as a security, and he being at the point of death, Thora, in innocence of the nature of the act and its consequences, had affixed

[1] The play is, of course, *A Doll's House;* Thora is Nora; and a happy ending has been added.

his name herself. Herein lies the motive of the plot. Helmer thinks that the money that saved his life was a gift from Thora's father and it is Thora's aim to keep the truth from him. Krogstad, having become incensed at Helmer for discharging him from the bank and at Thora for having failed in her intercessions in his behalf, threatens to inform the husband of the wife's forgery and, in her efforts to avert this, her attempts to be her usual, joyous self, with this dread hanging over her, take up most of the first two acts of the play. The drama opens promisingly. The first act was mainly introductory and with the exception that it might be less prolix, it serves its purpose well. The second act, on the whole, is very good. The interest is drawing to a focus. The letter from Krogstad to Helmer, informing him of his wife's crime, is actually in the house, deposited in the letter box, and it is the one last despairing effort of Thora—through her dancing, singing, anything —to divert her husband from the letters and protract the moment of her doom.

The third and last act, however, does not fulfill the promise of the first and second. It begins dramatically, but ends turgidly. There is a fine situation when, Helmer having retired to the next room to read his letters, Thora knows at last the time has come when he will learn her secret. Throwing her coat around her, she is about to hurry from the house and drown herself, when Helmer, rushing forth, stops her flight and denounces her in the most brutal and bitter manner, anathematizing her for ruining his name in the estimation of the world. Thora's ideal of her husband is thus rudely shattered, and she stands as if petrified, for she had been convinced that her husband, once learning of her crime, would avow it himself to shield her, and it was to prevent this sacrifice on his part that she determined to die. At this stage of affairs another letter comes from Krogstad, who having met with good fortune himself, resolved to cease his persecution and sends to Thora the forged document. It is Helmer's turn now to be astounded because his wife does not respond to his lordly overtures for a reconciliation. Thoroughly disillusioned as to his character, she withdraws, dons a street dress and announces her intention of leaving her husband forever. He expostulates, argues and pleads in vain, but finally, through the medium of the children, some indefinite talk about "religion," there is a reunion, a rushing together and a falling curtain on a happy family tableau. The principal inconsistency of the play is at this point. A woman, cherishing as high an ideal of her husband as Thora did and finding him as unworthy of it as Helmer was, cannot mount him again on his pinnacle through any such superficial means as here employed. In the original drama, Thora carries out the logical situation by leaving her husband. Probably after all the most consistent ending would be in her death.

The play is one of mental development bordering at times on the psychological and does not possess the intricacy or rapidity of action which best pleases the average American audience. In it, however, Mme. Modjeska has a character different from any other in her repertory, a character which calls on her subtlest divination and her most engaging talents. Her portrayal of the innocent, gay, true-hearted Thora is full of beauty and varying charm, reaching in the second act a nervous intensity and strength and yet maintaining a rare delicacy and grace which seem in the power of none so well as of this actress. In the final act Modjeska was the strength of every scene and in the first act her personation was delightful in its winsomeness and its changing, dainty color. The character, indeed, is a beautiful one, and in that pure womanliness, that exquisite art necessary for its interpretation, where is the actress so gifted as Modjeska? Modjeska, in truth, was the performance. It would be impossible to predict the success of *Thora* without her. The other characters are few and altogether subsidiary. Dr. Rank, by the way, who has nothing to do with the development of the play, in his mystic melancholy, his black crosses, etc., is thoroughly Norwegian.

Thora as a play will probably never become very popular with American audiences, but the charm of the character and of Mme. Modjeska's portrayal should insure it a continual life.

From *The Louisville Courier-Journal,*
December 8, 1883.

MARY ANDERSON

By J. RANKEN TOWSE

... N A T U R E endowed her with rare beneficence. When, as a mere girl, she first entered upon the stage, she presented a figure of classic and virginal purity that was almost ideal. Her tall, lithe form was at once stately and graceful, the poise of her head was stag-like, and her face was radiant with health, innocence, and dignified beauty. It was by the spell of her personal charms that she instantly made her way into the heart of the American public, and she retired to a happy and prosperous privacy when still at the height of her popularity, while that spell was yet potent. A finer type of young American womanhood could not easily be imagined. Like Lady Teazle, "bred wholly in the country," she was accepted at once as the representative American actress of her time, was fondly called "our Mary," and quickly became the object of a widespread affection and admiration that might, without much exaggeration, be called national. As a novice she was placed by her worshipers on a pinnacle from which she was never deposed. Her memory is still surrounded by a glamor which no one could wish to dispel. Her beauty, her spotless character, her graciousness, her intelligence, her refined manner, and her unquestionable dramatic instinct and ability contributed greatly to the honor and glory of the American stage while she adorned it; but for all that, she was never a great actress or a great artist. She does not belong in the same category with Charlotte Cushman, Janauschek, Modjeska, Clara Morris, or Edwin Booth.

In her early days, when she was first acclaimed as a great genius, she was manifestly a tyro, hastily and imperfectly drilled, crude and spasmodic in action, but armed with fascination, courage, ambition, and a remarkable faculty of declamation. Her voice was always one of the most potent weapons in her artistic armory. It was a rich contralto, thoroughly feminine, but uncommonly full, deep, supple, and melodious. She knew how to avail herself of its finest tones, and consequently her delivery of blank verse was not always proof against the charge of monotony—but she often employed them to splendid purpose. As she gained experience she grew in power of emotional expression and was able to reinforce vocal richness with that inner throb of feeling that implies, if it does not necessarily denote, inspiration, but she never succeeded in identifying herself with any of the first-rate tragedy parts which she undertook. Now and again, where she could bring all her natural gifts into full display, she made some admirable points and was, for the moment, wonderfully picturesque, imposing, majestic, or appealing. But she exhibited—I am speaking now of tragedy or deeply emotional parts—little versatility in method or variety of resource.

She had certain formulas in which she was proficient, and she applied them to corresponding types of situation with a deadly and unmodified reiteration. In the mechanism of her art she never advanced beyond a moderate proficiency. What she had learned to do she did well, but her executive ability was rigidly limited. It ceased to expand. In it she revealed neither invention nor ingenuity. She was always, solely and inevitably, Mary Anderson, and she reached her artistic boundaries when she had learned to express herself freely and fully. Thus she created no illusion of character, and was only fully successful when her part fitted her like a good glove. She had intelligence, a liberal measure of capacity, a sure comprehension of the finer feminine instincts and feelings, but she had not genius. In great parts, demanding imagination, passionate eloquence, or subtle discrimination, she was second-rate.

It is not necessary to dwell long upon her high tragic experiments, or even to mention all of them. Her Juliet was charming in the earlier acts, a little lacking, perhaps, in romantic coloring, but exquisite in its virginal faith and innocence. In the tragic climaxes it was impressive only in its picturesqueness and vocal power. It was a sympathetic but uninspired performance. In Sheil's *Evadne,* she was constantly beyond her depth in dealing with the complex emotions of the character, but her statuesque beauty, her sense of pose, and her declamatory vigor enabled her to fill the theatrical situations with considerable effect. In the final act she was at her best. In her white robes she was an ideal figure of maidenly grace, dignity, and purity. With her rich voice she gave the fullest value to the sonorous lines relating to the deeds of her ancestors, and her challenge to her royal persecutor was superb....

When she rashly ventured to challenge comparison with Charlotte

Cushman in the character of Meg Merrilies, she not only offered a conclusive demonstration of her own artistic inferiority, but a curious lack of histrionic intuition in her failure to make legitimate use of her own physical qualifications. Witnessing her performance, one would naturally suppose that she had never read *Guy Mannering*. Scott gives a minute description of his famous Gypsy Sybil. She was a masculine figure, six feet high, erect as a grenadier, with a voice like a man's. Mary Anderson, who had the stature, and the vigor, and the voice, chose to depict the formidable Meg as a withered, bent, and tottering old crone. The assumption of old age—which is not difficult—was not badly done, but by this wilful or ignorant misrepresentation she robbed the character of its proper material dimensions, which she could have supplied, as well as its spiritual significance, which she could not. Dramatic genius could never so flagrantly abuse an opportunity. What would not Cushman have given for those additional inches!

In the parts which really suited her—whose component elements were those of her own temperament and personality—Mary Anderson was wholly delightful. Her Galatea in W. S. Gilbert's admirable *Pygmalion and Galatea* was a charming performance, which reflected the spirit of the author in its various moods of humor, sarcasm, and pathos with delicate and artistic fidelity. As the statue she was so lovely an example of pure classic grace that the infatuation of Pygmalion was no cause for surprise. Her awakening to life was an exceedingly delicate and imaginative piece of pantomime. The naïveté of her innocence was perfect, pure unsophisticated curiosity and bepuzzlement, irresistibly true and piquant, without the slightest trace of artifice. Her timid, questioning, reflective, unsuspicious air, and her grave, gentle, tuneful voice, were all beautifully appropriate. Her treatment of the episode of the wounded fawn was exceedingly clever and veracious, full of tenderness and pity, and delightfully natural in its childlike shrinking from the notion of annihilating death. The embodiment was a most felicitous combination of the human, the poetic, and the idealistic. It could have been furnished only by a clever, refined, and good woman. Her Parthenia, in *Ingomar,* was a performance of the same type, marked by the same methods. It was an older Galatea, with a little more sophistication, a little more of the purely human and feminine, but the same spell of virginal freshness and innocence. A third impersonation which will always be cherished in the memories of those who saw it was her Perdita, in *The Winter's Tale,* instinct with the spirit of the springtime, buoyant with the joy of life, manifesting its happiness in a dance which was the very poetry of motion. In these three parts Mary Anderson found herself, in more senses than one, and they were the masterpieces of her theatrical gallery.

From *Sixty Years of the Theatre,*
(Funk and Wagnalls, 1916.)

EDWIN BOOTH

The Last Tragedian of His Era

By J. RANKEN TOWSE

... M R . L O C K R I D G E [1] holds that Edwin Booth (whom the writer saw in all his best known parts) is entitled to the credit of modifying the extravagances of the "old school," and forming, as it were, a connecting link between the old and the new. This is not correct. The Shakespearean drama and the older comedies (practically) disappeared from the stage at his withdrawal simply because there were no actors left capable of performing it. The "rot" had set in long before he left the stage. For the last twenty years of his career his supporting companies, except for two or three veterans, were often notoriously incompetent, even in his own theatre on Twenty-third Street. He was no manager. It was during his later alliance with Barrett and Modjeska that his representations were fairly satisfactory. This was due to Barrett who was a manager, a scholar, an idealist, and an indefatigable worker. Edwin himself, as was natural, was to all intents and purposes an actor of the school to which his father belonged, the school of the Keans, Macready, and Samuel Phelps, and he adopted largely its traditions and methods. But he had not the robustness, vocal or physical powers, or half-insane fury of his sire, who as Richard III is reported as having driven his Richmond from the stage into the orchestra seats. He was of slighter and more elegant form, only slightly above middle

[1] *Darling of Misfortune, Edwin Booth, 1833–1893,* by Richard Lockridge. New York, The Century Company. 1932.

height, while his face, with its luminous dark eyes and cleanly cut mouth, was singularly handsome, mobile, and expressive. The face of an actor.

And in the early days with his father, and afterwards in his varied experiences on the road—where he played everything from high tragedy to black-face—he had acquired an almost perfect mastery of theatrical technique. He knew every trick of the stage, and had been widely recognized as a coming man, when his brother's assassination of Lincoln drove him into retirement. That shock, doubtless, affected his character, increased his brooding and, possibly, modified his style. At any rate his Hamlet—the great success of his famous reappearance at the Winter Garden, in New York—must have been in striking contrast with that of the elephantine and thunderous Forrest. It was some time after that the present writer first saw it. By then it was a wonderfully finished, consistent and interesting, if scarcely inspired performance. It was graceful, refined, melancholy, philosophical, drily humorous and satirical, but it lacked fire at critical moments and real vitality. The soliloquies were beautifully spoken—his elocutionary skill was always a great asset—but in the "Oh, what a rogue," after the scene with the players, the note of true passion was wanting. There was nothing of the lover in his scene with Ophelia. He was admirable with Rosencrantz and Guildenstern, with the grave-diggers, and with Horatio, less happy in the burial scene with Laertes and in the closet scene with the Queen. In the final act he was spirited and pathetic. As a whole it was a notably fine embodiment, remarkable for its general consistency and artistic polish—the best of its generation. Personally, save for its unfortunate foreign intonation, the writer preferred the impersonation of Charles Fechter, not because of its blond wig— which was doubtless correct, in spite of the ridiculous fuss made over it—but because of its general form and character, its more romantic coloring, and its glow of human passion. And it had a flavor of originality. Booth's Hamlet followed traditional lines more closely, as did that of Forbes Robertson, of which the most striking attributes were dignity and eloquence. He was the last of the "old school" players, being linked with Samuel Phelps, of Sadler's Wells fame. Since his day the only Hamlet of note has been that of Walter Hampden, the most human of them all.

The strange thing about Edwin Booth is that, although his renown is associated chiefly with high tragedy, it was in melodramatic or romantic parts that he revealed his greatest powers of tragic expression. His Othello, even in its most wrathful moments, seemed pale and colorless beside the weighty and overwhelming Moor of Salvini. He showed none of the emotional power of E. L. Davenport or John McCullough in that character. He conducted the murder of Desdemona in the manner of a solemn sacrifice. The deed suggested little of the fury of maddened jealousy. But the impersonation, in its entirety, had salient merits in the technical finish, its consistency, oratorical perfection, and strokes of genuine pathos. The opening address to the Senate was beautifully delivered, but in the later scenes there was more of theatrical dexterity than of fire or inspiration. His Iago, probably his masterpiece, has rarely been equaled, never excelled. It was a triumph of subtle deviltry masked beneath an outward garb of brisk geniality. Only in the soliloquies was the inveterate and reasoned malignity exposed. It was an extraordinarily fine performance, which made the deception of Othello altogether plausible. His Macbeth, excellent in the scenes before and up to the murder of the King, and always marked with his invariable theatrical skill and admirable declamation, failed afterward to realize the furious desperation of the hag-ridden usurper. It was most impressive in its moments of pathos—as after the appearance of Banquo's ghost—but here his gentleness was scarcely in consonance with the actual situation. His Richard III was in strong contrast with that of the powerful John McCullough which followed the lines set by his own father and Edwin Forrest. It had less of sound and fury and more of subtlety and intellectuality. It had the main characteristics of his Iago, was a clever, interesting, but not highly impressive performance, of which the outstanding feature was the hypocrisy. He did not shine particularly in the part and practically abandoned it in his later years. In Lear—a character which no less an authority than Charles Lamb declared to be unactable—he was more fortunate. To say that he realized all the emotional vastness of Shakespeare's ideal would be absurd, but he made the old demented King a most memorable figure. In the opening act he carried himself with rude authority, and exhibited rising passion with eloquent gesture and his usual declamatory power. And in the delivery of the curse upon Goneril he reached a thrilling height of rage, which however savored rather of melodramatic fury than of tragic intensity. But it was exceedingly effective. It was in the mad scenes on the heath, with the Fool, that he was most successful. He played these with a fascinating blend of mild humor, deep pathos, and flashing satire. And he was admirable in the closing scene over the dead body of his daughter. The representation must be reckoned among his best.

With the incidents of his private life, his friends—among whom were many of eminence in literature, art, and commerce—and his avocations Mr. Lockridge in this book, as has been said already, deals so fully and advisedly that his report demands nothing but commendation. It may be questioned, however, whether it does not insist, somewhat too persistently, upon the undeniable weakness in Booth's character, his inherited tendency to drink. This was doubtless strengthened by the depression caused by the successive misfortunes which befell him. But he was not an habitual drunkard. His outbreaks of intemperance were spasmodical and rare, were followed by periods of dejection, and seldom affected his public performances, except upon one especially regrettable occasion. His domestic troubles, during his second marriage, were of a peculiarly bitter and harassing kind. If Mr. Lockridge was aware of these he deserves credit for the tactful and reticent way in which he refers to them. They were sufficient to madden a man of Edwin's former cruel experiences. It was a marvel that he was able to carry on. But in his closing years of retirement in the club which he had founded, among his professional and other friends, he was at peace, rich, honored, beloved, and happy—a fine ending of a brilliant but checquered career.

From *The Saturday Review of Literature,*
October 22, 1932.

CLARA MORRIS

By J. RANKEN TOWSE

...CLARA MORRIS is one of the very few American actresses to whom the gift of genius may be properly ascribed. It is by no means easy to define her place in any coldly critical category. She was, first and last, a natural born actress. If judged by her artistic equipment only, she could not establish claim to any very high place in the ranks of her contemporaries. She was far behind many of them in artistic cunning, but she distanced all of them in flashes of convincing realism and in poignancy of natural emotion. She was often barely respectable as an elocutionist, she was habitually crude, and occasionally unrefined, in pose, gesture, and utterance; she had distressful mannerisms, she could not or did not attempt to modify or disguise her individual personality, her range was limited—she could not soar into the upper regions of tragedy—but, nevertheless, she showed, especially in emotional crises, a strong grasp of diversified characters within her own boundaries and illuminated them, at intervals, with such a blaze of vivid truthfulness that, for the moment, she seemed to be perfectly identified with them.

Such effects, very rare upon the stage, may safely be accepted as proofs of dramatic genius, of which, of course, there are varying degrees. And Miss Morris's genius, while unmistakable, was of a very special and restricted order. It was not manifested in romance, in high comedy, or in the heroic emotions, whether good or evil, but shone out resplendently in the intensification of the commoner passions of ordinary human nature, and particularly in the depiction of pathetic suffering, whether mute or tearfully eloquent. As she never really succeeded, or came very near to success, in any great part, she can not be called a great actress. It is only in great parts, embodying lofty imagination, that demonstrations of a great interpretative faculty can be made. This test she failed to satisfy. But she was great as a realist in the exaggerated, false, or morbid emotionalism of the current French plays of her period, and displayed high intelligence in a considerable range of English drama. . . .

Her audacity [in playing Lady Macbeth] was largely in excess of her equipment, but she made no ridiculous failure. Neither in physique nor in declamatory power was she fitted for parts of tragic dignity and passion. And she did not attempt the impossible. "Look like the innocent flower, but be the serpent under it," was the line that furnished the keynote to her conception. She presented a slight, lithe figure, richly but plainly dressed, a girlish and, but for a certain hardness in the eyes and mouth, an innocent face, surmounted by a coronet and a mass of golden hair—a seductive and dangerous siren, full of lure and guile, amatory, callous, ambitious, and immoral. And such were the characteristics which she successfully portrayed. She did not dominate her husband, but humored, tempted and spurred him.

From the traditional notion of Lady Macbeth she was, of course, leagues away, but not much further than was Ellen Terry. Conservative critics rated her soundly, but her ideal was not entirely devoid of authoritative support. The great Sarah Siddons herself is said to have found warrant for it, but rejected it as unsuited to her majestic style. Henry Irving created a new Macbeth to harmonize with his own artistic limitations and personal idiosyncrasies. Miss Morris did the same thing; but we know that what is but a choleric word for a captain is flat blasphemy for the private soldier. Personally I believe that the true Lady Macbeth is to be found midway between the Morris-Terry and the Siddons-Cushman types. The latter is the grander and more imposing, but the former is more human and, perhaps, more subtle.

With the masses the more heroic embodiment will always take precedence. Miss Morris's assumption had at least the merits of originality, cleverness, and sustained interest. She was never conventional and she made many interesting points. Her elocution, inevitably, was sadly defective. Her reading of Macbeth's letter was, from the old point of view, tame, but it was natural and not ineffectual. In the soliloquy following it there was more of clairvoyant speculation than of murder. Her invocation to the spirits to unsex her was uttered with the concentrated intensity which she could always command. There was more of mockery than ferocity in her manner when she upbraided Macbeth for his vacillation. She almost laughed when she compared him with the "poor cat in the adage." After the murder, in taking the dagger from her demoralized lord, she made it plain that it was only her will-power that enabled her to overcome her own natural feminine weakness. In the banquet scene again she suggested with unerring skill the strain of an outward composure maintained by will-power under the stress of harrowing anxiety and dread. She signified her distress to the audience while offering a courteous front to her amazed guests as if the king's seizure were really the frequent infirmity she asserted it to be. But when the chamber had been cleared she exhibited complete nervous collapse, uttering a distressful wail which, however unauthorized, was wonderfully impressive; and her sleep-walking scene, wholly novel and modern, was intensely pathetic in its denotement of spiritual anguish. The personification as a whole lacked the regal, imperious, imaginative, and masculine qualities of Shakespeare's heroine—it was all woman—but it had brains and consistency, excited admiration and reflection, and, considering the limitations of the actress, it was a memorable achievement. . . .

She made a wonderful but somewhat unprofitable emotional display also in a condensed version of Nicholas Rowe's *Jane Shore*. Returning to the Union Square Theatre, she appeared in a Frenchified version of *East Lynne,* called *Miss Multon,* in which she made a tremendous hit. Nothing need be said of the play, although it was much better dramatically than some other variations of the story, whose essence is a cloying sentimentality. Miss Morris's acting in it was superb of its kind. As the unrecognized mother tortured by the innocent prattle of her own children, as the broken-hearted woman, desperately seeking reinstatement, fleeing in shame from the home she had polluted and abandoned, and in the closing death scene, she sounded all the depths of poignant pathos. In *Raymonde,* an adaptation of the *Mons. Alphonse* of the younger Dumas, she made another extraordinary display of pathos and passion, in the character of a wife with an unsuspected past, who betrays herself to her trusting husband when fate confronts her with her illegitimate child; while as Mercy Merrick in *The New Magdalen* she simply obliterated the performance of Ada Cavendish, the English actress, who was supposed to have made the part her own. In realistic pathos, though not in art, her Camille was the equal of Bernhardt's or Modjeska's. . . . In whatever play she appeared she was always the center of interest, except once, and that was when she played Rosalia in *La Morte Civile* in support of Salvini. Then, for once, she suffered eclipse.

From *Sixty Years of the Theatre.*
(Funk and Wagnalls, 1916.)

AUGUSTIN DALY'S COMPANY AND ADA REHAN

By J. RANKEN TOWSE

THE fifteen years between 1885 and 1900 saw Daly's Theatre in the height of its prosperity and in the beginning of its decadence.... Daly's actual achievement has been vastly overrated. There is very little solid foundation for the common belief that his contributions to the revival, or survival, of the literary and poetic drama were of any great or lasting value. It is true that he was a man of artistic tastes and impulses, and a most liberal, enterprising, and courageous manager, who could be daunted by no disaster, but was always ready with a fresh experiment. It is true that he had for many years the best light-comedy company in the country and that he was the author of many delightful entertainments, prepared and served in irreproachable fashion. But these, in the main, were of an entirely ephemeral and unimportant kind.

In some of his more ambitious undertakings, his sense of artistic propriety did not prevent him from resorting to some of the most mischievous practises of the purely commercial and speculative managers. He did not hesitate, for instance, to sacrifice artistic principle for the sake of "booming" a popular actress, to put on plays for whose proper interpretation his players were unqualified, to mangle the text in order to minimize their incompetency, or to offer attractive spectacle as a substitute for good acting. Some of the pieces that he produced were unmitigated trash, flagrant melodramatic absurdities, with no other possible object than to catch the mob. I have already alluded to the fact that, on some occasions, even his scenery was flashy rather than artistically appropriate and meritorious. On the whole, however, he shone in contrast with most of his contemporaries, and to this fact, probably, may be attributed a considerable proportion of the critical complaisance which he enjoyed. Thus much in the interest of truth and common sense, but I am indebted to him for too many agreeable and not unprofitable evenings to wish to linger upon this phase of his career.

At the period of which I am writing his principal players—at one time or another—included Ada Rehan (whose death has been so recent), John Drew, Otis Skinner, Effie Shannon, Arthur Bourchier, and Frank Worthing (also recently dead)—all of whom were to be "stars" in the near future—and Mrs. Gilbert, James Lewis, Charles Fisher, William Davidge, George Clarke, Harry Edwards, and Charles Wheatleigh, of an older generation.

The list speaks for itself. No such aggregation of competent performers in light contemporary comedy has been in existence since. Their coöperation in the long succession of comedies provided for them, mostly from foreign sources, by Mr. Daly was admirable in smoothness, rapidity, and sustained spirit. All these pieces, though varying in incident and plot, carried a strong family resemblance, and present review of them would be tedious. Among them may be mentioned *A Night Off,* Pinero's *The Magistrate, Nancy & Company, Love in Harness, The Railroad of Love, The Lottery of Love, Dandy Dick, The Golden Widow, The Last Word, Little Miss Million, Love on Crutches,* and *The Countess Gucki.*

In all of these, and others of less note, Ada Rehan, John Drew, James Lewis, and Mrs. Gilbert were the protagonists. Miss Rehan, from the first, was in her element in every variety of piquant, tender, mischievous, high-spirited, alluring, whimsical, and provocative girlhood. Her humor was infectious, her charm potent, her pertness delicious, her petulance pretty, and her flashes of ire or scorn brilliant. She improved rapidly in artistry, and to the intuition of a clever novice she quickly added the skill of the trained comedian. John Drew, a tyro when he first joined Daly, soon became one of the best of leading juveniles, in any sort of part that did not involve serious sentiment or deep feeling. Humor of a distinctive quality—cynical, satirical, or genial—especially effective in situations of serio-comic perplexity, he had inherited from his parents, and he gradually acquired a notable refinement of style, with uncommon neatness of execution and capacity of repose. In this heyday of Daly's he promised to grow into one of the most accomplished comedians of his era, but his long apprenticeship in one line of work was to prove a bar to his further progress. As a modern man of the world—the polished clubman, the wise mentor, the social diplomatist, the polite wooer—he excelled all competitors, but when he tried to pass beyond the boundaries of the drawing-room into the outer regions of poetic romance and the profounder human emotions, his equipment was insufficient and his habits so set and petrified by habit as to be no longer susceptible of growth. Inspiration, long confined, would not respond to the call of intelligence.

Mr. Daly, in 1880, effected a revival of *The Merry Wives of Windsor,* which he had first produced fifteen years before. He mounted and dressed it sumptuously, but his players, with few exceptions, were sadly out of perspective, their modern manners contrasting strangely with the old costumes and direct and vigorous speech. They used to play the warm-blooded farce as if it were an anemic social comedy of the present, dealing with fashionable foibles and artificial elegances, instead of a study of human nature in an Elizabethan townlet. Shakespeare would have been sorely puzzled to recognize in these dandified folk the old burgesses of Windsor in their lusty sylvan simplicity. Beyond question he would have paid a poet's tribute to the loveliness of Ada Rehan and Virginia Dreher, but he never would have suspected that these dazzling young beauties, in their silks and laces and sparkling gems, were those noted gossips, Mistress Ford and Mistress Page, whom Fat Jack himself, even in a letter of courtship, was compelled to admit were neither beautiful nor young. The Knight's tastes, it may be remembered, were not of the most fastidious kind.

The transformation of the husbands was no less complete. The fiery, jealous Ford, in the hands of John Drew, was a pretty fellow, an exquisite in dress, and a courtier in behavior, who, like Bottom's lion, roared like any sucking dove. The Page of Mr. Otis Skinner was a swaggering young prig, who might, for all his apparent years, have been the lover of his own daughter, Sweet Anne. The Falstaff of Charles Fisher—who now revealed the infirmities of age—was right in design, but bereft of unction and vitality. The Bardolph of Mr. Roberts had a red nose and that was all. The Pistol of George Parkes, gentlest of bullies, emitted little puffs and snorts, at intervals, with the decrepitude of an ancient bellows. James Lewis, quaintest and most delightful of comedians in his line, could do nothing with Slender. Mrs. Gilbert, who did nothing really ill, was hopelessly miscast in the part of Mrs. Quickly. The only really Shakespearean embodiment was John Wood's Nym, which, in its dry eccentricity, was a capital little study. The representation did not last long. There was no reason why it should. Upon its inevitable withdrawal there were the usual lamentations over the degeneracy of the public taste. The public was not at fault. It exhibited better judgment and greater reverence for Shakespeare than the critics, who professed to enjoy and admire such a spiritless parody of him.

Mr. Daly approached a Shakespearean success much more nearly in 1887, when he produced *The Taming of the Shrew,* with a luxurious setting and in something like the original form. The piece was simpler sailing for his company than *The Merry Wives,* and the general performance, in the circumstances, was fairly creditable, though the text, in many instances, presented insoluble problems to the speakers. Moreover, the play was a comparative novelty to the New York public, and as such was cordially accepted. As Katharine, Ada Rehan won a personal triumph, and the part remained long in her repertory. For myself, I must confess that I could never fully agree with the panegyrics bestowed upon her performance here and, afterward, in England. Undoubtedly, it was a good one—in some respects even brilliant, but I fancy that the personal fascination of the actress—which, in her prime, was very great—had much to do with the wide critical acceptance of it. Her Shrew was a superb figure, but to my mind she vulgarized the character somewhat unnecessarily.

It is true enough that, in the text, Katharine's unmanageable temper is described in words that would warrant almost any degree of coarseness and violence, but some allowance must be made for the bluntness and vigor of Elizabethan speech, and it should not be forgotten that Katharine was the daughter of a merchant prince, moved in "upper circles," so to speak, and, presumably, had the training of a gentlewoman in a period precise in its code of manners. On the whole, it is reasonable to suppose that she had her normal moments and that it was only in her tantrums that she became positively outrageous. The play itself, although it contains some notable blank verse, is not of very much consequence, but it would lose nothing in humor and gain in plausibility and interest with a higher conception of Katharine than that of a half-crazy virago. She ought to suggest some of the graces of her station, carry with her a certain personal distinction, and exhibit passion in varying degrees. Miss Rehan started her performance at the highest pitch of quivering indignation at her command, and thereby secured a most picturesque and effective entrance. She maintained herself at this level, or near it, with amazing energy, but the effort left her without any reserve force for climaxes. Consequently her performance was lacking in light and shade, and grew weaker instead of stronger toward the end. But it marked an upward step in her career. Mr. Drew played Petruchio with a gay audacity that met all the absolute requirements of the situation, although he was not an authoritative figure. . . .

Many eloquent encomiums were lavished upon the production of *Twelfth Night,* which Mr. Daly produced in 1893, and especially upon the Viola of Ada Rehan. I wish I could agree with them. Pictorially the representation was charming, but there honest praise must end. Most of the actors were unequal to the parts assigned them, and the general performance was devoid alike of romance and poetry. The character of Viola, charged with the most delicate and fanciful sentiment, was outside the range of Ada Rehan, except in those phases of it denoted in the comic vein. Her delivery of verse, whether blank or rhymed, was always curiously monotonous and inexpressive. She was fairly successful in the soliloquy after her first interview with Olivia, and the duel scene—of which, in accordance with silly tradition, she made roaring farce—but in the sentimental and poetic interludes her droning sing-song robbed the lines of nearly all their poetic essence. She was lacking, moreover, in that refined and measured grace of gesture and action essential to illusion in any attempt to embody a conception so ethereal and free from earthly grossness.

From *Sixty Years in the Theatre,*
(Funk and Wagnalls, 1916.)

JOHN BARRYMORE'S HAMLET

By J. RANKEN TOWSE

T H E newspaper critic who is called upon to write of a show so elaborate, and in many ways so superior, as this finds himself instantly confronted with a somewhat disagreeable dilemma. He has to choose between misleading his readers by partly concealing the truth, as he sees it, and seeming to speak ungraciously of a production upon which an infinite amount of care, money, and good taste—of a certain kind—

has been spent. And it should be added that it is a production which was received by a crowded house with much apparent satisfaction, apart from volleys of tempestuous applause, some of which suggested very strongly a fairly well organized claque. Moreover—to say the pleasant things first—there can be no doubt that it contained much that the most fastidious spectator could not fail to admire very heartily, even if there was more to make the older theatregoers and the worshippers of Shakespeare grieve. Very seldom, if ever, has a great play, even in the days of Irving or Beerbohm Tree, been presented with a more richly spectacular background. The stage pictures were nobly designed and gorgeously brilliant or impressively sombre in color, while every grouping had been arranged with a view to pictorial effect. The eye was continuously charmed by a succession of fresh beauties. Every precaution had been taken to secure an ideal representation except the important one of a vital interpretation of the text.

The lamentable fact is that Mr. Arthur Hopkins, whose artistic instincts and ambitions need not be disputed, while his liberality is beyond all question, has fallen into very much the same error that made his *Macbeth* so sad a disappointment. He has not yet realized the fact that a costly and luxurious setting does not disguise, but rather emphasizes, the weakness of a poor performance. Moreover, he has become infected with some of the pernicious theories of Gordon Craig, and of what is called, by utter misnomer, the "new art of the theatre," which, while comparatively innocuous in the case of modern exotic and abnormal drama, cannot be made to harmonize with the structure or the spirit of those great classics in which the realistic and the imaginative are combined in incomparable fashion. To attempt to modernize Shakespeare, to apply to his robust and soaring genius the finicking methods of a more artificial civilization, is not only futile but something worse than foolish.

Mr. Hopkins, in this representation, has not departed widely from the ordinary stage version—only adding or omitting a few lines here and there—but separates it into three main divisions, not a matter of vast importance. The foundation of his spectacle is one majestic set, a vast domed chamber inclosing most of the stage, with platforms and steps leading up through a lofty central arch to the open air beyond, and an eminence which served for the ramparts of the castle, and various other things. It was in what might be called this amphitheatre that his chief tableaux—court episodes, the play scene, the burial of Ophelia and the culminating tragedy—were displayed. For the connecting scenes he employed curtains, decorative to a degree but not invariably felicitous, while the front part of the stage he used as an apron, sometimes with curious effect, as in the prayer scene.

As a matter of simple fact this scenic scheme, with its blend of solid architectural structure and flowing draperies, expressly devised to simplify and expedite the action, did nothing of the sort, but, on the other hand, tended rather to delay and confuse it. But on this particular point it is impossible to dwell now. It must suffice to say that if the spectacular was served it was only too often at the cost of the destruction of all illusion. This was strikingly the case with regard to one of the most notable innovations of the whole spectacle, the abolition of the spectral Majesty of Denmark—"the corse, clad in complete steel." "My father in his habit as he lived," etc., etc.—and the substitution for it of a sort of incandescent comet, from the neighborhood of which proceeded sepulchral sounds, barely recognizable as fragments of some of the most sonorous and effective blank verse ever provided for recitation. It is difficult to speak of such wilful and senseless disregard and perversion of the text, with all its unmistakable implications, with even a pretence of civility. Art, forsooth! It was barbarous and childish.

Of this there may be more to say hereafter. It is time now to refer to the acting, which ought to be the prime object of consideration, but which, on this occasion, as in the precedent of *Macbeth,* but to a less disastrous extent, seems to have been regarded as a matter entirely subordinate to the scenery. First in order, naturally, comes the Prince of John Barrymore, and it must be borne in mind that this was a first performance. The chief impression conveyed by it—as was the case with his Richard III—was the obvious lack of tragic power. It was a clever, thoughtful, interesting, and fairly consistent impersonation, with an individuality all its own, but it reflected only one or two of the many facets in Hamlet's manysided character. In one sense it was original, for it was a distinctly personal interpretation: it was not blindly subservient to traditions, some of which are more honored in the breach than in the observance; it did not copy the special points of other actors, but the originality was of no distinctive value, and proceeded largely from what can only be regarded as mere self inter-pretation or an utter want of dramatic perception. The avoidance of special points, eagerly seized upon by preceding performers, may be set down as a virtue. At any rate it need not be ascribed to unacquaint-ance. Of the accurate, traditional, mechanical Hamlets we have had more than enough.

But the glaring and fatal defect of this embodiment was the total absence of the inspiring spirit, the alternating moods of philo-sophic brooding, of momentary energy and passion, of absorbing impulse and hesitant vacillation, of gracious badinage and biting satire, all the attributes clearly indicated by the text that contribute to the constitution of the soldier, courtier, scholar, and lover of which Ham-let is the epitome. In the quieter phases of it there was much to admire. It was intelligent and refined, if not princely, and in the abstracted quietude of the "to be or not to be" there was original and attractive naturalism, but, on the other hand, the delivery of the text, though clear, was marred in countless instances by misplaced or disregarded emphasis, while in the more passionate scenes, such as the encounter with the Ghost, the play scene, or the interview in his mother's closet, the lack of fire, or of anything resembling emotions of tragic intensity, robbed them of all vitality or impressiveness. Even when Mr. Barrymore was loud, his utterance had no ring of true passion. His tameness in some crises—as for example in the query "Is it the King?" —was indicative of an astonishing imperception.

His performance was not without its sympathetic appeal. It was the work of an attractive, earnest, and intelligent comedian laboring under a burden much too heavy for him, and as a whole was sadly ineffective. As much might be said truthfully of most of his associates. It looked very much as if they were performing under stern instructions to do nothing that might divert attention from the star. Tyrone Power, as the King, seemed to be hiding his light under a bushel. With his magnificent voice and stature and his Shakespearean experience, he certainly could have made him a more significant figure than he did. Sidney Mather gave voice and a measure of life to Laertes and Blanche Yurka was fairly efficient as Gertrude, but none of the actors appeared able to let themselves go. One of the very best performances of the evening—a really delightful bit—was the Grave-digger of Whitford Kane. Why John S. O'Brien should have been selected for Polonius or Rosalind Fuller for Ophelia goodness—and perhaps Mr. Hopkins—only knows. The play in this case was not the thing.

From The New York Evening Post,
November 17, 1922.

SOME NOTES ON THE THEATRE

By HENRY JAMES

I F one held the belief that there is any very intimate relation between the stage, as it stands in this country, and the general cause of American civilization, it would be more than our privilege, it would be our duty, as vigilant observers, to keep an attentive eye upon the theatres. For in New York, at least, these establishments have rarely been more active than during the past few weeks, and the moment would be highly opportune for drawing from the national diversions a critic's moral as to the national state of mind. In fact, however, we suspect that moralizing too rigidly here is a waste of ingenuity, inasmuch as the diversions in question are not especially national. New York possesses half-a-dozen theatres of the so-called first class, in addition to a host of play-houses of the baser sort, whose performances are dramatic only by that extension of the term under which the romances in the Sunday papers may be spoken of as literary. These theatres are all, for the time, working at high pressure. Each has brought forward its *pièce de résistance*. The trumpets are blown and the public is convoked. The public assembles in varying numbers—on the whole, it seems to us, in very goodly ones. The public evidently likes play-going, and is willing to pay for it—to pay a good deal, and to pay often. But except at the Fifth Avenue Theatre, it does not go with the expectation of seeing the mirror held up to nature as it knows nature—of seeing a reflection of its actual, local, immediate physiognomy. The mirror, as the theatres show it, has the image already stamped upon it—an Irish image, a French image, an English image. The French and English images indeed are multiplied, and an Italian image, we per-

ceive, looms above the horizon. The images may be true to an original
or not; the public doesn't care. It has gone to look and listen, to laugh
and cry—not to think. This is so true that we fancy it must have
resented even the very slight intellectual effort necessary for finding
Women of the Day at the Fifth Avenue as preposterous an attempt
to portray as it was a dreary attempt to entertain. Nevertheless, if the
theatre with us *is* a superficial institution, it shares the peculiarity
with other social phenomena, and the observer may commit as great
a fault in taking it too easily as in taking it too hard.

Our drama seems fated, when it repairs to foreign parts for its
types, to seek them first of all in the land of brogue and "bulls." A
cynic might say that it is our privilege to see Irish types enough in
the sacred glow of our domestic hearths, and that it is therefore rather
cruel to condemn us to find them so inveterately in that consoling
glamour of the footlights. But it is true that an Irish drama is always
agreeably exciting; whether on account of an inherent property in
the material or because it is generally written by Mr. Boucicault, we are
unable to say. *The Shaughraun* will, we suppose, have been the theatrical event of the season; and if a play was to run for four or five
months there might have been a much worse one for the purpose than
this. There is no particular writing in it, but there is an infinite amount
of acting, of scene-shifting, and of liveliness generally; and all this
goes on to the tune of the finest feelings possible. Love, devotion, self-
sacrifice, humble but heroic bravery, and brimming Irish *bonhomie*
and irony, are the chords that are touched, and all for five liberal acts,
with a great deal of very clever landscape painting in the background,
and with Mr. Boucicault, Mr. Montagu, Mr. Becket, and Miss Dyas
in the foreground. For Mr. Boucicault, both as author and actor, it is a
great triumph—especially as actor. His skill and shrewdness in knock-
ing together effective situations and spinning lively dialogue are certainly commendable: but his acting is simply exquisite. One is hard
cleverness, polished and flexible with use; the other is very like genius.
The character of the Shaughraun is very happily fancied, but the best
of the entertainment is to see the fancy that produced it still nightly
playing with it. One hears it said sometimes that an actor acts with
"authority"; certainly there is rarely a higher degree of authority than
this. Mr. Boucicault smiles too much, we think; he rather overdoes

the softness, the amiability, the innocence of his hero; but these ex-aggerations perhaps only deepen the charm of his rendering; for it was his happy thought to devise a figure which should absolutely, con-summately, and irresistibly please. It has pleased mightily.

The Two Orphans at the Union Square Theatre, a piece which has been running a race with the *Shaughraun* in popularity, is an American rendering of an elaborate French *drame* of the old "boule-vard" school. The original play ran all last winter in Paris, and fairly rejuvenated the rather defunct type to which it belonged. It is pro-digiously clever, and we doubt whether for the time and the money one spends it would be possible to give one fuller measure, pressed down and running over, of surprises, sensations, and bewilderments. What is offered at the Union Square is the mere gaunt, angular skele-ton of the original. The whole thing, both as to adaptation and ren-dering, is very brutally done. It hangs together as it can. There is no really delicate acting in the piece, with the exception, in a sense, of Miss Kate Claxton's representation of the blind maiden. She goes through the part with the pretty dismalness required, and with the enunciation of a young lady reciting a "piece" at a boarding-school. But *The Two Orphans* is worth seeing simply for the sake of sitting in one's place and feeling the quality of a couple of good old-fashioned *coups de théâtre* as your French playwright who really knows his busi-ness manages them. The first is when one of the Orphans, hearing in her garret the voice of the other, who is wandering in the street, sight-less and helpless, and singing a song addressed, through the mercy of chance, to her sister's ear, and being about to fly to her rescue, is arrested on her threshold by a *lettre de cachet*. The other is the cry of that sadly unwholesome cripple, Pierre (badly played, we should say, if the part were not in its nature an impossible one), when, after being trampled upon through the whole play, he turns upon his hulk-ing, blackguard brother: "As you say yourself, we come of a race that kills!" These are very telling strokes, but if you wait for them at the Union Square you pay for them well. You are kept in patience, it is true, by some very pretty scenery.

The Fifth Avenue Theatre, we believe, makes a specialty of "American comedy," eschews for the time at least Parisian orphans and heroic bog-trotters, and gives us our fellow-citizens in their habits as they live. Some one ought to be held morally accountable for such an unqualifiable mess of vulgarity as *Women of the Day*. It is a pity to talk about this thing, even explicitly to pass it by; but we believe it is one of a series, and under these circumstances one strikes out instinctively in self-defence. It was ghastly, monstrous, a positive nightmare. It ran for several weeks, and one wonders whether the public was an active or a merely passive accomplice. Did it like it, or did it simply endure it? The public at large is very ignorant and very good-natured, and anything is possible.

One is bound to regret, in the presence of such a phenomenon as *Women of the Day,* that the wholesome old fashion of hissing has in the English theatre fallen into disuse. It was of course liable to abuse; but what is one to say, on the other hand, of the spectator's patience? It would seem at least that, short of the privilege of absolute hissing (which ceases to be brutal only when it is directed at the play, and not at the performers), the disappointed, the deceived spectator ought to hold in his hand some instrument of respectful but uncompromising disapproval. We made this reflection as we watched the celebrated Mrs. Rousby, who has been interpreting historic blank-verse for a month at the Lyceum. It is hard to speak rigidly of so handsome a woman, but Mrs. Rousby's histrionic powers are about equivalent to those of some pretty trained animal—a pet lamb, say, or a white rabbit, or a snowy-breasted dove. Her acting is absolutely flat and weak —uninspired, untrained, unfinished. It was singular to see so extremely pretty a person take so little the critical chill off the atmosphere. Mrs. Rousby is distinctly incompetent. She has been followed at the same theatre by another English artist, a real artist this time—Mr. Toole. Mr. Toole has solved the problem of making low comedy charming. It must be admitted that in one of his parts—the Artful Dodger—the lowness is more apparent than the charm.

A more important dramatic enterprise than any we have mentioned has been the revival at Booth's Theatre, as a great spectacle, of *Henry V.* We can spare but a word to it. The play could be presented only as a kind of animated panorama, for it offers but the slenderest opportunities for acting. These all fall to the lot of Mr. George Rignold, a young English actor, who, as the victor of Agincourt, has made a very charming impression. He plays the part in the most natural fashion, looks it and wears it to perfection, and declaims its swelling harangues with admirable vigor and taste. He is worth looking at and listening to. The scenic splendors of the play have received many compliments, though, as such things go, they seem to us to have a number of weak spots. But even if they had fewer, they would still, to our sense, be founded on a fallacy. Illusion, as such an enterprise proposes to produce it, is absolutely beyond the compass of the stage. The compromise with verisimilitude is not materially slighter than in the simple days before "revivals" had come into fashion. To assent to this you have only to look at the grotesqueness of the hobby-horses on the field of Agincourt and at the uncovered rear of King Harry's troops, when they have occasion to retire under range of your opera-glass. We approve by all means of scenic splendors, but we would draw the line at invading armies. Mr. Rignold, as we say, however, really produces a very grateful illusion.

From *The Nation,*
March 11, 1875.

SALVINI'S OTHELLO

By HENRY JAMES

...SALVINI'S Othello is not more superficial than the law of self-preservation (on the actor's part) demands; there is, on the contrary, a tremendous depth of feeling in it, and the execution is brilliant —with the dusky brilliancy that is in the tone of the part—at every point. No more complete picture of passion can have been given to the stage in our day,—passion beginning in noble repose and spending itself in black insanity. Certain exquisite things are absent from it,—the gradations and transitions which Shakespeare has marked in a hundred places, the manly melancholy, the note of deep reflection, which is sounded as well as the note of passion. The pathos is perhaps a little crude; there is in all Shakespeare's sentiment a metaphysical side, which is hard to indicate and easy to miss. Salvini's rendering of the part is the portrait of an African by an Italian; a fact which should give the judicious spectator, in advance, the pitch of the performance. There is a class of persons to whom Italians and Africans have almost equally little to say, and such persons must have been sadly out of their account in going to see Salvini. I have done with strictures, and must only pay a hasty tribute to his splendor of execution. If those critics who dislike the Othello find it coarse (some people, apparently, are much surprised to discover that the representation of this tragedy is painful), there is at least not a weak spot in it from beginning to end. It has from the first the quality that thrills and excites, and this quality deepens with great strides to the magnificent climax. The last two acts constitute the finest piece of tragic acting that I know. I do not say it is the finest I can imagine, simply because a great English Othello would touch us more nearly still. But I have never seen a great English Othello, any more, unfortunately, than I have never seen a great English Macbeth. It is impossible to give an idea of the way in which Salvini gathers force as he goes, or of the superior use he makes of this force in the critical scenes of the play. Some of his tones, movements, attitudes, are ineffaceable; they have passed into the stock of common reference. I mean his tiger-like pacing at the back of the room, when, having brought Desdemona out of her bed, and put the width of the apartment between them, he strides to and fro, with his eyes fixed on her and filled with the light of her approaching doom. Then the still more tiger-like spring with which, after turning, flooded and frenzied by the truth, from the lifeless body of his victim, he traverses the chamber to reach Iago, with the mad impulse of destruction gathered into a single blow. He has sighted him, with the intentness of fate, for a terrible moment, while he is still on one knee beside Desdemona; and the manner in which the spectator sees him—or rather feels him—rise to his avenging leap is a sensation that takes its place among the most poignant the actor's art has ever given us. After this frantic dash, the one thing Othello can *do,* to relieve himself (the one thing, that is, save the last of all), he falls into a chair on the left of the stage, and lies there for some moments, prostrate, panting, helpless, annihilated, convulsed with long, inarticulate moans. Nothing could be finer than all this: the despair, the passion, the bewildered tumult of it, reach the high-water mark of dramatic expression. My remarks may suggest that Salvini's rage is too gross, too much that of a wounded animal; but in reality it does not fall into that excess. It is the rage of an African, but of a nature that remains generous to the end; and in spite of the tiger-paces and tiger-springs, there is through it all, to my sense at least, the tremor of a moral element. In the Othello, remarkable in so many respects, of Salvini's distinguished countryman, Ernesto Rossi, there is (as I remember it) a kind of bestial fury, which does much to sicken the English reader of the play. Rossi gloats in his tenderness and bellows in his pain. Salvini, though the simplicity, credulity, and impulsiveness of his personage are constantly before him, takes a higher line altogether; the personage is intensely human....

From *The Atlantic Monthly,*
March, 1883.

COQUELIN

By HENRY JAMES

...THE peculiarity of M. Coquelin's position, and the cause of the curiosity with which we shall have regarded the attitude of the public towards him, is in the fact that he offers no bribe whatever—none of the lures of youth or beauty or sex, or of an insinuating aspect, or of those that reside in a familiar domestic repertory. It is a question simply of appreciating or not appreciating his admirable talent, his magnificent execution....

M. Coquelin is not of a romantic type, and everything in him that meets the eye of the spectator would appear to have been formed for the broadest comedy. By a miracle of talent and industry he has forced his physical means to serve him also, and with equal felicity, in comedy that is not broad, but surpassingly delicate, and even in the finest pathetic and tragic effects. But to enjoy the refinement of M. Coquelin's acting the ear must be as open as the eye, must even be beforehand with it; and if that of the American public learns, or even shows an aptitude for learning, the lesson conveyed in his finest creations, the lesson that acting is an art and that art is style, the gain will have been something more than the sensation of the moment—it will have been an added perception....

The pathetic, the "interesting" (including, where need be, the romantic and even the heroic), and the extravagantly droll represent the two opposite ends of M. Coquelin's large gamut. He turns from one to the other, he ranges between them, with incomparable freedom and ease. Into the *emploi* of the impudent, extravagant serving-men of the old comedies,—the Mascarilles, the Scapins, the Frontins, the Crispins,—he stepped from the first with the assurance of a conqueror; from hand to foot, in face, in manner, in voice, in genius, he was cut out for them, and it is with his most successful efforts in this line that, for the public at large, his name has become synonymous. If his portrait is painted (perhaps it has been) for the *foyer* of the Comédie Française, it should be as the Mascarille of Molière's *L'Étourdi.*

I have an impression that this was the second part I saw him play, with Delaunay as the scatterbrained hero. Coquelin was dressed like a figure of the old Italian comedy, in great stripes of crimson and white, a little round cloak, a queer, inflated-looking cap, and breeches and hose of the same pattern. I can see him, I can hear him, the incarnation of humorous effrontery and agility, launching his prodigious voice over the footlights, fairly trumpeting his "points," and giving an unparalleled impression of life and joy. I have seen him in the part many times since then, and it has always seemed to me, with the exception of his astonishing incarnation of the false marquis in the *Précieuses Ridicules* (the valet, who in his master's finery, masquerades as a *bel-esprit*), the most exuberant in his repertory. Of this fantastic exuberance he is a rare master, and his command of it is doubly wonderful when one thinks of his command of effects which lie entirely in self-possess—effects of low tone, as painters say. The representative of Don Annibal in *L'Aventurière,* of Don César de Bazan in *Ruy Blas* (in both of which parts the actor is superb), is also the representative of various prose-talking, subdued gentlemen of to-day (the Duc de Septmonts, in *L'Étrangère* of the younger Dumas, the argumentative, didatic Thouvenin, in the same author's *Denise*) caught in various tight places, as gentlemen must be in a play, but with no accessories *à la Goya* to help them out. The interpreter of the tragic passion of Jean Dacier, which I have not seen for many years, is hidden in the stupendously comical and abject figure of M. Royal, the canting little pettifogger or *clerc d'huissier,* who appears in a single brief scene in the last act of *Tartuffe,* and into whom M. Coquelin, taking up the part for the first time in the autumn of 1885, infused an individuality of grotesqueness and baseness which gave him—all in the space of five minutes—one of his greatest triumphs.

The art of composition, in the various cases I have mentioned, is the same, but the subjects to which it is applied have nothing in common. I have heard people enunciate the singular proposition: "Coquelin has great talent—he does ever so many different things; but, I don't know—he is always Coquelin." He is indeed always Coquelin, which is a great mercy, considering what he possibly might have been. It is by being always Coquelin that he is able to be Jean Dacier one night and Don Annibal another. If it be meant by the remark I have just quoted that he makes Don Annibal resemble Jean Dacier, or gives the two personages something in common which they could not really have possessed, no criticism could well be less exact. What it really points to, I suppose, is the extreme definiteness and recognizableness, as it were, of the performer's execution, of his physical means, above all, of that voice which no manner of composing a particular character can well render a less astounding organ at one moment than at another. Don César is Coquelin and M. Thouvenin is Coquelin, because on the lips both of Don César and of M. Thouvenin there sits a faculty of vocalization, as one may call it, which is peculiar to the artist who embodies them, and surely one of the most marvelous the stage has ever known. It may be said that M. Coquelin's voice betrays him; that he cannot get away from it, and that whatever he does with it one is always reminded that only he can do such things. His voice, in short, perpetually, loudly identifies him. Its life and force are such that the auditor sometimes feels as if it were running away with him—taking a holiday, performing antics and gyrations on its own account. The only reproach it would ever occur to me to make to the possessor of it is that he perhaps occasionally loses the idea while he listens to the sound. But such an organ may well beguile the ear even of him who has toiled to forge and polish it; it is impossible to imagine anything more directly formed for the stage, where the prime necessity of every effort is that it shall "tell." When Coquelin speaks, the sound is not sweet and caressing, though it adapts itself beautifully, as I have hinted, to effects of gentleness and pathos; it has no analogy with the celebrated and delicious murmur of Delaunay, the enchanting cadences and

semitones of that artist, also so accomplished, so perfect. It is not primarily the voice of a lover, or rather (for I hold that any actor—such
is the indulgence of the public to this particular sentiment—may be a
lover with any voice) it is not primarily, like that of M. Delaunay, the
voice of love. There is no reason why it should have been, for the passion of love is not what M. Coquelin has usually had to represent.

He has usually had to represent the passion of impudence, and it
is, I think, not too much to say that it is in this portrayal that he has
won most of his greatest victories. His expression, his accent, give
him the highest commission for placing before us the social quality
which, I suppose, most conducts a man to success. The valets of
Molière and Regnard are nothing if not impudent; impudent are
Don César and Don Annibal; impudent, heroically impudent is
Figaro; impudent (as I remember him) M. Adolphe de Beaubourg
(in *Paul Forestier*); impudent the Duc de Septmonts; impudent even—
or at least decidedly impertinent—the copious moralist M. Thouvenin. . . .

If M. Coquelin's voice is not sweet, it is extraordinarily clear, firm,
and ringing, and it has an unsurpassable distinctness, a peculiar power
to carry. As I write I seem to hear it ascend like a rocket to the great
hushed dome of the theatre of the Rue de Richelieu. It vibrates, it
lashes the air, it seems to proceed from some mechanism still more
scientific than the human throat. In the great cumulative tirades of
the old comedy, the difficulties of which are pure sport for M. Coquelin,
it flings down the words, the verses, as a gamester precipitated by
a run of luck flings louis d'or upon the table. I am not sure that the
most perfect piece of acting that I have seen him achieve is not a prose
character, but it is certain that to appreciate to the full what is most
masterly in his form one must listen to and enjoy his delivery of
verse. That firmness touched with hardness, that easy confidence which
is only the product of the most determined study, shine forth in proportion as the problem becomes complicated. It does not, indeed,
as a general thing, become so psychologically in the old rhymed
parts; but in these parts the question of elocution, of diction, or even
simply the question of breath, bristles both with opportunities and
with dangers. Perhaps it would be most exact to say that wherever
M. Coquelin has a very long and composite speech to utter, be it verse

or prose, there one gets the cream of his talent. The longest speech in the French drama, not excepting the famous soliloquy of Figaro in the second comedy of Beaumarchais, and that of Charles V. in *Hernani* is, I should suppose, the discourse placed in the mouth of M. Thouvenin aforesaid in the last act of *Denise*. It occupies nearly four close pages in the octavo edition of the play, and if it is not a soliloquy it is a sermon, a homily, a treatise. An English or an American audience would have sunk into a settled gloom by the time the long rhythm of the thing had declared itself, and even at the Théâtre Français the presumption was against the actor's ability to bring safely into port a vessel drawing such a prodigious depth of water. M. Coquelin gave it life, light, color, movement, variety, interest, even excitement. One held one's breath, not exactly to hear what Thouvenin would say, but to hear how Coquelin would say it. Such a success as that seems to me to be the highest triumph of the actor's art, because it belongs to the very foundation, and to the most human part of it. On our own stage to *say* things is out of fashion, if for no other reason than that we must first have them to say. To *do* them, with a great reënforcement of chairs and tables, of traps and panoramas and other devices, is the most that our Anglo-Saxon star, of either sex, aspires to. The ear of the public, that exquisite critical sense which is two-thirds of the comedian's battle-field, has simply ceased to respond from want of use. And where, indeed, is the unfortunate comedian to learn how to speak? Is it the unfortunate public that is to teach him? Gone are the days when the evolution of a story could sit on the lips of an actor. The stage-carpenter and the dress-maker have relieved him long since of that responsibility....

From *The Century Magazine,*
January, 1887.

EDWARD HARRIGAN'S COMEDIES

By WILLIAM DEAN HOWELLS

...THE outlook is not hopeless, however. We will not speak of Mr. Gilbert's exquisite ironies; he is an Englishman, and we are talking now about the American drama, or non-drama; for, in spite of theatres lavishly complete in staging, and with all the sanitary arrangements exemplary—the air changed every fifteen minutes, and artificially refrigerated in the summer—we have still no drama. Yet we have the prospect of something of the kind, and naturally we have it in accordance with the existing conditions. We have an abundance of most amusing sketches and extravaganzas, embodying more or less of our grotesque life; and amongst these, saving the respect of all the gentilities, are Mr. Hoyt's *Rag Baby,* and other absurdities. But, most hopeful of all the promises, we have the plays of Mr. Edward Harrigan. Our one original contribution and addition to histrionic art was negro minstrelsy, which, primitive, simple, elemental, was out of our own soil, and had the characteristics that distinguish autochthonic conceptions. But that is a thing almost of the past, and we have now to do with a novel contribution to the drama, and not to the art of the drama. It is peculiarly interesting, because it is morally, though not materially, the contribution most possible under our peculiar circumstances, for it is the work of a man in whom the instincts of the author combat the theatre's traditions, and the actor's experience censures the author's literary vanity.

Mr. Harrigan writes, stages, and plays his pieces; he is his own playwright, manager, and comedian. He has his own theatre, and can risk his own plays in it, simply and cheaply, in contempt of the carpenter and upholsterer. Not that he does treat these useful personages with contempt, but he subordinates them. In his theatre the highly decorated husk and gilded shell are not everything, nor the kernel attenuated to the last degree of innutritiousness. But the setting is at the same time singularly perfect and entirely sufficient. Mr. Harrigan accurately realizes in his scenes what he realizes in his persons; that is, the actual life of this city. He cannot give it all; he can only give phases of it; and he has preferred to give its Irish-American phases in their rich and amusing variety, and some of its African and Teutonic phases. It is what we call low life, though whether it is essentially lower than fashionable life is another question. But what it is, it is; and it remains for others, if they can, to present other sides of our manifold life with equal perfection; Mr. Harrigan leaves a vast part of the vast field open. In his own province we think he cannot be surpassed. The art that sets before us all sorts and conditions of New York Irishmen, from the laborers in the street to the most powerful of the ward politicians and the genteelest of the ladies of that interesting race, is the art of Goldoni —the joyous yet conscientious art of the true dramatist in all times who loves the life he observes. The old Venetian filled his scene with the gondoliers, the serving-folk, the fish-women, the trades-people, the quacks, the idlers, the gamesters, of his city, and Mr. Harrigan shows us the street-cleaners and contractors, the grocery-men, the shysters, the politicians, the washer-women, the servant-girls, the truckmen, the policemen, the risen Irishman and Irish woman, of contemporary New York. Goldoni carried through scores of comedies the same characters, the masks of the older drama which he drove from the stage, and Mr. Harrigan instinctively repeats the same personages in his Mulligan series. Within his range the New Yorker is not less admirable than the Venetian. In fact, nothing could be better than the neatness, the fineness, with which the shades of character are given in Mr. Mulligan's Irish people; and this literary conscientiousness is supplemented by acting which is worthy of it. Mr. Harrigan is himself a player of the utmost naturalness, delicate, restrained, infallibly sympathetic; and we have seen no one on his stage who did not seem to have been trained to his part through entire sympathy and intelligence. In certain moments of *Dan's Tribulations* the illusion is so perfect that you lose the sense of being in the theatre; you are out of that world of conventions and traditions, and in the presence of the facts.

All the Irish aspects of life are treated affectionately by this artist, as we might expect from one of his name; but the colored aspects do not fare so well under his touch. Not all the Irish are good Irish, but all the colored people are bad colored people. They are of the gloomy, razor-bearing variety; full of short-sighted lies and prompt dishonesties, amusing always, but truculent and tricky; and the sunny sweetness which we all know in negro character is not there. We do not wholly object to the one-sided picture; it has its historical value; and so has the contemptuous prejudice of both Irish and negroes for the Italians, which comes out in the *Leather Patch;* that marks an epoch and characterizes a condition.

The *Leather Patch* is not nearly so good as the Mulligan series, though it has very good things in it. The author seems to have labored for incident and effect in a plot, whereas all that the heart asked of him was to keep his delicious Irish folks on the scene and keep them talking. As it is, some passages of the piece are extremely good; and it is as a whole in the good direction. The material is rude, very rude; we repeat that; it is the office or it is the will of this artist to work in that material; but it is the artist and not the material which makes the work of art. The error of the dramatist has been that he has at times not known how to hold his hand; he has given us the whole truth where part of it would have been enough; he might have spared us some shocking suggestions of the undertaking business. At other times he quite forgets his realism: the whole episode of the colored wake, with its plantation spirituals, is real and excellent; but when the old-clothes men and women of Chatham Street join in a chorus, one perceives that the theatre has come to the top, and the poet has lapsed.

In spite of such lapses, however, we recognize in Mr. Harrigan's work the spring of a true American comedy, the beginning of things which may be great things. We have more than intimated its limitations; let us say that whatever its offences, it is never, so far as we have seen it, indecent. The comedies of Edward Harrigan are, in fact, much decenter than the comedies of William Shakespeare.

They are like Shakespeare's plays, like Molière's plays, in being the work of a dramatist who is at the same time a manager and an actor. Possibly this is the only way we can have a drama of our own; it is not a bad way; and it is at least a very natural way. At any rate, loving reality as we do, we cannot do less than cordially welcome reality as we find it in Mr. Harrigan's comedies. Consciously or unconsciously, he is part of the great tendency toward the faithful representation of life which is now animating fiction.

From "The Editor's Study,"
Harper's New Monthly Magazine,
July, 1886.

STEELE MACKAYE'S *PAUL KAUVAR*

By NYM CRINKLE

MR. STEELE MACKAYE will appear this week with his grease paint on. He has been seen here as an actor on several occasions before and his efforts elicited all kinds of opinions. He has, in fact, been here before in the very rôle he is now about to assume.

Mr. MacKaye is a man of such emphatic personality that anything he does must attract attention. He has a large vibration, both in literature and in speech, and it is doubtful if theatrical audiences who measure him with their senses ever adjust the forces of the man right when they are propelled through the illusions of a stage character.

His work has now been submitted at the Standard Theatre long enough to the public to determine its staying power. It is a work of great propulsive power; of genuine creative ingenuity; of massive dramatic effectiveness; of broad cartoon effects and much elemental strength of passion. Without going any further into it at present to look after the inconsistencies, the incidental pathos, the empirical melodramatic use of human motives, let us rest for a moment on the distinctively broad lines and bold colors of the drama.

The moment we get the right perspective of the work and consent to look at it as a heroic fresco and not as an etching, we begin to see Mr. MacKaye's emphatic personality in it, and to understand how unlike it is to all the other work that is being done for the stage here. In the first place, it is the protest of a vigorous masculine talent against the æsthetic inanity of that American drama which, laid in Boston, always comes to New York to be hatched.

If you would see the goal of Mr. Howell's primrose path in dramaturgy you have got to go to the *Abbé Constantin*. If you want a shock of that wave of romanticism that set in with Victor Hugo's *Hernani,* you have got to go to *Paul Kauvar.*

It is simply a question of which you prefer. If you gauge literature with your night-key and the *Century Magazine* you will have it come without virtue and go without vice, and it will be a properly drear, inoffensive platitude, made up of friskiness, prudery and pomp. If you measure it by great desires, strong hopes, eager longings and vital impulses, you will put up with its ungloved finger tips on account of its biceps.

If your historic estimate of momentous events is that Julius Cæsar buttoned his shirt in front and St. Paul ate with his fingers and mended tents at Corinth, then you will prefer Erasmus to Luther and see more in Chesterfield than ever blazed in Cromwell. You will go to

Augustin Daly because the cut of his Greek Chiton is correct and you will avoid *Paul Kauvar* because the throes of a great nation are vulgar.

My friend Mr. Edgar Fawcett, who has written the best poem in the English language on a toad, pointed out the other night at the Nineteenth Century Club that Walt Whitman just missed being embalmed in the nurseries of good taste by committing the error of having something to say, and then adding the insult of saying it without eight-button gloves. This reminds one of an Indian agent's opinion of Custer's dash into the valley of death and over the barbarians to immortality—"If he'd gone round and compromised the thing there'd been money in it!"

Mr. Steele MacKaye, whatever else he may be, is not a "lisping hawthorn bud." He doesn't embroider such napkins as the *Abbé Constantin,* and he can't arrange such waxworks as *Elaine.* He can't stereoscope an emotion, but he can incarnate it if you give him people enough. If he cannot manicure a sentiment he can at least forge an idea.

It is true enough that this process gives us the clang of the smithy occasionally. But we get the scintillant iron, and behind it is the strong arm, ruddy at times with the tongues of Promethean fire. In our lady-like condition of good condition masculinity ought to be prized. We want the undaunted mettle that will bring forth male dramas only. It would help to put the lawn-tennis actors into training. It would develop virility in execution; it would possibly awaken the dead function of aggressiveness in thought and action and shame the automatism of precise littleness.

Anything like a comprehensive look at the work done for the stage must convince you that playwriting talent just now is effeminate. It is receptive, not seminal and procreative. Its best work pinnicky; given to minutiæ; patent in unessentials; looking after the swaddling clothes and ratite, not after the bones and bowels of the infant.

Mrs. Irving keeps house with English respectability. Mrs. Daly is like a dowager with fine, handsome daughters, who change their dresses and their bric-a-brac at every reception, but always wear their mother's set smile. The English lady scoured and scented Goethe. The American lady combed out Shakespeare. The respectability of the two great poets is now guaranteed by two great houses. "Warranted not to offend the best circles" is written all over them. Minerva wears the *chiton* and Aphrodite rises out of our set in proper underclothes.

It's amazing how much more money and pains a young man with one dress coat will spend to get into a set than he will to get into an essential. He does not know or care anything about Goethe's drama of human destiny, but he will talk you deaf about Mrs. Irving's delicacy of realism. He couldn't comprehend Shakespeare's mid kingdom of the air, but he has got the *chiton* burned into his soul. When good taste gets to this enervated Roman condition it is time for some barbarian to sweep down upon it and shake it up.

I should like to regard Mr. MacKaye as an Alario if I were not compelled to regard him as an artist. At all events, I like his heroics. There is a sinewy purpose to his drama, and he has tried the audacious experiment of substituting blood and iron for sweetness and light. I don't ask you to let the iron enter your soul if you will only let some of it get into your blood.

What you want is not taffeta but tonics. Half an hour on a mustang with Buffalo Bill would probably do you more good than a whole year with Prof. Adler.

Honestly, now, wouldn't you like to steal away from your set and eat with your knife for a while? Wouldn't you like to see man as he loves and hates and kills and overcomes? Aren't you a little tired of seeing him as he dissembles and compromises and trims and truckles? Doesn't your respectability weigh on you like a mortgage? Isn't the empiricism of good taste producing a slow but sure softening of your convictions and intentions?

What do you go on a ranch for? Why do you sail away to the north pole and plunge into the heart of Africa if you do not want to escape from Mrs. Grundy and Mrs. Daly? What do you encourage prize-fighting for and rush into athletics and sports for if it isn't the assertion of masculinity in you?

You are tired of sitting in a bay window and listening to Siegfried. Somehow you can't help feeling that morality is mucilaginous when it wants to make the punishment of criminals an æsthetic delight and tears down the best masters from the picture-dealers' walls, and æsthetics are drivelling when they make you count the stitches in the *chiton,* and society is a tyrant when it breaks down the safeguards of art to let its pets in and patronize them at the expense of the workers when they are in.

At all events you are entitled to a growl at the lady-like condition of things that ought to have preserved the destructive qualities of both sexes, to be of any value.

Masculine men are getting scarcer and scarcer in the drama. I think they are crowded out by sweetness and light. When Howells and his scholars made decoration and not character the test in art they invited the whole phalanx of incompetent gentility into the arena of hard work. They have been at it with their crochet needles ever since. You can wash some of their ability off with a sponge.

Do you suppose they are without any influence in art? Perhaps you think a mob does not interfere with pedestrianism.

I admire one thing in Steele MacKaye. He hasn't let down the pegs of his romanticism to please this fad. It has a lusty blare in it that is not of our hour, and his hero has got to be masculine or he will not fit the work.

Were you ever out all night in the great city? It's a curious experience.

Suppose you had only money enough to ride on the horse cars, and you see the city go through all the phases of extinction from 12 o'clock midnight. One by one the stragglers go home. The last song of the carousal dies out. The belated doctor, the tramp, the beggar disappear. The great streets yawn, and the lamps are ghostly. Now and then the step of a policeman. Then all is hushed. The millions are asleep. About 3 o'clock the crisis of dark desolation is supreme. The very nearness and numbers of the silent millions affect you strangely. The dead pause in so much life seems solemn.

You don't appreciate the æsthetic triumph of it. You fail to admire the perfect elimination of vulgarity. You watch for the first gray streaks above Long Island, and with them comes the first chirp of the milkman. Then follows the newsboy. How jocund is even this rude sign of life come back! Presently there is a stir, and then the great rude leviathan shakes himself in the dawn, and whistling, singing, praying, sets about his multitudinous vulgarities in the early sunlight.

After all, we can't shake ourselves clear of our human shackles. Life is the thing we want, and life only as it exists in men and women.

From *The World,*
February 19, 1888.

BRONSON HOWARD'S *SHENANDOAH*

By *EDWARD A. DITHMAR*

SHENANDOAH, an interesting drama dealing with the romantic side of life in the South during the Civil War, was received at the Star Theatre last night with a great demonstration of approval. Mr. Bronson Howard, the author, was called before the curtain twice during the evening and cheered vociferously; but the best tributes he received were the tears and laughter evoked by his play. The popular success of *Shenandoah* is as distinct and indisputable as that of *The Henrietta* after its first performance. The new play is not so cleverly constructed as that comedy of contemporary life; as an example of mere stage-craft, indeed, it has many defects which professional critics of the drama may be inclined to deplore. But the most blasé of habitual theatre-goers must admit that the pathos of Mr. Howard is moving, and that much of the humor he has put into his new play is true and irresistible.

Mr. Howard has painted his new picture of American life on a very large canvas. It is crowded with figures. In the background the bloody contest for the preservation of the Union is waging. The noise of the battle is heard during the action. The torch signals of the enemy flash from a distant mountain top in one of the climaxes and add pictorial effect to the dramatic situation. In another climax the ride of Phil Sheridan is depicted, that ride made immortal in verse by Thomas Buchanan Read. It is a stirring picture as the belated commander dashes down the Virginia road, and the skulkers of his army, inspired by the sight of him, forget their terror and rush wildly into the fight. But Mr. Howard has not depended upon these representations of actual incidents for the strength of his play. While the signal lights are flashing, and the Union Signal Corps are reading the enemy's secret by means of their code, captured at the cost of his life, by one of the dramatis personæ, the interest of the spectators is centred in the love and jealousy of the men and women in the foreground; and it is Colonel Kercheval West who is Mr. Howard's hero in the Shenandoah Valley, not Gen. Sheridan. The battle for the Nation is kept in the background, and the battle of a few human hearts is the subject of the play.

The various elements that make up *Shenandoah* are perfectly simple, but there are many of them—too many, in fact, for a well-constructed drama—and the story of the play could not be told intelligibly in a brief narrative. The artistic fault of the drama is complexity of interest. General Haverill's quarrel with his son, and his suspicion of his young wife; Colonel West's love for the spirited rebel girl, and her sacrifice for his sake; young Haverill's bravery and death; the Confederate Colonel's love for the Northern officer's sister, and the love of a brusque Yankee General's spoiled daughter for a stupid but good-hearted and finally heroic cavalry Captain must all be borne in mind by the spectator during the play; and his attention is diverted from these exhibitions of human nature by incidents that involve the brutal courage and dangerous malice of a Southern secret service officer and the woe of a forlorn young widow with a baby, (happily unseen,) who has grown big enough in the last act to wear trousers.

But Mr. Howard has told this complex story so well in neat, effective, often eloquent dialogue and picturesque action, that it is all interesting even if some of the elements are a trifle blurred in the general effect; and though the play—as a play—is not so commendable as *The Henrietta* and *Young Mrs. Winthrop,* it is a finer work in a literary sense than we can expect from any of our playwrights except Mr. Howard.

An uncommonly good company has been gathered together at the Star Theatre. Mr. Henry Miller plays one of the several heroes with plenty of energy and sufficient fervor. Miss Viola Allen plays the corresponding heroine in a sympathetic manner. Her performance is notably free from the affectation that used to mar her work. Mr. Wilton Lackaye, at last, has been called upon to act the part of an honorable man, and his portrayal of Gen. Haverill is natural, and agreeable, and effective. Mr. Harry Harwood contributes a delightful sketch of a brusque old soldier, and Mr. James O. Barrows ably seconds him as a faithful Irish Sergeant. Mr. John Kellerd as the only villain of the drama acts with nice discrimination and telling force. Mr. G. W. Bailey contributes a delicately-conceived performance as the erring son of Gen. Haverill who dies in the performance of military duty. Misses Dorothy Dorr, Nannette Comstock, Effie Shannon, and Alice Haines have suitable parts.

The play is handsomely mounted, and the Shenandoah Valley picture will be greatly admired. The details have been attended to with much care, even to the small items of mud on the boots of the soldiers. The stern, dilapidated butternuts who appear in one of the scenes under a flag of truce seem to belong to the soil. The author has spared no effort to emphasize the sentimental idea of the brotherhood of the contesting parties in our terrible war, and the recognition by individuals on either side of the natural ties which bound them to their foes. There are many telling lines in the play the burden of which is to that effect, and they are sure to evoke the applause of immigrants and sons of immigrants who have settled in this country since 1861. Of course the true drama of the Civil War will not be written in our time. Mr. Howard has made a popular play, which, happily, is good enough to deserve popularity, but he touches very lightly on the causes of the rebellion and the feelings that prevailed during that dreadful period, in spite of his background of carnage, his signal lights and bugle calls, and the fleeting vision of glorious Phil Sheridan on horse-back.

From *The New York Times,*
September 10, 1889.

JAMES A. HERNE'S *MARGARET FLEMING*

By *EDWARD A. DITHMAR*

MARGARET FLEMING, a play in five acts, written by James A. Herne, a well-known actor and stage manager, was presented in Palmer's Theatre yesterday afternoon. It was thus brought into the notice of the habitual and critical theatregoers of New York, who were largely represented in the audience, but it is not a new play. Some interest is attached to the piece because it was acted in Boston, in a hall, under the auspices of a few enthusiastic persons who contemplate the establishment in that city of an Independent Theatre; because it has been regarded by a select few as an example of what the drama that aims to depict contemporary life should be, and because that eminent and authoritative writer, William Dean Howells, has spoken very kindly, in print, of Mr. Herne as a playwright.

Margaret Fleming is, indeed, the quintessence of the commonplace. Its language is the colloquial English of the shops and the streets and the kitchen fire-place. Its personages are the every-day nonentities that some folks like to forget when they go to the theatre. It is constructed in defiance of the laws of Aristotle and Horatius Flaccus and Corneille and Hazlitt. It has two "situations," and two hours are required to develop the first, while the slow culmination of the second occupies another hour. Its incidental humor is quite as true to nature as the humor of Mr. Harrigan's farces, and of much the same quality; but it is not emphasized and set off by the lively songs and dances that have secured success to Harrigan. The life it portrays is sordid and mean, and its effect upon a sensitive mind is depressing.

The drama properly is poetry; the actor's highest task is to interpret poets. The love of the sexes is ever the dramatic poet's most fruitful theme. The theme is often debased on the stage. No one needs to be told that the modern drama is generally prose, not only in form but in spirit as well, and very poor prose at that. But the stage would be a stupid and useless thing if such plays as *Margaret Fleming* were to prevail. Mr. Herne is perfectly true to his present creed, which has been forced upon him, we fancy, by circumstances. Love is a mean thing in his play. Cleopatra does, indeed, live at Number Seven, while Anthony resides in Brunswick Square.

Yet there is merit to be found in the piece, if we take the playwright's point of view, which is the same point of view we take when we read the morning newspaper and buy meat at the butcher's shop. The piece is consistent. It is realistic in everything. We see human beings as they are. There are no soliloquies. The meditations of the characters are not spoken aloud. The author has steered clear of all the old conventions of the drama. The personages come and go naturally. It is easy to be natural in making a play without stirring climaxes and forcible dramatic situations.

The first scene of Act I. is the office of Philip Fleming, a gray-haired young man who drinks too much brandy. Philip has a young wife, a year-old baby, and a nice home to keep them in. He enters his office, removes his hat and overcoat, sits at his desk and reads his letters. A visitor is announced, one Joseph Fletcher, a vendor of soap, cough medicine, and cement for broken china. He was formerly an employe of Fleming, and the object of his call seems to be, principally, to get a drink of rum for nothing. A second caller is Dr. Larkin, Fleming's family physician, whose mission is more serious. Before he has a chance to impart it Fleming has a scene with the telephone. He talks with his wife about the baby's birthday and dinner, and also with the baby, who is understood to remark by telephone, "Ah goo."

Then Dr. Larkin is permitted to come to the point. He has been called to attend a poor woman, Lena Schmidt, in childbirth. She has been employed by Fleming. She has suffered greatly—the physician enters into particulars on that head. She has been delirious, and has unwittingly spoken the name of her betrayer. Fleming gets pale and nervous. The physician scowls and lectures, and threatens. Fleming is compelled to promise that he will visit the girl before she dies. Therefore he telephones to his wife that he cannot be home to the birthday dinner, takes a large drink of brandy, puts on his overcoat and cap, takes his umbrella, because it is raining now, and goes out.

In the second scene the home of Fleming is revealed. The baby has just had her bed-time bath, a custom to be condemned, by the way, because one tub bath a day is enough for a year-old child, and that in the morning. Mr. Herne should reconsider this highly dramatic point. Too much praise, however, could not be given to the pictorial accuracy of this scene. The display of linen, particularly of those articles of infant apparel known to women of all ages as "didies," is most impressive. Well, the child is put in its crib, and the German nurse tells a story of misery to the child's mother, Margaret Fleming. Her sister has gone astray, and is dying. The nurse vows vengeance on the betrayer when she learns his name. Mrs. Fleming gives her a "night off," so that she may go to her sister.

Then Margaret stands by the bedroom door and sings softly to the baby, who is restless. While she is singing Philip enters, wet, pale, agitated. His wife is worried by his ill looks, and prescribes hot lemon-ade, a mustard footbath, and extra blankets. A conversation between husband and wife here indicates the course she will pursue when she learns of her husband's perfidy. He is embarrassed in business, and has called a meeting of his creditors. Yet he has put $1,000 in a savings bank for the baby, and produces also a paid-up insurance policy on his life in the infant's favor. He has, moreover, settled his house upon his wife. These benevolent actions the wife rebukes somewhat sternly. The house must be sold, she says, and all his money must go to pay his debts.

In Act II. Philip is left, lying on the floor, playing with baby, who has a canton-flannel elephant and a woolly dog, while Margaret, hav-ing instructed the new cook about the 12-o'clock dinner, goes out. She is going, without Philip's knowledge, to see the dying girl, the nurse's sister. When she reaches the cottage where Lena Schmidt had found shelter the girl is dead. Her puny infant is starving. The girl's sister has found a letter, written by Lena to Philip Fleming, which tells the whole story. She shows it to Margaret in a burst of anger, and threatens to take Philip's life. The meddling physician is there to try to protect Margaret, and to tell her that she is in danger of blindness which is hereditary in her family, as certain maladies are hereditary in the families of Ibsen's characters. But Margaret can take care of her-self. She quiets the German woman by the influence of her own calm-ness, and sends a note to Philip demanding his presence at the cottage. Then she is left alone with the new-born infant, who is wailing piteously from hunger. Margaret is agitated, naturally; she is angry beyond words; all the hope has gone out of her life. Dr. Larkin would have told her not to try to nurse Lena's child at that moment. She ought to have known better herself. But it is after all Mr. Herne's fault. All realists encounter an impenetrable brick wall of fact sooner or later when writing for the stage. Poets have the poet's license. Well, Philip staggers into the room just as Margaret has decided what to do with the child, and the sagacious prompter rings down the curtain just in time.

The child dies, of course. Margaret, in a frenzy of grief, starts to return to her old home at Niagara Falls, forgetting her own child, forgetting even that her mother has been dead two years. There seems to be some poetic license in this. She is stricken blind, and passes seven months in an asylum at Utica, N. Y. Philip runs away and has a prolonged spree. Meanwhile the German nurse steals the child, returns to her worthless husband, Joe Fletcher, the peddler, and establishes herself in the grocery business in the north end of Boston. Both she and Joe drink a great deal, and the Fleming child carries beer from the adjacent barroom, drinks the foam because she likes it, and tells lies glibly. She is at length discovered, when she is five years old, by both her father, a prematurely old, enfeebled man, and her blind mother, who earns a living by selling school books on commission.

Philip and Margaret have never met since their separation. They meet at last in a street squabble over the child. They are arrested and taken to a police station along with the child and the Fletchers. A kindly Police Inspector, having heard their story, endeavors to effect a reconciliation by leaving the husband and wife together; but that is impossible. Margaret will not have a divorce, because she wants no more ceremony. She will not return to her husband. Her illusions are gone, and her heart, except for her child, seems to be stone. Her argument is seemingly unanswerable. "What would you do," she asks Philip, "if I had been unfaithful?"

The text is simple and direct and contains many unpleasant expressions not often heard on the stage. The character of Margaret is strongly drawn, but, if she is a logical personage, she is certainly a disagreeable one. Selfishness is her predominating trait. This rôle was excellently played by Katharine Corcoran Herne, a competent actress of large and varied experience, a graceful woman with a sweet Irish face and a musical Irish voice. Her acting was naturally faithful to her husband's ideal, and it is not likely that the part could be better played. But it is not pleasant to dwell upon the performance. Mrs. Herne would doubtless shine in poetical comedy.

Well-known members of Mr. Palmer's company, including Mr. Bell as Fleming, Mr. Holland as Dr. Larkin, Mr. Harris as Joe Fletcher, and Mr. Ramsay as the Police Inspector, were faultless in their respective parts. Miss Mattie Earle played the important and complex rôle of the German termagant with an unconvincing accent, but with considerable force and variety. The many minor parts were remarkably well acted, especially by two small boys, Hughes and Mowatt, Miss Helen Goold, Miss Adelaide Rowe, Mrs. Britton, and Miss Nellie Lingard, and the prattling child of the last half of the play was an exceedingly bright little girl named Viola Neill.

Margaret Fleming has thus come prominently into public notice. We doubt if it will stay. But, in the circumstances, it was worth trying, and Mr. Palmer certainly did nobly for it.

From *The New York Times,*
December 10, 1891.

BRET HARTE AND MR. HOWELLS AS DRAMATISTS

By BRANDER MATTHEWS

T H E misfortune hitherto of American dramatic literature has been that those who made plays did not make literature, and that those who made literature did not make plays. This, of course, is not universally true. There are exceptions. N. P. Willis, for instance, was one, and G. H. Boker is another. But in general the poets of America have not been playwrights, and the playwrights have not been poets. The playwrights have been incapable of poetry, and the poets have been unwilling to spend time and trouble in learning the trade of the playwright. The drama, so-called, split apart into "acting plays" and those unspeakable impossibilities—"dramas for the closet." But a change for the better is now impending, if it is not already upon us. We have noted with great pleasure a desire on the part of the younger American authors to grasp the olive crown of dramatic victory. Mr. Bryant, Mr. Longfellow, Mr. Lowell have not sought the stage. But Mr. Bayard Taylor is preparing an English play from the German. Mr. "Joaquin" Miller seeks to set the life of the Sierras upon the stage of the city. Mr. "Mark Twain" has produced his second play, and Mr. "Petroleum Vesuvius Nasby," leaving for the present the Confederate cross roads and Deacon Baskoms, is preparing his second dramatic attempt also, his first having failed as fully as Mr. Clemens's first succeeded, although it can hardly have been poorer as a play. *Two Men of Sandy Bar* has been tried in the light of the lamps and found wanting. It has no unity of plot. There is no singleness of purpose—no definite aim held firmly from the first scene to the last: all is veering and shifting. Faults like these are fatal to dramatic effect. There is none of the simplicity of central idea which a play needs as a man needs a backbone—and for the same reason. Single scenes scattered here and there recall the old charm of *The Luck of Roaring Camp* and the pathos of *The Outcasts of Poker Flat.* As a whole, the play is proof that Mr. Harte, on taking up the new and difficult profession of play-making, did not see its difficulties, and therefore did not devote himself to the overcoming of them. Mr. Howells is working on a wiser plan. As he taught himself to write novels, beginning with the simple sketch of *Their Wedding Journey,* until he reached the almost tragic climax of *A Foregone Conclusion,* so now he is teaching himself to write plays. He began with the dainty and delicate little comedy, the *Parlor Car* (included in the Vest Pocket Series), which he maligned greatly in calling a farce. And before writing *A Counterfeit Presentment,* now appearing in the *Atlantic,* and destined for the stage, he produced *Out of the Question.* Whether it would succeed or not in the theatre, we cannot of course tell; no test is sufficient short of the ordeal by fire—the glare of the footlights. Its story is simple and well handled; the interest is well sustained, the characters are well contrasted. But perhaps the effects are not quite broad enough; perhaps there is not color enough; perhaps the tone of the whole piece is too quiet; perhaps it is all too slight for the stage. Possibly, indeed, it was never intended to be acted. If this be so, if it were only a tentative essay in a new form, its success can be called complete. Mr. Howells has never worked with a lighter hand or a firmer touch than in many passages of this little comedy. To those who know the depth and the delicacy of Mr. Howells' former writings nothing more need be said.

From *The Library Table* (New York),
September 13, 1877.

ON PUTTING LITERATURE INTO THE DRAMA

By BRANDER MATTHEWS

W H E N the future historian of the American drama comes to deal with the final years of the nineteenth century and the early years of the twentieth, he will do well to record that the riper development in that period was retarded by three untoward events,—the premature deaths of Clyde Fitch and William Vaughn Moody and the premature birth of Bronson Howard.

Moody was a poet who was engaged in conscientiously acquiring the art of the playwright when his career was cut short; and if he had lived we should have had a right to reckon on a series of serious plays deep in purpose and expert in craftsmanship—plays in which we should find a fulfilment of the expectations aroused by the promising *Great Divide* and *Faith Healer*. Clyde Fitch ran a longer course; he was far more prolific; and he had to his credit half-a-dozen or half-a-score popular successes. But there was no one of his plays which sustained its entire action on the high level he had been able to attain in separate scenes when he was at his best. The third act of the *Girl with the Green Eyes* was a masterpiece of dramaturgic skill and of psychologic veracity, but it was followed by a fourth act so inept as to be beneath contempt. The Duke in the *Coronet of the Duchess* was a vital character created with real insight into human nature, but the play itself was false in motive and feeble in construction. Fitch was honestly ambitious; and he believed to the end that his best work was still before him.

As both Moody and Fitch were taken from us before they had achieved their full artistic maturity, we cannot even guess what ampler effort they might have put forth if they had been spared. But we can see that there was a definite loss to the American drama in the appearance of Bronson Howard a score of years too early. He had an unusual endowment for dramatic authorship; he had the instinct for theatrical effect; he had a keen sense of character; he had an individual insight into human nature; he had an intuitive understanding of the fundamental principles of playmaking; and he had a broad outlook on life. But he came to maturity and he did his best work in a period of rapid

149

transition,—in the years before the artificial methods of Sardou and of Boucicault had been supplanted by the sterner simplicity of Ibsen and of the host of latter-day playwrights who responded to the stimulus of Ibsen's masterly technic. The overt theatricality of the playmakers of half-a-century ago has now fallen into disrepute, for we expect today to find in our more ambitious dramas a less arbitrarily arranged story, a theme of more vital interest, handled with a more obvious veracity. We demand a more serious treatment of motive and an ampler vision of life.

These qualities we do not find in Bronson Howard's plays, clever as they were and amusing as they were. We cannot help confessing that they seem to us compounded according to an outworn formula. Their merits, undeniable as they are, strike us now as ingeniously theatrical rather than truly dramatic. These pieces were good in their own day; but they are not good enough to withstand the change in our standards. They are unfortunately old-fashioned, even if we can still admire the power and the felicity with which certain episodes are handled, like that in *Shenandoah,* where the soldier father all unwittingly conducts the funeral of his unrecognized son, a scene which is a little master-piece of unforced pathos. And the reason why these successful plays, the *Banker's Daughter, Young Mrs. Winthrop* and *The Henrietta* are out-of-date today is that they were up-to-date yesterday; they are what they are because their author conformed to the customs of his youth. But those who knew Bronson Howard personally can testify that he had it in him to write plays of a finer substance and of a solider truth than he was permitted to write in the changing epoch when he was at work. He was subdued to what he workt in; and he was born out of time. If he had come into this world forty years later he would have employed the simpler methods which are now acceptable; he would have dealt more sincerely with life; he would have been more truly dramatic without surrendering his theatrical effectiveness; he would have utilized more imaginatively his persistent and inquisitive observation of conduct and of character.

Most successful artists work rather by instinct than by rule; they achieve their results more or less unconscious of the laws they are obeying; and only a very few can be trusted to analize their own processes and to explain why they did what they did in the way they did. Bronson Howard was one of the small minority who could always give a reason for the faith that was in him. His methods were intuitive, of course, or they would not have accomplisht the result at which he was aiming; but they were also authenticated by his constant reflection upon the principles of playwriting. After he had been guided by his intuition he could explain to himself the reason why he had done what he had done. In other words, he had strengthened his native instinct by philosophic inquiry into the unvarying principles of playmaking.

From *Principles of Playmaking.*
(Scribner's, 1919.)

IBSEN THE INDIVIDUALIST

By JAMES GIBBONS HUNEKER

... A N ironic self-contradiction may be gleaned from a study of Ibsen; each play seems to deny the conclusions of the previous one. But when the entire field is surveyed in retrospect the smaller irregularities and deflections from the level melt into a harmonious picture. Ibsen is complex. Ibsen is confusing. In Ibsen there rage the thinker, the artist, the critic. These sometimes fail to amalgamate, and so the artistic precipitation is cloudy. He is a true Viking who always loves stormy weather; and, as Brandes said, "God is in his heart, but the devil is in his body." His is an emotional logic, if one may frame such an expression; and it would be in vain to search in his works for the *ataraxia* of the tranquil Greek philosopher. A dynamic grumbler, like Carlyle, he eventually contrives to orient himself; his dramas are only an escape from the ugly labyrinth of existence. If his characters are sick, so is latter-day life. The thinker often overrides the poet in him; and at times the dramatist, the pure *Theatermensch,* gets the bit between his teeth and nearly wrecks the psychologist. He acknowledges the existence of evil in the world, knows the house of evil, but has not tarried in it. Good must prevail in the end is the burden of his message, else he would not urge upon his fellow-beings the necessity of willing and doing.

The cold glamour of his moods is supplemented by the strong, sincere purpose underlying them. He feels, with Kierkegaard, that the average sensual man will ever "parry the ethical claim"; and if, in Flaubert's eyes, "man is bad because he is stupid," in Ibsen's "he is stupid because he is bad." "To will is to have to will," says his Maximus in *Emperor and Galilean.* This phrase is the capstone of the Ibsen structure. If he abhors the inflated phraseology of altruism, he is one with Herbert Spencer, who spoke of a relapse into egotism as the only thing which could make altruism enduring.

Felicity, then, with Ibsen is experience itself, not the result of experience. Life is a huge misunderstanding, and the Ibsen dramas hinge on misunderstandings—the conflict between the instinctive and the acquired, between the forces of heredity and of environment. Herein lies his preference for the drama of disordered wills. And touching on this accusation of morbidity and sickness, may there not be gleaned from Shakespeare and Goethe many mad, half-mad, and brain-sick men and women? The English poet's plays are a perfect storehouse of examples for the alienist. Hallucination that hardens into mania is delicately recorded by Ibsen; he notes with a surgeon's skilled eye the first slight decadence and the final entombment of the will. Furthermore, the chiefest malady of our age is that of the will enfeebled by lack of exercise, by inanition due to unsound education; and as he fingers our spiritual muscles he cries aloud their flabbiness. In men the pathologic symptoms are more marked than in women; hence the number of women in his dramas who assume dominant rôles—not that Ibsen has any particular sympathy with the New Woman, but because he has seen that the modern woman marks time better with the *zeitgeist* than her male complement.

Will, even though your will be disastrous in its outcome, but will, he insists; and yet demonstrates that only through self-surrender can come complete self-realization. To say "I am what I am," is the Ibsen *credo;* but this "*I*" must be tested in the fire of self-abnegation. To the average theologian all this rings suspiciously like the old-fashioned doctrine of salvation by good works. The Scotch leaven is strong in Ibsen. In his bones he is a moralist, in practice an artist. His power is that of the artist doubled by the profound moralist, the philosopher doubled by the dramatist; the crystallization in the plays of these antagonistic qualities constitutes the triumph of his genius.

From *Iconoclasts: A Book of Dramatists.*
(Scribner's, 1905.)

MARY GARDEN AS AN ACTRESS-SINGER

By JAMES GIBBONS HUNEKER

...MY dear friend and master, the late Remy de Gourmont, wrote that man differs from his fellow animals—he didn't say "lower"—because of the diversity of his aptitudes. Man is not the only organism that shows multiple personalities; even in plant life pigmentation and the power of developing new species prove that our vaunted superiorities are only relative. I may refer you to the experiments of Hugo de Vriès at the Botanical Gardens, Amsterdam, where the grand old Dutch scientist presented me with sixteen-leaf clover naturally developed, and grown between sunset and dawn; also an evening primrose—Æonthera Lamarckiana—which shoots into new flowers. Multiple personalities again. In the case of Mary Garden we call her artistic aptitudes "the gift of versatility." All distinguished actresses have this serpent-like facility of shedding their skin and taking on a fresh one at will. She is Cleopatra—with "serpent and scarab for sign"—or Mélisande, Phryne, or Monna Vanna; as Thaïs she is both saint and courtesan, her Salome breeds horror; and in the simplicities of Jean the Juggler of Notre Dame a Mary Garden, hitherto submerged, appears: tender, boyish, sweet, fantastic; a ray of moonshine has entered his head and made of him an irresponsible yet irresistibly charming youth.

Not without warrant is Karma believed in by people whose imagination cannot be penned behind the bars of Now. Before to-day was yesterday, and to traverse that Eternal Corridor of Time has been the fate of mankind. The Eternal Return—rather say, the Eternal Recommencement—mad as it seems, is not to be made mock of. It is always the same pair of eyes that peer through windows opening on infinity. What the Karmas of Mary Garden? In spirit-land what avatars! Is she the reincarnation of that Phryne of the "splendid scarlet sins," or the

Faustine who crowded into a moment the madness of joy and crime; or the recrudescence of a Sapho who turned her back on the Leucadian promontory, turned from the too masculine Phaon and sought her Anactoria, sought and wooed her with lyric sighs; has she recaptured, this extraordinary Mary of Aberdeen, the soul of Aspasia, who beguiled Pericles and artistic Athens with the sinuous irony of the serpent; and Gismonda, Louise, and Violetta, all those subtle sonorous sinners—was she in her anterior existence any or all of them? Did she know the glory that was Greece, the grandeur that was Rome? Henry James has warned us not to ask of an author why he selects a particular subject for treatment. It is a dangerous question to put; the answer might prove disconcerting. And with Miss Garden the same argument holds. Her preference for certain characters is probably dictated by reasons obscure even to herself. With her the play-instinct is imperious; it dominates her daylight hours, it overflows into her dream-life. Again the sounding motive of multiple personalities, Karma, subconsciousness, the profound core of human nature. And on the palette of her art there is the entire gamut of tones, from passionate purple to the iridescent delicacies of iris-grey.

That Mary Garden interprets a number of widely differentiated characters is a critical platitude. Chapter and verse might be given for her excellencies as well as her defects. Nor does she depend upon any technical formula or formulas. Versatility is her brevet of distinction. An astounding versatility. Now, the ways and means of the acting-singer are different from actors in the theatre. Dramatic values are altered. The optique of the opera shifts the stock attitudes, gestures, poses, and movements into another and more magnified dimension. Victor Maurel, master of all singing-actors, employed a sliding scale of values in his delineation of De Nevers, Don Giovanni, Iago, and Falstaff. His power of characterization enabled him to portray a Valentine true to type, nevertheless individual; and if there is a more banal figure on the operatic boards than Valentine, we do not know his name (perhaps Faust ... !). But every year the space that separates the lyric from the dramatic stage is shrinking. Richard Wagner was not the first composer to stress action; he is the latest, however, whose influence has been tremendously far-reaching. He insisted that the action should suit the singing word. To-day acting and singing are inextricably blended, and I can conceive of nothing more old-fashioned and outmoded than the Wagnerian music-drama as interpreted in the dramatic terms of the old Wagnerian singers. They walked, rather waddled, through the mystic mazes of the score, shouted or screamed the music, and generally were prodigious bores—except when Lilli Lehmann sang. After all, Wagner must be sung. When Jean de Reszke pictured a Tristan—a trifle of the carpet-knight—he both sang and acted. It was the beginning of the New Wagner, a totally changed Wagner, else his music-drama will remain in dusty pigeonholes. Debussy has sounded the modern key.

There is born, or reborn—nothing is new since the early Florentines—a New Opera, and in its train new methods of interpretation. Merely to sing well is as futile as attempting to act though voiceless. The modern trend is away from melodrama, whether Italian, French, or German; away from its antique, creaking machinery. Debussy patterned after Wagner for a time and then blazed new paths. As Serge Prokofieff so acutely observed to me: "In *Pelléas and Mélisande* Debussy rewrote *Tristan and Isolde.*" The emotional scale is transposed to fewer dynamic values and rhythms made more subtle; the action is shown as in a dream. The play's the thing, and reality is muffled. Elsewhere we have studied the Mélisande of Mary Garden. Like her Monna Vanna, it reveals the virtues and shortcomings of the New Opera. Too static for popular taste, it is nevertheless an escape from the tyranny of operatic convention. Like the rich we shall always have "grand opera" with us. It is the pabulum of the unmusical, the unthinking, the tasteless. Its theatricalisms are more depressing than Sardou's. The quintessence of art, or the arts, which the modern Frenchmen, above all, the new Russian composers (from the mighty Slavic races may come the artistic, perhaps the religious salvation of the world—for I am a believer in Dostoievsky's, not Tolstoy's, Christianity), are distilling into their work is for more auditors than the "ten superior persons scattered throughout the universe" of whom Huysmans wrote. There is a growing public that craves, demands, something different from the huge paraphernalia of crudely colored music, scenery, costume, lath and plaster, and vociferous singing. Oh, the dulness, the staleness, the brutal obviousness of it all! Every cadence with its semaphoric signalling, every phrase and its accompanying gesture. Poetry is slain at a stroke, the ear promise-crammed, but imagination goes hungry. The New Art—an art of precious essences, an evocation, an enchantment of the senses, a sixth sense—is our planetary ideal.

And in the New Opera Mary Garden is the supreme exemplar. She sounds the complex modern note. She does not represent, she evokes. She sings and she acts, and the densely woven web is impossible to disentangle. Her Gaelic temperament is of an intensity; she is white-hot, a human dynamo with sudden little retorsions that betray a tender, sensitive soul, through the brilliant, hard shell of an emerald personality; she is also the opal, with its chameleonic hues. Her rhythms are individual. Her artistic evolution may be traced. She stems from the Gallic theatre. She has studied Sarah Bernhardt and Yvette Guilbert —the perfect flowering of the "diseuse"—but she pins her faith to the effortless art of Eleonora Duse. The old contention that stirred Coquelin and Henry Irving does not interest her so much as does Duse. We have discussed the Coquelin-Irving crux: should an actor leave nothing to chance or should he improvise on the spur of high emotions?—that is what the question comes to. Miss Garden denied her adherence either to Coquelin or Irving. I asked her to give us a peep into her artistic cuisine while she prepared her sauces. Notwithstanding her refusal to let us participate in the brewing of her magic broth, I still believe that she sided with Coquelin. She is eminently cerebral. And yet her chief appeal is to the imagination. Not a stroke of her camel's-hair brush, not the boldest massing of colors, are left to chance. She knows the flaming way she came, she knows the misty return. Not a tone of her naturally rich, dark voice but takes on the tinting of the situation. This doesn't forbid a certain latitude for temperamental variations, which are plentiful at each of her performances. She knows tempo rubato and its value in moods. She has mastered, too, the difficult quality described by William Gillette as the First-time Illusion in Acting. Various are the Mary Gardens in her map of art.

And she is ours. Despite her Scottish birth she has remained invincibly Yankee. Despite long residence in her beloved Paris, enough American has rubbed off on her, and the resilient, dynamic, overflowing, and proud spirit that informs her art and character are American or nothing. Race counts. Can any good come out of our Nazareth of art? The answer is inevitable: Yes, Mary Garden. She is Our Mary.

Lyrically, dramatically ours, yet an orchid. Dear old Flaubert forcibly objected to Sarah Bernhardt being called "a social expression." But she was, and this despite her Dutch ancestry and the exotic strain in her blood. Miss Garden may not emphasize her American side, but it is the very skeleton of her artistic organism. Would that an Aubrey Beardsley lived to note in evanescent traceries her potent personality, a rare something that arouses the "emotion of recognition," but which we cannot define. "Come," said Berlioz to Legouvé in the early years of the third decade of the last century. "I am going to let you see something which you have never seen, and some one whom you shall never forget." Berlioz meant the playing and personality of Frédéric Chopin. Garden is leagues asunder from Chopin—who was the rarest apparition of his age; but as an intepretative artist she is rare enough for sympathetic writers to embalm in the amber of their pagan prose; definitely to pin to their pages this gorgeous dragon-fly.

From *Bedouins,*
(Scribner's, 1920).

MRS. LESLIE CARTER IN *ZAZA*

By NORMAN HAPGOOD

AFTER the third act of *Zaza,* which blew into the Garrick last night with a burst of scarlet trumpets, David Belasco made a speech. He reminded the audience, with tears in his larynx, that nine years ago a most unhappy woman flung herself at his feet and asked his "advice." She got it. Mr. Belasco then said: "There is one perfectly happy woman in the world to-night." That woman had reached the goal of every actor's ambition (while in New York), the approval of a New York audience. "She will, before she *retires,* send a telegram to a certain red-headed boy, telling him that you like her, and he will then know that he has no reason to be ashamed of his mother."

Bravo, Mr. Belasco. Did not every woman's heart in that vast throng thrill with yours and Mrs. Carter's when it remembered that, through plot and counterplot, through the divorce court and the awful verdict of the judge on the mother's relation to her child, her maternal

heart beat fondly on her offspring in this crowning hour of triumph?
Does anybody believe that David Belasco was born yesterday?

Through this touching mist of motherhood, behold the play which
enraptured a house full of polished rounders. The first act is a triumph
in stage management, especially in that kind of mechanical aid
to the drama in which Mr. Belasco and Mr. Gillette have set the
pace for the world, to the great astonishment of our British cousins.
The inside of a theatre is shown—the making of thunder, lightning,
wind, and galloping horses behind the scenes—with a dexterity and
attractive suggestion of accuracy apparently beyond improvement, and
the handling of the actors by Mr. Belasco, in building up the pictures,
points, and incidents, shows a master mechanic, even if in the main he
is but carrying out the lines of the French original. The authors, too,
have done their best work in this act. While the amusing exposure of
stage machinery is being accompanied by illustrations of the ways
found by actors to injure one another, the situation is easily put before
us in a series of events centering in the dressing room of the star, which
is exposed to the audience. To make the act still more full the situation
develops to the accompaniment of a poem by Skeats called *La Belle
Dame Sans Habit,* a very beautiful production to the soul of every true
rounder, exhibiting the stockings, arm, neck and back of the passionately maternal actress. She wishes to preëmpt the heart (or rather those
parts of the being which operate in kinds of love with which the heart
has no concern) of a definite male, and she goes through devices which
people who know say are realistic. They seemed to be, also. It was the
only time that a touch of nature seemed to make Mrs. Carter akin to
true art. The rest of her performance was a startling *tour de force,* but
in the first act we were really unable to detect any lack of conviction.

The second act let down like an express elevator, because after this
entrancing cornucopia of motion, novelty and naughtiness there was
offered a domestic scene in which Mr. Stevenson and Mrs. Carter
performed true love. Zaza, the wicked and of course irresistible music
hall singer, has known the spark divine, and is blissfully warming her
heart upon it. From this point on the machinery in Mrs. Carter shows,
and it is not as interesting or novel as the stage machinery in the first
act. A certain power she has—the power of limitless energy directed
by a master of the trade—but never for a moment does she suggest

those finer shades, those softer touches, that can be truly given only from an inner well of genuine feeling, of instinctive recreation of the emotions portrayed. You might as well engage Corot to teach a Philistine how to represent the poetry of morning. Mrs. Carter is a good actress, as actors go, and we have no desire to disguise it, but she is as hard as an arc light and as lacking in exquisitiveness as a turnip. She was good, therefore, in her outbreaks of fury and in her picture of low tempting, but in the scenes which mark her spiritual redemption, though she was correct, the soul of the thing was dead.

Zaza learns that the man for whose love she has become another woman is married and holds her as a toy, and she casts him off. After several years he returns to her music hall and she (in the English version) gives him a fine lecture on the higher sentiments. It is a strong play, not original after the first act, but dealing with facts of sterling interest presented with the firmness of professional skill. It is interesting. Nobody will be bored. It will run. The rounders will be delighted, the puritans will be shocked, and a few, of whom we confess ourselves a part, will shrug their shoulders and say "blessed are the commonplace, for they shall inherit a good deal." Anyone who is inclined to regret that a turnip should be viewed with such furor, may be able to add a glamour to the success by recalling the story of the redheaded boy.

From *The New York Commercial Advertiser,*
January 10, 1899.

RICHARD MANSFIELD'S *HENRY V*

By NORMAN HAPGOOD

HENRY V was so magnificently produced by Richard Mansfield at the Garden Theatre last night that it is hardly venturesome to prophesy a long and popular new lease of stage life for this, one of the least dramatic of Shakespeare's plays. Magnificence, however, while it is what carried the audience to storms of approval after the most spectacular scene, is by no means the only quality. Mr. Mansfield has decorated the play with such skill that the sweetness and majesty of it, the poetry which is its whole nature, instead of being crowded aside, seem to be only appropriately clothed. It is called on the programme a war play; but it is also a poem and a character portrait, and in this production, as in the drama itself, all three are blended.

The act which, almost innumerable times, sent up the curtain and called Mr. Mansfield before it, was not written by Shakespeare. It was not written by anybody, for it contained no words. The chorus, exquisitely rendered throughout by Florence Kahn, was made by the poet to say this:

> *But now behold,*
> *In the quick forge and working-house of thought,*
> *How London doth pour out her citizens!*
> *The mayor and all his brethren, in best sort,—*
> *Like to the senators of th' antique Rome,*
> *With the plebeians swarming at their heels,—*
> *Go forth, and fetch their conquering Caesar in.*

Upon that hint Mr. Mansfield, following Kean's example, trusted, not to the quick forge and working-house of thought, but to the improvement in stage machinery and the love of visible motion which dwells within the human breast. The whole fourth act, in this arrangement, was a scene in a London street, where the populace hailed the arriving troops, marching in battalions, with cross-bows, pikes and lances, passing rapidly forward through an arch in the rear and off through the crowd to the side. Now and again a soldier was joined by his wife or by a waiting maiden, and amidst the excitement of it all the harder side of war was suggested by one woman's fate: she rushed among the soldiers to ask one question, and then was carried senseless from the ranks. A dance of girls with flowers was one feature of the pageant, which ended with the entrance on the stage of King Henry on his battle horse.

Next to this in spectacular success was a picture of Henry's wedding to Katherine of France, which closed the evening. The tableau of the battle of Agincourt, although it was approved, was not so convincing a picture as the others, at least from the front of the house, the painted soldiers not competing adequately with the living ones.

Nobody can grudge the success gained by these spectacular features since they were well executed in themselves, not inharmonious with the drama, and the means whereby thousands will be led to spend an evening in the company of gorgeous language and noble sentiments.

The cutting of the text and rearrangement of the scenes was almost constantly felicitous. Passages of great length, except Henry's speeches, were dropped, as were those lines in which the meaning would not be immediately clear to a modern audience, and a few words which show a cruelty in King Henry incompatible, to our minds, with the kindlier movements of his heart. A mistake was surely made in not dropping the first scene between Katherine and Alice, for by making it part of the scene where the princess meets the king, the absurdity is introduced of having Katherine learn her first few nouns in English a few seconds before she addresses Henry in his own language. The ingenuousness was taken out of the chorus, and possibly that was prudent, in view of the nature of audiences; but a much better and less abrupt end to the chorus of the fourth act would be found at "a little touch of Harry in the night." Occasional words are changed in deference to religious sensibilities without injury to the play.

Mr. Mansfield's performance of Henry showed his skill as an actor to a high degree. Many players carefully choose rôles that fit their personalities. Not so Mr. Mansfield. Famous for satire and character parts, he now stood forth as a king who was half warrior and half saint, so that every stroke the actor made had to be with his talent against his natural physical characteristics. None the less he gave a performance of the extremely difficult rôle which was in every way worthy to stand among this able and varied actor's proudest achievements. To say that more poetry, more sweetness and more power might be put into Henry is true, but not very important, for Mr. Mansfield had something of each of these qualities, and he had so much gallantry, spirit, dignity and humor that no fair person who had built a somewhat different Henry out of Shakespeare could refuse to accept Mr. Mansfield's as fine and just. He began in a rather low key, and in his first two long speeches he dropped at the ends of lines, although both to the French herald and to the conspirators did he show much quiet dignity; but when he had thus saved his forces at the start he expended them with strong effect in the famous speech, "once more unto the breach, dear friends, once more," in which, standing before his bending army, which did "stand like greyhounds in the slips, straining upon the start," he gave the resounding words with heroic fervor and memorable aspect. Small of stature, and mental rather than passionate in temper, yet the actor subdued himself to his work and his art made him triumphant. The account of the horrors of war, delivered before the gates of Harfleur, could hardly be given with more truthful and determined calm, and the sudden charge to "open your gates," in the voice of prompt command, was admirably just. His second tired and friendly defiance to the herald, and his delivery of such sharp reflective lines as "God Almighty! There is some soul of goodness in things evil," could hardly be improved, and his speech on ceremony, which perhaps lacked the poignancy that some of us read in it, was full of a soldier's direct and honest meaning, and Henry was in Mr. Mansfield's acting, what he was in his own eyes, first of all a warrior. When he cheered his followers in the English camp with visions of the future glory of St. Crispin's day, the specially intelligent audience responded with applause born of their share in the actor's contagious gallantry. In his wooing and his marriage he was still the soldier, and the Saxon soldier, downright and commanding but with greater play of gayety and wit —a buoyant airiness that came with double force after the words and scenes of war. Mr. Mansfield here and there through the play sacrificed metre to modernity, perhaps with sufficient reason, but this was a trifle, and his strong, rapid and clear declamation was throughout one of his most apt and helpful weapons. . . .

The crowds were well drilled, and the only ensemble error was a tendency of the attending noblemen at both courts to act at certain points automatically as one man. Altogether, we may well take off our hats to Mr. Mansfield, both as actor and as liberal and ambitious manager, for putting on the stage, in spite of its inherent lack of drama, one of the most beautiful pieces of English literature, and so presenting it that the unwary may be pleased at the same time as the judicious.

From *The New York Commercial Advertiser,*
October 4, 1900.

"THE LIMIT OF STAGE INDECENCY"

Shaw's *Mrs. Warren's Profession*

''T H E L I D '' was lifted by Mr. Arnold Daly and "the limit" of
stage indecency reached last night in the Garrick Theatre in the
performance of one of Mr. George Bernard Shaw's "unpleasant
comedies" called *Mrs. Warren's Profession.*

"The limit of indecency" may seem pretty strong words, but they
are justified by the fact that the play is morally rotten. It makes no
difference that some of the lines may have been omitted and others
toned down; there was superabundance of foulness left. The whole
story of the play, the atmosphere surrounding it, the incidents, the
personalities of the characters are wholly immoral and degenerate.
The only way successfully to expurgate *Mrs. Warren's Profession* is
to cut the whole play out. You cannot have a clean pig stye. The play
is an insult to decency because—

It defends immorality.

It glorifies debauchery.

It besmirches the sacredness of a clergyman's calling.

It pictures children and parents living in calm observance of most
unholy relations.

And, worst of all, it countenances the most revolting form of
degeneracy, by flippantly discussing the marriage of brother and sister,
father and daughter, and makes the one supposedly moral character of
the play, a young girl, declare that choice of shame, instead of poverty
is eminently right.

These things cannot be denied. They are the main factors of the
story. Without them there would be no play. It is vileness and degeneracy brazenly considered. If New York's sense of shame is not aroused
to hot indignation at this theatrical insult, it is indeed in a sad plight.

This is an outline, or, rather, a suggestion of the story that Mr.
Arnold Daly saw fit to enact in the Garrick Theatre last night before
a morbidly curious audience that packed the theatre to suffocation,
and doubtless will continue to do so as long as the play is permitted
to be given.

Mrs. Warren, a child of the slums, has become a courtesan and is the mistress of several disreputable houses in Brussels, Berlin, Vienna and Budapest. Her profession has brought her wealth. She has a daughter, Vivian, educated in England in ignorance of her mother's real character, and who has achieved fame in college as a mathematician. This clever young daughter of a vile mother is in love with and is beloved by Frank, the flippant, good for nothing son of a prominent clergyman.

The mother goes to England to visit Vivian, and with her are two men, Praed, a mooning artist, with weak morals, and Crofts, a dissolute baronet, with no morals whatever. Crofts is the business partner of Mrs. Warren in her "profession." He is the capitalist who put up the money for her to start with.

Crofts would like to marry Vivian, but is in doubt about her parentage. He is not sure but that she is his own daughter. Nevertheless, he presses his suit through three acts. Possibly it is Praed, thinks Crofts, but Praed is quite sure that he (Praed) is not her father. They discuss the matter at length. As Crofts says, "It's very awkward to be uncertain about it"; that is, it is an awkward thing to marry your own child.

Then it develops that the clergyman was a former intimate of Mrs. Warren, and Crofts asserts that he must be Vivian's father. When the girl rejects his suit in favor of Frank he blocks the match by telling the young couple they are brother and sister, Frank's father, the clergyman, having been the girl's parent.

Mrs. Warren tells her daughter all the revolting details of her life of shame, and glories in it, as it saved her and "Liz," her sister, the drudgery of menial labor.

You may think that the pure and clever daughter is shocked, but forgives and tries to reclaim her mother. Not a bit of it. Her views coincide with those of her shameless parent, and Vivian admits that in the circumstances she herself would have considered licentiousness and sin quite the better choice. She almost envies the career of her aunt, who became rich through the ill gotten gains of the "profession" of shame and is posing now as the social leader in a cathedral town and the chaperon of young girls.

The clergyman, who, mind you, is not made by Mr. Shaw a deposed or unfrocked clergyman, but the spiritual and religious head of a large and prominent church, confesses himself to be a debauchee and a rake—a subject which father and son familiarly discuss and laugh over. The clergyman sits up all night with Crofts and becomes bestially intoxicated; then he starts in to write his sermon for the following day.

Frank, in love with Vivian, makes advances to Vivian's mother, whom he knows to be a lewd woman, and suggests that they go to the Continent together. And so on through the revolting story, until Vivian goes away to London to earn her own living and the other characters sink into obscurity in their old moral degradation.

Does not this literary muck leave a bad taste in the mouth? Does it not insult the moral intelligence of New York theatre-goers and outrage the decency of the New York stage?

There was not one redeeming feature about it last night, not one ray of sunshine, of cleanliness, to lighten up the moral darkness of situation and dialogue; not the semblance of a moral lesson pointed. As Letchmere says of his family in *Letty,* "We are rotten to the core," and the same might be said of the characters in *Mrs. Warren's Profession.*

The play was well acted from a technical standpoint by Mr. Daly as Frank, Miss Shaw as Mrs. Warren, and others of the cast; but while that is ordinarily cause for praise in a performance, it constituted an added sin to last night's production, for the better it was acted the more the impurity and degeneracy of the characters, the situations and the lines were made apparent. There were a few slight excisions made in the play as written, but what was left filled the house with the ill odor of evil suggestion, where it was not blatantly immoral.

After the third act Mr. Daly came before the curtain and made a speech in which he rather floundered as though he had forgotten what was committed to memory. He said that the play should only be seen by grown up people who could not be corrupted. Children might be kept to the old fashioned moral illusions, including Santa Claus and Washington.

"We have many theatres," he went on, "devoted to plays appealing to the romanticist or child—New York has even provided a hippodrome for such. But surely there should be room in New York for at least one theatre devoted to truth, however disagreeable truth may appear.

"This play is not presented as an entertainment, but as a dramatic sermon and an exposé of a social condition and an evil, which our purists attempt to ignore, and by ignoring, allow it to gain its strength. If Mr. Comstock devoted half the energy and time to providing soft beds, sweet food and clean linen to the poor of New York that he does to suppression of postal cards, we would have less immorality, for the logical reason that virtue would be robbing vice of its strongest features and attractiveness—comfort and health.

"It is a strange but true thing that everybody who has written to the newspapers, asking that this play be suppressed, has concluded the letter with the quaint statement, 'I know the play should be suppressed, although, of course, I have not read the book.' God has gifted these mortals with strange powers, indeed.

"If public opinion forces this theatre to close and this play to be withdrawn, it will be a sad commentary indeed upon twentieth century so-called civilization and our enlightened new country."

Then Mr. Daly retired amid vociferous applause from the double distilled Shawites present and the speculators who had tickets for sale for to-night—if there is to be any to-night for the play.

From *The New York Herald*,
October 31, 1905.

NOTE

Said the *Sun* for the same day, "If Mr. Daly had held to his original intention of playing the piece at a few matinees to invited guests, there might be some excuse for its production, but to throw so vile and unnecessary a concoction in the teeth of the public violates all canons of good art and common decency.... The play, in a word, smells to heaven. It is a dramatized stench." The *Times* observed: "Arnold Daly has made a serious mistake. *Mrs. Warren's Profession,* whatever its merits or demerits as a play for the closet, has absolutely no place in a theatre before a mixed assembly such as witnessed it at the Garrick last night.... Mr. Shaw takes a subject, decaying and reeking, and analyzes it for the edification of those whose unhealthy tastes find satisfaction in morbific suggestion." The *Evening Post* remarked, "There is nothing that is so offensive to the normal, clean and healthy mind as the affectation of a lofty motive in the commission of a mean and dirty action, and there was no more exasperating feature of the performance of Bernard Shaw's *Mrs. Warren's Profession* at the Garrick Theatre last evening than the false pretense, at once contemptible and abominable, which clothed the whole undertaking as a garment.... *Mrs. Warren's Profession* is one of those half-truths, which are ever the basest of lies—a composition primarily designed for mere sensation, in which all sense of veracity is lost in the mass of crude exaggeration and specious misrepresentation."

LANGDON MITCHELL'S *THE NEW YORK IDEA*

By JAMES METCALFE

R E V O L U T I O N is in the air. Nothing that ever was is as it should be. The wisdom of the ages is going to be set right by the superior wisdom of the present generation. We are the only children of light who ever existed, and at a single blow we are going to straighten out the sins of our fathers, even to the third and fourth generations going backwards.

That possibly might be the matrimonial moral of the new play written by Mr. Langdon Mitchell for Mrs. Fiske. It teaches that we Smart Alecks of the present generation are bound to revolutionize the marital relation at one fell swoop, just as we are going to change property relations by the election of one bad official to take the place of another bad official. We are going to correct the faults of one bad wife by marrying another who will be better because we don't know she'll be worse. In other terms, the right way to lower the temperature of the frying-pan is to jump into the fire.

Mr. Mitchell probably never intended to convey any such ideas. He simply voices the general discontent with the inherited uncharitable beliefs about the victims of ill-assorted marriages, and lays the blame on the American young women whose mothers have taught them that it's better to be smart than maternal. The evils of American non-maternity are voiced in a play which would be exactly described by the term farce-comedy if that description had not been usurped by Mr. Charles Hoyt to describe an entirely different kind of entertainment. The New York idea, by which Mr. Mitchell evidently means the

American idea, is, according to him, that matrimony among the richer or better class in this country means anything but maternity. Like most inexpert and amateur reformers, he expatiates on the evil without prescribing a remedy. The result, thanks to his wit, is a really clever and laugh-provoking, polite stage piece.

The New York Idea is very up to date. It makes fun of a religion which tries to make form take the place of truth. This is embodied in a fashionable clergyman who wears a gold cross on his watch-chain and books a tip on the races. It makes love and sentiment largely the result of previously imbibed high-balls. Its heroines are actuated by no higher motives than feminine spite, jealousy and craving for new sensations. Of course it is exaggerated, and, as it is entirely farcical and satirical, should not be taken too seriously. At the same time it voices one man's notions of social evils and is preached from the broad pulpit of the stage. Gentlemen like Mr. Mitchell do not appreciate, perhaps, the power of the medium at their command, and, therefore, do not stop to think that they should be careful, very careful, how they use it, lest they should sow evil in minds not able to understand the good they intend. He uses his medium to voice his discontent and stir up anarchy, when, more thoughtful and better studied, he might be quite as humorous and help to a rational solution of evils we all condemn.

The play is admirably acted. Mrs. Fiske herself still persists in faults of delivery which, with her artistic intelligence, she should be ashamed of. Her position is too firmly fixed to make it necessary for her to resort to any tricks of manner, and she lets them give the lie to the expertness and cleverness she has at her command. At the same time Mr. Mitchell has given her such a thoroughly artificial character to delineate that artificiality is not entirely out of place. The same description fits the Vida of which Marion Lea makes a triumph of characterization. Mr. Arliss's Englishman in America is a finished creation, and Mr. Clinton's clergyman of the "Four Hundred" is very clever exaggeration. Mr. John Mason is, as always, a perfectly satisfactory gentleman of the world. The remainder of the cast deserves more than passing mention for its excellencies.

The New York Idea isn't half as serious as a commentary on its teachings might suggest. It is laughable throughout and very well staged and acted.

From *Life,*
November 29, 1906.

DAYS WHEN NEW YORK WAS YOUNGER

Edward Sheldon's *Romance*

By JAMES METCALFE

W E are really getting old enough to have a picturesque past. Writers of the younger generation are beginning to discover it. The old plaint of our newness as a country, which drove our earlier writers and dramatists to locate their scenes in foreign or imaginary places, no longer serves as an excuse. Mr. Sheldon, the author of *Romance,* has to go back only a half century to find settings and costumes for his play which are more remote to his generation than the castle and cathedrals of France and Italy and the vistas of far Cathay were to the public of yesterday. Washington Square as a fashionable center, the Brevoort House as an exclusive hostelry and the Academy of Music as the shrine of New York's wealthy opera worshipers are to-day veritable antiquities. Mr. Clyde Fitch shadowed this approach to the antiquity of things American in *Captain Jinks,* but he was a bit early to use it for anything but light comedy. Mr. Sheldon has the talent to seize to-day upon this background for a more serious purpose.

From this on, as we grow older every day, and new generations with only recent memories are crowding on, the American dramatist should find his own country rich in material and coloring. Certainly the stage writer of fifty years hence will not be lacking in inspiration for the grotesque when he comes to picture the period of silliness and exaggeration in which we are living.

In *Romance,* Mr. Sheldon gives another example of his versatility, and with the boldness of youth shoulders a handicap which might have daunted an older dramatist. His prologue, which clearly shows that the play which is to follow cannot have a happy ending in the accepted sense, gives away his hand to his audience. It is known in advance that the hero and heroine are not to have a happy issue to their love affair, but it is to the author's credit that this previous knowledge does not dull the edge of interest in his story, nor blunt the curiosity as to how it will develop. A better use of modern stage mechanics, so there should have been no halt between the story the old bishop starts to tell in the prologue and its change from words to visual representation in the beginning of the play proper, would have helped tremendously the illusion the author seeks to create. A similar instantaneous relapse from the conclusion of the play to the scene of the epilogue would have saved the latter from its air of crudeness.

But neither prologue nor epilogue are of great importance except as theatric novelty and a method of creating atmosphere. From the noisy and absurd New Year's eve of to-day we are at once carried back to the time when Trinity's chimes could really be heard, and to a social function where the *Blue Danube* waltzes were being played as Strauss's latest. Into this entertainment is introduced a celebrated opera prima donna whose past is questioned by the gathering of that day more seriously than now we look into the antecedents of the opera singer whom the author has evidently taken as a prototype, and who has been gladly received by certain circles of present New York society. A young clergyman among the guests falls in love with the prima donna, and the story hangs upon her finding through the love he inspires in her that there is a difference between good and evil, so that eventually she sends him back to his duty in the church and for herself renounces the primrose path. The clergyman became the bishop of the prologue and epilogue, and this was his romance.

Of course Mr. Sheldon has enriched this slender story with episodes and decorated it with clever talk, besides giving it the distinction, not always found in successful plays on our stage, of having been written by an educated man familiar with the ways of well-bred persons. His clergyman hero is somewhat unconventional for the period of the play, and not entirely suggestive of the Episcopal cloth he wears. To some extent this may be the fault of Mr. Courtenay, who impersonates the Rev. Thomas Armstrong, and who may not be shrewd at differentiating the methods of clergymen of different denominations.

The principal character is that of the impulsive, spoiled and passionate young Italian prima donna pictured by Doris Keane. She

plays the part in dialect throughout, and her perfection in pronunciation, accent and intonation is a notable accomplishment in itself. In
her early days Mme. Cavallini has been a street singer, and in the
later days, when she has furs, jewels and a pet monkey, she retains
with her acquired manners just enough of swagger to suggest her
beginnings, and perhaps some of the intervening episodes. In these
aspects of the character Doris Keane was more successful than in the
emotional passages which called for more magnetic appeal. There is
no question of her ability as a character comedienne. The remainder
of the cast is competent, Mr. Anson making an impression as a New
York gentleman of the old school, and Gilda Varesi as an Italian
ex-prima donna descended to the position of servant and companion
to the heroine.

   Romance is of more importance in matter and manner than most
of the plays we see.

From *Life,*
February 27, 1913.

THE CASE OF CLYDE FITCH

By WALTER PRICHARD EATON

TO take Clyde Fitch seriously always surprised many serious people.
To take the theatre seriously always surprises many serious people, for
that matter—the theatre, that is, not of the printed page, not of the
so-called "literary drama," but the actual playhouse, where farces and
musical comedies, vaudeville and moving pictures, trivialities of all
sorts, jostle with Shakespeare and Ibsen in the long effort to amuse.
Now, Clyde Fitch was a man of that actual playhouse; his plays,
though several of them have found their way into type, were designed for the footlights with no thought of type in mind. They were
almost as much "produced" as written, for Mr. Fitch was his own
alert stage manager and shaped his pieces in rehearsal. They were, most
of them, frankly wrought to amuse, to entertain an audience in the
playhouse, to bring the immediate returns of popularity and patronage.
They were neither conceived nor considered as literature in the con-

ventional sense. Mr. Fitch was perfectly willing to be a dramatic tailor, to cut a part to the measure of a star, to adapt from the French or German, to "dramatize" novels. Mostly, he may fairly be said to have been concerned not so much with weaving a fabric as cutting a garment; mostly he wrought, it seemed to his critics, not so much from a central idea, from an impulse of self-expression, as from a purely theatrical impulse to "shape up" an entertaining story. He belonged to Broadway, not the library or the class room. . . .

It is obvious that what is most effective in the theatre need not be most effective in type, and what is the literature of the proscenium frame need not be the literature of the printed page. That a great many fine dramas are literature, in the formal sense, when printed—Sophocles, Shakespeare, Molière, Sheridan, Ibsen—does not prove that a great many fine dramas are not. At best, it proves, perhaps, that the finest dramas transcend the theatre. And even they are never quite satisfactory till played, never quite the same things, at any rate. For ordinary purposes, what is or is not literature in drama should in fairness be determined by the play's effectiveness and truth in actual presentation on the stage. The concession which the critic must make is this—he must learn to visualize the printed play as he reads, and judge it as literature by its stage value. He must understand that it is but the skeleton he has before him. To do this is difficult, but not impossible, the more as most printed plays have been acted. The critic of music would not dream of judging a symphony by the printed score, unless he had the technical ability to read it into sound.

If we apply this test to the work of Clyde Fitch it is impossible to deny it a place, and an important place, in the stage literature of America. His plays were never concerned with large personages nor profound passions. His comments on the pageant of social life which he depicted were never deep. His preoccupation with the idea of successful "entertainment" was a blemish on much of his work. Nevertheless, that work at its best caught truthfully the surface of the life depicted and occasionally, with a kind of smiling irony, plunged down below the crust; it was made fascinating by a boundless observation and individual by the touches of its author's sprightly fancy. Never stirring profoundly the beholder, and not infrequently annoying him by its petty devices of villainy to bring a situation about, it was yet work which gave much pleasure at the moment, was freshly and vitally contemporaneous, and has counted steadily as influence in the American theatre. The stage literature of to-day in this country is more truthful, more carefully observed, closer to life and more consistently a comment upon it (for merely to observe truthfully is to comment) than it was before Mr. Fitch began to write. In this development his work played a large and important part. It could not have done so had it not been truthful work, had it not been dramatic literature. And one is tempted to add it could not have done so had it been written with the printed page in mind. It is the men of the theatre who do its real work.

That the better of Mr. Fitch's plays were a comment upon life, a truthful comment, and hence literature, although in the main they were designed for purposes of theatrical entertainment, was due to the fact that his instinctive respect for the theatre was greater than that of the mere theatrical artificer on the one hand—Sardou, for instance, or perhaps Henri Bernstein or W. Somerset Maugham—and greater, on the other hand, than that of the usual "literary dramatist," self-styled, whom Mr. Fitch probably held in considerable contempt. His respect for the theatre was so great that he saw men and women in the world about him, heard conversations in his daily rambles, observed incidents and characters, in the light of possible stage material. It was not in him to divorce this daily reality from the theatre. If it was good enough for life, it was not too good for the drama nor too mean. This, when you come to think of it, is a high respect. And his respect for the theatre, also, was such that his wish was to appeal to its habitual audiences, to catch their ear and win their favor. For the dramatic cults, the associated "high brows," as they are known on Broadway, he cared not at all. That, at bottom, the desire for pecuniary gain had anything to do with this, all who knew Mr. Fitch can stoutly deny. It was an instinct with him. It led him, no doubt, into excesses of caricature or "comic relief" which marred even his best plays, as *The Truth*. But, on the other hand, it kept his work immediately and practically effective and enabled him to exert his influence along the only lines that were for him potential. Because he respected the actual theatre too much to give it less than reality, so far as he could, and because he respected the actual theatre too much to withdraw contemptuously from its verdicts, he made the actual theatre a better place within his own too brief lifetime, he helped to increase critical respect for it, and to refine popular appreciation....

Admitting...his limitations, his half-failures and incomplete realizations, we must at the same time admit his positive merits and, striking the balance, judge him as one whose contributions to stage literature possessed considerable truth and value of themselves, and have been of even more significance as influence and example. In the long array of his plays, stretching over a period of almost twenty years, will be found a varied record of the foibles and fashions of the hour, the turns of speech which characterized the fleeting seasons, our little local ways of looking at little things, the popular songs we were singing, the topics which were uppermost in our social chat, our taste in decoration, our amusements, the deeper interests, even, of our leisured classes; and always a portrait gallery of vividly drawn minor characters of great historic interest. Supplement the texts and stage directions of Mr. Fitch's plays with a collection of flash-light photographs of the original productions, to picture the costumes and settings (a collection of such stage photographs would be of great value to any historical library), and they will afford twenty, fifty, a hundred years hence a more authentic and vivid record of our American life from 1890 to 1910, so far as it was lived in the gayer parts of town, than any other documents, whether the files of the newspapers or the fiction of the hour. The minute and faithful gift of observation which was his gave Mr. Fitch's plays at once their most immediate appeal and their most lasting value. Ruskin long ago pointed out that the only "historical painting" which will have value for our descendants is our record of our own times. The same is true of drama. Our descendants will not care what we thought of the French Revolution or even of the Civil War. But what we thought of our own immediate surroundings will be to them of historic interest and worth. They, at least, will be glad that the best of Mr. Fitch's plays have been preserved in print.

And because his appeal was so immediate, because his success, due to his keen and sprightly observation, was so great, his influence on other dramatists, consciously or not, was far-reaching and for good. He encouraged a more subtle and painstaking stage-management—a reform that in America still has a long way to go. He taught the value of a seemly setting for a play, of accuracy and solidity of scenery. He encouraged by his success the choice of American subjects and the stage illustration of American manners. When he began to write, the percentage of native American dramas in a single season was very small, and the characters in them were often native only in name. To-day the percentage of native dramas produced in a given year far exceeds the percentage of foreign plays, and most of them are now concerned with contemporary themes and people with characters recognizably American. It is impossible, of course, to estimate Mr. Fitch's share in this result, but that it was considerably more than that of any other single man, no one familiar with American theatrical conditions can doubt.

A man of the actual theatre, with the failings as well as the virtues of a man of the theatre, without the consciousness of a prophet's call nor the intellectual assurance of a self-appointed leader, Clyde Fitch led by his practical success as a maker of popular plays which were also truthful plays. That those plays obeyed the tendency of the times and led the theatre still farther from poetry and true romance there is no question. The pendulum had to swing. It is still swinging. The mission of the theatre to-day is to give reflective realism a full and fair trial. So far as he could, Mr. Fitch instinctively made his plays realistic, he commented upon the life about him by showing it on the stage as he saw it, often through the glass of a kindly irony. Because truth always makes its way when it is not dully presented, he was popularly successful above most other playwrights. They studied the secrets of his success and wrote better plays themselves. The public—which never studies—felt the secrets of his success and demanded better plays. A man who has done this for the theatre need not fear that the theatre will forget him. But to deserve so well of the theatre, to have contributed so much to stage literature, is not yet, in popular estimation, to have become a man of letters. One is only left to speculate whether, after all, some acknowledged men of letters deserve so well of fame for any contributions they have made to vital truth in art.

From *At the New Theatre and Others.*
(Small, Maynard 1910.)

MOODY'S *"THE GREAT DIVIDE"*

By JOHN CORBIN

MR. WILLIAM VAUGHN MOODY'S new American drama, *The Great Divide,* which Henry Miller and Margaret Anglin presented last night at the Princess, is so bold and vital in theme, so subtly veracious and unaffectedly strong in the writing, that it is very hard in the few moments left by a tardy if excellent performance to speak of it in terms at once of justice and of moderation.

Yet it is abundantly clear that no play of the present season—a season unusually rich—has equalled it either in calibre or in execution, except only Pinero's *His House in Order.* And even this strikes less true and deep into the wells of human impulse and passion.

To say that it is the best product of the American drama thus far would doubtless be extravagant; yet the fact remains that it is inspired by precisely that fulness and wholesomeness of feeling, and is accomplished with precisely that technical firmness, the lack of which has thus far proved the cardinal defects of our most vivacious and amusing playwrights.

The fact is that Mr. Moody, who has already placed himself at the head of modern American poets, has not ceased to be a poet in essaying the stage—though his play is written in the simplest and most unaffected prose. And he has, furthermore, applied the finesse and precision essential in the true poetic craft to the no less rigid and requiring task of the dramatist. With the lesser order of writers it has been the lamentable custom to deal lightly in and insincerely with the theatre. Mr. Moody respects his new medium, copes with it courageously and with manful adherence to the simple truth of life, and masters it.

His theme is unusual—sensational, if you will. But it is unusual and sensational in the manner not of melodrama, but of true and original drama. The great divide of his title is the barrier which exists between the rigor and dry formality of old civilization and the larger and freer, if more brutal, impulses of the frontier.

An Eastern woman (Miss Anglin), left unprotected for a night on an Arizona ranch, is set upon by three drunken marauders, and to escape a worse fate promises to give herself in marriage to the least repulsive of them on condition that he will save her from the others. This Stephen Ghent (Mr. Miller) buys off one of his rivals, shoots up the other in equal combat and leads his Sabine Woman—that was Mr. Moody's original title for the piece—to the nearest Magistrate.

The second act shows how the shame of the transaction eats into the soul of the proud and puritanical woman, until she leaves her enforced husband to bring up their child in what to her is respectability. The final act, which takes place in New England, represents the triumph of the husband, whose sincere native honesty and strength have developed in contact with a refinement new to him. The great divide has ceased to exist and the Sabine Woman becomes a willing captive to primitive, wholesome passion.

A story which seems destined to melodrama and the false heroics of sentiment is treated with simplicity that verges always on bareness. There will be those no doubt who deprecate the boldness of the theme; but they will be the first to condemn the play as slow and dull.

The method throughout, in so far as a work of such simplicity can be said to have a method, is that of understatement. One sits up and takes notice because it all happens so much more naturally and subtly than it was possible to imagine. No phase in the conflict and development of the two souls is neglected, and no word rises above the utmost austerity of realism. Mr. Moody has the courage to be true, because he has the vision to see the truth in its deepest and most vital aspects.

The acting throughout was pitched in precisely the key the play demands. Miss Anglin has never been more precise in the portrayal of the finer shades of character, and though she has had showier and more sensational parts she has never been more poignantly emotional.

At the outset she denotes with consummate fineness the kindling of the Puritan maiden toward the freer and more vital life of the West. And even in her first horror of the deed of the half drunken and altogether reckless Ghent, she manages to denote her fascination before his rough manhood. It is in the second intermediate act that she rises to the fullest achievement, for here she has to display the opposing impulses blindly yet potently struggling within her for mastery. It was in *Zira* that she displayed the height of her powers. Here she develops their depth and subtlety.

Mr. Miller has never been more simple and sympathetically convincing. He spares no trait of the recklessness of the initial deed of violence, yet manages to win regard for its passional simplicity. And in the end, when shame and sorrow have transmuted his impulses into gold, the man he has become is still the child of the man he was. Under his touch dramatic character and dramatic emotion are one.

To Laura Hope Crews falls the part of a young married woman, the friend of the Sabine woman. It is full of amusing character and sprightly humor. At times it verges toward the function of a classical chorus. Polly Jordan is under suspicion of being the mouthpiece of Mr. Moody's thesis and his psychology. Yet the part is very naturally written, and as acted by Miss Crews takes on a high degree of lifelikeness and a humor which is as natural as it is effective in contrast with the prevailing sombreness of the play.

Robert Cummings was equally effective in the smaller part of a sensible and amusingly laconic miner in Ghent's employ, and Mrs. Thomas Whiffen portrayed a New England mother of the old school with her accustomed fidelity and accuracy in character.

Play and performance were applauded heartily and only too persistently. Both Mr. Moody and Mr. Miller were reluctantly forced to each make a brief speech. Beyond question the production is a popular success.

From *The New York Sun,*
October 4, 1906.

MOSCOW AND BROADWAY

By *JOHN CORBIN*

T H E R E are two stages of provincialism, equally objectionable. In one stage anything new from the outside world is condemned as licentious, irreligious, contrary to public interest and certain to shock Aunt Jane. In the other stage, anything new from the outside world is welcomed if only it seems to undermine the foundations of Church and State, play tenpins with the Ten Commandments—and offers the fair hope that Aunt Jane will expire in conniptions. Note the climax. What really matters is Aunt Jane. As the Ptolemaic astronomy was geocentric, so provincialism in either phase revolves about local opinion, established propriety. Of all phenomena the most disregarded by the provincial is simple truth. In a city genuinely cosmopolitan, if such a city is conceivable, things would stand or fall by their own inherent virtue, and if they stood they would stand more or less in due relation to all other things, irrespective of Aunt Jane.

With regard to the Moscow Art Theatre, New York has assumed the attitude cosmopolitan; but in its manner of doing so has it not been somewhat too strenuous, self-conscious? What if the chorus of adulation expressed only the second phase of provincialism? What if its true and underlying purpose were to bring the blush of shame to the cheek of Broadway—that thoroughfare serving in our parable as the local shock absorber?

These questions suggested themselves at a performance of *The Cherry Orchard,* admittedly the masterpiece of Anton Tchekhoff and chief cornerstone in the fame of the Moscow Art Theatre. Note that I speak only of questions. One cannot judge magisterially of a play, and especially of high comedy, which is accessible only in a somewhat pedestrian translation. Especially is it impossible to render verdict on a performance representing intimate phases of a life utterly alien. The touchstone of Stanislavsky's art is realism, and how shall we judge of that when we have never known the purported reality? The finest flavor of the comedian's style is, so to speak, the precise accent of his demeanor, and how shall one judge of the fitness of action to word, understanding no syllable of all that is said?

Yet, having praised without stint Stanislavsky's productions of *Tsar Fyodor* and *The Lower Depths,* we may perhaps be permitted to admit certain misgivings. Is *The Cherry Orchard* of a higher order than, let us say, *Loyalties* or *Rain?* Is the acting really superior to that in either of these productions, or in numerous productions of recent memory, from *Passions for Men* back to *Liliom* and *John Ferguson?* In the glad task of critically placing these Muscovite artists, let us not neglect due consideration of our own ablest and best.

Whether or not *The Cherry Orchard* is a great play, it is the work of a literary artist of the first order; make no mistake about that. Even in translation it induces a definite and perfectly original mood, peoples a world with a group of characters each one of whom is a clear-cut personality, yet is an integral, indispensable part of the whole. Like Turgeneff, Tchekhoff loves and admires the peasant, depicting him as stable in character, shrewd and not impractical; and, like Turgeneff, he is satirical of the Russian gentry and intelligentsia, attributing to them the Slavic vices of vanity, loquacity and futility. If Tchekhoff falls short of the incisiveness of Turgeneff's satire, he has a full measure of his poetic sensibility—more than his humor and sympathy in characterization.

In this play he symbolizes the old order by means of an ancient manor-house lying in the midst of a cherry orchard, once productive but now valued only for its acreage of gay blossoms in Spring. Its owners, a middle-aged brother and sister, also retain only the charm of the vanished day, its witchery and enchantment. Idle and self-indulgent, they have heavily mortgaged the home of their fathers—yet not so heavily that it is beyond the reach of a modicum of thrift and common-sense management. Passionate in their love for the old home, the old cherry trees, their minds flinch from any practical decision. The servants are still faithful, with a dog-like devotion. Old Firce, once himself a serf, even laments his freedom, referring to the year of his emancipation as the Year of Calamity. The son of an emancipated serf who has prospered in business pursues them with good advice, yet cannot bring them to say yes or no. And so the estate is sold at auction to this same loyal friend, to be divided into suburban residence plots— the sound of the axe echoing from the orchard even as the exiled gentry depart with their few belongings to spend the spare proceeds of the sale in Paris. After they have gone, old Firce (whom every one believes to have been placed, by some one else, in a home for the aged) comes into the dark and deserted living room and there dies alone and neglected.

In one sense of the word, this is no play at all. There is no visualized dramatic conflict—only an inward and spiritual struggle, vague and confused as such struggles commonly are. Once only is there a "situation" and "climax." While awaiting news of the fate of the cherry orchard, the spendthrift sister gives a dance for the countryside. Into the midst of the revel comes the serf's son, Lopakhin, flown with wine but not with insolence, to announce that orchard and manor house are his. That is all. In a word, we have the work of a novelist. Tchekhoff himself knew this, writing for the stage reluctantly, under pressure from Stanislavsky. For the essentials of drama he had no instinct. At most he had a sense of "good theatre" in creating mood and depicting character. *The Cherry Orchard* is a novel written for the stage. This is said by way of description, not adverse criticism. What the art of prose fiction has lost, the theatre has gained. It is doubtless true that the depths of human passion, the heights of spiritual triumph, are revealed only in dramatic conflict. In the "static" drama there are no Medeas, no Hamlets. Yet in this novelist's play we have a witchery of atmosphere, a novelty and variety of characterization, an authenticity, a poetic mood, worth a wilderness of less inspired dramatic struggles and situations and climaxes.

That is the play as one reads it. Stanislavsky's production has certain imperfections obvious to the most casual glance, with which, for the most part, I for one shall not quarrel, agreeing gladly with these Muscovites that the realism of scenic paint brush and stage carpentry is a negligible thing compared with the realism of the spirit. Yet to keep the record clear it must be set down that the two interiors are far below the standard of Broadway, while the outdoor set "before a tumbledown shrine" would scarcely pass muster in the Bowery. Almost equally negligible is the fact that the song of birds in the orchard, which pipes up when a window is raised, presently ceases, though the window remains open. One is glad enough to cut the aviary cackle and get on with the dialogue. With the representation of the cherry trees fault may be more legitimately found. These spindling trunks of five to ten years' growth, with flowering twigs tacked on, should be gnarled and ancient boles beneath a bridal veil of blossoms. That is necessary to suggest both the antiquity and the beauty of the orchard, its power to move the hearts of its ancient possessors, to evoke the intermittent spring of their tears. Stanislavsky's orchard recalls a line in an English satire on American rural melodrama: "Don't sell the old 'omestead, Jabez; it's bean in the fambly fourteen years." But these things, as Lord Bacon wrote of scenic masques and triumphs at the court of Elizabeth, "are but toys to come amongst such serious observations.... Away with such toys."

It is the acting of Stanislavsky's company in this play that gives us what is sometimes called pause. As regards the more purely Russian

and local characters, criticism is scarcely possible, these folk and their
milieu being so utterly alien and uncouth to us. In point of fact, the
governess Charlotte of Maria Ouspenskaya, the student Trofinoff of
Nikolai Podgorny, the self-made merchant Lopakhin of Leonid Leoni-
doff, the voluble and blundering Yopikhodoff of Ivan Moskvin, and
especially the old Firce of Vassily Luzhsky, seemed admirable—less
marvelous than performances in *The Lower Depths* only because the
characters were less stark in their outlines, and the situation in which
they moved less simple emotionally. But even at their highest valua-
tion, have we no actors capable of equally good work? A more serious
doubt arose with regard to the two leading characters, played by Olga
Knipper-Tchekhova and Stanislavsky himself. These are mundane
people—essentially Slavs, no doubt, yet creatures of a world that has
similar standards in all civilized countries.

It was Tchekhoff's intention that Stanislavsky should play the
middle-class merchant, Lopakhin, the serf's son who buys in the
orchard. It is a part for which the robust and stalwart director seems
eminently fitted. In a letter from Yalta on Oct. 30, 1903, Tchekhoff
said: "When I was writing Lopahin [sic] I thought of it as a part
for you. . . . Lopahin is a merchant, of course, but he is a very decent
person in every sense. He must behave with perfect decorum, like an
educated man, with no petty ways or tricks of any sort, and it seemed
to me that this part, the central one of the play, would come out brilliantly in your hands. . . . You must remember that Varya, a serious
and religious girl, is in love with Lopahin; she wouldn't be in love
with a mere money-grubber." In describing the merchant as the central
part of the play one senses the blandishment of an author who has
doubts as to the discretion of his director. In point of fact the central
parts of the play are the amiable, hare-brained Gaieff—or Gaiev, as
Tchekhoff spells it—and his flightily emotional sister. As if to be
prepared for fate, Tchekhoff wrote also: "If for any reason you don't
care for [Lopahin] take the part of Gaiev." Constance Garnett, who
translated the letters, says in a footnote, "Stanislavsky acted Lopahin";
but Oliver M. Sayler is more probably right in saying that he created
Gaieff.

Now, the impression one gets of Gaieff when reading the translation is fundamentally different from the visual impression of Stanislavsky's performance. There one perceives a flighty, mercurial simpleton who delivers pseudo-philosophic, pseudo-poetic mouthings at an old cupboard, to the humorous disgust of his relatives; who punctuates conversation that is serious with playing imaginary pocket billiard shots: "Red to the centre; blue carroms to the corner!" Fundamentally the character is admirably real; but superficially it is of the theatre, earmarked in that artificial manner practiced in the early plays of Arthur Wing Pinero. What Stanislavsky accomplished in the phrasing of his lines, in those subtler strokes of psychology that are lost upon ignorant ears, I have no means of knowing; but it is fairly obvious that the herculean presence of the director and his vigorous, vibrant voice, so eloquent of an orderly mind and an unshakable will, are ill-adapted to suggest the will-o'-the-wisp brain and uncontrolled moods of this attenuated aristocrat.

Mutatis mutandis, precisely the same is true of the Ranevskaya of Olga Knipper-Tchekhova. In the text one reads of a woman of the lighter Parisian world, the prey to febrile, disjointed emotions. At one moment she is bewailing the death of an only child long years ago, at another she is irresistibly drawn to a faithless lover in Paris who, as she knows too well, cares only for the money he can force from her. Now she is all tears at the thought of losing the cherry orchard and in the next moment gives a gold piece to a drunken tramp. How much of this the speech of the actress may suggest deponent sayeth not, but little or nothing of it was suggested by her Junoesque form and demeanor.

If these be flaws, was there anything like them in the casting of *John Ferguson,* of *Liliom,* of *Passions for Men?* Supposing that the scenic investiture and the casting of *The Cherry Orchard* were more nearly perfect, would the play have more of the atmosphere, more of human living revealed, than one finds in *Rain?* I am raising a question, not answering it. But it is a question one must ponder deeply before using this production of light, atmospheric character comedy as a reproach to our native theatre.

More surely than anything else, a reiteration of false praise and provincial obsequiousness will eventually discredit the splendid example of a living ensemble, of imaginative realism, which the Moscow company has given us in *Tsar Fyodor* and *The Lower Depths*.

From *The New York Times,*
January 28, 1923.

EUGENE WALTER'S *"THE EASIEST WAY"*

By *ALAN DALE*

A W E A K little drab of a vacuous, aimless woman, too puerile to be moral, and almost too cowardly to be brazenly immoral, pitted against two lovers—one a type of the bestial Broadway booze-feeder, representing immorality, the other the figure of a vigorous Lothario, suggesting non-morality—made out a sensational case at the Stuyvesant Theatre last night, in a play called *The Easiest Way*. It purported to sketch the familiar picture of the theatre-woman, struggling for her virtue amid the alleged temptations of Broadway—temptations that are popularly supposed to begin at the lobster-palace and end at the devil, but which last night began at the devil and ended at the lobster-palace. It did sketch this picture, with daubs of color, splashes of verity and a dazzling varnish of candor at which a sophisticated audience laughed last night, at which a less sophisticated audience might feel impelled to grieve. But this is a big community, and there are all sorts of people in it. The duty of the critic need not be to preach. Let him tell, and be satisfied at that.

In the dialogue last night the sophisms of a courtesan, bold and untrammelled, were received as though they were outbursts of pure comedy, priceless gems of uncorroded wit, while the interjectional profanity of one of the men was rippled out as though it were the prettiest persiflage of an intelligent commentator. But there are all sorts of people, and all sorts of plays for them. At the outset it may be said that *The Easiest Way* is not a play for the Young Person. Let us make that emphatic, and, having made it so, may we consider that our duty is done.

Laura Murdock, who is the mistress of the Broadway lounger—his type will be familiar to every first-nighter—falls in love with a $30 per week reporter and gives up everything for his sake. He is to go away and make a fortune for her. She is to continue her work in the theatre. If she is not an actress, she is, at least, as Mr. Clyde Fitch would say, on the stage.

If the psychology of such people be a study—and possibly it is— I may here say that a very false note plays havoc with Mr. Eugene Walter's remarkable trio. For the young reporter knows Laura's life; he is quite aware that she is the mistress of Brockton. Just the same he offers to marry her. He goes further. He is introduced by her to Brockton; he talks with Brockton; he tells his plans to Brockton. He has a long scene with Brockton. He is not repelled by him. He even enters into a compact with him, and swears that when Laura leaves him he will let Brockton know, in return for information of a similar brand from the other.

Even the courtesan, and the Broadway loafer, and the lobster-palace hanger-on are shown to have some spark of decency about their constitution. But this reporter loses all sympathy as he finishes his cigar with Brockton. What reporter, even one calloused by the nausea of the Thaw and the Hains cases, would consent to plead to a Broadway loafer for the hand of his mistress in lawful marriage?

This was the real weak spot in a strong case. It was strong in every sense of the word. The girl tries poverty in a garret. She does not like it. She cannot get an engagement. She lacks the powerful influence that women of her kind demand. She is down to her last cent. Then the courtesan arrives, and pours the tricks of the trade into her ears. Such perfect, candid revelation has rarely been heard on the stage. It is the very familiar plea of the courtesan in her contempt for the men who despise her, but pay for her gowns. And Laura, down to her last cent, weak, vacillating, broken—listens. She goes back to Brockton.

A slight effort is made to enlist sympathy for Laura. It does not succeed, or, if it does, it is due to the admirably simple and unaffected work of Miss Frances Starr. When next we see Laura she has all the "luxury" that she feels necessary—the "luxury" that pessimists are fond of supposing that women must have, and the hankering for which is presumed to show their inferiority to men.

Laura is completely un-moral. She lies to her lover, to whom she swore she had advised the young reporter of her change of plans. And later she lies to the reporter. He returns rich, and anxious to marry her. Then there is a good deal of a "cut up" between the three. They are three fine instances of the human animal. The spectacle is sensational, though scarcely educational.

At the end she is left by the reporter to her unshakable affinity, and—to Rector's. One wonders why two men were so unduly interested in such a woman. One wonders all the time why the genial Broadway bloke was so cussedly addicted to such a whining, flabby little imbecile. But such things are. Such things have been shown to be. Such things are continually being shown to be. Men commit murder—only for fast women, never for the good ones, or the intelligent ones, or the bright ones. One wonders just the same. It is one's privilege to wonder. Laura Murdock is a despicable type, but a real one. So is the Broadway beast. The only absurdity is the reportorial lover, who is ridiculously drawn.

But *The Easiest Way* was watched with engrossed attention. It was not unlike cases that we have had dished up for us time and again in the "courts." Exactly why we should revel in them on the stage may not be explained here. The play was so well done and so forcefully presented that it gripped. It was ugly, unpleasant, distressing—anything you like—also more—but it gripped. It will be discussed in various ways. Some will grow indignant, which is, of course, ludicrous, but not interesting. Others will laugh, which is more difficult. A few will talk only of its dramatic trend, which is the safest talk of all. It is un-moral; it is Broadway; it is a vivid section of vicious life—but nobody need go to see it unless they like. This is a free country. People are not driven to the play. If the Young Person buys tickets for *The Easiest Way,* it is a pity—just that. The Old Person can take care of himself. *The Easiest Way* will not hurt his hard head.

Belasco has staged this piece in a way that is simply a wonder. The detail, the touches, the atmosphere are absolutely perfect. It is a triumph of stage management. I have seen garrets, and boarding-house rooms, and the squalid resorts of the shabby genteel a thousand times, but never did I see anything so unmistakable as Laura Murdock's "furnished room" in Act II. Its wall paper, its ceiling, its sordid appurtenances, its "decorations," its owner, were indescribably real. This room alone beats any stage setting I have ever looked at (and I have looked at one or two). The room in the "expensive hotel" was a gorgeous picture.

Miss Frances has arrived. She got there last night. Her work was so fine, so simply.rendered, so perfectly executed that she need be told it emphatically. This puts her job in *The Rose of the Rancho* on the blink. At one time she gave an exhibition of pathos that was irresistible—when nothing in the dialogue or the situation led one to expect it. There were only six people in the cast. Edward H. Robins, as the reporter, was the least good. The others—Joseph Kilgour, William Sampson, Laura Nelson Hall (who covered herself with glory) and Emma Dunn—were all superfine.

The Easiest Way is certainly a "slice of life."

From *The New York American,*
January 20, 1909.

A MINOR POET OF BROADWAY

George M. Cohan

By ARTHUR RUHL

I F New York had a Montmartre and Mr. George Cohan were a Frenchman, one can almost imagine him wearing baggy clothes and a Windsor tie, and stalking up and down between the tables of his *café chantant* of an evening, singing his songs of Broadway. People would take him seriously, admire his lyrics because they were so "instinct" with the spirit of a certain curious fringe of society, and words and music would doubtless be published in limited de-luxe editions for circulation among the literati.

Mr. Cohan is a talented young man. He can dance in a way to charm wild beasts from their dens and make them sit up and wonder; he expresses the feelings of a certain metropolitan type as does no one else, and he not only sings and acts his pieces, but also writes their words and music. People who would naturally derive no pleasure from that conglomeration of noise and cheapness of which his musical plays superficially consist are often baffled to explain the odd fascination of Mr. Cohan's personal work. It seems to consist very much in the sin-

cerity and artistic conviction with which he does the precise thing
that you yourself probably would try not to do. He neither attempts to
impersonate the gentleman in the narrower sense of the word, nor,
on the other hand, to hide his own personality behind some such broad
character part as the traditional Bowery tough boy. Instead he assumes
the cheap sophistication of the blasé racing tout or book-maker, sings
through his nose practically on one note, wears clothes that just miss
being the real thing—in short, pitches everything in the key of slangy
cynicism and cheapness characteristic of that curious half-world which
foregathers at Forty-second Street and the shady side of Broadway.
So clever a person could doubtless assume a superficial refinement for
stage purpose if he wanted to. Mr. Cohan apparently doesn't; apparently he has carefully worked out a "method" aimed at sublimated
cheapness, and got away with it.

In *Forty-Five Minutes from Broadway,* a curiously uneven conglomeration of "musical comedy," puns, and melodrama, ostensibly
designed as a vehicle for the familiar humor of Miss Fay Templeton,
Mr. Cohan has created in Kid Burns a character rather broader than
he himself impersonates, but typical of his point of view. The Kid is
"secretary" to a young millionaire who has just taken a house at New
Rochelle, and through him the spectator views that suburb—not as it
is, probably, but as it might appear in the day-dream of some good-
humored book-maker or wire-tapper lounging of a summer afternoon
in the shade of the Metropole. As the Kid sings:

> *Only forty-five minutes from Broadway. Think of the*
> *changes it brings,*
> *For the short time it takes, what a difference it makes*
> *in the ways of the people and things.*

His droll amazement at the ease with which he can "get a laugh"
with the stalest line—"all the old stuff goes here"—his genuine desperation at the inability of the suburbanites to understand his nimble slang
—"You've gotta talk baby-talk to these guys—all they can understand
is pantomime"—these and similar observations are given such sincerity
and earnestness, such an almost pathetic appeal, by the quiet-voiced,
lazily good-humored, plaintive Kid that for the moment the home-

sickness of this parasite of the town, as he thinks of himself, "standin'
at the corner of Forty-second Street, smokin' a fi'-cent Cremo cigar, an'
waitin' for the next race to come in," seems important. His principal
song, with the lullaby-like refrain coming at the end of each verse—
"only forty-five minutes from Broadway"—and Mr. Victor Moore's
singing of it, are perfect of their kind. The emotion which makes the
lights of Broadway the sun of one's existence, and its fatuous and
premeditated gayety the music of one's soul, is not a heroic one, but
to a certain corner of the world it is exceedingly real. And in Kid
Burns Mr. Moore and Mr. Cohan unite in very entertainingly expressing it....

January, 1906.

Mr. Cohan keeps developing. He not only sings of Broadway,
but he is getting to be a sort of song-bird and prophet of that frank
materialism characteristic of a certain side of New York, and, indeed,
of America. It is for this reason that his *Get-Rich-Quick Wallingford,*
which he has arranged from stories written by Mr. George Randolph
Chester for one of the magazines, is a much more genuine expression
of his audience's notions of fun than anything a Falstaff might do, and
for them, at least, a more satisfying form of art....

There is a certain special pleasure to be derived from any spontaneous art. Shakespeare's audiences liked to eat and drink, so they were
amused at a sort of Gargantuan eater and drinker. Mr. Cohan's audiences like to make money, and it is natural that they should be
amused by a man who makes it with absurd easiness and a light heart.

December, 1908.

In *Broadway Jones,* Mr. Cohan discards songs, chorus girls, and
his own dances, and offers himself as a regular actor. One can easily
imagine a stranger to America, inspecting us for the first time, finding
this the freshest and most characteristic exhibit of our theatres. Polite
comedy, such as Mr. Drew presents, timely melodrama, like *Within the
Law,* musical plays—all these things are but imitations or duplications
of things done just as well or better abroad. *Broadway Jones,* though
but a flower of the Broadway asphalt, is wholly of the soil....

Without Mr. Cohan's childlike cocksureness, without his clothes

and his walk and his hat tipped over one eye and his way of talking
through his nose, this unregenerate child of Broadway would lose half
his charm. Mr. Cohan's more or less consciously elaborated surface
"cheapness" actually makes his characters more likable by taking them
into the region of caricature where ordinary judgments are disarmed.
The black patent-leather shoes with tan tops and the nasal monotone
have a relation to reality similar to that of the action of the play—
express a similar taste and trust. The surface is farcical, but through the
heightened light we see more clearly the genuine feeling beneath—
the poetry, so to speak, of this quaint cheapness and vulgarity. Again,
Mr. Cohan becomes its voice. The theatre, the play, and the principal
part are his, and he does not rely, as far as I can recall, on a word of
spoken slang. We may be writing about Mr. Cohan's "third period"
or "later manner" before he gets through.

February, 1910.

From *Second Nights.*
(Scribner's, 1914.)

Folks have complained of late, and I think with justice, that the
Guild was a bit too inclined to express the acrid criticisms and complaints of a not very representative or significant minority. And Mr.
O'Neill's plays have not infrequently been marred by a humorless
overaccent, which, in the case of a dramatist less gifted and forceful,
would have been described as sophomoric. But in *Ah, Wilderness!* we
have the Guild, being as "American" as the most orthodox could ask,
without in the least sacrificing its quality, while Mr. O'Neill, also
without being any the less himself, writes as humorously and understandingly of a perfectly normal American father, mother, son and the
latter's adolescent flounderings with the world and his first love as if
he were a contemporary of George Ade and John McCutcheon and
had been brought up in Indiana!

On top of all this we have Mr. Cohan, once a Minor Poet of
Broadway, in the limited and parochial sense of the latter word, with
a brown derby cocked over one eye, a nasal accent, and blindness and
contempt for everything forty-five minutes away from Times Square,
now, not suddenly, to be sure, but more urbanely and authoritatively
than ever before, taking the part of what might be described as not

merely the American, in the fullest sense of the word, but almost the "universal" father.

From *The New York Herald-Tribune,*
October 15, 1933.

THEMES IN THE THEATRE

By CLAYTON HAMILTON

AS THE final curtain falls upon the majority of the plays that somehow get themselves presented in the theatres of New York, the critical observer feels tempted to ask the playwright that simple question of young Peterkin in Robert Southey's ballad, *After Blenheim,*— "Now tell us what 't was all about"; and he suffers an uncomfortable feeling that the playwright will be obliged to answer in the words of old Kaspar, "Why, that I cannot tell." The critic has viewed a semblance of a dramatic struggle between puppets on the stage; but what they fought each other for he cannot well make out. And it is evident, in the majority of cases, that the playwright could not tell him if he would, for the reason that the playwright does not know. Not even the author can know what a play is all about when the play isn't about anything. And this, it must be admitted, is precisely what is wrong with the majority of the plays that are shown in our theatres, especially with plays written by American authors. They are not about anything; or, to say the matter more technically, they haven't any theme.

By a theme is meant some eternal principle, or truth, of human life—such a truth as might be stated by a man of philosophic mind in an abstract and general proposition—which the dramatist contrives to convey to his auditors concretely by embodying it in the particular details of his play. These details must be so selected as to represent at every point some phase of the central and informing truth, and no incidents or characters must be shown which are not directly or indirectly representative of the one thing which, in that particular piece, the author has to say. The great plays of the world have all grown endogenously from a single, central idea; or, to vary the figure, they have been spun like spider-webs, filament after filament, out of a central living source. But most of our native playwrights seem seldom to experience this necessary process of the imagination which creates. Instead of working from the inside out, they work from the outside in. They gather up a haphazard handful of theatric situations and try to string them together into a story; they congregate an ill-assorted company of characters and try to achieve a play by letting them talk to each other. Many of our playwrights are endowed with a sense of situation; several of them have a gift for characterisation, or at least for caricature; and most of them can write easy and natural dialogue, especially in slang. But very few of them start out with something to say, as Mr. Moody started out in *The Great Divide* and Mr. Thomas in *The Witching Hour.*

When a play is really about something, it is always possible for the critic to state the theme of it in a single sentence. Thus, the theme of *The Witching Hour* is that every thought is in itself an act, and that therefore thinking has the virtue, and to some extent the power, of action. Every character in the piece was invented to embody some phase of this central proposition, and every incident was devised to represent this abstract truth concretely. Similarly, it would be easy to state in a single sentence the theme of *Le Tartuffe,* or of *Othello,* or of *Ghosts.* But who, after seeing four out of five of the American plays that are produced upon Broadway, could possibly tell in a single sentence what they were about? What, for instance—to mention only plays which did not fail—was *Via Wireless* about, or *The Fighting Hope,* or even *The Man from Home?* Each of these was in some ways an interesting entertainment; but each was valueless as drama, because none of them conveyed to its auditors a theme which they might remember and weave into the texture of their lives. . . .

Most of our American playwrights, like Juliet in the balcony scene, speak, yet they say nothing. They represent facts, but fail to reveal truths. What they lack is purpose. They collect, instead of meditating; they invent, instead of wondering; they are clever, instead of being real. They are avid of details: they regard the part as greater than the whole. They deal with outsides and surfaces, not with centralities and profundities. They value acts more than they value the meanings of acts; they forget that it is in the motive rather than in the deed that Life is to be looked for. For Life is a matter of thinking and of feeling; all art is merely Living, and is significant only in so far as it reveals the Life that prompted it. Give us less of Living, more of Life, must ever be the cry of earnest criticism. Enough of these multitudinous, multifarious facts: tell us single, simple truths. Give us more themes, and fewer fabrics of shreds and patches.

From The Theory of the Theatre,
(Henry Holt & Co., Inc., 1910.)

A NOTE ON TRAGEDY

By LUDWIG LEWISOHN

IT has been said many times, and always with an air of authority, that there is no tragedy in the modern drama. And since tragedy, in the minds of most educated people, is hazily but quite firmly connected with the mishaps of noble and mythical personages, the statement has been widely accepted as true. Thus very tawdry Shakespearean revivals are received with a traditional reverence for the sternest and noblest of all the art-forms that is consciously withheld from *Ghosts* or *Justice* or *The Weavers*. Placid people in college towns consider these plays painful. They hasten to pay their respects to awkward chantings of Gilbert Murray's Swinburnian verses and approve the pleasant mildness of the pity and terror native to the Attic stage. The very innocuousness of these entertainments as well as the pain that Ibsen and Hauptmann inflict should give them pause. Pity and terror are strong words and stand for strong things. But our public replies in the comfortable words of its most respectable critics that tragedy has ceased to be written.

These critics reveal a noteworthy state of mind. They are aware that tragedy cuts to the quick of life and springs from the innermost depth of human thinking because it must always seek to deal in some intelligible way with the problem of evil. But since it is most comfortable to believe that problem to have been solved, they avert their faces from a reopening of the eternal question and declare that the answer of the Greeks and the Elizabethans is final. They are also aware, though more dimly, that all tragedy involves moral judgments. And since they are unaccustomed to make such judgments, except by the light of standards quite rigid and quite antecedent to experience, they are bewildered by a type of tragic drama that transfers its crises from the deeds of men to the very criteria of moral judgment, from guilt under a law to the arraignment of the law itself.

Macbeth represents in art and life their favorite tragic situation. They can understand a gross and open crime meeting a violent punishment. When, as in *King Lear,* the case is not so plain, they dwell long and emphatically on the old man's weaknesses in order to find satisfaction in his doom. In the presence of every tragic protagonist of the modern drama they are tempted to play the part of Job's comforters. They are eager to impute to him an absoluteness of guilt which shall, by implication, justify their own moral world and the doctrine of moral violence by which they live. The identical instinct which in war causes men to blacken the enemy's character in order to justify their tribal rage and hate, persuades the conventional critic to deny the character of tragedy to every action in which disaster does not follow upon crime. Yet, rightly looked upon, man in every tragic situation is a Job, incapable and unconscious of any degree of voluntary guilt that can justify a suffering as sharp and constant as his own.

Thus modern tragedy does not deal with wrong and just vengeance, which are both, if conceived absolutely, pure fictions of our deep-rooted desire for superiority and violence. It is inspired by compassion. But compassion without complacency is still, alas, a very rare emotion. And it seeks to derive the tragic element in human life from the mistakes and self-imposed compulsions, not from the sins, of men. The central idea of *Ghosts,* for instance, is not concerned with the sin of the father that is visited upon the son. It is concerned, as Ibsen sought to make abundantly clear, with Mrs. Alving's fatal conformity to a social tradition that did not represent the pureness of her will. Her tragic mistake arises from her failure to break the law. The ultimate and absolute guilt is in the blind, collective lust of mankind for the formulation and indiscriminate enforcement of external laws.

To such a conception of the moral world, tragedy has but recently attained. That both the critical and the public intelligence should lag far behind is inevitable. Every morning's paper proclaims a world whose moral pattern is formed of terrible blacks and glaring whites. How should people gladly endure the endless and pain-touched gray of modern tragedy? They understand the Greek conception of men who violated the inscrutable will of gods; they understand the renaissance conception that a breach of the universal moral law sanctioned and set forth by God, needed to be punished. They can even endure such situations as that of Claudio and Isabella in the terrible third act of *Measure for Measure.* For that unhappy brother and sister never question the right of the arbitrary power that caused so cruel a dilemma, nor doubt the absolute validity of the virtue that is named. These two strike at each other's hearts and never at the bars of the monstrous cage that holds them prisoner. Do they not, therefore, rise almost to the dignity of symbols of that moral world in which the majority of men still live?

But it is precisely with the bars of the cage that modern tragedy is so largely and necessarily concerned. It cannot deal with guilt in the older sense. For guilt involves an absolute moral judgment. That, in its turn, involves an absolute standard. And a literally absolute standard is unthinkable without a super-human sanction. Even such a sanction, however, would leave the flexible and enlightened spirit in the lurch. For if it were not constantly self-interpretative by some method of progressive and objectively embodied revelation, its interpretation would again become a mere matter of human opinion, and the absoluteness of moral guilt would again be gravely jeopardized. Not only must God have spoken; He would need to speak anew each day. The war has overwhelmingly illustrated how infinitely alien such obvious reflections still are to the temper of humanity. We must have guilt. Else how, without utter shame, could we endure punitive prisons and gibbets and battles? Is it surprising that audiences are cold to Ibsen and Hauptmann and Galsworthy, and that good critics who are also righteous and angry men deny their plays the character of tragedy?

But the bars of the absolutist cage are not so bright and firm as they were once. The conception of unrelieved guilt and overwhelming vengeance has just played on the stage of history a part so monstrous that its very name will ring to future ages with immitigable contrition and grief. And thus in the serener realm of art the modern idea of tragedy is very sure to make its gradual appeal to the hearts of men. Guilt and punishment will be definitely banished to melodrama, where they belong. Tragedy will seek increasingly to understand our failures and our sorrows. It will excite pity for our common fate; the terror it inspires will be a terror lest we wrong our brother or violate his will, not lest we share his guilt and incur his punishment. It will seek its final note of reconciliation not by delivering another victim to an outraged God or an angry tribe, but through a profound sense of that community of human suffering which all force deepens and all freedom assuages.

From *The Nation,* May 31, 1919
Reprinted in *The Drama and the Stage.*
(Harcourt, Brace, 1922.)

CREATIVE IRONY

Mr. Rice's *The Adding Machine*

By LUDWIG LEWISOHN

EXPRESSIONISM has two chief aims: to fling the inner life of the dramatic figures immediately upon the stage; to synthesize, instead of describing, their world and their universe into symbolic visions that shall sum up whole histories, moralities, cosmogonies in a brief minute and a fleeting scene. If this form of art is to be effective and beautiful, it must be very sensitive and very severe at once. Beneath it must be fundamental brainwork, thinking as resilient as steel and as clean cut as agate. The symbolic masses must glow with a clear irradiation from within. Otherwise all is murky and muddled. You can describe fragmentarily and produce fragments of truth. Realism does not commit you to any whole. In expressionism the antecedent intellectual grasp of your entire material must be firm, definite, complete. Everything must be thought out and thought through. This is what, despite moments of the highest brilliancy and glow, Mr. Eugene O'Neill did not do in *The Hairy Ape.* This is what, in a harder, drier, less poetical vein, Mr. Elmer Rice has actually succeeded in doing in *The Adding Machine.*

Mr. Rice's vision of the world may infuriate you. There were people behind me at the Garrick who first grumbled and then cursed politely. You cannot miss it; you cannot withdraw yourself from its coherence and completeness. Examine his play scene by scene, symbol by symbol. The structure stands. There are no holes in its roof. It gives you the pleasure of both poetry and science, the warm beauty of life and love, the icy delight of mathematics. I am aware of the fact—critics should make this confession oftener—that my profound sympathy with Mr. Rice's substance necessarily colored my reaction to his play. Not, however, to its form, not to the heartening fact that here is an American drama with no lose ends or ragged edges or silly last-act compromises, retractions, reconciliations. The work, on its own ground, in its own mood, is honest, finished, sound.

What Mr. Rice has to tell us is not new. But creative literature, I hasten to add, need not have novelty. What Edgar Lee Masters, Sinclair Lewis, Sherwood Anderson, Zona Gale, what the whole new American literature of moral protest has told us, is also told here. This particular world of ours deliberately hides or chokes with dust and ashes the very sources of human life. It has made fetishes of ugliness and monotony and intolerance. It has given to these fetishes high-sounding names. It is wedded to denial and has made a pact with death. From the intolerable repressions of Mr. Zero's life flames one explosion of the nerves. But it is an explosion of the sickened nerves only. Slavery is in his soul. He is, in reality, doomed to add figures, doomed to chant in unison the pack-formulæ so terribly and hauntingly projected in the third scene. He cannot stay in the Elysian Fields with Swift and Rabelais and the great company of the confessors of life and light. He cannot hear the music which is the music of life. The place is not respectable. It is no place for him. He "beats it"—beats it back to an eternal adding machine, back finally to an earth where slavery is his eternal portion and hope an ironic delusion. Mr. Rice is terribly bitter, terribly relentless. There is the other murderer in the Elysian Fields who turned upon the torment of his life, who was so steeped in hell that he thought it heaven, who now thirsts for flames to burn away the guilt of his one moment of blind protest and dumb liberation. Only to the shabby office girl a better knowledge is given. In the woman soul alone Mr. Rice sees a ray of beauty. She wanted

Zero to fulfil her womanhood even on earth; she hears the music of life at once. Hers are courage and insight and love.

It is not just to speak of the Theatre Guild's production of this play in the ordinary sense of that word. How much or how little Mr. Rice had in his stage directions concerning the scenic embodiment of his vision I do not know. It is clear, however, that there has been here an imaginative collaboration between dramatist and producer which is not necessary in the case of a realistic play. It is necessary here. And the results are extraordinarily telling and beautiful. There is, for instance, the place of justice to which poor Zero is brought. The tall windows are crooked; the railing is crooked. But the lines are not crinkled. To the perverse vision they may seem straight. They lean diagonally. The judge is petrified. He is literally of stone. The mob cries "guilty"; a dead heart deals out mercilessness and calls it justice. Not all the scenes are as finely conceived as this. But all have been designed by an imagination packed with close thinking, profoundly akin to the imagination that shaped the play itself. The acting is in the same mood of absorption in the author's intention. Here, too, is creative collaboration. Mr. Dudley Digges gives the finest performance since his Henry Clegg. And here he is more varied, more expressive. He makes shabbiness of body and soul true to every dusty detail and also a thing of cosmic dread. Miss Helen Westley has her accustomed edge and veracity, Miss Margaret Wycherly her pathos and yearning, Mr. Louis Calvert his depth and richness of reality. Mr. Edgar G. Robinson and Miss Elise Bartlett contribute to the strange eloquence of this play and production which constitute, without question, one of the major achievements in the entire field of the American arts.

From *The Nation,*
April 4, 1923.

JOHN BARRYMORE AS RICHARD III

By FRANCIS HACKETT

SHAKESPEARE is still the dramaturgic Octopus. A good actor may escape him for a long time, but for ever?—never. The old convention is too strong in the Anglo-American theatre, and all the

Ibsens and Sheldons in the world haven't changed it. If you want to be hall-marked as a great actor, don't content yourself with great acting. Arrange for Shakespeare. It is the theatrical equivalent of a snowy Christmas, a big church wedding or a ticket to the Firemen's Ball.

It had to be Shakespeare—and John Barrymore could no longer escape it—there are good reasons why he should have made it *Richard III*. It would have been better if it had come in some other season than the one that saw *Ruddigore* staged in New York. *Richard III* and *Ruddigore* are too similarly homicidal not to compel comparison. But even with that cruel daylight pouring on *Richard,* it was manifestly the play for Mr. Barrymore. He might have begun with *Hamlet*—not a long theatrical step from his work in *Redemption* and *Peter Ibbetson* and *Justice*—but Richard suited much better his genuine passion for effect. He had to accept deformity, it is true, but he has long been educating his public to the possibilities of the sinister, the beauties of the *fleur du mal,* and Richard's deformity gave him a weapon right to his hand. He had, besides, in Robert Edmond Jones and Arthur Hopkins just the producers of Shakespeare that this country has previously grafted from England. *Richard III* offered a fresher and wider field to the talents of all three.

The outcome is, in the literal sense, superb. It does not seem very much, perhaps, that John Barrymore had to correct and sublimate an ugly slovenliness in diction and a lazy colloquialness in manner—the natural marks of a spoiled theatrical Prince Hal. These he has certainly eliminated, and with magnificence. The nose, an excellent olfactory but a poor elocutionary contrivance, has at last been subordinated by Mr. Barrymore to its humbler uses. His voice is now beautifully placed, deep and sonorous and free. And his body, once a rather shiftless tenement, is now a mansion, or rather a house in which there are many mansions. He is so master of his craft today that he can give Richard III two lame legs, both the right and the left legs short at will, and he shifts from one to the other so subtly that only a shrew could detect him. His face is endlessly and marvelously expressive. He is sweet to the point of effeminacy; crafty to the edge of the diabolic; uneasy and turbid as a leaden sea; open and soulful as an innocent; mean as a worm; pious as an undertaker; cruel as the fang of a snake. And all with such eager facility that the human strain of such a performance hardly comes to mind.

This is superb, and carried off in a superb setting. The sixteen scenes are taken from *Henry VI* and *Richard III* conjoined and then carpentered. But each scene is a visual surprise, a scenic bomb-shell. In the later stages—around midnight, to be accurate—one began to recognize some of the components of the explosion—to detect, so to speak, the old tomato can. The Tower of London could be observed in the gloom, holding up the boulders of Richmond's camp down in the country. So, also, the outer walls of the Tower became the inner walls by the aid of a few noble hangings. But oh! the costumes. Except in the case of Richard, Mr. Jones did not lavish them absurdly, he simply invested them heroically and to great purpose. There was one piece of stuff worth going again to behold—the dress of Lady Anne, whom Richard murders off-stage.

But a passion for effect is a very dangerous passion in a one-man show like *Richard III,* and I confess that with all the pride of the eye and pride of the ear I never could serenely forget that this was John Barrymore playing Shakespeare. Once, during the much curtailed speech of Richmond (Raymond Bloomer), I felt the exaltation which is communicable by Shakespeare above all the other acted poets; but for the most part, even during the astounding ingenuity of the wooing (played so seductively by Miss Robbins as well as Barrymore), and even during the grandstand play in Richard's tent, I kept thinking, "Yes, this is the Big Show, this is Buffalo Bill Shakespeare, but I do not find myself translated. Lower my threshold, I beseech thee, o Shakespeare. Pour thy spirit upon me, or I faint."

Why does anyone fail to feel this splendor, when most people are verbally efflorescent after seeing *Richard III?* I think it is partly because Mr. Barrymore lays it on so thick, and also because Shakespeare does the same. Richard begins by explaining to you that he is a particularly bad man, and that he is going to kill somebody every day before breakfast. And his badness, of which he assures you, is due to his mighty ambition. He is going to be king, despite his sisters and his cousins and his aunts, and if at any time he seems to be off guard and human it mustn't be taken seriously, because he is so particularly double-dyed and bad. Well, after that elaborate explanation, I feel as everybody feels after the card-trick is explained. Very clever, but let us move on to something else. The unsophistication of Shakespeare's method is fatal to my sense of reality. And when I see the two dear little princes come on the stage to be slaughtered—after all the brothers and elder statesmen and what-not—I marvel more at Richard's homicidal preciosity than at the fate of Richard and Edward. At each appearance of Richard I think, "here comes the Bad Man, whose number is up now?" And I wait hoping against hope that some cross-grained citizen will shy a brick at him, to end his relentless automatic career.

Because of the odium it attaches to the family life of kings and queens I am, as a democrat, predisposed to *Richard III*. But the plot, the psychology, the history, seem to me infantile; and I feel too responsible in the presence of Shakespeare to go the full limit of his and my own infantility. This is, perhaps, regrettable. With John Barrymore so versatile and Robert Edmond Jones so fecund, it is a pity not to be transported into their splendid-horrible world. Yet I cannot help believing that they are partly to blame. The great fact about imagination is its coyness. A child that can be imaginative with a stick and string may be surfeited with a barrel-ful of toys. The pomposity and ostentation of *Richard III* has not the happiest effect of one's imagination. It is true that John Barrymore has a wealth of corrective devices—grossness and humor, sly hypocrisy and wit, and in the end an acknowledgment that evil is not the good he bargained for. But what devices can correct Shakespeare's monstrosity? That is inherent in *Richard III,* however it may bait the ear and the eye.

And I have one further grievance against Shakespeare—his medieval insistence on the loathsomeness of a cripple. He is artist enough to put the words in Richard's own mouth, but it is Shakespeare pandering to herd-instinct, nothing less. It is enforcing the old brutal cave-notion that a cripple is necessarily maleficent. Richard's description of his entering the world feet foremost is meant to be disgusting. Shakespeare should reap the disgust. Are we led to understand Richard? No, only to moralize over him. Thus platitude makes cowards of us all.

From *The New Republic,*
March 24, 1920.

THE JONES-BARRYMORE-HOPKINS *MACBETH*

By KENNETH MACGOWAN

I F the past three months in the New York Theatre have demonstrated anything, they have demonstrated the possibility and the necessity of great acting on our stage. They might have been expected to demonstrate the power of the new stagecraft; for Robert E. Jones, Norman-Bel Geddes, and Rollo Peters have followed Lee Simonson in a series of most interesting and stimulating productions, ending with a staging of *Macbeth* by Jones that is more extraordinary and significant than any other single production which I have seen or heard of in twenty years. In the face of such work by new artists, the power and supremacy of the actor—after the playwright the chief prime factor in the theatre from the earliest days—were reasserted and reemphasised, not alone by such fine acting as Julia Arthur, Margaret Wycherly, Augustin Duncan, Carroll McComas, Lawrence Grossmith, George Arliss, William Faversham, Mrs. Fiske, and Laurette Taylor have given us, but by the consequences to Jones's *Macbeth* of the dull and tedious performance of Lionel Barrymore. The art of the theatre is not the art of the decorator—as the decorators themselves know full well. Without superb acting and superb direction, no real progress in the art is possible. America has its artists now, not many perhaps but as good in their ways as any that Europe can offer. It has some unusually good actors, and a director or two of insight and ability. But without permanent companies and repertory theatres in which these three types of talent can come to know one another and achieve fusion, the difficulties that stand in the way of our reaching the fullest and finest art of the theatre are still gigantic.

I am convinced that *Macbeth,* as Robert E. Jones has visualized it for Arthur Hopkins's courageous revival, is essentially an epoch-making production. It is not the highest point in a developing tradition of beauty, suggestion, synthesis. It is the beginning of something new. It cuts off the past and locks the future just as surely as did *Hernani.* It has not annihilated the old tradition, as did that great first romantic drama of France, and it will be a long time before critics and public see how inevitably progress in the future must lie along the lines suggested by this production. The reason is very simple: the acting centre of the play failed to glow with the luminosity which this extraordinary production demanded. Had John Barrymore played Macbeth, had Ben-Ami acted the part, if in fact any actor of first-rate ability had appeared against Jones's backgrounds, I am certain that the evening of February seventeenth would have been evident to everyone as an occasion of the very highest significance in the calendar of the American theatre.

Elsewhere in this issue appear reproductions of the principal sketches made by Robert E. Jones for *Macbeth,* together with two studies from models. These need perhaps two explanations. The first is philosophic, and touches Jones's purpose. Throughout his production he has attempted through significant form to create an abstract background expressing the spiritual relationships of the play. He has seen as the dominant element of *Macbeth* the abnormal influence of the powers symbolized by Shakespeare in the witches. He has tried to visualize the superhuman nature of these mystic forces in gigantic masks appearing high in the air above the blasted heath. Through the rest of the play he has placed upon the stage very simple and abstract forms to carry the mood induced by the supernatural influences which seize and dominate the characters constantly throughout *Macbeth.* These bits of settings are, to him, things projected by the masked forces upon the action of the play.

A second explanation must deal with the actual materials of the production. The short scenes, mainly of a narrative nature, which pass elsewhere than at Inverness or Dunsinane, are acted at the front of the stage against a draped curtain of canvas falling in stiff folds and beautifully executed by Robert Bergman—whose painting has been so important to the success of most of the newer artists—a curtain of dully-burnished gold which takes the light in uncommonly beautiful ways. The main portions of the drama, the more important portions, are acted upon a deep stage surrounded by dimly seen black hangings. For the first scene of the witches there are only the three silver masks hanging above and three similarly masked figures in red standing motionless in a pool of light below. For most of the scenes in Inverness, Jones uses one or two sets of arches, curiously and disturbingly aslant. These develop in dramatic force as the course of the play alters. When

Macbeth is reaching the highest point of his success the two groups seem to lunge upward and away toward triumph. In the last scenes, when he hears of the coming of Birnam wood, only one set of arches remains and it seems almost toppling to the ground. Other abstract shapes are handled similarly. For the sleep-walking scene there are a series of arched window frames set about the stage, through which and against which Lady Macbeth appears. The throne of the banquet scene is backed crazily by brooding and malignant shapes. All these elements are handled in the barest and simplest grays, with an occasional dull red like the backing of the throne. They are lit by sharp beams of light that come, as it were, from the spirits in the void and make patterns of the air. The costumes are of the simplest materials and of primary colors; yet never has Jones shown more power and beauty in such work.

From the settings alone, I carry away three impressions. First, from the front scenes and from the costumes and the clear cut, exactly finished quality of the whole production, a sense of absolute beauty. Second, from the sleep-walking scene, an unearthly impression of a pearly dream-world such as I have never had. Third, from the dominating shapes of the bits of setting a sensation of terrible, overpowering obsession. These are the shapes that suggest not realities but unconscious forces. The characteristic form employed is the distorted gothic arch. Repeated in shields, conical helmets and spears, it is like the dull point of a murderous dagger. Twisted as it is, it impresses upon the mind the deadly and thwarted ambition with which the sisters obsess Macbeth.

Of the purpose of Jones there is nothing to be said. He has merely set out to give us scenery to suggest an emotional idea, instead of a physical reality. By so much he has cut off sharply from the methods and ideas of the whole new movement in stage decoration. His method is an abstraction of spiritual reality. The only measure of it can be its success in achieving what it sets out to do.

On that score there must be many reservations. Personally, I believe that Jones erred in his method of keeping the super-human and dominating quality of the forces of the heath before us. I think he should have concentrated more attention on the masks. I think the witches should have been practically invisible; or at most only as

dim as they appear in the tongue of flame which mounts in the caul-
dron scene. Doubtless in the first scene on the heath he wished to
insist on the identity of the red figures and the large masks, by
similarly masking them. Actually, our preconceptions as to the appearances of the witches and Shakespeare's own lines of description jar
frightfully with the birdlike figures in red. If only the masks in the
air were clearly seen, and if they were retained as visible, dominating
symbols above all the other scenes of the play where the influence
of the witches is felt, I think the whole idea of the production would
be much more clearly evident. You will note from the sketch of the
banquet scene that it was apparently Jones's intention to use the
masks in this manner for this particular episode. That he did not do
this and repeat the effect in other scenes, seems to me one of the
blunders that make the production as a whole puzzling and incon-
clusive to so many.

These are the only blunders of Jones. The rest must be charged
to acting and direction. In general the fault of Arthur Hopkins's direction is the fault of too slow a pace and too static a treatment of the
people on the stage. This is only a fault perhaps because of the still
greater fault of the leading actor, Lionel Barrymore. If he possessed
the spiritual fire and strength that the part demands, the slow pace
might not be evident. Certainly if he did not give so absolutely tedious
and unimaginative a performance, few would find the background
anything but an exciting and immensely stimulating part of the drama
enacted. As it is, Barrymore plods heavily through the long play, dwelling endlessly on every vowel, never for a moment simulating any
natural emotion appropriate to Macbeth. It is his Neri of *The Jest*
sobered a bit and shorn of his more intriguing violence. It is a performance on a dead level. Macbeth's moments of terror and anguish
seem hardly more than heavier accents of a slow and laboriously
rumbling beat of the voice. Audiences that came looking for a Macbeth
and a Barrymore were cheated of their satisfaction and fell back on
cursing the settings. Never had a production called so for acting or
been so ready to support it and raise it aloft; but without such acting,
never was a production so vulnerable to popular prejudices.

The truth of what I say was clearly evident I feel in the response
of the audiences to those moments when Julia Arthur had the stage

and the action to herself. Her performance is by no means inspired; it does not partake of the true quality of the spiritual obsession of the setting. But it is fine enough to show, in the quick response of the audiences, that real acting could have turned Jones's work from a liability into an asset so far as the popular reaction goes. This is even clearer, perhaps, in the case of E. J. Ballantine's very fine performance as Malcolm. But I cannot help feeling that if Barrymore could only do as much with his part as the rest of a generally excellent cast do with theirs, it would be enough to carry this production to a remarkable and an epoch-making success.

From *The Theatre Arts Magazine*
April, 1921

MR. HAMPDEN AS SHYLOCK

O. W. FIRKINS

T H E R E are three things to be said at the outset about Mr. Hampden's Shylock. It is squalid; it is aged; it is (in parts) unbalanced or hysterical. The text does not require Shylock to be all or any of these things;[1] it does not forbid him to be any or all of the three. There is not the smallest probability in the supposition that all three of these traits were gratifying to an Elizabethan audience. There is grave doubt whether any one of them actually recommends the play to an audience of our time. In points where Shakespeare is elastic, perhaps the twentieth century has as good a right to its preference as the sixteenth. Shakespeare's authority is valid everywhere, but the Globe has hardly the right to dictate to the Broadhurst.

What are the traits common to all Shylocks—the inseparable or universal traits? Avarice, revenge, cruelty—to which stubbornness and masterfulness may be added. Strength in evil—that is the character in a nutshell; and the feeling it evokes is horror. Add squalor, add infirmity, add hysteria, and the horror is diminished; part of it is replaced by loathing. Horror as a literary value includes respect. Horror looks up; pity looks down. Put Shylock at our feet; make him

---

[1] The Tubal scene may fairly be called hysterical, but Mr. Hampden extends the hysteria to other parts.

abject in the etymological sense: and you lighten the horror and augment the pity. That is the net result of Mr. Hampden's work. His Shylock begets no consternation; he is not felt as a power. Logically, he
may be formidable, but, æsthetically, he is not terrifying. The strength
of the portrayal lies in its vivid reflex of Shylock's pain. The pity is real,
though it is an impatient, reluctant, half-averted pity, a pity that breeds
relief when Shylock finally disappears and gives the play a chance to
be itself again. For Shylock, an alien in his own city, is in a sense a
stranger to his own play, and he is doubly a stranger when he is
acted by Mr. Hampden. Let us look into the meaning of this fact.

The *Merchant of Venice* is probably the first of all Shakespearean
plays in the expression of joyous and beautiful vitality as the animus
of a community. The lady in Belmont is richly left, and she is fair,
and more than fair, wondrously virtuous; and in the play itself as in
the lady the beauty and the riches and the virtues are piled up in
bright exuberance and delectable profusion. The play can not stop
when its work is done; no, it must needs add a delicious afterpiece
in which farce appears for the first and last time under moonlight, and
to this afterpiece it must prefix a prologue, two, three prologues, which
inlay the skies with gold and broider the air with music. Into this
play steps Shylock. How? Was the porter bribed or drowsy? I admit
fully the legitimacy of contrast, but the contrast in this drama is unusual. There is no wider chasm to be sure between Shylock and Portia
than between Caliban and Miranda. But while Caliban is opposed to
Miranda, he is not opposed to the *Tempest;* the *Tempest* is built for
Calibans and Mirandas alike; there is both steerage and first cabin
in the ship. But in the *Merchant of Venice* all that is not Shylock is
anti-Shylock, and this all is strong enough to create a highly composed
and firmly concentrated effect which the presence of Shylock disturbs
and deranges.

Shylock, then, costs the play a good deal. His worth is more than
his cost, much more. Still, that is no reason for not reducing the cost
as much as possible, and the latitude Shakespeare has given to the
actor by making the part short and divesting it of hampering particulars enables the actor to reduce that cost materially. He can widen or
lessen the estrangement of Shylock from the play. Let us help ourselves to an analogy. If you dramatize Satan in heaven after the revolt

but before the fall, you must dramatize him as Lucifer. The devil, as he was understood, let us say, by Maggie Tulliver or Thrawn Janet, would not be an antithesis to the City of God; he would be a smutch. It is useless to plead contrast; a sooty Lucifer, a tailed Lucifer, would merely distract contrast from its proper object, the moral abyss between the rebel and his God. Now Shakespeare has been so obligingly inexplicit or noncommittal that (within certain limits which the intelligent reader may be trusted to supply for himself) it is possible to play Shylock either as Lucifer or as Launcelot Gobbo's foul fiend, either as a malign force of redoubtable intensity, or as a buzzard or hyena. In London or New York he might fitly enough be the foul fiend, but in Venice, Portia's Venice, which is a kind of sublunary heaven, there is a distinct advantage in playing him as Lucifer. Mr. Hampden declined that advantage. If any one insists on specifications, to play Shylock as Lucifer means to emphasize the vitality, the intellect, and the occasional dignity, and to avoid all the degradations in person, age, voice, carriage, temperament, or apparel as to which the text is not peremptory and explicit.

The performance, apart from Mr. Hampden, was unequal and fluctuating. The scenes were rearranged with a fearlessness, which, excusable for the most part, involved at one point a gross affront to probability. Miss Mary Hall was a warm, sensuous, half-Oriental Portia, lively, as it were, on a basis of indolence, or, if you prefer, physically and temperamentally sluggish, while youthfully and mentally vivacious. She was felicitous in the talk with Nerissa and acceptable generally, but in the trial scene she allowed Portia, not only to imitate, but to parody, the doctor. That Portia, for the sake of stroking herself or mocking herself, would risk the verisimilitude of a comedy on which Antonio's life depends is a theory that assails Portia's intelligence and condemns Miss Hall's. The Gratiano of Mr. Hannam Clark seemed like an imitation of a roysterer by a puritan; if he stumbled into *Twelfth Night,* it is questionable whether Sir Toby Belch or Malvolio would take him by the arm.

From *The Weekly Review,*
May 28, 1921.

EUGENE O'NEILL'S *BEYOND THE HORIZON*

By HEYWOOD BROUN

EUGENE O'NEILL'S *Beyond the Horizon,* which was produced at a special matinee at the Morosco Theatre yesterday, is a significant and interesting play by a young author who does not as yet know all the tricks. Fortunately, he therefore avoids many of the conventional shoddy stratagems, but at the same time there is an occasional clumsiness which mars his fine intent and achievement. Nevertheless, the play deserves a place among the noteworthy achievements of native authors. It is frankly and uncompromisingly a tragedy. A happy ending would be unthinkable, but O'Neill has gone a little way toward an opposite extreme and insisted on polishing off his play with certain tragic happenings which are not quite relevant to his theme.

His story concerns two farm boys, Robert and Andrew, closely knit, though widely varying in type. Robert longs to be free of the grind of the farm and to find adventure and release in the far-off places. Incidentally, his health has not been good, so his family agrees when he accepts the invitation of a seafaring uncle to take a long voyage around the world on a sailing craft. The very day before his departure he finds that he is beloved by the daughter of the neighboring farmer. He had thought about her romantically but reservedly, since he believed that she cared for his brother. Her sudden confession that he is the one she loves sweeps him off his feet momentarily and he decides to stay on the farm. The brother, chagrined to find himself not favored, takes his place on the voyage.

The girl and the boy marry and he makes a fearful mess of farming. And he finds that he had made a mess of life as well, for the girl discovers that, after all, it was the competent Andrew whom she loved all the time. In a bitter scene she upbraids him with his uselessness and tells him that when Andrew returns he can take to the road if he chooses and let Andrew run the farm. On his return, however, Andrew soon shows that he is entirely cured of his youthful love, and in a single day he is off again to seize a business opportunity in the Argentine. The luckless couple muddle along on the farm and things go from bad to worse, until in the last act Robert dies of consumption and finds his chance at last to escape from the little valley and go to the far places.

Of course, the fundamental tragedy of the play lies in the fate of the incompetent dreamer forced to battle with the land for a living against every inclination and ability. His disease and death are entirely fortuitous and indeed they lessen the poignancy of his fate, which would have had more force of fear and pity if the author had left him still engaged in his hopeless and thankless task of keeping on and on in the dreary grind. The hero is much too deliberate in dying and the last act is further marred by the addition of a scene which is unnecessary, and which compels a wait at a time when the tension is seriously impaired by the fall of the curtain.

O'Neill begins crudely but honestly and frankly with a scene in which two of his chief characters sit down and tell the audience the things they ought to know, but after this preliminary scene the play gathers pace and power, and until the final act it is a magnificent piece of work, a play in which the happenings are of compelling interest, and more than that a play in which the point of view of every one concerned is concisely and clearly set forth in terms of drama. Every body who saw the best of O'Neill's short plays when they were given by the Washington Square, the Greenwich Village or the Provincetown Players realized that he had an extraordinary ability to write true and absorbing dialogue. He has done it better than ever in *Beyond the Horizon.* His characters talk like real people and yet the process of selection has been so shrewd that there is none of the deadening dullness of the merely literal and photographic.

The power of the play is tremendous, but there is no sense of the author's arbitrarily moving pawns about into implausible situations to thrill an audience. It is as honest and sincere as it is artistic. In the last act we found a distinct let-down, in spite of some splendid writing for the theater, because O'Neill has by then become so carried away with his theme that he has not been able to hold it at arm's length and slash and cut in the light of the fact that audiences are human and fallible and demand a brevity in the relation of all happenings which keep them in the theatre after 5 in the afternoon or 11 at night. And more than that, as we have said, it does not seem to us that the progress of the hero's disease is an inevitable part of his tragic career.

The play is to be presented again at a matinee on February 4 and again on February 6. It is to be hoped that a theatre will soon be found at which the play may be put on for a regular run, since it is by far the best serious play which any American author has written for years. It is pleasant to record this, for, in a measure, *Beyond the Horizon* offers a justification for all reviewers who went down to the various little alley theatres and shouted loudly about some of the work which was done there. O'Neill's short plays have received such recognition for several years and yet we feel certain that when his long play achieves the success which it deserves, and which it is pretty sure to get, the author will be hailed as a brand new playwright who has just been discovered. His first production on Broadway will be set down as his dramatic birth in spite of such splendid forerunners as *Bound East for Cardiff* and *Where the Cross Is Made*.

It is to be hoped that when the play goes on for a regular run most of the present company may be retained, for the performance is one of exceptional skill. Richard Bennett as the hero seems to us to play better than ever before, and there also are performances of an unusually high order by Louise Closser Hale, Helen MacKellar and Erville Alderson, not forgetting good work by Edwin Arnold, Max Mitzel and a child actress called Elfin Finn. In speaking of the fact that O'Neill is still somewhat impractical in the theatre it is worth noting that he provides this child shall be two years old. Of course the little actress is perhaps ten or twelve, but then it seems to us that we remember other actresses in the theatre who have played rôles even further removed from their actual age.

From *The New York Tribune,*
February 4, 1920.

GEORGE KELLY'S *THE SHOW-OFF*

By HEYWOOD BROUN

I MIGHT as well begin boldly and say that *The Show-Off* is the best comedy which has yet been written by an American. To be sure, it departs quite radically in many respects from the form which has been associated traditionally with comedy. Critics who hold by old standards may point out that it is less lavish with incident than many another native play in the same mood, but they can hardly argue that human personality has ever been made more vivid, more truthful and more complete in the American theatre.

No one can question the authenticity of Aubrey Piper. He moves under his own steam from the moment the curtain rises. At no time does one feel that the hand of the playwright is still on the wheel directing the character to move in this direction or that in order to suit the exigencies of the story. And it seems to me that there is soundness in the scheme whereby the author makes some one character a concern above that of the tale itself. I am no longer drawn to the play "with a big idea" or the comedy constructed for the sake of a single telling scene. When an author works from such a blueprint he must almost inevitably find it necessary to scrunch and whittle his characters now and then to make them fit into his plot scheme. He must bulldoze a little. He must regiment his folk and Prussianize them.

No such interference is visited upon Aubrey Piper of *The Show-Off*. He sets the pace and the story follows. This man is no creature born within the wings of the theatre. We have sat desk to desk with him in offices. He has bumped against us in the subway and as like as not he lives in the flat just across the hall. He has been wrenched out of life.

But there is one more test which must be met by a play if it is to live among drama of the first order. The playwright has done a great deal if he has been able to create a living, breathing, individual human being. He must do more. At some point in the story this fictional man or woman must stand as a symbol of all mankind. There should be in him some recognizable common factor of humanity. And Aubrey meets the test. He brings to us the realization of the toughness of human fibre. In him there glints the glorious truth that personality endures against the blows of circumstance.

When I was in college much was said to us about the playwright's obligation to show the development of character. I hold that this obligation is imaginary and should be generally discarded for the sake of truth. As a matter of fact, it seems to me that human beings are moulded early and that their later history is largely an account of the manner in which fate breaks its fingernails in vain efforts to claw them into new habits of thought. The Aubrey Piper whom we see at the close of *The Show-Off* is precisely the same person who stalked into the first act. He has not changed. We know him better and more intimately because we have seen his reaction to various emotional stimuli, but the development has been in the minds of the audience and not in the soul of Aubrey.

Personally I came to like Aubrey exceedingly before the evening was done. I think that George Kelly has succeeded magnificently in this respect. It is essential that the audience should come in time to have a friendliness for the central figure of the comedy. But this is no easy task. Special pleading will not avail and Kelly does not employ it. An author, like a judge or a baseball umpire, is under obligation to preserve at least the appearance of neutrality. He may not lean down from Olympus too palpably to pat some favorite character on the head. Tenderness he may have—indeed we think it becomes the dramatist—but it must be shown subtly. The sleight-of-hand ought to be fast and skilful enough to deceive the human eye.

And so we have it here. George Kelly builds up the case for Aubrey Piper by countless small strokes. By degrees he opens up the heart of the man. There he stands—liar, braggart, egotist, but the very consistency of his faults colors them with magnificence. From Prometheus down, mankind has chosen for its heroes men who stood pat. "Be yourself, Mother Fisher," cries Aubrey to his mother-in-law in times of stress, and it is a slogan which he has taken to heart. There is no need for anyone to say "be yourself, Aubrey." He never is tempted for a moment to be anything else.

Of course, it may truthfully be said that Aubrey lives in a fantastic dream world of his own creation, but once he has built his world he stands by it. God himself has done no more.

From *The Show-Off*
(Little, Brown), 1925.

CHARLES FROHMAN

By MONTROSE J. MOSES

CHARLES FROHMAN, as he stood upon the deck of the sinking Lusitania, spoke of death as a beautiful adventure. His last attitude was one of calmness, his last utterance was one of few words. This well affords a key to the character of the man—a personality of great mystery to the public at large, a man of simple manner and retiring disposition to those who knew him.

There is nothing more burned out than a bare record of theatrical activity. Yet, though Charles Frohman had little time to do more than to live a theatrical life, his personality endeared him to all of his associates, and represented to them honest dealings, thorough good faith, sympathy, and agreeable humor. If he refused to show himself before the curtain, it was partly because of his lameness, but a great deal because he was by nature modest and willing to let his work speak for him. If, with many of his "stars," he contented himself with verbal agreements, he not only exhibited such faith as existed during a long association between Joseph Jefferson and Edwin Booth, but he established the bond of his word, leaving the actor free to meet conditions as they arose.

Charles Frohman lived in a significant period, as far as the theatre is concerned. He was struggling in his youth to gain a foothold just at the moment when managers like Wallack and Daly were approaching the end of their days; just when the old type of play, represented by Boucicault and Sardou on one hand, and French and German farces on the other, was to give way to realistic treatment. He began his endeavors when the theatre, as a business, was largely disorganized; when companies outside the chief cities went forth in doubt as to their fate, oftenest that of being stranded.

Looking back over the life of Charles Frohman, it may be safely claimed that he brought system and stability into the theatre, helping to turn actors from vagabonds into professional beings. Though he did not strictly adhere to the policy of the business man, Frohman helped to make it possible for the playhouse to be run on legitimate lines of accounting. Out of this condition there followed more prosperous times for the actor, who had larger salaries and who became a business asset to be exploited as a "star," and there came into being a theatrical monopoly as distinct and as potent for evil as any commercial organization could be. In the "star" system, Frohman placed his absolute trust; to the evils of the syndicate such as existed nearly twenty years ago he could not have given his absolute sanction, though he was affiliated with the organized booking offices, and persistently remained silent when questioned as to their methods and practices.

Born in Ohio fifty-five years ago, his boyhood was one of struggle and privation. His first jobs were in newspaper offices, where his brother Daniel started his worthy career. His first organized venture was with Haverley's Minstrels, at the head of which troupe he used often to march. Out west he came in contact with David Belasco, who was struggling in California, and there arose between the two a friendship which even years of estrangement could not destroy, as witness the recent revival of *The Celebrated Case,* under their joint management. It was under Frohman that Belasco had some of his early ventures brought east; it was through Frohman and his other brother, Gustave, that Belasco went east to see Daniel Frohman, who was then managing the Madison Square Theatre in New York. This resulted in Belasco's becoming stage-manager of that famous little house, with its famous stock company, while Charles looked after the road interests.

But he was also looking further and seeing the opportunities that the road presented for larger ventures. The bare theatrical facts in the life of Charles Frohman all point to his exceptional business foresight, which could see where the theatre was trending, and make the most of it. From 1877 to 1888, these formative forces were at work. Belasco was struggling to make good in New York; Alf Hayman (Charles Frohman's largest associate) was "advance" man for W. J. Florence— Jefferson's contemporary; "C. F." was going here and there, now in pocket and now out of pocket, appealing to McVicker, Hooley, Stetson, and McGuire—the managers of the day—for aid when he needed it.

It was with an American play, however, Bronson Howard's *Shenandoah,* that Frohman made his first financial success, and from 1888, therefore, may date the rise of the manager. Thenceforth he was always hunting around for a theatre of his own, looking enviously upon those managers who could boast of established homes, and finally turning an old church on Twenty-third Street into some sort of an auditorium. For that house—now Proctor's—Belasco and Henry DeMille wrote *Men and Women,* and the significant feature of the cast was the appearance of Maude Adams in an unassuming rôle. The Frohman theatrical planet sailed into its place, however, with the opening of the Empire Theatre in 1893, and here, again, Belasco, in collaboration with Franklin Fyles, was asked to write the initial piece, with the result that *The Girl I Left Behind Me* was produced.

Under the influence of the Madison Square Theatre, where the stock company had maintained a high level of acting and ensemble work, both Charles and Daniel Frohman went forth imbued with a liking for the system. The results are theatrical history. In New York there has never been, since the disappearance of the little Lyceum Theatre on Fourth Avenue, an organization so dedicated to healthy amusement and good acting as the one maintained for many years by Daniel Frohman, unless it be the Empire Stock Company, which Charles Frohman established. The days of association in the theatre have changed as far as New York is concerned, and both the Frohman brothers saw this change taking place. But to the credit of Charles, he kept an atmosphere at his Empire, and he established a policy of running it which has kept it out of the matter-of-fact atmosphere of most of our places of amusement—the atmosphere of "pay two dollars and get a seat."

From the moment he became established in his Empire Theatre, Frohman had to conform to the new commercialism which he had helped to establish. But he was in an anomalous position. When the syndicate was at its greatest power "C. F." was also at his height, and people truly said that he was the largest part of the strength of the organization—that if he withdrew, the octopus would fall asunder. And they were right. But doubtless Frohman was also right in not deserting the pirate ship. He was too good a business man to give up a system until there was a better system to go to.

As far as he was concerned, his word was his bond; he took a fatherly pride in his "people"—such actors and actresses as Viola Allen, Henry Miller, William Faversham, John Drew, Maude Adams, Margaret Anglin, Ethel Barrymore, and Charles Richman. Yearly he began making his trips abroad, returning in July with promises which were mostly fulfilled. And while abroad he was making friends with dramatists on the Continent and in England, and they were all promising him manuscripts for years in advance, until no one other than Frohman could touch Pinero, Henry Arthur Jones, Hubert Henry Davies, Barrie, R. C. Carton, and a host of others. Both in New York and London it was not long before he was managing many theatres.

It is unfortunate that Frohman had to bear the stigma of a discredited system, for he was above it and beyond it. His life's opportunity had been disorganized theatrical business, which he struggled to put in order. He helped to build up a theatrical circuit; he helped to build up the "star" idea; he was one of the biggest monopolists among his associates, but he was a monopolist with good intent, and his actors and dramatists in their recent tributes show that. At a critical period, when the American stage was being deluged with plays from abroad, and our papers were asking for the American drama, Charles Frohman was not as eager to show the pioneer spirit as he was to maintain a certain excellent level at his theatres.

As a manager he was a citizen of the world, and when one saw on the playbills "Charles Frohman presents," one was sure that there would be no attempt to fool the public, however mistaken "C. F.'s" judgment in the choice of plays might be. When all is told, he did give the public pieces by Gillette, Clyde Fitch, Augustus Thomas, and at the time of his death he seems to have had great faith in Edward Sheldon, as well as Justus Miles Forman, who went down with him. But his most evident pleasure was to deal with his English playwrights of established reputation.

Whether or not theatrical things in America were—for experimental purposes—more or less cut and dried to Charles Frohman, his greatest sacrifices to the cause of art were made in London, when he established his Repertory Theatre at the Duke of York, February 21, 1910. Rumor has it that J. M. Barrie, who was associated with Mr. Frohman in the enterprise, lost nearly a million dollars. But the failure of the experiment somehow revealed the fact that public taste is not as ideal as one would have it; and it showed Mr. Frohman's willingness on his part to give a chance to such pieces as George Meredith's *The Sentimentalist* and Elizabeth Baker's *Chains*. The experimental side of him in America was evident twice,—not counting, for instance, his mistaken notions of "all-star" revivals,—when he sent Miss Adams to Yale University for an outdoor production of *Twelfth Night* and to Harvard for a gigantic spectacle of Schiller's *Joan of Arc,* for which he received official thanks and she the degree of M.A.

Mr. Frohman was a man of pet theories and special tastes. I think there was something more than his business foresight which made him rely with such genuine expectancy on Barrie; there was something in common between the manager, the playwright and Maude Adams, a quality of character which the literary critic calls "charm." Friends of Charles Frohman speak of his Barriesque characteristics. There was something more than pose in his repertory experiment. Certainly, by the results, there was no foresight. I believe that all the younger men—Galsworthy, Masefield, Maugham, Hubert Henry Davies— could tell of the non-commercialism of the man. The very fact that he died poor is sufficient indication that Charles Frohman was not in the theatre business entirely for what he could get out of it; it is also indication of the fact that in the theatre business the manager has all to risk as far as the immediate expenditure of money is concerned; that it costs to run any sort of a theatre of standing and comfort.

Mr. Frohman was not in the strict sense a creative stage-manager; his were more or less organized productions. Instead of holding every-thing in the palm of his hand, he gave out parts of the work to different heads of departments, and they attended to the work for him. It is one thing to come to final rehearsals, and another to be personally responsible for each step of the way. And that is the one thing, to my mind, which detracted from the managerial policy of "C. F.," and which kept him out of the same category with Augustin Daly and Lester Wallack.

From *The Bellman,*
May 29, 1915.

A PLEA FOR FOLK BASIS IN AMERICAN DRAMA

By MONTROSE J. MOSES

I H A D a conversation at one time with an historian who was writing an introduction for a group of pictures dealing with the American Theatre. "What I'm going to do," he said enthusiastically, "is to begin with the Indian rituals, and show how the American drama sprang from them." I hated to spoil that man's enthusiasm, I hated to disrupt his academic love of tracing phenomena from the seed to the flower, I hated to have to confess that there was no such basic beginning to American drama, despite the fact that the Indians have their corn dances, their war and death ceremonies, their hymns to the rising sun, and their reverence for Manito.

I gave this man long arguments about the dependence of the American theatre on Britain; I outlined for him the joy with which Augustin Daly and A. M. Palmer—our early but famous theatre managers—ransacked the farce trash-baskets of France and Germany, and refurbished the flimsy situations for American consumption. "But certainly," he argued, "our native actors must have learned something of costuming and make-up from the Indian!" I bethought me of Edwin Forrest's gaudy headdress as Metamora, and the long row of cigar Indian imitations I had seen in the weak line of Western dramas, which used to be called typically American, and I smiled.

· This smile was met by a sharp retort. "Look at Eugene O'Neill's masks in *The Great God Brown;* surely here one finds traces of the Indian ceremonial masks." I wonder if O'Neill ever thought, when he wrote that play, of the Choctaws and the Eries. I don't believe so. I think he was nearer Æschylus than the Chief of the Crowfeet. I really don't think he considered either. I feel that he was seeking for new ways of expressing new psychological states rather than of reviving any old custom or making use of any native decoration.

No, as much as I should like to find a folklore basis for the American drama, I can detect no basis at all before the beginning of the so-called renaissance in our theatre. Then a self-conscious realization of the poverty of our foundations made us go back to the soil, and it is only recently that the strictly native drama has begun to flourish. Drama is not folk speech; it is folk passion, and in contemplating the peculiar way of expressing that passion, one gets to the bone of local life and local outlook. A few "Ahs" for "I" will not make a Southern play any more than "by goshes" scattered through the dialogue make a New England play....

Foreigners who came over to visit us in the early years went back and said our manners were those of the Indians; all the more reason, therefore, that our New York social dramas should assume the manners of Mayfair, just to show the English that we knew a drawing-room when we met one. That point of view doesn't worry me about the American theatre. But what does seem a shame is that for so many decades, though we have made stabs at depicting Yankee types, and cowboys and miners and mountaineers, we really didn't seem to know them. We let slip their folk quality. Our drama in the past has touched the soil as lightly as we touch it when, by train, we roll from one State to another. Our dramatists have become as nonchalant as that about it. Even in *Outside Looking In* it didn't very much matter where the action ventured, though specific indications gave the locale as North Dakota and Montana. The only thing that counted was that it was somewhere West.

There is no more significant date in American letters than the year of the publication of *Uncle Remus*. There was, in this collection of tales, a mixture of folklore and of creative art that set something going in the American mind. From about 1882, the American soil began to tremble and bear fruit. New England, the Kentucky Mountains, the Southern Negro, the South itself, were discovered literally, taken from the mists of conventionalized romanticism, and looked at with a sympathetically realistic eye. This soil was the true basis for a folk literature, but, unfortunately, for some years to come, no American theatre was built on that soil, eager to claim it.

We made faint stabs at the prairie soul in *The Great Divide;* we showed a Bret Harte loyalty in Belasco's *The Girl of the Golden West;* we romanticised without a spark of reality and truth about the mountaineer in *The Trail of the Lonesome Pine;* our Negro conception was not up-from-slavery but still down-at-slavery in slow, drawling, insignificant Southern war plays. Even our sense of dialogue peculiar to locality was rather weak. The cry against Uncle Remus was that he was hard to read. We became impatient whenever the native stuff of value began to raise its head. Those who didn't like the New England stories of Mary E. Wilkins and Sarah Orne Jewett —forerunners of such a play as *The Detour*—called them drab and plain level; the reading public were still hankering after Lords and Ladies. That is why they read so persistently the paper backed novels of the Duchess. *The Arundel Motto* and *Lady Audley's Secret* for them! ...

The Negro gave a picturesque addition to plantation life in the South; his paternalistic comfort somewhat compensated for his moral degradation. His folk tradition began to flower on Southern soil; his picturesque tribal differences were evident in the rice fields of South Carolina and in the canebrakes of Louisiana. The Southern kitchen rang with the hymns of the cook; the Southern cotton fields swung with the communal songs of the cotton pickers; the banjo was a re-crudescence of tribal music. For an instant the theatre reached out for this phenomenon and Negro Minstrelsy was the result. It was provocative of a sincere creativeness. But the fault with minstrelsy was that it did not remain true to its basic origin, a fault characteristic of so much of our American drama. We soon found the black-faced minstrel singing Irish love songs. All that is left of the halcyon days of minstrelsy is the old plantation lyric.

What is really happening in the American theatre is this: nearly three hundred years after its beginning in this country, it has started building its native foundations. The planted settler didn't write *Hiawatha;* he was more likely to rest from his labors—as in the case of George Sandys—by sitting down in the primæval forest and translating Ovid's *Metamorphoses.* We are now resurrecting what we should have taken cognizance of long ago. Sculptors are picturing our broad-breasted pioneer mothers, who never were recreated on our stage as they should have been; mural painters are coloring panoramas of our national youth which the theatre ignored as material for drama; the folk song musician is recording spirituals and chanties and mining songs which have only now and then filtered through into our *entr'acte* music and the radio. We have been inclined to let our native dramatic material go to waste.

And the curious thing is that we have realized our shortcomings with a benign indifference. Whenever we meet with the real thing in the theatre we thrill over its sincerity, its picturesqueness, its richness of human interpretation, its rightness as truth. Out in South Dakota, down in North Carolina, far across to California, Professor Frederick Koch has told the ambitious drama student: "Don't write about Piccadilly, where you have never been, or about Fifth Avenue, which is not your Main Street. But write what you know around you, make use of the soil beneath your feet, of the tradition in your heart, of the struggle in your soul, of the breath of your hills. Sing not the syncopation of Irving Berlin but the age-old crooning songs that have come from generation to generation down your family life."

There are many like Koch who have become conscious of how far from the soil the American theatre has travelled. Susan Glaspell, Eugene O'Neill, Paul Green, DuBose Heyward, and now Marc Connelly have shown us the harvest ahead of us. I can't connect—as that Professor wanted me to—the beginnings of our theatre with the tomahawk, though I believe our literary artist has foolishly denied the tragic significance of that weapon. It does seem to me a sad commentary that all the theatre of the past could draw from the clanking chains of slavery was the melodramatic lithograph of a dramatized *Uncle Tom's Cabin,* which slid, by the way, in locality from Kentucky to New Orleans.

Even if no one had thought of the significance of *The Green Pastures* as a milestone in the history of American drama, that play could not have done other than grip attention by its sweeping sincerity and its folk humor and dignity. But when I witnessed it, I was additionally entranced, for I saw in this visualization of simple minds a gorgeous utilization of those things at our very threshold which the American theatre has so blindly ignored. Paul Green's *In Abraham's Bosom,* Eugene O'Neill's *The Emperor Jones,* the Heywards' *Porgy* and now *The Green Pastures* are to the theatre what Joel Chandler Harris's *Uncle Remus* was to American literature of 1882. . . .

And what are we finding in this folk quality? That there is a universality in the poetic glamour of folklore; that this poetry is bringing back to the stage, with the aid of scenic design and direction, a certain flow of words that give to the actor more scope; that allow him to rise above the mere reserve of ordinary conversation. Notice this in most of Eugene O'Neill's plays. There is a universal appeal in any folk basis which somehow lifts the play out of its definite locale, and makes it available to all countries....

I am not pleading for our dramatists to be finicky in this matter of giving every play a local habitation. We find no Indian war paint in Walt Whitman, but a consciousness of a common urge in a young democracy. We find no blatant Americanism in Emerson, yet he showed us our American soul. It is that consciousness which Dvořák suggested in his *The New World Symphony,* wherein he made use of Negro spirituals.

Locality is not wholly a matter of peculiar speech. We do not want plays that need glossaries. We do not wish our actors taught race phonetics. Maeterlinck, not able to speak English, learned his first American lecture by a phonetic system, and broke down dismally. Eliza Doolittle, in Shaw's *Pygmalion,* taught to be a lady by accent as well as by manner, when she was overcome with natural feeling threw to the four winds all she had learned, and reverted to the life and manner she knew. Under such strong emotion the basic life returns. And my contention is that if our American dramatists wrote more often out of strong emotion, they would realize that locality, climate, tradition, play not a little, inconsiderable part in the lives of the people they are writing about.

From *North American Review,*
January, 1931.

PHILIP BARRY

By *MONTROSE J. MOSES*

I T I S difficult to place Philip Barry in a category. We hear from him at intervals with a play which bears the stamp of his own personality, which reveals his own lightsome style. And the rest is silence. Then we know that he is either at his home in Cannes or at his home in Westchester, working on some fantastic humor of his. We gather that he came from Rochester, New York, where he was born in 1896; that he went to public and private schools. We are told that he clerked in the State Department in Washington, only to be shifted to the United States Embassy in London. And from that diplomatic atmosphere he turned to Yale and then to the beneficent guidance of George Pierce Baker, at Harvard, where he was to add luster to Workshop 47. There he remained from 1919 to 1922. It was there, during his second year, that he was awarded the Richard Herndon Prize of five hundred dollars for *You and I,* which was given a production.

This was the first that Broadway heard of Philip Barry. But he had been writing before. Burns Mantle has unearthed titles of plays he must have wheedled from the silent Barry; and from such research we find that a one-acter of his was performed by the Yale Dramatic Association, which, in the face of his identification with the Harvard Baker régime, brings further to light that he was actually graduated from Yale, in 1919. Barry has spent very little time writing about himself; he never defends his plays; he never attempts to explain them. He moves in the pages of the press, a veritable fiction character of his own, making his stage people brothers and sisters of his own generation, and playing with them gently. There is no term you could apply to some of his stage people that you could not apply to Barry himself. You are charmed by their tenderness, by their irrelevancy, by what John Anderson, the dramatic critic, termed their "shimmering idiocy." So, too, are you charmed by Philip Barry.

His plays are really Barry in quest of himself. There is no American dramatist of the same stamp. He cannot take life too soberly; he shadow-boxes with ideas and philosophies, he writes the most exquisite dialogue, he can be absurdly childish and delicately serious. His gossamer plays are shot through with patterns of ideas always in the bud, and the ideas are never given a chance to become full blown. His stories are spider webs of quaint spinning, with problematic knots which help to hold the dramas together. His seriousness is never left alone a minute; the puckered brow is chased by the inexhaustible good humor. If he should consider himself, Philip Barry would find his youth in his plays.

Which brings me to the point I have in mind. We must picture Barry as young: tomorrow he will be older, and while it will be difficult for him to alter his style, while his mind we hope will never lose its quaint conceits, while his dialogue will not, we trust, lose its facility, its ease and grace, he may recognize the importance of being earnest. Whatever the Philip Barry of the future, the charm of the young man will always be authentic biographical data; and only by that youthful portrait of the young man will we be able at a later date to judge his plays, from *You and I* through *The Animal Kingdom*.

Barry hovers over his plays with an unmistakable fancy wand, and even if he does not completely justify his means, they are holding as sheer entertainment. Problems have a fascination for him, but his mental habit is to toss them deftly back and forth in care-free dialogue; and he is not so much concerned with solutions as he is with wit and quick response. A quick retort turneth away wrath—and this tendency on Barry's part makes him a lovable writer, if not always a potent dramatist. I think sometimes there is method in his disjointed incidentals; unsteady thinking though it may seem, the flavor of a solution is often more lasting than the solution itself. Amidst tender confusion, positiveness is out of place. It is because of the lack of definiteness, the refusal to take Barry's fantasy at its full, that Laurette Taylor failed to see the problem in *In a Garden,* when she appeared in it. It is because of fantastic fooling in *White Wings*—a breezy, pathetic picturing of the street-cleaning days of New York in the gay Nineties—that it lingered so short a while on the stage. Philip Barry was not at first a lucky star for the managers. But with the advent of *Paris Bound*—and the two plays that followed, *Holiday* and *Hotel Universe*—he more definitely found a foothold in our theatre.

I do not know whether Barry ever thought, while writing these plays, that they might represent a trilogy of youth. But I take them as such. If so considered, they may stand together as commentary on his own era. They are held close by a similar mannerism, and certain fooling which sparkles in *Holiday* crops up again in *Hotel Universe,* showing a bitter agony which comes with immaturity. Once upon a time, Barry and Elmer Rice, exiled abroad in order to escape the cloying rush of American life, collaborated in a play called *Cock Robin.* It seemed strange to see a play of Elmer Rice's later on and to come away, thinking persistently of Philip Barry. But that is exactly what *The Left Bank* did to me—it made me ponder on the illusive charm of Barry and on the intellectualized, sober statement of reality in Rice,

which Barry always so lightly evades. Both playwrights have dealt
with the younger generation, have used their vocabulary. That vocabulary and the philosophies which were expressed by it nearly ran
away with the group living under the roof of the *Hotel Universe.* Let
us analyze the situation.

The younger generation which came out of the War had its
bitter cracks against everything; they set out to repudiate the world
as it was; they left from their calculations entirely any illusions that
might have been ready at hand for them; they were not sure of anything, but they were willing and anxious to think of everything. What
they knew for a certainty was that they had had enough of what
they called the "older generation," which had bungled the world into
a great social and economic mess; they were—in other words—out on
a voyage of new discovery.

If they had taken anything with them in their mental kit other
than rebellion, they might not have so easily fallen into morbidity.
If they had been willing to pause by the roadside, to spend a week-
end with themselves as they were fundamentally, and to chart the
seven seas of existence, they might not have turned so violently against
the life they finally came to live, after they turned against the life
of the older generation. As I see it, that is the entire philosophical
matrix in Philip Barry's plays. In *Paris Bound,* youth married gains
its experience, becomes ripened in the spirit of compromise. In *Holiday,* youth fights against the pressure of life that would strangle
the *joie de vivre.* In *Hotel Universe,* youth is fagged. Barry would
substitute a sense of fun for the vacuous living of the older generation. "Life is exciting," exclaims Youth. "Life is an exacting business,"
exclaims the older generation. Barry's plays have about them the
atmosphere of youthful excitement. In *Holiday* the exclamation is,
"We are all grand at seventeen." What is the disillusionment in *Hotel
Universe?*

Plays of the younger generation, with which we have been deluged for many years past, all seem to agree upon the restlessness of
the rebel. *Holiday* is restless. But, even though the rebel, who re-
pudiates the conventions of society, goes out to think bravely about
life, he soon realizes that thinking about life is not living, and the

two points of view sometimes end in disillusionment. So we have the poignant moments in *Hotel Universe.*

After the War, young people looked upon the world as hideous; they could not square their own questions with any of the answers offered by their elders. They became violently interested in the problems of why they were here and whither they were going. That is a typical youthful attitude of the past decade, of all decades. They have debated the morality preached in the pulpit and have been witness to the repudiation of that morality as exploited in the newspapers. So, the restless group that Philip Barry introduces in *Hotel Universe* is but the reflection of that awful drifting uncertainty into which rebelliousness so often takes us. Barry's characters express their doubts because they have only a smattering connection with the permanent things of the universe. They distrust any permanency whatsoever. They would not work on schedule time because they wish an untried schedule for life of their very own, that would make life worth living. In *Holiday,* the hero decides that it were best for people to let fresh air into life while it is young; to take a holiday first and to work afterwards.

In this spirit, young people are willing to risk everything. They are sometimes willing to risk death, and, in a moment of despondency, they are willing even to take life as a sacrifice. They do not yet know the value of ease; they only know that they must go quickly through the adventure. One of the characters in *Hotel Universe* contemplates killing himself, and an older, a wiser being tells him that things may change—why do it? He is sufficiently knowing of the younger generation not to say to this young person: "*You* may change. In this world there is a certain law of maturity which comes from experience; you are in a state of flux; you know nothing of the certainty of calm."

Not one of Barry's characters but is thus drawn rebellious. In most of his dramas, with a flash or two, he suggests that there is a practical side to life which, humorous though it may be in dialogue, serves also its purpose as a stabilizer of excessive energy. One of his people says: "While there is life there is rent to pay": in itself a wisecrack, but representing a point of view which might serve to bring back a rebellious spirit to a point of rest. For a point of rest is as necessary in life as it is, according to Ruskin and Coventry Patmore, in art.

After the War, the younger generation cried out: "We have had enough," meaning enough of the old-time bungling. Our dramatists are giving hint that in some respects that same generation, looking back on its rebelliousness, is again saying: "We have had enough. We will take stock of what we have gained, of what we have lost. There is time to recapture some of the things we hastily threw overboard when we rebelled."

All this tumble of living, discussed so sensationally in the papers of the day, is by no means steadying to the so-called younger generation. Philip Barry has reflected this unsteadiness in his plays. He has used both the positive and negative characteristics of the time. He does not answer any questions. But he gives the panorama with a thread of narrative that oftentimes is very thin; the reward is that he always has at his disposal a beautifully light touch of fancifully quaint humor.

From *Representative American Dramas.*
(Little, Brown, 1934).

LEGEND'S END—DAVID BELASCO

By GEORGE JEAN NATHAN

TO applaud the practice of Mr. David Belasco in expending infinite care and time in perfecting the production of so empty and bootless a play as *Little Lady in Blue* is akin to an admiration for the sort of adult who triumphantly expends painstaking effort and time in putting together the several hundred little pieces of a jig-saw puzzle. That such veneration is as without foundation as a tent is probably perfectly well appreciated by the folk who participate in it, yet the Belasco tradition dies hard and of that tradition this particular veneration is, one may believe, something in the nature of a death rattle. It is as if they who stand by the bed-side, at a bit of a loss what nice to say, murmur gently, "But anyway—he had a good heart."

It is perhaps now a dozen years since the Belasco legend slid off the well-oiled ways and sailed gaudily forth, with flags flying and guns booming, into the gullibilities of the American public—a public already celebrated for having swallowed in high clover Madame

Janauschek as a great artist, Richmond Pearson Hobson as a great naval strategist, Hamlin Garland as a great novelist, Tom Sharkey as a great prize-fighter and May Yohe as a great beauty. Nurtured by the gentleman himself with an even more scrupulous cunning than Barnum exercised in the exploitation of Jenny Lind, the Russian press bureau in preliminary *missa cantata* of the genius of Admiral Rodjest-venski or Mr. Ziegfeld in the glorification of Lillian Lorraine, the tradition fattened with the years and, fattening, established its creator in the American mind as a leading figure in the world's theatre.

To the fattening of this tradition, Mr. Belasco was tireless in contributing albumenoids of various and succulent genres. First, by way of bequeathing to himself an air of aloof austerity and monastic meditation, he discarded the ordinary habiliments of commerce and by the simple device of turning his collar hind end foremost, made of himself a sort of Broadway Rasputin, a creature for awe and pointings and whisperings. Arrayed so, he strode as a messiah among the peasants and, by putting on a show in a barn in El Paso, Texas, brought down the wrath of these æsthetes upon the sack-suited infidels of the Syndicate who very probably because his show wasn't so good or so much of a drawing-card in El Paso as the Byrne Brothers' *Eight Bells,* denied him their El Paso mosque on the theory that if Mrs. Leslie Carter was a great artist then the whole darned artist business was Greek to them and they would just as lief take their chances on getting simultaneously into the Hall of Fame and the First National Bank with Nellie McHenry.

But this Belasco, a sapient fellow withal, knew well what he was about. The thing worked like a charm. And the yokelry, egged on by the ever naïve and infatuated St. William Winter and other such credulous emotionals, raised cries of persecution and Belasco became, overnight, the martyred Dreyfus of the American drama. High-salaried press agents who knew how suavely to soule and roget and bartlett were commissioned now to fashion compositions to be signed by Belasco and spread discreetly in the more literary gazettes. And by way of augmenting the aloofness, the mystery, the remote melancholy and the artistic temperament of him, the monsignor sold now his old swivel chair, his old desk light with the green shade and the chromo of Ned Harrigan that hung on the wall and bought to

take their places a Ming dais, an altar candle-stick and a copy of the
Mona Lisa. Carpets ankle-deep were laid upon the floor, the blinds
were drawn and Vantine's entire stock of joss sticks set to smell up
the place with a passionate Oriental effluvium. In that corner, a single
wax taper, inserted artistically in a Limoges seidel, illumined the
chamber with its ecclesiastic glow, and in that was glimpsed a single
narcissus in a wistful pot. Upon the inlaid onyx commode that served
as a desk rested carelessly a framed photograph of Dante, with the
inscription "To my warm friend, Dave, in token of his services in
the cause of art"—and duly autographed by the poet in that peculiar
and unmistakable flowing hand of his. Outside the heavy bird's-eye
maple door studded with big brass thumb-tacks, two small coloured
bellboys, impressed into service from a nearby hostelry and outfitted
with green turbans and yellow togas, were made to sit cross-legged
like twin gods of the mountain. And atop the door, to be set melodi-
ously ringing at appropriate moments by a push-button neighbourly
to Mr. Belasco's great toe, was arranged a set of chimes.

This restful chamber was christened a "studio" and, so was the
news given out, it was here, amid these classic inspirations, that the
Belasco withdrew from the sordid, work-a-day world to woo the muse.
Among the muses that Belasco wooed in these surroundings was the
muse of dramatic criticism, for here were bidden from time to time,
with much flourish and ado, much subtle greasing and tony flim-flam,
the newspaper theatrical writers. One at a time, and after much stun-
ning hocus-pocus, were these gentlemen received. When they entered,
Mr. Belasco was invariably seen to be seated on the Ming dais, fore-
finger to brow, in attitude of profound and impressive meditation. All
was still as the tomb and dim, and but the thin spirals of the burning
joss sticks disturbed the solemn lull. Presently, as from a distance,
though in reality hidden under the dais, a music box began a sweet and
mellow lay. And as the music died away, a press-agent, secreted behind a heavy purple Beloochistan portière at R 1, made sweet sounds
on a small whistle filled with water as of a canary singing.

Suddenly then, as if startled out of deep reverie, would the surprised Belasco become aware of his guest's presence. As some kindly
and generous emperor, the Belasco would deign now bid the fellow near
his throne and, putting the fellow at his ease, would express to the

fellow his vast admiration for the fellow's critical and literary abilities and beseech his advice on how best to end the second act of the play he was even then working on. Allowing ample time for the grease to sink in good and deep, the Belasco would then descend in queenly abandon from the dais and sink wearily into the tufts of the Louis XIV *chaise* before the Louis XV table, meanwhile adroitly pressing the button under the table with his toe and setting the chimes over the door to dulcet playing. Followed now, *penseroso,* a lament on the crass commercialism of the theatre, ending up, *allegro,* with a quotation from Shakespeare and another from a recent article written by the visitor.... An hour later, the newspaper writer might be seen on the highway cutting one of his old friends dead.... And the following Sunday might be seen in his gazette a six column article attesting to the extraordinary intelligence, learning, discernment, taste, artistry, and genius generally of David Belasco, *maître* and wizard *extraordinaire* of the American theatre.

Gradually the legend, nursed and coddled now by an affectionately inscribed card at Yuletide, now it may be by a rarebit *à deux,* now mayhap by an irresistibly polite note of thanks for a favourable bit of written comment, spread its wings in Forty-fourth Street and flew with loud flutter far and wide across the countryside. Did the tradition perchance periodically show signs of drooping, then were *apéritifs* hustled to its reviving in the shape of a couple of recherché lamps hoisted in the aisles during the intermissions or in the shape of one of Gorham's country-house dinner gongs to signal the curtain's rise or in the shape of Reinhardt's old trick of sackcloth hangings for the boxes and proscenium during the presentation of a play of pious countenance or, more recently, in the shape of a series of profound essays on artistic stage illumination and like subjects (signed by Mr. Belasco, but written by Mr. Louis DeFoe) and in the shape of a legend-boosting autobiography written for the Belasco signature by a needy member of the Drama League.

As has been said, this ingenuous bait worked like magic and the yokelry swallowed it hook and sinker. For this Belasco was a clever man—the cleverest, and by all odds, in the native theatre—and, doubtless chuckling up his sleeve, for it is impossible to imagine him deceived by his own tin-pantaloonery, he witnessed the canonization of his simple humbug and through that simple humbug the canonization of himself by the absorbent rhapsodists. But this was yesterday.

Already there is considerable evidence, even in the newspapers, of a grievous *lèse majesté*. One observes a profane grinning and head-shaking. And the Belasco legend shows signs of soon going to the foot of the class to join its comrades, the stork and Santa Claus, Friedmann the tuberculosis curer and Eusapia Palladino, Doctor Cook and Gran-ville-Barker, Augustus Thomas the Dean and the Mann Act, black hose with white feet and Swiss vermouth, eugenics and neutrality, Rabin-dranath Tagore and the Russian Army.

What now is becoming belatedly apparent to the hoaxed Hazlittry and its proselytes has of course been familiar these many years to every one else. The facts, bereft of Ming sofas and perfumed punk sticks, are these. During his activity as a producer, Mr. Belasco has produced not one-fifteenth so many worthy plays as the late Charles Frohman pro-duced during a precisely corresponding period. Mr. Belasco has pro-duced *The Easiest Way, The Concert* and *The Phantom Rival*—three meritorious plays: so much and no more. As against these lonely three, he has presented an astounding procession of show-shop piffle includ-ing such things as *The Governor's Lady, The Woman, Seven Chances, The Fighting Hope, Alias, The Rose of the Rancho, Adrea, The War-rens of Virginia, A Good Little Devil, The Heart of Maryland, May Blossom, Peter Grimm, The Music Master, The Case of Becky, The Heart of Wetona, Men and Women, The Grand Army Man, The Wife, The Very Minute, Little Lady in Blue....* A show-shop peg higher, but certainly of not authentic stature, have been his presenta-tions such as *The Darling of the Gods,* shilling melodrama in Morocco binding; *The Lily,* one of the least interesting specimens of the modern French problem play; *The Boomerang,* a pleasant but unimportant trifle; *The Auctioneer,* not to be compared with the Montague Glass dramaturgy.... The financial success of most of these plays has, of course, no more relevance to the question of their artistic status than the financial success of the novels of A. N. and C. M. Williamson has to theirs.

During a like and parallel period of managerial activity, Charles Frohman, on the other hand, produced any number of plays of the order of *Peter Pan, Mid-Channel, The Legend of Leonora, L'Aiglon,*

The Silver Box, Alice-Sit-by-the-Fire, Preserving Mr. Panmure, The Twelve Pound Look, The Admirable Crichton, The Mollusc, The Hypocrites, His House in Order, A Wife Without a Smile, Trelawny of the Wells, The Importance of Being Earnest, Chantecler, The Tyranny of Tears—the plays of such as Ibsen, Shakespeare, Pinero, Rostand, Barrie, Fitch, Chambers, Galsworthy, Jones, Wilde and Ade as opposed to the Belasco catalogue of William C. DeMilles, Roi Megrues, Edward J. Lockes, John Meehans, Lee Arthurs, Wigney Percyvals, Willard Macks, Richard Walton Tullys and Victor Mapeses.

And Charles Frohman was and is not the only one. Winthrop Ames, who has been producing plays but a very short time in comparison with the lengthy career of Belasco, has in that brief period achieved a vastly more important position for himself through the presentation of such works as *Anatol, Strife, The Pigeon, Prunella, L'Enfant Prodigue, Old Heidelberg, Rutherford and Son, Sister Beatrice, The Thunderbolt, The Piper.* . . . William Faversham, during his few years as a producer, has done *The World and His Wife, The Faun, Othello, Julius Cæsar, Herod* and *Getting Married,* an honourable record marred only by the *flon flon* called *The Hawk.* True enough, these producers have also on occasion presented plays quite as seedy as those presented by Mr. Belasco, yet such plays have in their repertoire been the exception, certainly not, as with Mr. Belasco, the rule. . . .

To compare Belasco with such men afield as Antoine or Stanislavsky or Reinhardt—a fruity frolic of the newspapers—is to compare Holbrook Blinn with Max Maurey, Ned Wayburn with Meyerholdt or Butler Davenport with Victor Barnowsky. (Indeed, I do Mr. Wayburn, at least, something of an injustice. Mr. Wayburn has brought a great deal more to the music show stage than Mr. Belasco has brought to the dramatic.) Such comparisons are of course altogether too absurd to call for serious notice. These producers are as far removed from Belasco as is Mr. Ziegfeld from Al Reeves, or as is Arthur Hopkins from Corse Payton. A mere glance at their records, records brave with the production of fine drama, development of fine acting and successful research and innovation in stagecraft, is sufficient to shrivel to the vanishing point even the best of Belasco's achievements. Beside such men, beside even such second-rate producers as Granville-Barker or von Fassmann or Roebbeling, Belasco is a schoolboy in the art of the theatre. And beside the inventiveness and imagination of such as Marstersteig, Gordon Craig, Adolph Linnebach, or Hagemann, his inventiveness and imagination seem so much chintz. . . . But these are facts to be found by the bad sailor in the most accessible books of reference and I pose as no apothecary of news.

Mr. Belasco has contributed one—and only one—thing for judicious praise to the American theatre. He has brought to that theatre a standard of tidiness in production and maturation of manuscript, a standard that has discouraged to no little extent that theatre's erstwhile not uncommon frowzy hustle and slipshod manner of presentation. But what else? His plays, in the main, have been the sentimental vapourings of third- and fourth-rate writers. He has produced none of the classics; he has produced not a single modern first-rate British play or French play or German play; he has produced but two Austrian plays and one of these he deleted of its two most striking factors; he has encouraged no young American talent and those young Americans whom he has encouraged, he has encouraged to write not dramatic literature but so-called sure-fire shows, lending to their manuscripts his fecund aid in devising superficial hokums and punches and other such stuffs of the two dollar vaudevilles; he has developed, in all his career, but one actress, Miss Frances Starr; he has developed, in all his career, but a single actor, David Warfield—and this single actor he has long since stunted by casting him year in and year out in revivals of the lucrative trash of Lee Arthur and Charles Klein.

Upon what, then, does his eminence rest? The circusing, after the manner of Oscar Hammerstein, of an inferior actress who had come before the public notice through a sensational divorce case; the promulgation, as original, of a system of stage lighting that had been in use a long time before all over Germany and had already been borrowed by producers in the theatre in Russia; the promulgation, also as original, of a so-called ultra-realismus in stage settings which dates back to Charles Kean in the 1850's and which was elaborated to very nearly its present painful proportions by Otto Brahm in Berlin, if I am not mistaken, as far back as 1888 and carried even further two years later in the Moscow Art Theatre; the divulgation, also as original, in 1902, of a scenic treatment of such a play as *The Darling of the Gods,* already familiar to youthful students of a stage that years before had been occupied by Franz Ebert, Adolph Zink and the other imported lilliputians in an extravaganza called *The Magic Doll.*

I have been Mr. Belasco's guest in his theatres these many years. He has, with unfailing courtesy, regularly invited me to review his efforts and, with an equal courtesy, has uniformly assigned to the reception of my tender upholstery a most comfortable and well-placed seat—unlike the rude Mr. John Cort who always, with shrewd and uncanny precision, sits me in an ulterior pew without any stuffing in it and, to boot, directly behind a very fat gentleman guest who is given, particularly at tense dramatic moments, to stupendous and disconcerting nose-blowings. I admire Mr. Belasco as a showman—he is probably the best and certainly the most successful in the Anglo-American dramatic theatre. Indeed, if ever I write a bad play, I promise him the first refusal of it. I admire him for having gauged the American *esthetik* as probably no other showman since Adam Forepaugh and Barnum has gauged it. And I admire him, further, for having done several really good things really well. But, though he has been ever to me an urbane host and though ever he has subtly flattered my sense of humour by hesitating to bid me inspect his "studio" or his first-edition E. Phillips Oppenheims or his collection of Byzantine soup ladles, I cannot but believe, albeit unmannerly, that he has by his many counterfeits worked a vast and thorough ill to the American playhouse and its drama. And I cannot but further believe that his legend is ending to the brightening of a new and more understanding dawn in the native theatre.

From *Mr. George Jean Nathan Presents*
(Knopf, 1917).

DRAMA AS AN ART

By GEORGE JEAN NATHAN

"CONVICTIONS," said Nietzsche, "are prisons." Critical "theories," with negligible exception, seek to denude the arts of their splendid, gipsy gauds and to force them instead to don so many duplicated black and white striped uniforms. Of all the arts, drama has suffered most in this regard. Its critics, from the time of Aristotle, have bound and fettered it, and have then urged it impassionedly to soar. Yet, despite its shackles, it has triumphed, and each triumph has been a derision of one of its most famous and distinguished critics. It triumphed, through Shakespeare, over Aristotle; it triumphed, through Molière, over Castelvetro; it triumphed, through Lemercier, over Diderot; it triumphed, through Lessing, over Voltaire; it triumphed, through Ibsen, over Flaubert; it has triumphed, through Hauptmann, over Sarcey and, through Schnitzler and Bernard Shaw, over Mr. Archer. The truth perhaps is that drama is an art as flexible as the imaginations of its audiences. It is no more to be bound by rules and theories than such imaginations are to be bound by rules and theories. Who is so all-wise that he may say by what rules or set of rules living imaginations and imaginations yet unborn are to be fanned into theatrical flame? "Imagination," Samuel Johnson's words apply to auditor as to artist, "a licentious and vagrant faculty, unsusceptible of limitations and impatient of restraint, has always endeavoured to baffle the logician, to perplex the confines of distinction, and burst the inclosures of regularity." And further, "There is therefore scarcely any species of writing of which we can tell what is its essence, and what are its constituents; every new genius produces some innovation which, when invented and approved, subverts the rules which the practice of foregoing authors had established."

Does the play interest, and whom? This seems to me to be the only doctrine of dramatic criticism that is capable of supporting itself soundly. First, does the play interest? In other words, how far has the dramatist succeeded in expressing himself, and the materials before him, intelligently, eloquently, symmetrically, beautifully? So much for the criticism of the dramatist as an artist. In the second place, whom does the play interest? Does it interest inferior persons, or does it interest cultivated and artistically sensitive persons? So much for the criticism of the artist as a dramatist.

The major difficulty with critics of the drama has always been that, having once positively enunciated their critical credos, they have been constrained to devote their entire subsequent enterprise and ingenuity to defending the fallacies therein. Since a considerable num-

ber of these critics have been, and are, extraordinarily shrewd and ingenious men, these defences of error have often been contrived with
such persuasive dexterity and reasonableness that they have endured
beyond the more sound doctrines of less deft critics, doctrines which,
being sound, have suffered the rebuffs that gaunt, grim logic, ever
unprepossessing and unhypnotic, suffers always. "I hope that I am
right; if I am not right, I am still right," said Brunetière. "Mr. William
Archer is not only, like myself, a convinced, inflexible determinist,"
Henry Arthur Jones has written, "I am persuaded that he is also,
unlike myself, a consistent one. I am sure he takes care that his practice agrees with his opinions—even when they are wrong." Dramatic
criticism is an attempt to formulate rules of conduct for the lovable,
wayward, charming, wilful vagabond that is the drama. For the drama
is an art with a feather in its cap and an ironic smile upon its lips,
sauntering impudently over forbidden lawns and through closed lanes
into the hearts of those of us children of the world who have never
grown up. Beside literature, it is the Mother Goose of the arts: a gorgeous and empurpled Mother Goose for the fireside of impressible and
romantic youth that, looking upward, leans ever hushed and expectant
at the knee of life. It is a fairy tale told realistically, a true story told
as romance. It is the lullaby of disillusion, the chimes without the
cathedral, the fears and hopes and dreams and passions of those who
cannot fully fear and hope and dream and flame of themselves.

"The drama must have reality," so Mr. P. P. Howe in his engaging
volume of *Dramatic Portraits,* "but the first essential to our understanding of an art is that we should not believe it to be actual life. The
spectator who shouts his warning and advice to the heroine when the
villain is approaching is, in the theatre, the only true believer in the
hand of God; and he is liable to find it in a drama lower than the best."
The art of the drama is one which imposes upon drama the obligation of depicting at once the inner processes of life realistically, and the
external aspects of life delusively. Properly and sympathetically to
appreciate the drama, one must look upon it synchronously with two
different eyes: the one arguing against the other as to the truth of what
it sees, and triumphing over this doubtful other with the full force
of its sophistry. Again inevitably to quote Coleridge, "Stage presenta-
tions are to produce a sort of temporary half-faith, which the spectator

encourages in himself and supports by a voluntary contribution on his own part, because he knows that it is at all times in his power to see the thing as it really is. Thus the true stage illusion as to a forest scene consists, not in the mind's judging it to be a forest, but in its remission of the judgment that it is not a forest." This obviously applies to drama as well as to dramatic investiture. One never for a moment believes absolutely that Mr. John Barrymore is Richard III; one merely agrees, for the sake of Shakespeare, who has written the play, and Mr. Hopkins, who has cast it, that Mr. John Barrymore is Richard III, that one may receive the ocular, aural and mental sensations for which one has paid three dollars and a half. Nor does one for a moment believe that Mr. Walter Hampden, whom that very evening one has seen dividing a brobdingnagian dish of goulash with Mr. Oliver Herford in the Players' Club and discussing the prospects of the White Sox, is actually speaking extemporaneously the rare verbal embroideries of Shakespeare; or that Miss Ethel Barrymore who is billed in front of Browne's Chop House to take a star part in the Actors' Equity Association's benefit, is really the queen of a distant kingdom.

The dramatist, in the theatre, is not a worker of actualities, but in the essence of actualities that filters through the self-deception of his spectators. There is no such thing as realism in the theatre: there is only mimicry of realism. There is no such thing as romance in the theatre: there is only mimicry of romance. There is no such thing as an automatic dramatic susceptibility in a theatre audience: there is only a volitional dramatic susceptibility. Thus, it is absurd to speak of the drama holding the mirror up to nature; all that the drama can do is to hold nature up to its own peculiar mirror which, like that in a pleasure-park carousel, amusingly fattens up nature, or shrinks it, yet does not at any time render it unrecognizable. One does not go to the theatre to see life and nature; one goes to see the particular way in which life and nature happen to look to a cultivated, imaginative and entertaining man who happens, in turn, to be a playwright. Drama is the surprising pulling of a perfectly obvious, every-day rabbit out of a perfectly obvious, every-day silk hat. The spectator has seen thousands of rabbits and thousands of silk hats, but he has never seen a silk hat that had a rabbit concealed in it, and he is curious about it.

But if drama is essentially mimetic, so also—as Professor Gilbert Murray implies—is criticism essentially mimetic in that it is representative of the work criticized. It is conceivable that one may criticize Mr. Ziegfeld's *Follies* in terms of the *Philoctetes* of Theodectes—I myself have been guilty of even more exceptional feats; it is not only conceivable, but of common occurrence, for certain of our academic American critics to criticize the plays of Mr. Shaw in terms of Scribe and Sardou, and with a perfectly straight face; but criticism in general is a chameleon that takes on something of the colour of the pattern upon which it imposes itself. There is drama in Horace's *Epistola ad Pisones,* a criticism of drama. There is the spirit of comedy in Hazlitt's essay *On the Comic Writers of the Last Century.* Dryden's *Essay on Dramatic Poesy* is poetry. There is something of the music of Chopin in Huneker's critical essays on Chopin, and some of Mary Garden's spectacular histrionism in his essay on her acting. Walkley, criticizing *L'Enfant Prodigue,* uses the pen of Pierrot. Criticism, more than drama with her mirror toward nature, holds the mirror up to the nature of the work it criticizes. Its end is the revivification of the passion of art which has been spent in its behalf, but under the terms laid down by Plato. Its aim is to reconstruct a great work of art on a diminutive scale, that eyes which are not capable of gazing on high may have it within the reach of their vision. Its aim is to play again all the full richness of the artist's emotional organ tones, in so far as is possible, on the cold cerebral xylophone that is criticism's deficient instrument. In the accomplishment of these aims, it is bound by no laws that art is not bound by. There is but one rule: there are no rules. Art laughs at locksmiths.

It has been a favourite diversion of critics since Aristotle's day to argue that drama is drama, whether one reads it from a printed page or sees it enacted in a theatre. Great drama, they announce, is great drama whether it ever be acted or not; "it speaks with the same voice in solitude as in crowds"; and "all the more then"—again I quote Mr. Spingarn—"will the drama itself 'even apart from representation and actors,' as old Aristotle puts it, speak with its highest power to the imagination fitted to understand and receive it." Upon this point of view much of the academic criticism of drama has been based. But may we not well reply that, for all the fact that Shakespeare would still be the greatest dramatist who ever lived had he never been played in the theatre, so, too, would Bach still be the greatest composer who ever lived had his compositions never been played at all? If drama is not meant for actors, may we not also argue that music is not meant for instruments? Are not such expedients less sound criticism than clever evasion of sound criticism: a frolicsome and agreeable straddling of the æsthetic see-saw? There is the printed drama—criticize it. There is the same drama acted—criticize it. Why quibble? Sometimes, as in the case of *Gioconda* and Duse, they are one. Well and good. Sometimes, as in the case of *Chantecler* and Maude Adams, they are not one. Well and good. But where, in either case, the confusion that the critics lay such stress upon? These critics deal not with theories, but with mere words. They take two dozen empty words and adroitly seek therewith to fashion a fecund theory. The result is—words. "Words which," said Ruskin, "if they are not watched, will do deadly work sometimes. There are masked words droning and skulking about us just now... (there never were so many, owing to the teaching of catechisms and phrases at school instead of human meanings) ... there never were creatures of prey so mischievous, never diplomatists so cunning, never poisoners so deadly, as these masked words: they are the unjust stewards of men's ideas...."

From *The Critic and the Drama*
(Knopf, 1922.)

A TRIBUTE TO FLORENZ ZIEGFELD

By *GILBERT SELDES*

T H E incurable romanticist, George Jean Nathan, was the first to speak boldly in print and establish the rule of the silver-limbed, implacable Aphrodite in the theatre of Florenz Ziegfeld; and the equally incurable realist, Heywood Broun, has discovered that it isn't so. Mr. Nathan, obsessed by the idea that the world in general, and America in particular, goes to any extreme to conceal its interest in sex, really did a service to humanity by pointing out that there *were* beautiful girls in revues and that these girls constituted one of the main reasons for the attendance of men at the performances. Mr. Broun, sensing a lack of abandon and frenzy in the modern bacchanale, says, simply, that it isn't so, and implies that any one who could get a thrill out of that—! Like the king in that story of Hans Christian Andersen, of which Mr. Broun is inordinately fond, the girls haven't any clothes on; and this little child, noticing the fact, is dreadfully disappointed.

Now Mr. Ziegfeld is, in the opinion of those who work for him, a genius, and can well afford to say, "A plague on both your houses," for he has built up what he himself calls a national institution, glorifying, not degrading, the American girl (*pauvre petite*). He can afford to look with complacency upon undergraduates charging upon his theatre in the anticipation of unholy delights, and forced to bear the clownings of Eddie Cantor or the wise sayings of Will Rogers; then he can turn to Dr. John Roach Straton who, having heard from Mr. Broun that the *Follies* are chaste, approaches to see some monstrosity of a classic ballet and hears the vast decent sensuality of a jazz number instead.

Mr. Ziegfeld has lived through so much—through the period when it was believed indecent to be undressed and through the manlier period when nudity was contrasted with nakedness (it is the basis of a sort of Y. M. C. A. æsthetics that the nude is always pure) and through the long period, 1911-15, when the reviewers discovered the superior attractiveness of the stockinged leg; art in the shape of Joseph Urban has left a permanent mark upon him, and he has trafficked in strange seas for numbers and devices; what was vulgar and what was delicate, boresome and thrilling, having all passed through his hands; he has sent genius whistling down the wind to the vaudeville stage and built up new successes with secondary material; the storehouses are littered with the gaudy monuments of his imitators. And all the time the secret of his success has been staring Broadway in the face....

There are, if you count the chorus individually, about a hundred reasons for seeing a revue; there is only one reason for thinking about it, and that is that at one point, and only one point, the revue touches upon art. The revue as a production manifests the same impatience with half measures, with boggling, with the good enough and the nearly successful, which every great artist feels, or pretends to feel, in regard to his own work. It shows a mania for perfection; it aspires to be precise and definite, it corresponds to those *de luxe* railway trains which are always exactly on time, to the millions of spare parts that always fit, to the ease of commerce when there is a fixed price; jazz or symphony may sound from the orchestra pit, but underneath is the real tone of the revue, the steady, incorruptible purr of the dynamo. And with the possible exception of architecture, *via* the back door of construction, the revue is the most notable place in which this great American dislike of bungling, the real pleasure in a thing perfectly done, apply even vaguely to the arts.

If you can bring into focus, simultaneously, a good revue and a production of grand opera at the Metropolitan Opera House, the superiority of the lesser art is striking. Like the revue, grand opera is composed of elements drawn from many sources; like the revue, success depends on the fusion of these elements into a new unit, through the highest skill in production. And this sort of perfection the Metropolitan not only never achieves—it is actually absolved in advance from the necessity of attempting it. I am aware that it has the highest-paid singers, the best orchestra, some of the best conductors, dancers and stage hands, and the worst scenery in the world, in addition to an exceptionally astute impresario; but the production of these elements is so haphazard and clumsy that if any revue-producer hit as low a level in his work, he would be stoned off Broadway. Yet the Metropolitan is considered a great institution and complacently permitted to run at a loss, because its material is ART.

The same thing is true in other fields—in producing serious plays, in writing great novels, we will stand for a second-rateness we would not for a moment abide in the construction of a bridge or the making of an omelette, or the production of a revue. And because in a revue the bunk doesn't carry, the revue is one of the few places you can go with the assurance that the thing, however tawdry in itself, will be well done. If it is tawdry, it is so in keeping with the taste of its patrons, and without pretense; whereas in the major arts—no matter how magnificent the masquerade of Art may be—the taste of a production is usually several notches below the taste of the patrons.

The good revue pleases the eye, the ear, and the pulse; the very good revue does this *so well that it pleases the mind*. It operates in that equivocal zone where a thing does not have to be funny—it need only sound funny; nor be beautiful if it can for a fleeting moment appear beautiful. It does not have to send them away laughing or even whistling; all it needs to do is to keep the perceptions of the audience fully engaged all the time, and the evaporation of its pleasures will bring the audience back again and again.

The secret I have alluded to is how to create the atmosphere of seeming—and Mr. Ziegfeld knows the secret in every detail. In brief, he makes everything appear perfect by a consummate smoothness of production. Undoubtedly ten or fifteen other people help in this— I use Mr. Ziegfeld's name because in the end he is responsible for the kind of show put out in his name and because the smoothness I refer to goes far beyond the mechanism of the stage or skill in directing a chorus. It is not the smoothness of a connecting rod running in oil, but of a batter where all the ingredients are so promptly introduced and so thoroughly integrated that in the end a man may stand up and say, This is a Show. Everyone with a grain of sense knows that Mr. Urban can make all the sets for a production and Mr. Berlin write all the music; Mr. Ziegfeld has the added grain to see that if he's going to have a great variety of things and people, he had better divide his *décor* and his music among many different talents.

There have been funnier revues and revues more pleasing to the eye and revues with far better popular music; nowhere have all the necessary ingredients appeared to such a high average of advantage. Mr. Anderson could barely keep Bert Savoy within the bounds of a revue; the Music Box collapses entirely as a revue at a few dance steps by Bobby Clark. But Ziegfeld as early as 1910 was able to throw together Harry Watson (Young Kid Battling Dugan, nowadays, in vaudeville), Fannie Brice, Anna Held, Bert Williams, and Lillian Lorraine and, as if to prove that he was none the less producing a revue, bring down his curtain on a set-piece of "Our American Colleges." And twelve years later, with Will Rogers and Gilda Gray and Victor Herbert and Ring Lardner, he is still producing a revue and brings both curtains down on his chorus—once *en masse* and the second time undressing for the street in silhouette.

I cannot estimate the amount of satisfaction which since those early days Mr. Ziegfeld has provided. My own memories do not go back to the actual productions in which Anna Held figured; I recall only the virtuous indignation of elderly people and my own mixed feelings of curiosity and disgust when I overheard reports of the goings-on. But from the time I begin to remember them until to-day there has always been a peculiar quality of pleasure in the Ziegfeld shows, and the uninterrupted supply of things pleasant to see and entertaining to hear, has been admirable. Mr. Ziegfeld has never been actually courageous; his novelties are never more audacious than, say, radio-lite costumes or an Urban backdrop. He is apparently pledged to the tedious set-pieces which are supposed to be artistic—the Ben Ali Haggin effects, the Fan in Many Lands or the ballet of A Night in Statuary Hall with the discobolus coming to life and the arms of the Venus de Milo miraculously restored. There are years, too, in which Mr. Ziegfeld, discovering new talent, follows but one vein and leaves his shows so much in one tone that a slight depression sets in. Mr. Edmund Wilson, in the *Dial,* repeats the plaint of Mr. Heywood Broun in the *World*—that the *Follies* are frigid—the girls are all straight, the ballet becomes a drill, the very laughs are organized and mechanical. Well, it happens to be the function of the Ziegfeld *Follies* to be Apollonic, not Dionysian; the leap and the cry of the bacchanale give way to the song and dance, and when we want the true frenzy we have to go elsewhere. I doubt whether even the success of the negro shows will frighten Ziegfeld into mingling with his other elements some that will be riotous and wild; the best they can do will be to prevent Ziegfeld from growing too utterly "refined." He tends at this moment to quiet fun of the Lardner type and the occasional horseplay with which he accentuates this murmur, this smile, is usually unsuccessful. I am, myself, more moved by broader strokes than his, but I recognize that Ziegfeld, and not the producers of *Shuffle Along,* is in the main current of our development—that we tend to a mechanically perfect society in which we will either master the machine or be enslaved by it. And the only way to master it—since we cannot escape—will be by understanding it in every detail. That is exactly Mr. Ziegfeld's present preoccupation.

From *The Seven Lively Arts*
(Harper, 1924).

WHAT PRICE GLORY?

By ALEXANDER WOOLLCOTT

NO war play written in the English language since the German guns boomed under the walls of Liege, ten years ago, has been so true, so alive, so salty and so richly satisfying as the piece called *What Price Glory?,* which was produced last evening by Arthur Hopkins.

The premiere marked the reopening of the eventful Plymouth Theatre, and though a good many lines have been spouted and a good many curtains have gone frantically up and down since the middle of last month, the first night of *What Price Glory?* may be said to have inaugurated the theatrical season of 1924-1925. The first audience gave the play such a welcome as we have seldom seen matched in these many years of Broadway. Among those who, after the final curtain, remained quietly in their seats and roared was your correspondent.

The play is the joint work of Maxwell Anderson and Laurence Stallings, both members of the editorial staff of the *New York World,* more frequently known on such glowing occasions as "a morning newspaper." Mr. Anderson is the man whose tragedy, *White Desert,* served notice on us all that an interesting newcomer had started to write for the American stage. Presumably Mr. Stallings, sometime Captain of the United States Marines on duty in Belleau Wood, supplied the color. He was there.

And out of this fertile collaboration has come a play which smells of the war as it was really fought, which is alive with tough, verminous leathernecks as they really talked and thought and looked there in the cellars of Bouresches or in the little, evil smelling villages not far from La Ferte-sous-Jouarre. Compared with these men, who have their little day in the three acts of *What Price Glory?,* all the other stage officers and soldiers that have charged upon us from the embattled dressing rooms of Broadway have seemed to step glistening from some magazine cover painted in the thick of a Chicago studio.

The play really concerns itself with a murderous but not altogether unenjoyable duel between a captain and his top sergeant. And their complete oblivion of any world beyond the limits of the fox holes where they have burrowed or the village where they are billeted gives the play at once an isolation and a truth that is of immeasurable value.

Indeed the war falls back and leaves these two silhouetted against the skyline. There is this sergeant who has soldiered nonchalantly in every town from Vera Cruz to Pekin, "from the halls of Montezuma to the shores of Tripoli." There is this captain, who is as tough as leather, who takes to battle like a duck to water (to coin a phrase), but who is troubled in a fight when the powers that be supply him only with little boys who have no business there at all. There are these two and a serene French hussy in their billet town, just as there was a Spanish jade between them once in Manila and a pretty Chinese girl in Pekin.

The war, its immensity and its folly and its crushing evidence of human failure, is no more mentioned than it would be mentioned in a fine artist's painting of Belleau Wood. Yet, in the tremendous irony of the comedy and in the sardonic laughter which fills its every scene, there is more said about the war than in all the editorials on the subject which, if placed end to end, would reach nowhere.

There has been some preliminary hanky-panky about the rough talk in which the play abounds, and indeed we are making such progress in this respect that the cussing in *Rain* seems to have reached to the prettiness of *Daddy Long Legs*. You may be sure there has been some editing, for the American stage is not yet ready for the undiluted speech of the United States Marines. Indeed the favorite participial utterance of that distinguished corps is not once heard in the length and breadth of *What Price Glory?* It need only be recorded that the effect of true soldier talk is achieved by some happy selective process—far better achieved, for instance, than it was in *Three Soldiers* or in the truncated frenzies of *The Hairy Ape*.

It remains to be said that the second act, which is the battle scene, is so marked a subsidence in the march of the play as to have the effect of an intermezzo. But it is vividly interesting in its own right.

It remains also to be said that Mr. Hopkins has cast and directed the play expertly, with Louis Wolheim and William Boyd doing the best work of their years in the theatre. And there is fine work by Leyla Georgie, Fuller Mellish, Jr., George Tobias, Sidney Elliott and J. Merrill Holmes. It remains also to be said that the writer of this review intends to see *What Price Glory?* on every spare night for the rest of the season. The theatre in that time is not likely to offer better fare.

From *The New York Evening Sun*,
September 6, 1924.

AN AMERICAN TRAGEDY

By ALEXANDER WOOLLCOTT

THEY tell me that Horace Liveright, our doughty fellow towns-man who not only published *An American Tragedy* as a novel but also engineered its present success upon the stage, has decided to attend no more performances of the play. His reason for this stupefying renunciation, it seems, is that the play as performed nightly at the Longacre (matinees Wednesday and Saturday) moves him too pro-foundly. Each time he has attended a performance the Liveright depths have been so shaken that next day he was just a wreck.

Now, if all has gone as planned, the mighty Dreiser himself, but recently returned from foreign parts, has at last seen this puppet show contrived from his overwhelming novel. And it would not surprise me a bit to hear that he too would refrain from a return visit to the Longacre. Indeed, I would even learn without amazement that he had sworn off after the second act. I do not know how perceptive a playgoer Theodore Dreiser is, but I should think the mess the theatre has made of *An American Tragedy* would permanently impair his health.

It seems to me a gauche, spasmodic, almost childishly concocted melodrama, preposterously miscast. It is, I might add, a great success.

Nor can its conspicuous rush of trade be dismissed as the mere temporary stampede of the ardent Dreiserites to see their cherished book done into a play. After all, the sales of *An American Tragedy* to date come to something less than 52,000 copies, and besides in the audience in which I was embedded on Thursday night I doubt if one in fifty had ever heard of Theodore Dreiser. Indeed, after listening to the entr'acte chatter and looking at the faces agape and breathing hard in my vicinity, I was moved to wonder whether my neighbors had recently read anything more taxing than the memoirs of the reticent Mrs. Browning. From this audience the capitally written and well acted seduction scene in Roberta Alden's mean little bedroom elicited a hubbub that was neither laughter nor tears nor protest. It was just a chorus of squeals and in a dim light the Longacre rather suggested a large, emotion-swept sty.

To get as many of the bare facts of the book into a play as possible, Patrick Kearney had to pack tight, and then sit on the lid. The resultant telescoping of the story had the odd effect of transforming Dreiser's puzzled, storm-tossed, inert bit of American driftwood into an intensive Lothario. Indeed, as the play, with the nimbleness of a mountain goat, leaped from Roberta's dingy bed to Sondra's pillowy sofa on Thursday night, I could hear the dilettante bookworms around me murmuring: "Gee, that kid is cert'n'y a fast worker. That's what he is, a fast worker. Yes, sir, a fast worker."

It seems to me too that Morgan Farley was the worst imaginable choice for the central rôle. That, of course, is a faint exaggeration. One would prefer him, let us say, to Louis Mann in the rôle. Or Gail Kane. But he does come near to being the exact opposite of the quality which Dreiser's work called for. It is a trifle too much like casting Clifton Webb as Huckleberry Finn.

As every one knows, *An American Tragedy* had its origins in the arrest, trial and execution of an ornery young nobody named Chester Gillette. What led Dreiser into the field of that murder and bade him fence it in as his own was its great normality, its suggestion of disaster happening to the folks across the street. This was no Thaw case, lunatic spawn of the white lights, no Leopold and Loeb case, monstrously peopled as with creatures from some nether world. When, twenty years ago, the hapless Chester Gillette pushed poor Grace

Brown beneath those whispering Adirondack waters, we were all sick with the sense that it was one of us who had done this thing. And Dreiser, brooding on what unperceived, casual wrong turning must have sent this drifting youth to the death house instead of to the brotherhood of Rotary, wrought at last the plodding epic called *An American Tragedy*. It is a great book, great in proportion as it earns the tacit sub-title "Even as You and I." The play called for an actor who would suggest implicitly the average humdrum American youngster. Mr. Farley is a museum piece.

In addition to this natural handicap, his performance seemed to me quite distressing. He is a great one to dart about, being wistful with his elbows. And dramatic schools should be led in droves to watch one scene of his as an admonishing example. That is the scene in which the play tries to reproduce from the book the slow, sick, floundering indecision by which the plan to do away with Roberta rises like a shape of mist in Clyde's miasmic torment.

First Clyde is discovered alone in his lodgings. Enter landlady, equipped with newspaper to read aloud to him an account of a drowning in Big Bittern Lake, a canoe upsetting, a girl's death. As soon as he is left alone, Clyde must seize the paper and read it to himself and, since Mr. Farley is the kind of actor who expresses even mild surprise by wrenching his face out of drawing, you can imagine the playground for the emotions which that mobile face becomes during this reading. A playground? Nay, a Coney Island for the emotions, with merry-go-rounds, loop-the-loops and everything. Then, in case the audience should not be any too bright, Clyde next hurls the paper to the floor, trembles violently, then picks the paper up again with the agility of a slow motion picture, points to the article in the manner of a show window demonstrator and even says out loud: "Roberta cannot swim." He then shudders six times. If an intelligence test of subsequent audiences should indicate that even this is insufficient, I would suggest that Mr. Farley then lie face down on the floor and do an Australian crawl stroke as just another helpful hint.

From *The New York World,* October 25, 1926.
[Reprinted in *Going to Pieces.* (Putnam, 1928.)]

LILLIAN GISH'S CAMILLE

By ALEXANDER WOOLLCOTT

HERE are some program notes set down by one who is uneasily aware that he has already become an Old Playgoer. At least I feel a growing kinship with the aged banker who once wrote me that, beginning with Samuel Phelps at Clerkenwell, he had seen seventy-eight Macbeths and that, as I could well imagine, Walter Hampden was the worst of the lot. There comes a time when such a one totters off to a fresh revival with the acquisitive eagerness of a maniacal philatelist in pursuit of a fugitive Nicaraguan. In short, he goes only to complete his set. Thus I suspect it was chiefly as an irrational collector of theatrical memorabilia that I hied me to New Haven one day last week to see the tear-stained relic which the young man who wrote it called *The Camellia Lady*. The audience was recruited to a considerable extent from the undergraduate body at Yale. Then Boardman Robinson was there because his son was playing a footman in Act One—a footman who, by Act Four, had joined the *jeunesse dorée* and, unless my eyes deceived me, was dancing heartlessly in the gambling hell on the night of Marguerite's great humiliation. Also present—in New Haven, that is, not in the gambling hell—was Thornton Wilder, there because he had never chanced to see the play before. But scattered throughout the theatre were enough of us incorrigible old-timers to have justified some such notice in the program as "Wheel-chairs at Eleven."

It would be a satisfaction, I thought, to see the lovelorn Marguerite played, for once in a way, by a young actress who, in her own person, would suggest the cool, sweet, fragile, phthisic courtesan that the younger Dumas had in mind when he wrote the play. That was Alphonsine Plessis who, doing business under the name of Marie Duplessis, was once, for a little time, the talk of Paris. Dumas, *fils,* had an affair with her which his father was able to break up without having to appeal to her better nature. He broke it up by the more prosaic device of treating his son to the expense of a trip to Spain. By the time the youth returned to Paris, his lady lay buried in Montmartre Cemetery where you can see her grave today. While he was busy covering it with camellias and himself with reproaches, the poor girl's creditors were auctioning off the contents of her flat. Sundry agitated old gentlemen from the Faubourg St.-Germain bid high for such desks and cabinets as might conceivably shelter the letters they had been so careless as to write her. All this was noted with fine English disapproval by Mr. Dickens, who was in Paris at the time, and who, bless his heart, went off, buckety-buckety, to attend the sale.

The grief of the bereft Dumas took the form of a novel, and from that he made the play which was first acted in this country by Jean Davenport under the title of *Camille: or The Fate of a Coquette*. It was then successfully taken over by the lovely Matilda Heron, who translated her own version but still clung to the preposterous Davenport title, which has always bewildered the French. (Miss Heron's grandson, by the way, has made a name for himself in the theatre, said name being Gilbert Miller.) From the first, America delighted in *Camille,* and up to thirty years ago most of the actresses, foreign as well as native, played the part at one time or another—even Modjeska, despite William Winter's plea to her that she not degrade her art by portraying a fallen woman, and despite the pitfalls of a Polish accent which necessitated her crying out "Armong, I loaf you!" The Marguerite Gautier of Dumas's imagination was a wasted, waxen girl who died when she was twenty, but she was so often depicted in Nineteenth-Century America by robust actresses in full bloom that I suppose most people grew to think of her as one who had died of gluttony.

Then I suspect I was drawn to the ticket booth of this latest revival by an incurable wonder about Lillian Gish. A mockingly elusive phenomenon, Miss Gish. Was she a good actress? Was she an actress at all? After seeing the pastel wraith which she substituted for the smouldering Helena of *Uncle Vanya,* I rather thought not. But she was so grotesquely miscast as the disastrous woman in that lovely play that I went to *Camille* with an open mind. It is still open.

I do not envy the task of the reviewers who must try to make an intelligible report on that baffling performance. It will be easy enough to describe its obvious shortcomings, its emotional emptiness, the pinched little voice which reduces all her colloquies to an arid prattle. One has the illusion of watching *Camille* played by a small-town high-school girl. This is part of an abiding immaturity which one finds difficult to describe in such words as will distinguish it from arrested development. It is the immaturity of a pressed flower—sweet, cherishable, withered. It has a gnomelike unrelation to the processes of life and death. It has the pathos of little bronze dancing boots, come upon suddenly in an old trunk. It is the ghost of something that has passed this way—the exquisite print of a fern in an immemorial rock. It is of a quality for which I can find no words. As you see.

Then, when one has said all that, how shall one find other words for certain moments of loveliness which, by sorcery, she does impart to this fond and foolish old play? All around her in the death scene there is a shining light which the puzzled electrician cannot account for. And when she retreats into the garden in Auteuil, there passes over her a shadow as delicate and fleeting as the reflection of a cloud in the mirror of a quiet lake. Or am I babbling? I really do not know how to translate into print the tantalizing mystery of Lillian Gish. I do wish America had never been wired for sound.

Even so, I shall buy me a ticket when next she treads the boards in our town in another play. Even after seeing *Camille*. Even after reading that astounding opus of Albert Bigelow Paine's declining years, *Life and Lillian Gish,* which, insofar as I have had the strength to examine it, seems to me, in a quiet way, the most sickening book of our time.

From *The New Yorker,* October 22, 1932.
Reprinted in *While Rome Burns* (Viking Press, 1934).

SUSAN GLASPELL'S *THE VERGE*

By *STARK YOUNG*

NO play of Susan Glaspell's can be passed over quite so snippily as most of the reviewers have done with *The Verge;* for Miss Glaspell is one of the few people we have in our theatre who are watching the surface of life to find new contents and material.

The Verge turns around the life of a woman who is conceived by the author as having a certain clarity of vision beyond the common;

a Nietzschean woman, though not a conscious disciple; a mystic and a revolutionary; who because of all this is isolated from the people around her; tries to break from them and from herself. Meanwhile because she is so far from them perhaps, she attracts the men about her; she is something connected with their dreams, and their short flights from the daily actual. With her gift for science this woman feeds her violent absorption in herself and in her chances to break through to some other form of life. She is not the practical scientist working with experiments for solid results; nor is she the purely scientific investigator, for she makes discoveries partly by intuition, as Goethe did or Leonardo or Strindberg. She makes no separations in the universe and so looks through her observations of nature to the one life that runs through all things; and she lives in the conviction that what is true in nature may be true in human beings also. And so working on the de Vries theory of the development of species, she sees that plants break up, explode, and from this mutation when there is the right combination of individuals and environment, a new species may appear which will be isolated from the rest and carry life with it from the life it left. And so the dream possesses her that perhaps she can be this individual in the midst of her own species, may suffer isolation and be split away into a new life, having exploded her species as the plants do theirs because something in them knows that they have gone as far as they can go. All of which, obviously, is hard to state in words or character; but it bears on the newer psychology and is worth while trying, unless the theatre plans to go on dodging the modern ego.

If you listen closely to the lines you can hear all this. But if you give your attention to the acting of *The Verge* at the Provincetown Theatre you will meet with confusion. The Provincetown idea at the outset was to stick to amateurs in presenting plays; to approach something perhaps more in the nature of readings. It is a thousand pities they ever departed from this. Mr. Reese as the husband was so ingenuously unprofessional that he left you quite free to hear the lines whose meaning he could not act. Miss Glaspell's fine conception of Claire's gardener, a plant himself, following mutely her will, was not much hurt by Mr. Hallet's getting between it and us; and that daughter, bolstered with exactly the cant and pietistic humanitarianism and glib platitude that goes in young ladies' colleges just now, came out well enough with Miss Berry in it. Miss Wycherly did more than anyone else to throw the play off.

To begin with, the production works overtime in that first act; the place rattles too much with the wind, the clouds in the sky overwork, the actors do too much, the comedy comes out perplexing; and Miss Wycherly is all these things together. In the play there is an ominous comedy around something that is isolated, apart, that is driven to eccentricity, but that burns and glows and fascinates by its intensity of living. The part of the woman there should be seen with a certain single, pristine unity; the power and charm of her must come from the fixedness of her soul and the intangible poetry of her outline. The rôle should be played quietly, transparently, continuously; flashes of wit and shy defence and hot feeling but all flowing continuous and deep within. The movement should appear always from the spirit, the focus of the body following slowly after, almost absent in this infinite absorption. Miss Wycherly plays what the actor will play, his art; he feels that he must do something. She fidgets her arms neurotically; she is a conscious oddity; she has force but it is an erratic force. She gets all the afflictions but none of the point. And she is even coquettish, and swings her knees, and Forest of Ardens around like a British Rosalind, as if in fact we were going to have a comedy. I could not help remembering Miss Blair on the same stage last year in that first act of Diff'rent, that stiff little body stuffed into its awkward dress, the heavy, plain hair, the arms awkward and solemn, standing there repeating the same awkward little phrases over and over again, as she herself was repeated over and over again in the stiff lines of her little figure; how pathetic it was, and tense, and withdrawn! But yet, if we believe in good intentions—which really mean nothing in art—all I have said about Miss Wycherly must be untrue. You can see that she is sincerely trying after the part, is a serious artist, profoundly striving. Very well then, let's say she works too hard at it. She forgets what Æschylus knew, who said that all that gods work is effortless and calm. Her efforts drive out the gods that are visiting this woman and leave only problems and oddities and confusion.

The most completely done thing about The Verge is the love scene. In it there is a mixture of matter that is fresh on our stage, is at the same time scientific, vivid, intimate, and searching; and through all these is exciting. And what's more, this immediacy and truth and freshness make an excitement that is the same as that which good poetry has always achieved with its method and imagery. Miss Wycherly does fine work here, when she lies on the sofa in that amazing tower and says so quietly and beautifully the words that are struggling to find themselves. She knows how to do that. But once she got on her feet, she insisted and debated too much and was jerkier than ever. And these neurotic gestures were unfortunately heightened by the gleaming mass of sequins or beads or whatever it was that spread over her gown at the knees and extravagantly echoed the body and elbows.

As to the play itself its chief trouble is a lack of sufficient articulation, accentuation. And there are also too many words and phrases that run toward cant, too much about otherness, farness and so on, which could be cut down for good taste, and so assure us that the author confined them to the character and the moment and knew their doubtful nature. But the main idea of *The Verge* provokes the imagination and sense of wonder, and supplies that reminder of the strange and unguessed in life that is the source of all art. Such a play is an experiment, and nobody can expect it to spring full blown and perfect from the author's forehead. Art forever dilates its being with new matter, new life. And this in time finds its right form; since soul is form and doth the body make, as Spenser says. Prattling about new forms in the theatre and then fighting any attempt at new material is a poor game. We shall never have new form without having first the new matter, of which the soul becomes at length the form.

From *The New Republic,*
December 7, 1921.

A LETTER TO DUSE

By STARK YOUNG

M A D A M E : We are told here that you are coming and that you are not coming. I saw you some years ago in *La Gioconda,* in *Paolo and Francesca,* in *La Citta Morta* and in *Magda,* before you withdrew from the stage. And now that you have returned to the theatre and are playing in Genoa and Turin and Florence, we are hoping in America that you will come again. We hear that you go on the stage with only the glamour of your intense sincerity, without any puppetry, with small make-up, with your gray hair, admitting life as it stands in you under the sad laws of time, and showing to all who will read it there the writing on you of your real and ideal living. One knows that you would do that, that like a great artist you would admit your medium for what it is and work within it.

Those who have never seen you, madame, have heard how you played. They have heard how you seemed to put into the art of acting a modernity so simple and translucent that it seemed as old as the theatre. They have heard of the oneness of your art, the quiver and directness of your playing. They have heard how single your quality was, though the rôles might vary, as the light is single in which the various world is revealed. They have noticed that people who have understood you wish somehow to protect you, as if one were shy about your exquisiteness. And they have seen your photograph.

The face, madame, that they see there holds them. It has something more moving than the more immediately poetic or outwardly beautiful can be; what this face has is a kind of realism of tragic beauty. It has in it the thing that is most terrible and that we worship in life, that last and exquisite thing in life, a supreme response to it. We look at your face and feel that a sob is there, but withheld through the force of the general and universal poignancy and tragic intelligence behind it. Madame, whenever I read Dante, the picture of you keeps coming before my eyes.

The reader of our English poetry coming fresh on Dante for the first time, turns his hungry and astonished eyes on a passage like that of the two lovers who went together and seemed so light on the wind; and reads

"Amor condusse noi ad una morte."

and then Francesca's words when they read how the beloved smile was kissed by such a lover, and this one who never should be divided from her kissed her mouth all trembling,

"Quando legemmo il disiato riso
esser baciato da cotanto amante,
questi, che mai da me non sia diviso,
la bocca mi bació tutto tremante":

And a long way farther on in the book he comes on those lines about human desires and the end of day, the hour when longing returns to sailors and penetrates the heart, *intenerisce il core,* the day that they have said good-by to their sweet friends; and the new wanderer, *lo novo peregrin,* is pierced with love if he hears far-off bells that seem to weep the dying day. And the reader is amazed. Never before has he read anything in poetry so close, so free, so tender and direct and pitiful and exact.

Madame, that poetry has the permeation, the tender exactitude, that is your art. And like that poetry it might have happened yesterday, it might not happen until to-morrow, the thing I remember as your acting.

Madame, we need you in America to remind us that for every man there is only his kind of truth to make in the end any sense for him. The only purpose for him is that which, to use Dante's phrase, will give him wax to light him to his summit. The rest is competition, tricks, unrest, and satiety without exercise. You force into everything the soul of its reality; and so expose its truth or its incapacity and falseness. Whatever kind of part you take, romantic, rollicking comic, poetic, or highly naturalistic, you give the same truth to it by living out and bringing to completion its characteristic quality. Your art is your own perpetual dilation of reality. You have no false purposes, you never conclude, you never solve, you only create and reveal. Most of all, madame, our young actors need you.

These young actors, plenty of them, have talent, have dreams. But they are confused. They see promiscuous advertising and press comment that seem to assure them that they may follow as great artists actors who have nothing to go on but personality, insolence, ignorance, or superficial charm or good luck. These young actors have few good models of anything except success. They hear on all sides that acting copies nature, that their business is to reproduce what they see in life. And so they try, the better of them, to copy nature before they have eyes to see it with. They are given parts that seem by mere resemblance and the accident of individual characteristics to fit them, and they are kept in these parts. They are told practical points and try to carry those points out in order to carry themselves over the footlights and beyond to the electric signs over the doors. These young actors want to get on, that is only human. But they need to learn to express what they themselves have to express; they need to lean on life, not on expedients. They need to see that in you always there is something that the great artists must always have, something that baffles, something withheld. What we get in you, madame, is only the echo of all you are. And this will teach them the emptiness of the poor little show of themselves that they make. You are the artist and the performance is yours; but behind all that, as the world of nature is behind a flower, is you. You are an actor but first you are yourself.

Madame, you can teach these young actors what realism is. They are confused. Half a century of prose and thin science and problems have taught them that realism is the matter-of-fact, the provable and visible and immediately logical. They think that realism is brutality, is the journalistic, the photographic or the drab. In modern drama they have learned a self-conscious social sense; they become not so much artists as they do judges. Those who cannot create have been obliged to solve.

Madame, you know what realism is. To you, from the very start, the theatre, as Huysmans said of schools in literature, is neither realistic nor poetic; it is only good or bad, true or false. Your realism has commanded both sides. The stubbornest realists found it true beyond their wildest preaching and formulas. What you gave them they could never have discovered but could always recognize. The poets flocked to you because your kind of truth was theirs; like them, you created a soul in reality.

Madame, your realism does not accept the surface of things and does not accept your own body, but forces these toward a more intricate and luminous expression of the life hidden within. Your realism begins with the pressure of life from within out, the permeation of the entire object with its spiritual actuality. And so in your art feeling becomes plastic, as if you were the sculptor of your own soul. One seems to see in your presence radiance, spirit, something like music and falling wind, a strange identity with trees and air and light. But at the same time one seems to hear the sound of the blood in your veins. Your words seem to come to us through your blood. The underlying, intense, and most urgent and beautiful precision of your art gives us the tremendous shock and quiver of life. And to such a realism as this, a formal or poetic art comes as natural as a gesture to a living hand; it meets no sudden break, but is a consummation of the truth that was present, though in a less degree, from the very start. From your Hedda Gabler to your Francesca would be a continuous line.

Madame, you, of all artists in the theatre, know that, seen most deeply, life becomes a dream; there is so much of our own reality added to it that nowhere out of ourselves can it exist. And your kind of realism easily becomes mystical; it renders everything, and because it is so exact, so patient and so infinite can give back their mystery to things and make them like a dream again.

From *The Flower in Drama*.
(Scribner's, 1923.)

ABIE'S IRISH ROSE BULLETINS

By ROBERT C. BENCHLEY

AFTER *Abie's Irish Rose* opened in New York on February 21, 1926, Mr. Benchley's first report of it in *Life* ran as follows: *"Abie's Irish Rose* is the kind of play in which a Jewish boy, wanting to marry an Irish girl named Rosemary Murphy, tells his orthodox father that her name is Rosie Murphesky, and the wedding proceeds. Any further information, if such could be necessary, will be furnished at the old offices of *Puck,* the comic weekly which flourished in the 'nineties. Although the paper is no longer in existence, there must be some old retainer still about the premises who could tell you everything that is in *Abie's Irish Rose."*

Thereafter, for the five long years, Mr. Benchley was faced with the problem of describing the play in different terms for each week's issue of *Life* in his Confidential Guide. It is from these numerous "tabloid critiques" that the following selection has been made.

1922

FULTON THEATRE

Something awful.
Among the season's worst.
Eighty-ton fun.

REPUBLIC THEATRE

Comic supplement stuff.
Made up of jokes from the files of *Puck* when McKinley was running for President the first time.
People laugh at this every night, which explains why a democracy can never be a success.
Just about as low as good, clean fun can get.
Contains everything of the period except a character who says, "Skiddoo."
It takes all kinds of people to make a world and a lot of them seem to like this.
For the people who like the "funnies."
Well, it seems there was a Jew and an Irishman walking down the street....

1923

Denounced continuously as cheap by this department since last May, but apparently unconscious of the fact.
The management sent us some pencils for Christmas; so maybe it isn't so bad after all.
We give up.
The success of this shows that the older a joke is, the better they like it.
Where do the people come from who keep this going? You don't see them out in the daytime.
The fact that there are enough people to keep this going explains why Hylan is Mayor of New York.

Showing that the Jews and the Irish crack equally old jokes.

The kind of comedy you eat peanuts at.

In its second year, God forbid.

The country's most popular comedy, constituting a reflection on either this department or the country.

America's favorite comedy, which accounts for the number of shaved necks on the street.

Judging from the thousands who see and like this play, Henry Ford has a good chance of being our next President.

1924

In another two or three years we'll have this play driven out of town.

Answer to J. M. B.'s query: No, this was not written by Sir James Barrie.

Shall we join the ladies?

The one thing that will keep us from being President of the United States.

Heigh-ho!

An interesting revival of one of America's old favorites.

Fill this in for yourself. You know the idea.

The play which made Edwin Booth famous.

My, my, here it is November again!

Come on, now! A joke's a joke.

And a Merry Christmas to you, Miss Nichols!

1925

Contest line (in guide) closes at midnight, or at the latest, quarter past midnight, on Jan. 8. At present, Mr. Arthur Marx is leading with "No worse than a bad cold."

The Phoenicians were among the early settlers of Britain.

Thirty days have September, April, June and November. All the rest have thirty-one, excepting February alone.

They put an end to the six-day bicycle races by tearing down Madison Square Garden. How about a nice, big office building on the present site of the Republic theatre?

The oldest profession in the world.

There are 5,280 feet in a mile.

We will settle for $5,000.

The big Michael Arlen hit.

So's your old man.

See Hebrews 13:8.

We understand that a performance of this play in modern dress is now under way.

1926

Dun't esk.

Closing soon (Only fooling).

And that, my dears, is how I came to marry your grandfather.

From *Life,* 1922 to 1926.

O'NEILL'S *MOURNING BECOMES ELECTRA*

By ROBERT C. BENCHLEY

I N the midst of the acclaim with which Eugene O'Neill is being so justly hailed for his latest and most gigantic *tour de force, Mourning Becomes Electra,* and in the confusion of cross-references to the Greek dramatists from whom he derived his grim and overpowering story, are we not forgetting one very important source of his inspiration, without which he might perhaps have been just a builder of word-mountains? Was there not standing in the wings of the Guild Theatre, on that momentous opening night, the ghost of an old actor in a white wig, with drawn sword, who looked on proudly as the titanic drama unfolded itself, scene by scene, and who murmured, with perhaps just the suggestion of a chuckle: "That's good, son! Give 'em the old Theatre!"? The actor I refer to needs no introduction to the older boys and girls here tonight—Mr. James O'Neill, "The Count of Monte Cristo" and the father of our present hero.

Let us stop all this scowling talk about "the inevitability of the Greek tragedy" and "O'Neill's masterly grasp of the eternal verities" and let us admit that the reason why we sat for six hours straining to hear each line through the ten-watt acoustics of the Guild Theatre was because *Mourning Becomes Electra* is filled with good, old-fashioned, spine-curling melodrama. It is his precious inheritance from his trouper-father, his father who counted "One," "Two," "Three" as he destroyed his respective victims, one at the curtain to each act; it is his supreme sense of the Theatre in its most elementary appeal, which allows Eugene O'Neill to stand us on our heads (perhaps our heads would have been more comfortable) and keep us there from five in the afternoon until almost midnight. In this tremendous play he gives us not one thing that is new, and he gives us nothing to think about (unless we are just beginning to think), but he does thrill the bejeezus out of us, just as his father used to, and that is what we go to the theatre for.

Just run over in your mind the big scenes in *Mourning Becomes Electra*. A daughter upbraiding her mother for adultery, the mother plotting with her lover the murder of her husband, the poisoning of the husband and the discovery of the tablets in the fainting mother's hand, the placing of the tablets on the breast of the corpse to frighten the mother into a confession (and what a scene *that* was!), the brother and sister peering down the hatch of a sailing ship to spy on the mother and later to murder her lover, and the tense moments of waiting for the offstage shots which would tell of the successive suicides of the mother and the brother. Greek tragedy, my eye! The idea may have been the Greeks', but the hand is the hand of Monte Cristo. If the Greek idea of revenge, murder, incest, and suicide is so thrilling, why isn't Margaret Anglin busier than she is? *Mourning Becomes Electra* is just the old Greek story put into not particularly convincing New England talk, but it is a hundred times better show than "Electra" because O'Neill has a God-given inheritance of melodramatic sense. So let's stop kidding ourselves about the Verities and the Unities and take a grand, stupendous thriller when we find it and let it go at that.

In the face of such an overwhelming victory over Time, Space, and the Daily Press as that which Mr. O'Neill has won, it is perhaps puny in a single commentator to admit such a personal reaction as fatigue during the last of the three sections of the drama (for they are *not* three plays, as advertised, but one play in fourteen successive acts). But, willing as the spirit may be to take punishment, the human frame is not equipped for such a session as that which is imposed upon it in the Guild Theatre (at any rate, mine isn't, and I have a pretty good equipment), and, starting with a pretty bad scene (go ahead, strike me dead, Jove!) of comic relief at the beginning of the section called *The Haunted,* I began to be cushion-conscious. This uneasiness was heightened as I saw approaching that margin of Diminishing Returns in Tragedy which I alone seem to be conscious of in O'Neill's dramas, when one more fell swoop of Fate, one more killing, one more father in love with one more daughter, or one more sister in love with one more brother, and the whole thing becomes just a bit ridiculous. It was when I saw those magnificent scenes of the middle section becoming confused with a grand finale of bad comedy, incest, and extra suicide that Miss Brady's agonized cry, "I couldn't bear another death!," struck home, and I began to realize that, for me personally, *Mourning Becomes Electra* was getting to be just about one hour too long. I know that this is a purely individual and unworthy reaction, quite out of place in what should be a serious review of a great masterpiece, but, as this page is nothing if not personal, I am setting it down. And the final scene of all, in which Electra, or Lavinia, closes herself up in the great New England Greek temple for the rest of her unhappy life, content that mourning is her *métier,* made up for everything.

And now we come to Miss Brady and to Alla Nazimova and to all the rest of the splendid cast which the Theatre Guild has assembled to do homage to Mr. O'Neill's *magnum opus.* Without them, and without Robert Edmond Jones's superb settings, I am not so sure just how effective this drama would be. I can imagine its being pretty bad, as a matter of fact, if only moderately well done. We thrill to the scenes between the mother and daughter on the steps of the cold New England mansion, but how much credit do we give to Mr. Jones and to Mr. Moeller, who gave us this picture of two women in black on the white steps of a Greek temple? (It may have been so nominated in the 'script, but without Mr. Jones to give it being, it might have remained just a stage-direction.) Alice Brady has at last come into her own, in voice and bearing the perfect Electra, and Nazimova, in spite of her Russian accent, which rings so strangely in Suffolk County, made so much of the sinning Clytemnestra that the drama lost much when she withdrew into the shades of the House of Mannon never to return. Earle Larimore, too, as Orin-Orestes, gave the rôle a human quality which could hardly have been expected in the writing, and Thomas Chalmers, with an opera-trained speaking voice, not only overcame the trick sound-currents of the theatre but gave a healthy robustness to the rather murky proceedings which was reassuring, as long as it lasted. Lee Baker, the first of a long string of entries to die, may have seemed a little stiff, but I suspect that it was a rather stiff part. In short, Philip Moeller in his direction, and the cast in their interpretation, and especially Mr. Jones in his settings, all did more than their share to raise Mr. O'Neill to the undisputed, and probably for a long time uncontested, eminence of the First Dramatist of Our Time. Not that he wasn't there already, but it is good to be sure.

But while we are on our feet, let us drink once again to the Count of Monte Cristo.

From *The New Yorker*,
November 7, 1931.

EUGENE O'NEILL

By JOSEPH WOOD KRUTCH

. . . T H E group with which O'Neill came in touch at Provincetown was a group which knew far better what it did not want than what it did. All its members were determined to do something in the theatre and they were determined that this something should not be what was ordinarily done there, so that, for them, the first requirement of any play was that it should be "different." But insofar as they and the other young experimenters in the theatre had a definite tendency, it was in the direction, first, of realism and, second, of social protest. They wanted to present life as it is, even if that meant a good deal that was shocking and unpleasant, and they wanted also to expose the injustices, hypocrisies and cruelties of society.

Now though even the earliest of O'Neill's plays reveal a reaching out for something more than this, they might also be easily interpreted in accordance with this pattern. First of all came the series of one-act pieces, a number of which dealt with the sea and some of which, at least, might have been described as stark and bitter realism. The first of his full-length plays to achieve a New York production, namely, *Beyond the Horizon* (1920), is even more clearly in the tradition of realism, for it not only deals grimly with the life of the farmer but ends on that note of complete and unrelieved frustration, so characteristic of the earlier classic of the modern drama, but so unlike the note of high tragedy to be found in O'Neill's latest work. *Anna Christie,* a first version of which was the next of his important plays to be written, is also predominantly realistic and even the highly imaginative and poetic *The Emperor Jones,* like the later *All God's Chillun Got Wings,* could be and was taken as O'Neill's contribution to the study of "the Negro problem." So, too, *The Hairy Ape* was interpreted as a work of revolutionary propaganda, cast in the new "expressionistic" form.

Obviously each of these plays was, however, something more than it seemed to be. The early sea sketches had in them a strong strain of imaginative poetry and represent the first attempt of their author to find in life some value discoverable only below its surface. So, too, each of the others revealed at some point or other his feeling that the drama did not justify itself unless it did something more than reproduce facts from life, and each of them—especially *The Emperor Jones* and *The Hairy Ape*—is touched by a visionary ecstasy. It was, however, *Desire Under the Elms* (1924) which first revealed clearly the kind of artistic problem with which O'Neill's genius was destined to grapple.

Outwardly this play is concerned with certain violent events in the life of a family of puritan New Englanders. Outwardly it is a realistic, if heightened, study of the manners, morals and psychological processes of a definite society. But it is impossible not to realize that O'Neill is here interested less in New England as such than in an aspect of the eternal tragedy of man and his passions. He chose that particular time and particular place partly because he knew something about them; partly because the stern repression of New England customs make the kind of explosion with which he proposed to deal particularly picturesque and particularly violent;

but chiefly because it is necessary to give every dramatic story *some* local habitation and name. All questions concerning the accuracy or inaccuracy of any detail are essentially almost as irrelevant as similar questions would be in connection with one of Shakespeare's Roman plays. The events really occur out of place and out of time.

The Great God Brown, the next of his successful plays, should have removed any lingering doubt of the fact that O'Neill's concern was not with either the literal accidents of contemporary life or the local problems of our day. Here the use of masks emphasized that the *dramatis personæ* were not to be taken as simple individuals and the contemporary aspects of the struggle between a genius and a "success" were subordinated to the symbolical presentation of an eternal story of aspiration and frustration. Despite the author's own published explanation, it remains the most puzzling of all his plays, but in the half-despairing, half-exultant cry of its hero, "I've loved, lusted, won and lost, sung and wept" is suggested O'Neill's central theme—the effort to transform into some peace-giving beauty the crude and obvious fact that life is vivid and restless and exciting and terrible. He is not concerned with saying that it is. He is concerned with the effort to get beyond the fact.

Many words have been wasted in discussing the outward devices —masks, expressionistic settings, etc.—which O'Neill has used in his efforts to transcend literal realism. Far fewer have been used in the much more important effort to discover just what it is that he has been trying to achieve through these often startling methods. Nearly every unfavorable criticism of his work may be traced to some mis-apprehension of his intention and we cannot judge him truly without realizing that he has set himself a task different in kind from that which the contemporary playwright commonly undertakes.

As for myself, I find my mind going constantly back to a remark which he once let fall in conversation. "Most modern plays," he said, "are concerned with the relation between man and man, but that does not interest me at all. I am interested only in the relation between man and God." And to this may be added a much fuller statement of the same attitude which is to be found in a letter quoted in the *Intimate Notebooks* of George Jean Nathan. "The playwright today [writes O'Neill] must dig at the roots of the sickness of today as he feels it—the death of the old God and the failure of science and materialism to give any satisfying new one for the surviving primitive religious instinct to find a meaning for life in, and to comfort its fears of death with. It seems to me that anyone trying to do big work nowadays must have this big subject behind all the little subjects of his plays or novels, or he is simply scribbling around the surface of things and has no more real status than a parlor entertainer."

In *Lazarus Laughed* O'Neill gave lyrical expression to this conception through the ecstasy of a group of "lost" human beings brought suddenly into contact with a man of faith; in *Dynamo* he treated the theme directly through the story of a materialist who so literally worshipped the mysterious force of electricity that he finally immolated himself upon the altar of a gigantic generator. Since this particular play was not a success on the stage, its author dropped the project which he had entertained of carrying the theme through a trilogy on Religion, but the determination to make Art fulfil the function which Religion is no longer able to fulfil had already found expression in *Strange Interlude* and was soon to find it again in the latest and perhaps the greatest of his plays, *Mourning Becomes Electra.*

Like the hero of *The Great God Brown,* all the characters in both of these dramas can truthfully say, "I've loved, lusted, won and lost, sung and wept." But absorbing as each of these things is, it is never, for a human being, quite enough. He needs to feel that loving and lusting, singing and weeping, mean something beyond themselves, that there is some justification in the nature of things for that importance which they have for him. And if religion—the belief in a supernatural power capable of investing them with meaning—has decayed, then man must discover some attitude toward himself capable of investing him once more with the dignity he has lost. *Strange Interlude* and *Mourning Becomes Electra* are essentially efforts to do just that—to achieve the self-justifying grandeur of tragedy without having recourse to any conceptions, religious or otherwise, which the mind of the modern man cannot sincerely entertain.

In both, the intellectual framework is supplied by Freudian psychology. All that happens is capable of being interpreted in terms of "complexes," "repressions," and "fixations," but there could, nevertheless, be no error more fundamental than the error of assuming that the ultimate purpose of the plays is to illustrate the all-sufficient adequacy of any such interpretation. Like every great tragic writer, O'Neill must accept the premises of his audience, and it so happens that those premises are not the premises of ancient Greece or Elizabethan England but the premises of modern psychology. They, better than any other, represent the "world view" of today and they, as a matter of fact, constitute the only inclusive theory of human conduct which would not render any drama based upon it anachronistic or "poetic" in the very sense that O'Neill is most anxious to avoid. But they are the foundation, not the structure, the beginning, not the end, of what the dramatist has to say. The greatness of the plays lies in the fact that they achieve a grandeur which their rational framework is impotent even to suggest. Man, deprived of the importance which Religion conferred when it made him important to the universe as a whole, here raises himself by his own bootstraps, and by the very strength and articulateness of his passions asserts the dignity which a rationalistic psychology denies him.

Of the two trilogies *Strange Interlude* is the more discursive, brooding and "novelistic." All the incidents are discussed, viewed from various angles, and commented upon by various characters. The effect is to combine to a remarkable extent the vivid directness of the drama with the more intricate texture of the modern novel, and, indeed, the play brought to the stage certain subtleties which only the novel had hitherto seemed capable of suggesting. On the other hand, *Mourning Becomes Electra* returns to a more conventional dramatic method. The story sweeps forward with a speed and directness reminiscent of the great tragedies of the past, and for that very reason, perhaps, it may be taken as a sign that the author has advanced one step beyond *Strange Interlude* in his effort to discover the modern equivalent for Æschylus or Shakespeare.

As its title suggests, the fable follows, almost incident for incident, the main outlines of the Greek story. Though O'Neill has set the action in New England just after the Civil War, his Clytemnestra murders Agamemnon and his Electra persuades Orestes to bring about the death of their common mother. Nor do such changes as are necessarily made in the motivation of the characters so much modify the effect of the story as merely restore that effect by translating the story into terms which we can fully comprehend. It is true that Electra loves her father and that Orestes loves his mother in a fashion which the Greeks either did not understand or, at least, did not specify. It is true also that the play implies that the psychological quirks responsible for the tragedy are the result of a conflict between puritanism and healthy love. But this is merely the way in which we understand such situations, and the fact remains that these things are *merely* implied, that the implications exist for the sake of the play, not the play for the sake of the implications. It is, moreover, this fact more than any other which indicates something very important in the nature of O'Neill's achievement. Hitherto most of our best plays have been—of necessity perhaps—concerned primarily with the exposition and defense of their intellectual or moral or psychological backgrounds. They have been written to demonstrate that it was legitimate to understand or judge men in the new ways characteristic of our time. But O'Neill has succeeded in writing a great play in which a reversal of this emphasis has taken place at last.

Because its thesis is taken for granted, it has no thesis. It is no more an exposition or defense of a modern psychological conception than Æschylus is an exposition or defense of the tenets of the Greek religion, even though it does accept the one as Æschylus accepts the other. It is on the other hand—and like all supremely great pieces of literature—primarily about the passions and primarily addressed to our interest in them. Once more we have a great play which does not "mean" anything in the sense that the plays of Ibsen or Shaw or Galsworthy usually mean something, but one which does, on the contrary, mean the same thing that *Œdipus* and *Hamlet* and *Macbeth* mean—namely, that human beings are great and terrible creatures when they are in the grip of great passions, and that the spectacle of them is not only absorbing but also and at once horrible and cleansing.

Nineteenth-century critics of Shakespeare said that his plays were like the facts of nature, and though this statement has no intellectual content it does imply something concerning the attitude which we adopt toward *Mourning Becomes Electra* as well as toward Shakespeare. Our arguments and our analyses are unimportant so long as we attempt to discover in them the secret of our interest. What we do is merely to accept these fables as though they were facts and sit amazed by the height and the depth of human passions, by the grandeur and meanness of human deeds. No one knows exactly what it means to be "purged by pity and terror," but for that very reason, perhaps, one returns to the phrase.

To find in the play any lack at all one must compare it with the very greatest works of dramatic literature, but when one does compare it with *Hamlet* or *Macbeth,* one realizes that it does lack just one thing and that that thing is language—words as thrilling as the action which accompanies them. Take, for example, the scene in which Orin (Orestes) stands beside the bier of his father and apostrophizes the body laid there. No one can deny that the speech is a good one, but what one desires with an almost agonizing desire is something not merely good but something incredibly magnificent, something like "Tomorrow and tomorrow and tomorrow..." or "I could a tale unfold whose lightest word..." If by some miracle such words could come, the situation would not be unworthy of them. Here is a scenario to which the most soaring eloquence and the most profound poetry are appropriate, and if it were granted us we should be swept aloft as no Anglo-Saxon audience since Shakespeare's time has had an opportunity to be. But no modern is capable of language really worthy of O'Neill's play, and the lack of that one thing is the penalty we must pay for living in an age which is not equal to more than prose. Nor is it to be supposed that I make this reservation merely for the purpose of saying that Mr. O'Neill's play is not so good as the best of Shakespeare; I make it, on the contrary, in order to indicate where one must go in order to find a worthy comparison.

True tragedy may be defined as a dramatic work in which the outward failure of the principal personage is compensated for by the dignity and greatness of his character. But if this definition be accepted, then it must be recognized that the art of tragic writing was lost for many generations. Neither the frigid rhetorical exercises of the Victorians nor the sociological treatises of Ibsen and his followers are tragic in the true sense. The former lack the power to seem real enough to stir us deeply; the latter are too thoroughly pervaded by a sense of human littleness to be other than melancholy and dispiriting. O'Neill is almost alone among modern dramatic writers in possessing what appears to be an instinctive perception of what a modern tragedy would have to be.

Unlike the plays of "literary" playwrights, his dramas have nothing archaic about them. They do not seek the support of a poetic faith in any of the conceptions which served the classical dramatists but are no longer valid for us. They are, on the contrary, almost cynically "modern" in their acceptance of a rationalistic view of man and the universe. Yet he has created his characters upon so large a scale that their downfall is made once more to seem not merely pathetic, but terrible.

> From the Preface to *Nine Plays by Eugene O'Neill*
> (The Random House, 1933).

THE COMIC WISDOM OF S. N. BEHRMAN

By JOSEPH WOOD KRUTCH

W H E N the Theatre Guild produced *The Second Man* in the fall of 1928 S. N. Behrman was totally unknown. Since then he has written only two other plays which achieved an outstanding success, but there is no American dramatist who has more clearly defined or more convincingly defended an individual and specific talent. It is, as we shall see, difficult to discover in the rather commonplace incidents of his career any explanation of the fact that the whole cast of his mind should be as different as it is from that of any of his fellows, but from the very beginning it was evident that he had accepted and assimilated the Comic Spirit so successfully that he could write with a consistent clarity of thought and feeling unrivaled on our stage. With us farce, burlesque, sentimental romance, and even satire are common enough. They are, as a matter of fact, natural expressions of that superficial tendency toward irreverence which overlays the fundamental earnestness of the American character. Embarrassed by deep feeling or true comedy, we take refuge in the horse-play of farce or the ambiguities of "sophisticated" romance, where the most skittish of characters generally end by rediscovering a sentimentalized version of the eternal verities. But the remarkable thing about Mr. Behrman is the unerring

way in which his mind cut through the inconsistency of these compromises, the clarity with which he realized that we must ultimately
make our choice between judging men by their heroism or judging
them by their intelligence, and the unfailing articulateness with which
he defends his determination to choose the second alternative.

Several other American playwrights have hesitated upon the brink
of the decision. One or two of them—Sidney Howard and Robert
Sherwood, for instance—have written individual plays which all but
defined their attitude and, indeed, Edwin Justin Mayer's almost unknown *Children of Darkness* is a masterpiece which may some day
be rediscovered. But Mr. Behrman alone has been clear, persistent, and
undeviating; he alone has emerged from the group by virtue of a surprising intellectual quality. One might have predicted him a generation
hence. One might have foreseen that a definition as clear as his was
bound to emerge and that someone in America would be bound to
write comedy in the classical tradition—for the simple reason that
such comedy is the inevitable product of a certain stage in the development of any nation's civilization. But the amazing thing was his
sudden unexpected emergence from obscurity with both attitude and
technical skill fully formed.

The public was given no opportunity to discover Mr. Behrman
until he had completely discovered himself, and *The Second Man* was
not only a mature play—quite as good as anything he has written
since—but actually a comedy about Comedy and therefore, by implication, the announcement of a program. All its accidental qualities were,
of course, those common to nearly every work which even approaches
the type of which it represents the fully developed form. The locale
was luxurious, the people privileged enough to spend most of their
time adjusting amorous or other complications, and the conversation
sparkling with wit. But the theme was the Comic Spirit itself and the
hero a man forced to make that decision between the heroic and the
merely intelligent which must be made before comedy really begins.

Like Mr. Behrman himself, his hero belongs to a society which
still pretends rather unsuccessfully to affirm its faith in moral ideals.
Romantic love, for example, is still theoretically so tremendous a thing
that no man or woman worthy of the name would hesitate to give up
everything else in its favor. Life, below even the frivolous surface of

fashionable existence, is supposed to be real and supposed to be earnest. But our hero—a second-rate story writer—has brains enough to know, not only that his stories are second rate, but also that he does not really believe what he is supposed to believe. He can strike the heroic attitude, but the steam is not really there. A "second man" inside himself whispers the counsel of prudence and common sense, tells him that he does not really prefer love to comfort, or exaltation to pleasure. The only integrity he has is the only one which is necessary to a comic hero—the one which makes it impossible for him either to be a conscious hypocrite on the one hand or, on the other, so to befuddle himself with sentiment as to conceal from even his own mind the fact that he is making one choice while pretending to make the other.

In terms of action the result is that he sends packing the determined flapper who wants to marry him and returns to the wealthy mistress who can support him in the luxury to which he has been accustomed. "I suppose it's dreadful to take money from a woman. But why it's worse than taking it from a man I don't know. Do you?" Incidentally, and in the course of this action, the result is also to develop with bold clarity the whole philosophy of a hero who has surrendered the effort to be heroic and is ready to explain without equivocation why such as he must take themselves and the world as they find them without either trying to pretend that they are different or trying to make them so. The originality of the whole—so far as our particular stage is concerned—consists just in the fact that the play neither shirks the logic of its own conclusions nor presents itself as a simple "shocker" but remains essentially "serious" in the sense that it accepts and defends the premises of all pure comedy. "Life is a tragedy to those who feel and a comedy to those who think." Follow the emotions and you may reach ecstasy; but if you cannot do that, then listen to the dictates of common sense and there is a very good chance that you will be comfortable—even, God willing, witty besides.

Mr. Behrman has concealed from the public the inner history of his development and has not, so far as I am aware, told us even what literary influences helped him upon the way to his exceptional maturity, or enabled him to reach so quickly the core of a problem towards which most of our dramatic writers are still only feeling their way. The records say that he was born in Worcester, Massachusetts, and that, as a stage-struck youth, he managed to get as far as Fourteenth Street, New York, by appearing as an actor in a vaudeville skit which he himself had written. Then he attended Clark University and enrolled in Professor Baker's famous course at Harvard. But since then the outward events of his career have been much like those in the careers of half the men connected with the New York theatre. For a period he worked on the *Times* and for a period he acted as a theatrical press-agent—being connected in that capacity with the resounding success of *Broadway*. Since his first play he has spent a good deal of time in Hollywood and he ought, it would seem, to share the weaknesses as well as the strengths of the typical Broadway group into which he seems so obviously to fit. But by now it is evident that *The Second Man* was no accident. He shows no tendency to become submerged in the common tradition, to write merely in the current manner. Instead, each of his succeeding plays has been quite obviously the product of the same talent and the same integral attitude.

It is true that once—in the comedy-drama *Meteor*—he fumbled the intended effect for the very reason that he had, apparently, not thought the situation through to the point where it could be stated in purely intellectual terms. This history of a rebellious and disorganized genius seen through the eyes of a bewildered but admiring acquaintance is not pure comedy because it is suffused with a sense of wonder, because its subject is a mystery, whereas comedy, almost by definition, admits no mysteries and adopts *nil admirari* as its motto. But since that time Mr. Behrman has not faltered. He made a delightful play out of the delightful English *conte Serena Blandish* and then, in *Brief Moment* and *Biography,* he extended his demonstration of the comic solution to the problem of civilized living.

Each of these plays—and especially the last—enjoyed a considerable run. At least *Biography,* moreover, was generally recognized by critics as one of the outstanding plays of the season. And yet neither, I think, was taken unreservedly to its bosom by the general public or given quite the wholehearted approval accorded to certain other plays less relentlessly consistent in tone. The comic attitude—like any other consistent attitude—cannot be undeviatingly maintained without involving a certain austerity. The moment inevitably comes when it would be easier to relax for a moment the critical intelligence and to

pluck some pleasant flower of sentiment or—in other words—to pretend that some compromise is possible between the romantic hero and
the comic one. But Mr. Behrman never allows himself to be betrayed
by any such weakness and he pays the penalty of seeming a little dry
and hard to those pseudo-sophisticates who adore the tear behind the
smile because they insist upon eating their cake and having it too.
Just as they giggle when they find themselves unable to sustain the
level of O'Neill's exaltation—unable, that is to say, to accept the logic
of his demand that life be consistently interpreted in terms of the
highest feeling possible to it—so, too, they are almost equally though
less consciously baffled by Behrman's persistent anti-heroicism. Comedy
and tragedy alike are essentially aristocratic; only the forms in between are thoroughly popular.

Brief Moment is concerned with a very rich, intelligent, and disillusioned young man who marries a cabaret singer because he fancies
her somehow "elemental," and then discovers that she is all too capable
of becoming a very convincing imitation of the women of his own class
—not only by adopting all their manners, but by developing a genuine
enthusiasm for all the manifestations of fashionable pseudo-culture.
One of its points, therefore, is that those "simple souls" which sometimes fascinate the too complicated are really less "beyond" than simply
not yet "up to" the follies from which they seem so refreshingly free;
but the real theme of the play is larger. Its hero is an inhabitant of that
Wasteland described in so many contemporary poems and novels. He
is the heir of all our culture, the end product of education and privilege, eclectically familiar with so many enthusiasms and faiths that
there is none to which he can give a real allegiance. But instead of ges-
turing magniloquently in the void, instead of trying, like most of his
prototypes in contemporary literature, to turn his predicament into
tragedy despite the obvious absence of the necessary tragic exaltation,
he is content, first to analyze the situation intellectually and then to
compensate for the absence of ecstasy by the cultivation of that grace
and wit which no one can be too sophisticated to achieve.

Biography is again the vehicle for a comment made by the Comic
Spirit upon one of the predicaments of contemporary life. Its heroine is
a mediocre portrait painter with a genius for comely living. Her
dilemma arises out of the apparent necessity of choosing between two

men—the one a likable but abandoned opportunist in public life, the other a financial revolutionary idealist. Her solution is ultimately to choose neither, and the play is essentially her defense of her right to be a spectator and to cultivate the spectator's virtue—a detached tolerance. The revolutionist says everything which can be said against her attitude. He denounces it as, at bottom, only a compound of indolence and cowardice which parades as a superiority when it is really responsible for the continuance of all the injustices of the world which the intelligent profess themselves too "wise" to correct. But the heroine sticks to her contention that a contemplative, understanding neutrality is "right" for her. She may be wholly ineffectual. The world's work may be done by persons less reasonable and less amiable than she. But wit and tolerance are forms of beauty and, as such, their own excuse for being.

Mr. Behrman's plays are obviously "artificial"—both in the sense that they deal with an artificial and privileged section of society and in the sense that the characters themselves are less real persons than idealized embodiments of intelligence and wit. No person was ever so triple plated with the armor of comic intelligence as his hero; no society ever existed in which all problems were solved—as in his plays they are—when good sense had analyzed them. Just as the tragic writer endows all his characters with his own gift of poetry, so Mr. Behrman endows all his with his own gift for the phrase which lays bare to the mind a meaning which emotion has been unable to disentangle. No drawing room ever existed in which people talked so well or acted so sensibly at last, but this idealization is the final business of comedy. It first deflates man's aspirations and pretensions, accepting the inevitable failure of his attempt to live by his passions or up to his enthusiasms. But when it has done this, it demonstrates what is still left to him—his intelligence, his wit, his tolerance, and his grace—and then, finally, it imagines with what charm he could live if he were freed, not merely from the stern necessities of the struggle for physical existence, but also from the perverse and unexpected quixoticisms of his heart.

From *The Nation,*
July 19, 1933.

THE GREEN PASTURES

By R. DANA SKINNER

I DO NOT share entirely the general unrestrained enthusiasm for Marc Connelly's notable play. Few plays of recent years have loosed such a torrent of emotional praise from at least one section of the critical press. The vocabulary of several of our leading critics seemed to crack under the strain of trying, for the first time in months, to express a genuine stir of feeling and intellect. Only here and there was the small voice of discrimination raised to point out the ways wherein Mr. Connelly had failed to achieve a masterpiece of classic proportions.

This, I submit, was an unusual state of affairs. Our press critics are not easily reduced to an emotional pulp, nor easily prodded to a sincerity of praise which, by their own confession, beggars words. Yet the play which did this, and more, is simply a representation of the Negro's idea of heaven and of the world in the days when "God walked the earth in the likeness of a man." In view of some objections I have to make to the method and to certain underlying ideas of the play, it is only fair to let the author state his purpose in his own patently sincere words. The play is an attempt, writes Mr. Connelly, "to present certain aspects of a living religion in the terms of its believers. The religion is that of thousands of Negroes in the deep South. With terrific spiritual hunger and the greatest humility these untutored black Christians—many of whom can not even read the book which is the treasure house of their faith—have adapted the contents of the Bible to the consistencies of their everyday lives."

Further, they "accept the Old Testament as a chronicle of wonders which happened to people like themselves in vague but actual places, and of rules of conduct, true acceptance of which will lead them to a tangible, three-dimensional heaven. In this heaven, if one has been born in a district where fish frys are popular, the angels do have magnificent fish frys through an eternity somewhat resembling a series of earthly holidays. The Lord Jehovah will be the promised Comforter, a just but compassionate Patriarch, the Summation of all the virtues His follower has observed in the human beings about him.

278

The Lord may look like the reverend Mr. DuBois, as our Sunday school teacher speculates in the play, or He may resemble another believer's own grandfather. In any event, His face will have an earthly familiarity to one who has come for his reward." Now the most conspicuous failure of *The Green Pastures* lies in not achieving this very simple theme which Mr. Connelly outlines with such clarity and sympathy—a theme, certainly, to which no one familiar with the mediaeval morality and miracle plays could take exception. The veil between the finite and the infinite will always be such that man will seek to represent the unknown, whether in art or in the recesses of his mind, as somehow like the known. Even the most abstract philosophers and the most advanced scientists cling to the need of objective illustration of their ideas. The upheaval in science today, for example, is largely due to the difficulty of creating mechanical models of the atom. Philosophers living in space and time have had the utmost concern in trying to find words to describe concepts of God in terms that imply neither space nor time. Anthropomorphism is purely a matter of degree and not—as those who gently patronize the illiterate Negro imply—a distinct cleavage in viewpoint between the primitive and the educated. We can afford, then, to treat the mental images of the Negro with sympathy, understanding and tenderness. We may discard all thought of irreverence in the gentle familiarity these images imply with things divine. But what we cannot accept, either emotionally or intellectually, is a mixture of images, a scrambling of pictures which we may easily ascribe to the Negro mind of the deep South with other pictures obviously concocted, on behalf of the Negro, by a sophisticated mind of New York. This is a sin against real simplicity—and it is this which mars what might have been the great beauty of Mr. Connelly's work.

The pattern of the play starts with a Sunday school lesson on the book of Genesis for a group of Negro children. One of them asks what God looks like. The preacher replies that no one knows exactly, but that he himself has always imagined God must look like the Reverend Mr. DuBois, a famous Negro preacher of his own youth. Soon after this, the scene shifts to heaven—during one of those celestial fish frys Mr. Connelly mentions in his explanation. It is, of course, a Negro heaven, in which the Lord moves about in the dignified semblance of old Mr. DuBois in a frock coat. From then on, we follow the scenes of creation, of the fall of man, of the Deluge and the Ark, of the exile in Egypt and of the winning of the promised land—all in terms of supposedly Negro images in which the modern and the ancient are mixed with a forced naïveté. Some of the scenes are simple and moving, the more so because of the rich accompaniment of Negro spirituals. But the general mood—and here is something which must be felt even more than sensed through reason—is one of unconscious patronizing, as if the author were constantly asking the audience the question, "Isn't this childlike simplicity utterly charming and captivating?"

Moreover, there are many scenes in which the images, as I have suggested, are distinctly false. I can only compare them to the rich man's idea of "roughing it" to that deliberate effort at simple living which consists in traveling back to nature in a Pullman car, in hiring an expert chef as camp cook, and in calling a steam-heated log cabin a "shack." In other words, many of the scenes have a spurious simplicity forced upon them, a feeling which is not simple at all but, under surface appearances, highly complex, and mentally exacting. Other scenes again have a distinctly satirical twist; and throughout the play there is a lack of that solemn grandeur which, in my limited experience, even the most uneducated Negro mind attributes to things Divine. It is characteristic of the truly simple mind to exaggerate greatness, to run to excess in hero worship. It is the boy brought up in the slums who imagines every rich man's house to be a marble and gold palace. It may be as Mr. Connelly indicates, that the Negro imagines the business office of the Lord to be a tiny room with a couple of stiff backed chairs and a roll-top desk; but I doubt it. The majesty and panoply of the throne are much more in keeping with the dreams of the naïve and the humble. It is precisely the sophisticate who suspects behind the trappings of royalty the banal domestic life of the king. The simple or the childlike mind conceives of the king at breakfast in ermine and wearing his crown. I cannot imagine that the Negro, even of the deep South, thinks of Jehovah in commonplace surroundings, any more than the Jewish people themselves expected the King of Kings to be born in a manger. It is the person of Christ—with Whom this play does not deal except in one final intimation—

Whom the mind of the child clothes in the familiar simplicity of humble friendship.

At all events, childlike faith, no matter how humble, can never be truly and honestly conveyed except by those who share it, if not in its pictorial images, at least in its flaming essence, if not in its particular idiom, then certainly in its universal language. This sharing of the faith expressed permeates every instant of the mediaeval miracle plays, and the feeling of such a tenth century playwright as the nun, Hrotsvitha, to whom Rosamond Gilder devotes a well merited chapter in her vivid book, *Enter the Actress*. Unfortunately, *The Green Pastures* impresses one (perhaps quite wrongly in which case the author's technique alone is at fault) as being written by a playwright who undoubtedly has a deep respect for but does not share the essential qualities of the childlike faith of the Negro people of the deep South. It is remarkable that the play should have been written at all, and more remarkable that it should have been produced, and with such distinguished success. But it is not the equivalent, in our own day, of the plays that grew up around the mediaeval Church. Such a play remains to be written in the new creative period we are about to enter.

From *The Commonweal*, reprinted in "Our Changing Theatre" (Lincoln MacVeagh: The Dial Press, 1913).

ELMER RICE'S *STREET SCENE*

By JOHN ANDERSON

OUT of the clutter and racket and brownstone complacency of any New York side street Elmer Rice has wrought this new play called *Street Scene*, which William A. Brady, Ltd., presented last night in the Playhouse. It is a play which builds engrossing trivialities into a drama that is rich and compelling and catches in the wide reaches of its curbside panorama the comedy and heartbreak that lie a few steps up from the sidewalks of New York.

For his purposes Mr. Rice makes most of it spill onto the stoop and into the street evicting his drama into the presence of the audience by due process of a blistering night in June. It is too hot to stay indoors, so the Kaplans and Fiorentinos, and Maurrants, and all the rest of the stolid tenement, sprawl themselves and their lives across the stage on what is a marvelous and immense duplicate of No. 246 East or West Anywhere.

You can almost feel that mysterious grit that sifts all over Manhattan, sifting into the theatre, and hear its crunch as it eddies into the tattle and fuss of these people. It is like spying upon the neighbors with earphones and binoculars, and out of all the casual talk and incident Mr. Rice snatches with gusto and compassion the tawdry little items which stack up into an unusual and memorable evening.

A great, gaping house bestrides the stage, leaving only a narrow margin for area and sidewalk between audience and its inscrutable façade. It is as gauntly impersonal as vital statistics, merely a place where there are people and births, and marriages and deaths forever in endless succession. Even the talk that flows endlessly along it, and in and out of its windows, is as old and worn and battered with use as its sagging steps, as tattered as the grimy curtains hanging in the breathless night. It is the stencil of conversation everywhere, the ready-to-wear stuff in which these folks dress their love and hate, and pride and humor, for the jaunty chit-chat pillowed on a window ledge.

Presently out of its talk about old man Kaplan's communism, the third floor front's impending baby, or how much ice, presently, I say, out of all this and the clatter of milk bottles and baby carriages, this matter of Mrs. Maurrant and a collector for the milk company emerges with the far-off threat of tragedy like the sound of the elevated at the end of the street, rising to a roar and dying away again. When it dies down Mrs. Maurrant and her lover have been shot by the drunken husband, and little Rose Maurrant, sobbing on the doorstep, is giving up the phony promises of a stage career and the love of Sam Kaplan, just to drift down the street. And a new couple is seeing the supe. about taking the vacant apartment.

It is as casual as that, with the enormous unconcern of people who play in the streets, and grow up and live their lives in them. Call it photographic if you like; call it the baldest sort of realism, it remains, nevertheless, tremendously effective and deeply moving. It has the compulsion of overwhelming details, or acute observation and the zest of simple humors and ways. And there is, out of it, the frank, unwinking ugliness that Edward Hopper, for instance, can set down on canvas and make utterly beautiful. Here it all is, somehow life itself, come amazingly to life and captured in three hours on a stage, and it is an achievement remarkable enough to arouse interest even in a neglected theatre.

Not all of it, of course, is as wonderful as that. As director Mr. Rice has caressed some of the scenes overlong, and slowed them up, and left in conversations and details which another, working over the same script without an author's tenderness, might have omitted.

He has, though, a gorgeous cast, which gives it life and vitality wherever it touches. Beulah Bondi, who was so good in *Saturday's Children* and so amusing in *Cock Robin,* turns out a gossipy busybody with remarkable detail and rare effect. Miss Erin O'Brien-Moore was excellent at the business of Maurrant's daughter, and gave her chief scene a tremulous intensity that left the audience on what seemed the verge of tears. There is a quick, brilliantly realized portrait by Leo Bulgakov, and much helpful work by Mary Servoss, Horace Braham, Robert Kelly and George Humbert.

They bring the whole thing into the acute focus of intelligent acting along Mr. Mielziner's impressively realistic set, and help greatly to make *Street Scene* as lively, as sad and as cruel as any State.

From The New York Evening Journal,
January 11, 1929.

SHAW'S *TOO TRUE TO BE GOOD*

By JOHN ANDERSON

I N a passage of eloquent and simple writing which redeemed a fairly unnecessary book Miss Violet Hunt described affectionately some years ago the scene of W. H. Hudson's death; how suddenly his whole faith as a naturalist left him stricken and silent before his own extinction, and how he just sat in the dark, alone.

Something of that immensely stirring mixture of intellect and emotion lies at the core of Shaw's latest play, *Too True to Be Good,* which the Theatre Guild has produced in the Guild Theatre. It is a play about its author's own disillusion, and that process, now that he is an old man, seems to have had more emotional effect upon him than all the passionate work of his life.

Shaw stirred emotionally is a fresh sight, and an extraordinary one which gives this ridiculous, makeshift and deliberately knock-about drama a curious distinction. It is garrulous, tiresome, brilliant, idiotic, and even, at times, inept out of a sort of weary disinclination. But the one thing it is beyond any other Shaw play is heart-breaking. I don't see how anyone can see it without being moved to sadness at the spectacle of a man who has devoted his life to reason renouncing his faith. It suggests the tragedy of a man clearing out the desk where he has done his lifetime's work, going through the pigeonholes and tearing up, tearing up as discarded and useless and then throwing the fragmentary lot high in the air to watch the pieces glitter as they flutter down—intellectual confetti.

That cloud of falling opinions is *Too True to Be Good* and as a dramatic structure it is just about as haphazard and miscellaneous as all that. But in a way even that seems part of the whole statement, as if Shaw felt his personal tragedy worth just about the dignity and precise arrangement of a musical comedy plot. It is the inevitable Pagliacci—laugh, clown, laugh motive, Mr. Shaw sitting among the mountainous sticks of all those erstwhile dazzling skyrockets asking himself sadly, "What of it?" In a world where the atheist says in the play you can no longer believe even in disbelief, we are all lost, tumbling helter-skelter into the bottomless pit.

But before shrugging off his puppets Mr. Shaw can't resist one more twist to all the tails he has been tying into knots these many years. War, medicine, the church, morals, and so on and so forth are trotted out to get the inevitable Shavian kick in their ultimate pants.

"You can't divide a man's conscience into a war department and a peace department." "I was inoculated against influenza four years ago and have had it only four times since." " 'Safety First' is the cry of those who never cross the street." "Make any statement that is so true that it has been staring us all in the face all our lives, and the whole world will rise up and passionately contradict you. Tell a bold and simple lie, and they will swarm out to swear its proof."

These are fair samples of the dialogue which, as anyone can see, is cut to the old blue prints and stewed in the old formulas. They give the show its razzle-dazzle when it gets it, trick it out with all the grease paint which Shaw used to daub upon the face of his world—grease paint which now, apparently, is turning rancid.

Behind them is a story, if such coherence can be attached to a wayward piece of maundering, that begins in the sick room of a wealthy young woman who is destroyed by her relatives, coddled, badgered, and broken until she produces symptoms, more or less in self-protection. Her nurse almost kicks the mother out of the room, announces that she expects a young man, and then, when he arrives, informs the patient that they plan to steal her jewels. Instead, however, they persuade her to steal them herself, split the swag, and let them kidnap her to some fantastic island to which England immediately sends a punitive expedition, run by a private who has risen to a colonelcy three times, but resigned each time because his commission interfered with his real army work, a contention further illuminated by the actual commander spending all his time painting water colors.

Without much more excuse or by your leave than it takes to line up the jokesters in a minstrel show Shaw rigs his people up on the beach and unleashes their tongues. Words and a little fur fly for two acts during which it is obvious that Shaw has put deep emotion into his writing and made it a sort of sequel, a despairing sequel, to *Heartbreak House.* That play represented the Europe of Tchekhov's *The Cherry Orchard,* and showed the irresponsibility, laziness, and sheer futility of the presumably responsible class, the land-owners, governors, etc.

"Even those who lived within their incomes," he says in the preface, "were really kept going by their solicitors and agents, being unable to manage an estate or run a business without continual prompting from those who have to learn how to do such things or starve."

That same preface, in its reference to Woodrow Wilson, suggests at least a kinship with the present play, for Shaw had in 1919 the feeling of Wilson's tragedy and linked his own to it prophetically. "Before the humble and contrite heart ceases to be despised the President and I, being of the same age, will be dotards. In the meantime there is, for him, another history to write; for me, another comedy to stage. Perhaps, after all, that is what wars are for, and what historians and playwrights are for. If men will not learn until their lessons are written in blood, why blood they must have, their own for preference."

Even that bitterness over Heartbreak-Cherry-Orchard-Europe carried at least the implications that there were lessons for men to learn, lessons which, presumably, would make them saner, more sensible, more civilized and useful men. Somehow in the urgency and power of those days Shaw, whether he believed it or not, created the impression that perhaps argument and persuasion could at least show the general direction of truth. He stood up and pointed, shouting at the top of his lungs.

Now he lets his good pointing arm sink wearily to his side, knowing not which way to point. Nothing is sure, and Shaw no longer cocksure. In an Einstein universe that bends when it feels like it, and the planet Mercury sways off "to warm his hands at the sun" all is caprice, and in a world of caprice there are no rules, no truths, nothing but the pit that is as bottomless as Shaw's vocabulary.

Wherefore this play achieves a significance totally at variance with its inherent drama, or its actual statement. Until the end the despairing tone of it is half-hidden in the rowdy slapstick. But then, in a speech of five minutes, done brilliantly by Hugh Sinclair, Shaw rises in magnificent and melancholy splendor and affirms the futility of It All. There is nothing like it, since it is a sort of egoistic torture of the ego. It is on the grand scale because it is abdication of one of the tallest personal thrones in the world. William Archer taunted Shaw once with the statement that all Shaw's characters were immortal, and triumphed even over death. Certainly he could not call this triumph.

From *The Arts Weekly,*
April 16, 1932.

O'NEILL'S *DAYS WITHOUT END*

By JOHN ANDERSON

MR. O'NEILL merged from the *Ah, Wilderness* mood of adolescent memories last night to resume his old soul-searching, the quest which has led him into such self-tortured dramas as *The Fountain, The Great God Brown,* and *Dynamo.* In *Days Without End,* which the Guild presents at Henry Miller's Theatre, he hits at last the road which has loomed beyond his horizon for many years, the road which in this hurried midnight examination, seems to be spiritually and emotionally, the sawdust trail. I take it to be the old-time religion at which Mr. O'Neill arrives after three acts of self-conscious, unmoving, and generally embarrassing discourse upon the nature of Faith. His hero is on his knees before a crucifix, his masked spirit of evil dead on the floor beside him, and the remnants of a pretty bad play strewn about in the wreckage of what sounds like an emotional binge. The Guild invests it with all solemnity, gives it benefit of Simonson's excellent settings, and illuminates it with an extraordinary performance by Earle Larimore. But to no avail; it remains Mr. O'Neill in his most difficult and trying aspect.

Some six or seven years ago when Mr. O'Neill was singing an ecstatic paganism in *The Fountain* I predicted that he would, dramatically anyway, ultimately return to the church. But no one could have predicted, except after seeing *Dynamo,* that he would return in such disorder. I mean no disrespect for his beliefs, if this new play is to be taken personally, for a man's beliefs are his own—until he writes a play about them. The gentlemen who sat on the rooftops at Patchogue some years ago, waiting for the end of the world in their nightgowns, had full privileges to do as they pleased. In fact, they may have been right.

Mr. O'Neill's fundamental error, dramatically, lies in the notion that Faith is an intellectual process to be touched through words. Its very point, I take it, is that it lies beyond reason. His own hero prays for the "gift of Faith" as something which he cannot reach by his own mental processes.

Thus in the theatre the existence of Faith in a character, or the

achievement of Faith on the stage, is not dramatic in O'Neill's intellectual sense. It is not the climax of a rational dramatic process such as
you might make of a man working three acts to understand the Einstein Theory and finally getting it, and so lifting the mortgage or
crying "The world is mine." It is a thing you have or you haven't, and
to that extent it is a personal miracle. Mr. O'Neill calls *Days Without
End* a modern miracle play, and then writes not a simple, graceful
miracle but a sort of Sunday school debate with Q. E. D. attached
at the end. And to weaken the play further the debate is couched in
the tritest sort of dramatic formulas.

His central character is John Loving, a successful man, who finds
himself, after a life of questioning rebellion, peacefully married, and
working on a novel which is obviously autobiographical. It is the story
of a young man, brought up a devout Catholic, who spurned God
when his parents died, took up atheism and such, and finally, in his
beautiful wife, found a God of Love. But impelled by his Evil Spirit
he dishonored even that deity, and when his wife finds out his sin he
torments himself as she lies dying in the next room, unable to forgive
him.

O'Neill returns to a mixture of the *Strange Interlude* technique
and the mask business of *The Great God Brown*. This Evil Spirit or
"Damned Soul" of John Loving is embodied on the stage by Stanley
Ridges, hideously made up for grotesque effect, who never leaves Mr.
Larimore's presence. He is the personification of the aside. He speaks
the lines sometimes for John Loving; sometimes Mr. Larimore speaks
them. When John Loving is in the throes of spiritual agony their
dialogue monkeyshines become a joint debate, between the Gold Dust
Twins, or as some irreverent wag remarked in the intermission, a
session between Mr. Loving and his spiritual stooge.

It is this devil that is finally cast out at the end, through the inter-
cession of a priest, and Loving returns triumphantly to his old faith
Safe in Abraham's bosom. There is the intimation, at least, that Mrs.
Loving will get well and that God is love.

My objections to all this have not, I repeat, anything whatever to
do with the nature of O'Neill's faith, or of Loving's conversion. They
are based on the suspicion that it is all dramatically phony; that
O'Neill has substituted some florid emotion, and some muddy think-

ing for the dignity and simplicity of religious conviction. It is the place for poetry, not bombast; humility, not melodramatics.

The Guild has given this, under Philip Moeller's brilliant direction, one of its finest productions—even if it is wasted. The mechanical problem of two actors playing the double nature of one character is solved with unbelievable subtlety by Mr. Ridges and Mr. Larimore in superbly integrated performances. Mr. Larimore, in the more difficult rôle, does by far the finest work of his career, and one of the best jobs of this or any season. Robert Loraine, as the patient, kindly, sweetly reasoning priest, his uncle, gives a performance that is rich, balanced, and well sustained. Selena Royle, after getting past some bad spots of wifely banality, contributes an excellent scene before she takes to her deathbed, and Ilka Chase gives a sharp and vivid sketch of the talkative friend who happened to sin with Loving when dat ol' debbil in him was uppermost.

But *Days Without End* sounds like part of that religious trilogy which O'Neill started to write in *Dynamo* and which he had apparently abandoned. It seems a pity it wasn't, for while it is interesting as a phase of O'Neill's development, its values are more clinically personal than dramatic or stirring.

From *The New York Evening Journal*,
January 9, 1934.

IN PRAISE OF ED WYNN, COMIC

By BROOKS ATKINSON

E D W Y N N enjoys certain advantages that are denied to the common race of men. In a world in which few are doing what they might do best, Wynn is doing exactly what suits him in the style that communicates him perfectly. He is the greatest buffoon of the day in the vein of pure comedy. Such a man is not only to be enjoyed as the perfect fool and entertainer, but also to be envied for his good fortune; the fates, which are often so damnably capricious, have conspired to put him where he belongs. In private life Wynn is likable, earnest and frank, and mighty good company. But it is on the stage that his true genius comes into being. When the lisping nitwit emerges from the wings, with those quizzical eyebrows, that driveling, but singularly ingratiating smile and the eternal mummery of his costumes, Ed Wynn comes into full command of his creative powers, and performs the transcendent feat of magic that is the true art of the theatre. He becomes an imaginative figure. This is Ed Wynn after he has been breathed upon by the gods who create laughter.

There are, he says, two kinds of comedians: the gag comedian who tells jokes which you may repeat afterward without destroying their flavor, and the method comedian, who must be seen, and whose jokes are no good apart from himself. Wynn is both kinds, although he may not realize it. His gags have become notorious. His inventions of the hinged coffee spoon that will not destroy the eyesight when left in the cup, the windshield wiper to be served with grapefruit and the typewriter carriage for eating corn on the cob remain among the treasures of modern civilization. Other similar treasures are the automatic cigar-lighter, that carries its supplementary box of matches; the non-wrinkling nightgown, as scanty as a waist; the philosophical mouse-trap, closed all over; the cash drawer that closes before you can rob it; the piano velocipede; the cuckoo-clock fiddle. His two-man horse, which is a pack-animal of gags, carries a pocket-flask on the hip and a repair kit in the saddle bags. Applying modern methods to old-fashioned veterinarianism, Wynn raises the horse's hind quarters on an automobile jack. The dynamic liver-medicine and hair-restorer and the bag of Bull Durham tobacco dropped into a tea-cup by mistake, and the puns and bungled pronunciations are likewise the baggage of the gag comedian. Does he know what an amethyst is? Certainly. An amethyst, says this lisper, is a man who doesn't believe in God. Groucho Marx is not more lavishly equipped with gags.

But, you are saying, amusing as these gags may be in themselves, they are not to be considered apart from Ed Wynn once he has laid his hands on them. And that is true. Once he has used them they are gags impregnated with the unearthly fire of Wynnism; there is a creative process involved in his use of suitable material. "Genius is the ability to become at will a child again," as some one of consequence remarked, perhaps the author of *A Child's Garden of Verses* or the author of *Peter Pan*. At any rate, Wynn's gibes represent a sort of marriage of Mother Goose and Artemus Ward.

Transforming them into fantasy may be a matter of instinct to a fool who is generally known to be the perfect one, but Wynn is also a conscious propagandist for the imaginative theatre. Such artistic principles as naturalistic acting, holding the mirror up to life, he regards as apostasy. It is no reflection upon the vividness and anguish of *Street Scene* and *Journey's End* to remark that the quintessence of theatre is make-believe, as *The Green Pastures* revealed to the satisfaction of everyone. Wynn is our greatest stage comedian, not because he believes that theatre is make-believe, but because he lives in the sphere of make-believe when he is on the stage. A man's principles are of no value unless he lives them.

Just how an actor is to go about enkindling the imaginations of his audience would be a useful thing to know and to publish. Some actors have that gift; some actors lack it. Obviously, it has some relation to personal magnetism. But it is at least certain that one way to enkindle the imagination in others is to have it one's self, and to perform in one's own mind the feat required of the audience. In *Simple Simon* Wynn did that notably in one absurd number in which he imitated first one horse, then two horses and finally twenty horses prancing across the stage. As a matter of fact, there was no imitation about it whatsoever. Wynn rushed helter-skelter across the stage. But he began each excursion with so much serious premeditation, confessing that it was so long since he imitated a horse that he was not sure he remembered how to do it, or remarking, innocently enough, that it is hard for one man to know how two horses feel, that you were almost persuaded to see some equine significance in his awkward comic tumbling.

He has, furthermore, the rambling, spontaneous mannerism of the story teller. He hesitates, chuckles and repeats himself. Instead of paring his jokes down to glib thrusts, he is discursive about them. Most comedians would declare that Bruce's hair tonic is vigorous enough to turn a grapefruit into a cocoanut and consider the crack well exploited. But Wynn turns it into a story, making it an expression of character. "Is Bruce's hair tonic good?" he exclaims with as much indignation as his amiable personality can muster. "I'll tell you how good Bruce's hair tonic is. The other day I spilled some on a grapefruit and sold it for a cocoanut."

Like all good story-tellers, he appeals to your affections as the surest way to your heart. He listens to his colleagues on the stage with rapt admiration. Although he is the star, he preserves a certain humility toward those who merely feed him or serve as his foils. He has consideration for his audience. Lest he offend the tender sensibilities of the children who have come to see him, he has renounced the cigar smoking which hitherto was an integral part of his fantastic characterizations. (Apparently the hip flask does not matter.) "He's adorable," murmurs the perspiring dowager in the row behind who would normally be indignant about the silliness of such material as he presents. For sheer creative conception, the American musical stage has nothing superior to Harpo Marx's red-haired satyr and slap-stick fiend. But Ed Wynn's genius, combined with his capacity for taking infinite pains, has turned the reproachful epithet of "The Perfect Fool" into an expression of popular endearment. In the vein of pure comedy he is our greatest buffoon.

From *The New York Times,*
March 16, 1930.

THE GREEN PASTURES

By BROOKS ATKINSON

F R O M almost any point of view, *The Green Pastures,* which was put on at the Mansfield last evening, is a play of surpassing beauty. As comedy, fantasy, folklore, religion, poetry, theatre—it hardly matters which. For occasionally there comes a time when those names hardly matter in comparison with the sublime beauty of the complete impression. And Marc Connelly has lifted his fable of the Lord walking on the earth to those exalted heights where utter simplicity in religious conception produces a play of great emotional depth and spiritual exaltation—in fact the divine comedy of the modern theatre.

It has been suggested by Roark Bradford's volume of two years ago, entitled, *Ol' Man Adam an' His Chillun,* being the tales they tell about the time when the Lord walked on the earth like a natural man. It has been described as Uncle Remus's "Story of the Bible." In eighteen scenes it follows the chronicle of biblical history as ignorant religious negroes of the South might conceive it in childish terms of their personal experience. Beginning with the disarming vignette of a darky preacher teaching a class of negro children the main events of the Lord's creation, it moves swiftly into the fantastic comedy of a vision of heaven in terms of a fried-fish party, progresses to celestial drama of heartbreaking sincerity and concludes on a note of exhilarating faith. For everything that he has taken from Mr. Bradford's volume Mr. Connelly contributes stuff of the finest imaginative splendor. You might not expect so much from an unpretentious negro fable. The beauty of the writing, the humility of the performance put the theatre to its highest use.

Mr. Connelly has made the transition from negro comedy to universal drama by the effortless process of increasing emphasis upon the enduring themes. At first you are delighted by the naïve incongruities of the spectacle—the negro angels at their fried-fish party, the tiny pickaninny in whose throat a fish bone gets lodged, the Lord in his private office cautioning Gabriel not to blow his horn, Noah blowing the steamboat whistle on the Ark, the elephants clambering up the gangplank. All through the play these magnificent strokes of imaginative comedy make *The Green Pastures* a rare piece of work.

But hardly has the fried-fish party among the angels gotten under way before you realize that Mr. Connelly's play has nobler projects in mind. In fact, it has the Lord as its principal figure. Dressed in the formal garb of a parson, with his long coat and white tie, he is unpretentious. Even in his speech he is of humble origin. But straightway you perceive he is a good man—the fusion of all the dumb, artless hopes of an ignorant people whose simple faith sustains them. He is a Lord of infinite mercy. There is a reverential moment when he creates the earth and rears up Adam in the sweetness of a new garden. There are moments of anxiety when, walking on the earth, he shakes his head sadly, and remarks, "Bad business. I don't like the way things are going at all." "What seems to be the main trouble?" he inquires of Noah. "Well, the chief trouble seems to be," Noah replies, "that the district is wide open." There are moments of rudely expressed glory when the Lord rewards Moses for his faithful service, and moments of wrath when the Lord denounces the Babylonians. And more: there are moments when even the great Lord of creation suffers with the suffering of the world. "Being God is no bed of roses," he remarks wearily to Gabriel. He is a simple man and a good man. In the end he is not above learning himself.

Probably this is the quality that exalts *The Green Pastures* into drama of great pith and moment. Putting the Lord on the stage in such simple terms that your imagination is stimulated into a transfigurating conception of sheer, universal goodness—that is Mr. Connelly's finest achievement. During the eighteen scenes he introduces harmonious material. The spirituals sung as chorals as the scenes are being changed carry the mood forward to the next episode. And Robert Edmond Jones, who has an imagination of his own, has designed settings that give the theme a vaulting impetus. But the Lord, walking humbly through Heaven and on the earth, telling folks to enjoy themselves, gives the play its divine compassion.

The cast and chorus include about ninety-five negro performers. Under Mr. Connelly's direction they have been molded into a finely tuned performance. Most of them appear on the stage too briefly to leave a personal impression. But the humbleness of Alonzo Fenderson as Moses and of Tutt Whitney as Noah, the rapt wonder of Daniel L. Haynes as Adam and the reverent comedy of Wesley Hill as Gabriel are performances of note. As the Lord, Richard B. Harrison has the part of greatest responsibility. He plays it with the mute grandeur of complete simplicity. This is a paternal and lovable creation. When amid a thousand worries he walks to the celestial window, looks about with an air of anxiety, orders the sun to be "a might cooler," and then remarks appreciatively, "That's nice," you believe in him implicitly. In fact, you believe in the entire play; it is belief incarnadined. Such things are truer than the truth.

From *The New York Times,*
February 27, 1929.

KATHARINE CORNELL IN *THE BARRETTS*

By *BROOKS ATKINSON*

I F Katharine Cornell continues to put her genius to some creditable use, as she is now doing in *The Barretts of Wimpole Street,* she will be not only a great actress but a great force in the theatre. She is already one of the two foremost actresses in this country, despite the sultry stuff in which she has been recently appearing. Bad plays do not necessarily poison genius. Other actresses of first rank before her have indulged themselves in cheap, malodorous joint-pieces without jeopardizing their standing. And during the last five years, when Miss Cornell has been flinging herself away on such brummagem as *The Green Hat, The Letter* and *Dishonored Lady,* or on such incom- petent hack-work as the dramatization of *The Age of Innocence,* no one has disputed her genius as an actress. As Sydney Fairfield in *A Bill of Divorcement,* as Candida in Shaw's play, as Mary Fitton in *Will Shakespeare,* she had already given sufficient evidence of that.

In a generation that admires good plays, and has a remarkable talent for recognizing merit in playwriting, one of the conditions of great acting is a certain fastidiousness in the selection of vehicles. When a good actress stoops to bad plays, or considers plays only in terms of the stellar part, we all feel that she has let us down. We are all critics and we all know when an actress is merely appearing. Be- fore we surrender completely we like to be assured that, in addition to the immortal fire of all memorable acting, a great actress has courage and versatility enough to play with genius in more than one key. Not in all keys; no one expects her to play a cockney as brilliantly as a queen, although Lynn Fontanne has done that, and by appearing exclusively in plays of some distinction she has grown steadily in stature and established herself at the top of her profession. For one of the things we now expect of our finest actresses is a sense of respon- sibility. No one can fairly exist by himself for himself in such an entangled profession as the theatre; every one in the profession is affected, either vitally or remotely, by what his colleagues are doing. Being an actress who is still growing and who can still choose her future, quite independently, Miss Cornell has the power to leave her mark plain on the drama as well as the theatre. Whether she stands for something or nothing depends entirely upon her.

In the fire of her playing Miss Cornell has the one gift most essential to the great actress. Whatever she does is charged with excitement. Her presence is pulsatile and electric. We are caught up in magnetism the instant she appears, and we are passionately interested to know what she is going to do or say. Through all the strut and artifice of *The Age of Innocence,* the personal fortunes of Miss Cornell's Ellen Olenska seemed like matters of vital importance. In *The Green Hat, The Letter* and *Dishonored Lady* she compelled us to regard the principal character as the victim not of a playwright, but of the gods who had isolated this one mortal for special persecution. Miss Cornell gave these parts the beaten fury of epic heroines. In her playing Iris Fenwick shared with Electra the malevolence of unearthly persecution, and this was so not from anything we knew but from everything that we felt.

Miss Cornell is also a studious actress who designs her parts scrupulously; there is architecture as well as stir in her playing. Her voice may not be beautiful in itself, but it is laden with passion and it can lick at the dialogue like a flame. She uses it like a musical instrument. She plays on many stops. You can hear in the sound of the notes she strikes things that she never says. Likewise, the pleading mobility of her gestures and the transfixed look that is in her eyes when she stares away from a scene into the corner or across the footlights have a prescience of destiny.... Back comes this analysis to the beginning again. Although Miss Cornell is an actress who plans her characterizations and consciously designs the structure of her playing, any discussion of her art must eventually content itself with acknowledging the strange forebodings of her personality. She has disciplined it like an artist, but the unearthly spirit of her playing counts most.

As Elizabeth Barrett, the chief character in Rudolph Besier's *The Barretts of Wimpole Street,* Miss Cornell has one of the great stories of the world to unfold. It is chiefly the story of a daughter who escapes from a despotic father after he has tormented her beyond endurance and betrayed an incestuous impulse in his affection for her. Although Mr. Besier has never specifically named the nature of Edward Moulton-Barrett's feeling for Elizabeth, the direction of the current performance does not leave the point in doubt. Edward Barrett's ugly response to his niece's flirtation in the middle of the play and the morbidness with which he appeals to Elizabeth's mercy in the last act make the issue clear. The acting boldly interprets the hints that are lurking in the script. . . .

Miss Cornell's Elizabeth Barrett is her masterpiece. After all these years of cheap trumpery Miss Cornell has found the sort of character she can illuminate best. Her Elizabeth is a lady of rare spirit—leading a full, alert life on the threshold of death; triumphantly serene in the face of suffering and unhappiness; tremulously responsive to a love that she hardly dares claim as her own. Miss Cornell is not a bravura actress; she does not subdue her audiences or dazzle them; she keeps everything she does firmly in hand. But her Elizabeth gives you a feeling of exaltation when you stumble out of the theatre, where great things have been happening, into the nervous hubbub of Broadway.

From *The New York Times*,
February 22, 1932.

OF THEE I SING

By BROOKS ATKINSON

F O R some time now the musical stage has been acquiring intelligence and artistry. More than a year ago *Three's a Crowd* began the task of modernizing the revue. Last Spring *The Band Wagon* finished that particular branch of pioneering by reproducing the lithe, agile, stinging tempo of the age in a carousal of splendors. It was, and still is for at least another Gotham fortnight, the work of George S. Kaufman and Howard Dietz, wordsmithies; Arthur Schwarz, tunesmithy, and Hassard Short, smithy of the stage spectacle. During the present season something has been accomplished toward revitalizing the musical comedy stage. *The Cat and the Fiddle* has drawn a distinction between operetta and the song-and-dance arcade.

In *Of Thee I Sing,* which opened eight days ago, George S. Kaufman and Morrie Ryskind have substituted for the doddering musical comedy plot a taut and lethal satire of national politics, and George

Gershwin has composed a score that sings in many voices, simmers with ideas and tells the story more resourcefully than the book. Despite a Supreme Court of the United States that behaves as skittishly as the peers of highest station, *Of Thee I Sing* is no Gilbert and Sullivan palimpsest, for the humorous elegances of Gilbert and the idyllic melodies of Sullivan belong to an era that is dead. *Of Thee I Sing* is shrill and galvanic. It is written and produced in a nerve-twanging key. It attacks with the rapier and the club indiscriminately. In short, it is the musical hit of the season.

As political satirists Mr. Kaufman, Mr. Ryskind and Mr. Gershwin in the orchestra pit are devastating and hilarious, meaning no good. Never has there been such a belaboring of our self-seeking and pettifogging government. Never were the party campaign managers such a ruffianly, illiterate parcel of mountebanks, nor the Western Senators so otiose and grandiloquent, nor the Southerns so whinnying. Never was a Vice-President so comically superfluous. Never was the body politic so animal and stupid. From the moment the curtain lifts on a raffish assembly of campaign managers in a tawdry hotel bedroom *Of Thee I Sing* whacks every head in sight in an outrageous brawl of malignant buffoonery. The authors of *Of Thee I Sing* have translated government into bedlam.

At the risk of repeating what must be already the common tattle of the town let this column recount the story of a Vice-President's heart-breaking dilemma. For the Vice-President is that tear-choked, wobbly-headed Victor Moore whose tottering clowneries appeal to both the affections and the risibilities. Mr. Moore has always had great difficulty in getting his feet firmly planted on any corner of this globe. As a Vice-President his position is more nebulous than ever and his sweet disposition makes him uproariously useless. After the campaign managers have gravely nominated a suitable nonentity for Vice-President they cannot remember either his name or his face. As a matter of fact, Alexander Throttlebottom is rather an elusive name. They do not recognize Mr. Throttlebottom when he happily comes to headquarters; they try to throw him out of the room.

After some pathetic confusion he identifies himself. Every one is embarrassed and bewildered. But he tries his best to comprehend the political program. "Excuse me, gentlemen," he timidly inquires, "what party are we?" When the candidate for Vice-President becomes a thorough nuisance the campaign managers persuade him to hide away until after the election. The President is elected; the new government is installed; official business begins with a rumble. Still no one misses the Vice-President of the United States. In fact, he might never have come into the public eye again except for a lucky accident. While sight-seeing in the White House as an identified member of a party of tourists he learns for the first time that the Vice-President is supposed to preside over the Senate. There at last is a place where he can be comfortably tucked away. And that is how it comes about that Victor Moore finally has the delirious pleasure of meeting the President face to face and of presiding over the Senate with the bewildered benignance of a happy child. This whole episode, in the writing and the playing, is a masterpiece of sympathetic, humorous satire.

Merely to conceive the National Government in terms of knavery and ebullient ignorance is to create the most damaging sort of satire at once. It releases a good deal of a citizen's normal alarm over the daily menace of a Congress in session. But the authors of *Of Thee I Sing,* including Ira Gershwin, who has written capital lyrics, have a genius for coining lines. It is "tift and tift" all evening. It is thrust and retort. In the instance of the election bulletins thrown on the screen, it is a brilliant hugger-mugger of allusions and grotesqueries. For the bulletins show how logical it is to incorporate George Washington, Roxy, A Friend of Roxy's, Babe Ruth, Mae West and Mickey Mouse on equal terms in a national design of personalities. Now, the danger of indiscriminate wise-cracking is the repercussion it can set up through a long evening. The wise-crack in a long series has no buoyancy. It is flat and hard, striking you in the same spot each time, and unless your nerves are uncommonly rugged you are likely to grow tired of it. To me the unremitting jocosity of the last half of this lampoon grows wearisome.

Furthermore, a political satire in musical comedy form is, by all the laws of logic, not exempt from the duties of musical comedy plot-making. Toward the end of *Of Thee I Sing* musical comedy rears its ugly head and dictates a conclusion that is political satire only at second hand. News has swept through all the country that the President's bride is to become a mother. The hour is at hand. Great is the rejoicing thereat. The Supreme Court goes into impromptu session. The Ambassador from France delivers an eleventh hour ultimatum from his country. The trumpeters blow forth a mighty fanfare. Twins are announced. And then the President's bride is rolled on from the wings in a florid bed for the concluding scene, which looks like nothing so much as the gaudy finale of a routine musical show. And to me *Of Thee I Sing* is no longer political satire in that concluding episode, but old-line musical comedy, leaving a sour taste in the mouth.

Let that conclude the bill of exceptions. For the joyous fact remains that *Of Thee I Sing* has very nearly succeeded in liberating the musical comedy stage from the mawkish and feeble-minded formula that has long been considered inevitable. It is funnier than the government, and not nearly so dangerous.

From *The New York Times,*
January 3, 1931.

OTIS SKINNER

By JOHN MASON BROWN

T H E play is *The Honor of the Family,* the scene the Booth Theatre, the date, December 25, 1926. It is the third time Otis Skinner has appeared in this dramatization of Balzac's *La Rabouilleuse,* and the second time he has dug into his trunk to revive it. Twenty years have passed since the curtain first rang upon it in New Rochelle, twenty years and Mr. Skinner is an older man and the play—as is the way of things—a much, much older play. The middle of the first act has already slipped by. Now the curtain seems imminent, and nothing has happened to catch the eye or rivet the attention. The scenery is a little shoddy, but not nearly as much so as the writing. And the cast is none too good. Though the actors are dressed in the costumes of 1824, they do not wear them, but are merely covered by them. In fact, both the play and the performance are wooden and incredible—as dead as the de Mauprat subplot in *Richelieu* and of just about the same vintage. Who cares whether that plotting couple on the stage will make away with the old French miser's money? It all seems too silly, too archaic, too dull—and anyway this is Christmas.

But at just the moment when you may be reaching for your hat, or suppressing a yawn that makes your eardrums ache, things begin to happen. A man swaggers past the window at the back. Yes, that is all, but it is enough to make you swallow your yawn and forget you ever had a hat. Enough because—and we are forced to feel it—the brief passing of that man is more than obedience to a stage direction. The distance he has covered may be only a simple six feet or so. But there is no tape that can measure his crossing, because it is not a matter of distance but of the creation of character. With that brief appearance at the window blood has suddenly been pumped through the anæmic veins of this old melodrama, not mere mortal blood, of course, but the blood that is red with the redder corpuscles of the theatre. Not only has a character been summarized in a passing glance, but he has been catapulted across the footlights to all of us from the remotest depths of the backstage, from that very position in fact at which most of the younger actors, who like to hug the footlights, are ill at ease, but at which the veterans feel triumphantly secure.

If at that moment you suddenly find yourself sitting upright, without knowing or caring what has become of your programme; if Christmas has fled your mind without your dismissing it, it is because of the brave, salty figure of swash-buckling romance this man cuts as he swaggers by the window. From the battered high-hat sitting cockily aslant his head, and the greatcoat tightly bundled around his body, to the cane he swings with the air of a major-domo, this stout Ratapoil seems the most blustering of benevolent villains. In no time he is past the window, and has stomped his way on to the stage, confronting that heartless couple which is conspiring for old Rouget's money. Now we can see him better—note those slightly moth-eaten eyebrows, follow the ends of his moustache as they mount skyward, observe his bulging red cheeks, and that nose which seems a tattered poppy in their midst. We can follow, too, the energetic manner in which this Colonel Bridau swings up and down the stage, and enjoy that walk of his which is the finest bluster in roosterdom.

In a twinkling our cares are gone. We no longer think about the rent-day worries. We have even forgotten the half hour or more of dullness through which we have sat. In a twinkling, too, it seems to us that the old miser is really being cheated, and his being cheated begins to matter. We know no one like this jolly rascal who has come to Rouget's defense ever trod the earth. But we do not mind that, except to regret it. This is the way in which all villains should be treated. This Bridau's swagger is the swagger all of us have hidden in hearts, a hang-over from childhood, when within ourselves we were still brave non-conformists, when each of us rebelled at good behavior and, hating the respectable gentry of Nottinghamshire, gave our affections to Robin Hood and all the other lovable bandits who had stout cudgels in their hands. "Bang" goes Bridau's cane, thumping down on the table like the crack of doom—and we chortle with delight. Out comes his warning to the conspirators—an absurd, preposterous warning if you like, but you do not stop to say so then. Up comes a cigar to his mouth, driven home so grandly that it seems the finest gesture of arrogance this small world knows. And, with a final jaunty pat on the top of his high-hat, calculated to set it at an even cockier angle on the side of his head, off stalks this Bridau for a stroll.

It has taken but a minute, "less than a minute" Otis Skinner assures us in *Footlights and Spotlights,* but it lasts a lifetime in the memory of those who have seen it. By its memorability and the sense of importance it conveys while it is happening, this short second of Philippe Bridau offers an excellent illustration of the difference between coming on to a stage and making an entrance. Any mortal with feet, crutches, a wheel chair or a nurse can come on to the stage. And almost anyone can—and many modern actors do—slink from a door and slip into the nearest chair with a desperate sense of thankfulness. But locomotion followed by a squat is not an entrance. An entrance is made of entirely different stuff. It is the first "point" an actor scores, a dramatic moment in itself—studied, built up and sustained—which usually rumbles in the wings long before it bursts into view but which, when once made, defies any eye to leave it. Call it a kind of pillage, a hold-up staged in public, if you will. Admit the silliness to which some of the older actors have pushed it in their vanity. Laugh at the way in which some of them loved to swoop down on a play, and tuck it and its cast into their vest pockets, even while they were bludgeoning the audience. But realize that life is not its model, nor etiquette its guide. It is a trick, of course, but therein lies its special glory when it comes off. It is the theatre of the actor at its most militant, but to succeed—as this entrance of Bridau succeeds—it demands an actor behind it, no ordinary actor, but a personality and a technician who is able to carry it through.

Otis Skinner not only carries the entrance of this Bridau through with a triumphant flourish, but, even while he is making it, or whipping the rest of the old melodrama into life, we are carried beyond realism into that theatre of not so long ago, which modern realism has all but extinguished. Watch him in *The Honor of the Family,* see him in *Kismet, Blood and Sand, The Merry Wives, Henry IV* or in the Quinteros' gentle comedy, *100 Years Old,* and you are aware that you are facing a method which is not common on our contemporary stage. It is a veteran's method, sure in its devices, conscious of its "points" and certain in making them—at a time at which "points" are more or less looked down on by the moderns. It is character acting enlarged beyond the ordinary; bold, romantic, mellow but high-tensioned. It admits no moments of loafing and is never more active than when some one else is speaking. Like Mrs. Fiske, Mr. Skinner listens with his whole body, toys with his handkerchief, and "ahs" and "ums" his way through the speeches he must hear. And like Mrs. Fiske he is one of the most authoritative of our older actors, schooled in a different school, born of a different tradition.

Behind him lies more than a half century of the richest and most varied experience our stage has known. Read his *Footlights and Spotlights*—the wisest and most illuminating of our actors' autobiographies since Joseph Jefferson wrote his—and you will see what is the background for his authority. Here is a man, the son of a Universalist minister, who was given his first letter of introduction to managers by no less a person than the great P. T. Barnum himself. It was in 1877 that he made his first professional début as an old negro in a play called *Woodleigh* at the Philadelphia Museum. "There was no part I did not play," he tells us, writing of that first year at the museum when, counting "doubles," he appeared in ninety-two parts between October and June. "Even sex was no bar, for I was sometimes clapped into skirts for nigger wenches and coarse old hags. I scowled as villains, stormed as heavy fathers, dashed about in light comedy, squirmed in character parts, grimaced in the comics, and tottered as the Pantaloon in the pantomime." That was the beginning, and it was the kind of initiation which no modern player is granted. In the years that followed he acted with Lotta Crabtree, with John McCullough, Edwin Booth, Mary Anderson, Madame Janauschek, Lawrence Barrett; barnstormed Leadville when it was "wide open"; was a member of Augustin Daly's famous company with Mrs. Gilbert, May Irwin, John Drew and Ada Rehan; played Henry VIII to Modjeska's Katharine, Orlando to her Rosalind, Shylock to her Portia, Macbeth to her Lady; was Petruchio to Ada Rehan's Katharine; had his fling at "the inevitable Hamlet"; tried his own hand at management—and all this before the later-day Otis Skinner emerged, the Otis Skinner that Charles Frohman presented, the Otis Skinner of the *Count de Grammont, The Harvester, The Duel, Kismet, Mister Antonio* and *The Honor of the Family.*

When he plays his swaggering villains, his Bridaus and his Kismets, or even when he is seen as the old gentleman whose birthday is the plot of the Quinteros' *100 Years Old,* the background of that experience shows through the acting of this man who "never did like Kings," and who is at his best as rogues. See his fine Falstaff, watch that "valiant Jack" he acted in the Players' Revival of *Henry IV* rather than that far less glorious comico that Shakespeare put into *The Merry Wives,* and you understand just what "the great tradition" can mean in poise, in manner and authority. You understand, too, how Mr. Skinner has domesticated it, house-broken it to modern needs. Above all the "stars" of the Players' Revival, and the unwieldy chronicle-history they made of the play, rose the Falstaff of Mr. Skinner, dominating the entire stage and giving the only life the revival possessed to his scenes at the Boar's Head Tavern. He was not awed by Shakespeare, nor embarrassed because he had to don a costume other than his business suit. Nor was he the slave to hoary convention. He went his own way when he wanted, but always with the surety of one who knows the past before breaking with it.

It was a delight to see an actor unafraid to tackle the comic passages in Shakespeare, and able to keep them comic. His Sir John was no mere funny fat fellow, depending upon his padding for his laughs. He was a rotund old devil of the taverns; self-indulgent and gluttonous, and yet possessed of an alchemy of pathos that made him lovable beyond his faults. He was sensed as character, appraised in the terms of his theatre values, his "points," and, like Mr. Skinner's Bridau, catapulted across the footlights. He showed the unction of this veteran, his glowing vitality, and betrayed, too, that, though he had scrapped the fustian of "the old tradition," he had—luckily for all of us—salvaged its authority.

From *Upstage: The American Theatre in Performance* (W. W. Norton, 1930).

THE CONSTANT SINNER

Mae West of Stage and Screen

By JOHN MASON BROWN

T H E R E is nothing of the nun about Miss West. The characters she plays are children of the wide open places. The sisterhood they belong to is without shame, and Miss West invariably presented as the least reticent member of the order. Margie LaMont in *Sex* was a dishonorable woman. Babe Gordon, in *The Constant Sinner* was a dishonorable woman. Diamond Lil was and is a dishonorable woman. So have they all been, all dishonorable women. The perfume of the honky-tonk has followed in their wake.

These unregenerate Thaïses of the Tenderloin that Miss West loves to play—and plays so grandly—move in a world that has little or no relation to life. Crimes which are real enough are committed all around them. Men are shot, white slavers caught, counterfeiters exposed, dopesters die miserable deaths, and jailbirds escape from behind thick steel bars. But everything that happens has about it the heightened unreality of a waterfront ballad. That, as Mr. Galsworthy used to remark, is where the fun comes in.

One reason for this is, of course, that it is Miss West around whom all the sinful solar systems of her plots revolve. And Miss West is a magnificently incredible person. She conquers a bit too easily. Her predatory triumphs have an immediacy about them which mere mortals are forced not only to question but to envy. One slight roll of her

Police Gazette figure, four measured tosses of her unholy head, and every man for miles around is supposed to be hers. The effect she has on them is no less instantaneous than was the Medusa's, but, unlike that other figure in mythology, she does not turn her victims into stone.

There is something delightfully anachronistic about Miss West; something that belongs to the frontiersman's idea of fun, to the days of free lunch counters, and yet that has about it the imperiousness of a vanished race of regal sirens. There is an opulence about Miss West's person which the world cannot but admire in these lean times. There is, too, a cloudless certainty about her—and her wiles—which wins respect in these darkly doubting days.

The truth is Miss West is that rarest of all species among contemporary artists. She is a pre-Freudian. A Miocene mammal is scarcely more difficult to find. She is a survival of the most tightly fitted. Her approach to what Mr. Hammond has dubbed the "obstinate urge" is as simple as her dress is ornate. To her sex is sex, and that is all there is to it, or, for that matter, to life. She has no inhibitions. It would be grossly unfair to accuse her of being an introvert. No psycho-analysts are needed to point the way to release for her. She is her own guide down a very narrow but winding path. Her books are not her best friends. To misquote George Ade, she is a bad girl who needs no help.

She also happens to be a grand performer, an actress who has perfected a style of her own. On stage or screen she is not only a whole show, but a side show in herself. She has a voice like no other voice that has ever been heard, and a method of delivery that no one else can claim. Her voice is choked, and has a sneer in it which is obviously directed at all the hearthside virtues. But, just as obviously, it is warm. It is the smoke that escapes from a slow fire.

She shakes speeches out of her mouth as if they were dice being rolled with terrifying deliberation from a box. Her sentences writhe like serpents. She can turn the simplest statement into a scorching insinuation; make an innocent "Hello, boys" sound like a traveling salesman's idea of *The Decameron*. Vocally, she is a hootchie-kootchie artist. The course she steers is always down the midway. In fact, her lack of subtlety is the most subtle thing about her.

Constant sinner that she may like to pretend she is, Miss West has her redeeming virtues. She has a sense of humor. Her exploits as a saleswoman of sex benefit by being exaggerated until they belong to the mock epic class. Both as authoress and as actress, she continues the Paul Bunyan tradition. She seems to recoil with an almost gun-like precision after each of her more tawdry speeches, and make her own comment (which is the comment of modernity) upon them, even while she continues to play them seriously. She has a certain air of going slumming in her own plays. She makes passion palatable to a puritan public by making even its intensity ludicrous. She burlesques sex as uproariously as John Held Jr.'s woodcuts spoof the nineties. By managing to date it, by putting it in the museum class, by substituting fake fangs for real ones, she has conquered Hollywood, even as she once conquered Broadway.

Contrary to the teachings of the moralists, her vicious heroines may always be triumphant. But they are so unreal that they do not matter. And, anyway, there is no virtue in her plays to be rewarded. No wonder, therefore, that Miss West has become America's newest sweetheart. She has probably known for years that America could be "had." And now the reports are that she "has" it.

From *The New York Evening Post*,
March 25, 1933.

MRS. FISKE IN A FARCE

By ROBERT GARLAND

T H A T Great Lady of the Theatre, that High Class Low Comedienne, that Grand Old Trouper whose name is Mrs. Fiske has returned once more to town. This time you'll find her in Mr. Erlanger's West Forty-fourth Street showshop, lending distinction to a shaky little play and acting circles around the younger generation.

But pay no attention to anything I say in connection with the Great Lady of the Theatre, the High Class Low Comedienne, the Grand Old Trouper. Where Mrs. Fiske is concerned, I am in no way responsible. In these prejudiced and unreliable eyes, she can do no wrong. When she made a joke out of Mrs. Alving and a bum out of Mrs. Malaprop, it was quite all right with me. As a matter of fact, she could star herself in a dramatization of the telephone directory and I would praise her. For there is something about her which delights me, something I have never been able to get into words. But it is a very real something which can take a shaky little play such as Mr. Fred Ballard's *Ladies of the Jury* and transform it into a glittering and glamorous evening's entertainment.

If you've a memory for such things you may recall that the Mr. Ballard who is responsible for *Ladies of the Jury* is the Mr. Ballard who was responsible for the *Believe Me, Xantippe* in which Mr. John Barrymore once played. But that was years ago. Labelled a "comedy," the piece which has found its way into Mr. Erlanger's playhouse is nothing of the kind. It's a farce, a little uncertain, a little incredible, a little thin around the edges.

In it is Mrs. Livingston Baldwin Crane, an important female in an unimportant community. This time it is Rosevale, New Jersey. A lovely lady is on trial for the murder of her rich and elderly husband, and the jury which has been selected to try her is composed of both men and women. Among the latter is Mrs. Crane. In the jury room she and she alone believes in the lovely lady's innocence. It is, as she takes pains to tell you, her woman's intuition. Nothing can convince her that the young Mrs. Gordon, who was formerly Miss Yvette Yvet of the chorus, shot and killed the man who was fool enough to marry her. What, in her eyes, is the evidence? And the comic story the playwright sets out to tell is the comic story of how Mrs. Crane swings all the jury to her side and sends young Mrs. Gordon out into the world free and blameless.

From the outset Mrs. Fiske crashes into this with gusto. She uses the resources of the Great Lady of the Theatre, of the High Class Low Comedienne, of the Grand Old Trouper. The result is in these eyes delightful. You tell yourself that if Mrs. Livingston Baldwin Crane could never win over those Jersey jurymen, Mrs. Fiske could. She could win them over as easily as she won over last night's audience.

After an illness of three years, Mr. Wilton Lackaye returns to Broadway as Judge Fish, the distinguished gentleman who says

"Objection overruled," pounds on his desk for order and receives such kisses as Mrs. Fiske, pretending to be Mrs. Livingston Baldwin Crane, sees fit to blow in his direction. It's a pleasure to have Mr. Lackaye around again. The others do nicely, thank you. Well, then, as nicely as might be expected. Miss Hallie Manning is amusing in a broad, burlesque way as Mayme Mixter, a member of the jury. Mr. Sardis Lawrence is first-rate as Spencer B. Dazey, the foreman. Miss Germaine Giroux, as the delectable defendant, handles her big scene effectively. Mr. George Tawde is quite all right as Andrew MacKair, an uncelebrated Scotsman.

But *Ladies of the Jury* is Mrs. Fiske, first, last and always. That is why I like it, why I like it, in fact, tremendously.

From *The New York World-Telegram,*
October 22, 1929.

MISS CROTHERS'S *"AS HUSBANDS GO"*

By ROBERT GARLAND

THERE were tears and cheers and speech-making last night in Mr. John Golden's personal showshop when Miss Rachel Crothers's latest comedy had its first Manhattan showing in the presence of an eighteen-karat audience which couldn't get enough of it. The title of the piece is *As Husbands Go*. And, between the first line and the last, there is no small amount of the effective intermingling of Main Street and Park Avenue which, in play after play, has served Miss Crothers well. That is to remind you that America's leading lady-playwright manages to be smart without being snooty, sentimental without being sappy, funny without being flip.... It's not only what Miss Crothers says that counts. It's what she leaves unsaid, as well.

What she does say in *As Husbands Go* is that Paris is France, Dubuque is Iowa and never the twain shall meet. Each, in its own way, is excellent. But, if it is, what seems good and proper in the shadow of Notre Dame is something else again in the shadow of St. Raphael's Cathedral. Or vice versa, as the wise ones word it.... It's all in a spirit of nice clean fun, but, as it goes along you pause to shed a furtive tear or tell yourself how true this, that or the other observation is.

As stories go, Miss Crothers's is the slightest.... And, although it's cavilling to say so, I've the feeling that, having got her leading characters into a jam, the playwright cheats a little when she comes to getting them out of it.... It's the drunken scene I'm referring to, a scene which, in itself, is expert and hilarious. But, when you think things over, it remains outside the real body of the play. And it's in a tawdrier tempo. Be this as it may, Miss Crothers relates the tale of how two ladies of Dubuque find themselves alone in Paris. Alone, that is, save for a couple of other fellows who happen not to be their husbands.... It is Mrs. Charles Lingard who's in the more precarious predicament, for while Mrs. Emmie Sykes is by way of being a widow, she herself is a hundred per cent American queen-in-her-own-home with an open-faced hundred per cent American husband waiting with outstretched arms in their dear Iowa home.

The point is that the ladies throw their new French bonnets over the American windmill and bring their boy-friends back with them. For a while, the complications which ensue in that dear Dubuque are cheerful, tearful and arresting. So all that remains to be said is that a good part of the acting is pretty near perfection.... The best is that of Miss Catherine Doucet, who does nobly by the Mrs. Emmie Sykes whose imported boy-friend goes by the name of Hippolitus Lomi. She has only to point her finger and "Even he" to—if you'll pardon the argot—stop the show. Miss Lily Cahill is lovely to look at and lovelier to listen to as Mrs. Charlie Lingard.

The others, too, are more or less as they should be.... Mr. Jay Fassett is forthright as the faithful Charlie Lingard. Against your better judgment, you're made to believe that successful bankers are like that—but only in Iowa! Miss Marjorie Lytell as Peggy Sykes is the Hard-soft modern maiden. Mr. Robert Foulk is amusing in a small rôle which might be smaller without him. And a Master Eddie Wragge is sincere and moving as a lonely lad named Wilbur.

But by this time you've discovered that *As Husbands Go* is one of the things to see. It is, anyway.... It is clean without being too clean, it is adult without being too adult, it is replete with humor, humanity and a sense of what might just as well be spoken of as proportion.

From *The New York World-Telegram*,
March 6, 1931.

RHAPSODY IN RED

John Howard Lawson's *Processional*

By GILBERT W. GABRIEL

O N E can be purposely ridiculous, but only accidentally sublime. Out of that rude march of events and meanings, wilful absurdity, gross tragedy, the ranking, blood-knuckled stuff of a sarcastic vaudeville which makes up *Processional* darts ever so often a line, a phrase of such beauty and burning as lights up the whole parade with wonderment. There is the awe of genius in this new production by the Theatre Guild. There is the misery of genius still inchoate and fumbling for its forms.

John Howard Lawson is the young American responsible for *Roger Bloomer,* which the Equity Players of a past season held aloft and then let drop hissing into the sea of forgetfulness. Thomas Seltzer, the publisher, salvaged it and established the reading worth of it, at any rate. He will publish this second of Mr. Lawson's plays, too, and then—mark the day down—there will be another such trumpeting abroad of the glorious quirk, arch, soaring and stinging of Mr. Lawson's words and concepts.

In his drama there is a newspaper man who must "tell the world." So, in turn, must we. We owe the report that never in all our business of dwelling among audiences have we seen a play so sullenly accepted by its hearers. Sometimes we wondered whether they heard at all. What Mr. Lawson meant to be deliberately cheap and tawdry yanked their ears occasionally. Most of the time they sat in glum affront at the temerity of an American gone imaginative and rid of the four-square limits of the stage. If only they had risen in fury and howled this "jazz symphony" out of town we should be surer of its ultimate grandeur.

That is Mr. Lawson's subtitle to his *Processional*. And it is precisely that, and all of that:—"A jazz symphony of American life!" In a day when jazz is already numbered with the minuet, and when the psycho-shimmyists are looking back on it amusedly as a state of mind successfully dissolved, it is thrilling to meet up with this translation of it into a vivid, vulgar, hip-swaying, heart-pounding travesty of that same state of mind. The nice little English encyclopedist who defined jazz as "nigger rhythms eccentrically accentuated for the sake of the American dance hall" would be troubled, perhaps, to know of one American who stood a little way apart from the merry-go-rounding mass and asked himself:—"What's wrong with this picture?"

Mr. Lawson does not answer his own question, though. He shows you the cheap, brassy, tragical, comical, cruel, persevering carnival of life in a West Virginia mining town. It is your own affair to drain away the blare of it and then to find the warm throb of a living race. It is your part to strain your eyes at his gauze sheets of burlesque diorama, awkward and lurid daubs of a small-town nightmare, and to discern behind each of them Man in all his nakedness, wretchedness and bravery. The author himself is magnificently contemptuous about what you see and hear. His *Processional* must pass. He must keep it thumping. If the whip in his hand flicks your own face, too, he is equally unsentimental about it.

Out of this sardonic scramble, like a trombone's ruddy, breathy notes coming out of an orchestra of discords, comes the main theme of Dynamite Jim, a mountain native, jailed by the law and order bunch for participating in the miners' strike. He escapes—as absurdly as romantically. He bayonets a poor, shivering soldier who wants to arrest him. He flees to his mother's barn, flees off again from there. In the black mouth of a mine he rapes the jingly-hearted young daughter of old Isaac Cohen, the town store keeper. Soldiers surround him again, he flees a last time. His mother and the young girl, herself about to become the mother of his child, are mourning him for hanged six months later. He comes home to them, saved, blind, dumbly frustrated. The scene between him and the girl there is pure, concentrated lyricism—a stenographic hurtling of moving loveliness.

Yet, to either side of this unbandaging of poetry the scheme festers with bitterest, loudest nonsense. The Klan comes into the mess, a Klan unmasked as a ballet-dancing lot of Jews, negroes and what-nots, to bawl in competition with the laborers, the soldiery, the high-hatters. It ends, as it begins, in boozy bleating and parade.

Until we can quote accurately from the book we hesitate to tamper with the startle that lies in so many of Mr. Lawson's lines. They are more characterization than independent epigrams, anyhow. They sum up, mock, apostrophize, with one short chortle apiece. When, for instance, some one begins to bait old Isaac Cohen he answers only:— "Your children's children will be saying, 'Oi, oi.'" Brilliant bits of wit are cast into the pot with some of the scabbiest roustabout joshing that ever slunk out of the Bowery. Mr. Lawson doesn't care. He boils them all up together into an Esau's birthright, a mess of clangorous challenge.

The boiling point is not always sustained, that is true. The machinery which manufactures energy beneath it does not always meet, cog to cog, and pulley to wheel, as it should. Coördination flies off the handle in the whirling of so much quick, fierce thought.

The staging and action could not keep pace with the author's thinking, last night. Yet Mr. Moeller and Mr. Gorelick have done their keen parts towards giving *Processional* firm tread and provocative capers. They have realized more than novelty from it. The cast is altogether good. Another day will let us do more than mention George Abbott, free from the tosh of *Lazybones* and rising to real stature here; June Walker's fine playing of the ungartered Sadie; Donald Macdonald's debonair performance as the newspaper man, and others in smaller but no less remarkable bits.

Processional is a Rhapsody in Red. How many Americans will be willing to hear it?

From *The Telegram-Mail,*
January 13, 1925.

SIDNEY HOWARD'S *THE SILVER CORD*

By GILBERT W. GABRIEL

WRITING of scalpel keenness has gone into *The Silver Cord,* the latest play for the Guild's performing in the John Golden Theatre. It is a play for the mature, the unafraid; and to them it guarantees

an evening of excitive truths and rare dramatic instinct. It undoubtedly fulfills Sidney Howard's promise of shrewd, compelling playmaking as have none of his pieces since the dulcet days of *They Knew
What They Wanted*. It can claim the honors of his best work.

When "spring comes round again next year," and Mothers' Day
blows in on the spicy breath of carnations and nutted bonbons, we
shall all indulge in the same fond carols as of yore. Our mother love,
as Harvey O'Higgins once imparted to us, is one of the deepest wells
from which the American temperament draws its sentiment. But
meanwhile, in such a play as *The Silver Cord*, Mr. Howard will have
said a healthy lot of things about mothers and sons, and our world
will be a bit wiser—nor necessarily sadder—for their uttering. Indeed,
here is a theme that we had naked need to see put well upon our
stage.

It is a theme the native novelists have been gnawing at with great
subjective gusto, these several recent seasons: the theme of the blight of
motherhood, the worrying, belittling, devastating love of a mother for
her grown sons. Mr. Howard takes it to grimmer lengths, gouges it
out of wretcheder causes than I have ever seen used in prim print. He
makes straight for Freud, and lets you have in frank, infuriated biolo-
gist's terms just what it was that Mother wanted.

For this drama of the silver cord which must be loosed and the
golden bowl which must be broken before the *Familia Phelps* wins
back its peace and self-respect is an embattling study of two sons in
the coils of an Œdipus Duplex. The silver cord involved is not so much
Biblical as umbilical.

It comes to a powerfully ironic end. The married son has the
means of escape, the fortitude, too. The other, only engaged, throws
away all chances of normalcy with his fiancee, oozes out into a state
of complete marshmallow, and when last seen is burying his noddle
back upon his mother's triumphant breast.

Mr. Howard makes it easy for himself—and for you—by endow-
ing this second son with a hopeless number of the outward and more
obvious marks of sissydom. Also by turning the mother into a silly sort
of semi-Mrs. Malaprop. No great objection is necessary. They are true
to type, these two, and to the fine rancor which dramatic license
heartily allows. And it *is* fine rancor, too—fine enough to be fair and

let the mother have her innings in a defense double-edged with good emotional intentions. Have respect for this scrupulousness of character drawing by Mr. Howard. Here, as it could not in his *Lucky Sam McCarver,* it wins, something warmer than respect, too.

For *The Silver Cord* is put together with better plan, more forceful purpose, than any on the Howard list. Certainly, as a piece of play building, it makes his *Ned McCobb's Daughter*—due to alternate with it in coming weeks—seem mortarless and haphazard. Its acts open upon excellent notes, humorous, natural, inviting, and each of them closes upon ringing, right, tight drama. The talk is fresh in its comedy, forthright in its denunciations, lithe at its engrossing business of putting things plainly, craftily, understandingly.

The piece has the added advantage of successful acting and canny direction by John Cromwell. On the piano rack—unless distances misled me—I saw precisely such music of Nevins and MacDowell as Mrs. Phelps would certainly love to play. Details were as guarded as that throughout. A young husband about to go to bed had his next day's clothes all laid out in the immemorial manner of young husbands.

Margalo Gillmore has a rich chance at the sorrows of the discarded fiancee—and richly merits it. Her performance races up to sheer loveliness. Elizabeth Risdon is back at last in a rôle worth her intelligence's time. Earle Larimore and Elliot Cabot are both better as the brothers than merely good. Laura Hope Crews, who has not been with the Guild since the wreck of the *Ariadne,* is a comedienne doing her gravest for a grave impasse—and often enough doing it persuasively. If I picture Mrs. Phelps as an entirely other person, that is my fault, probably, not Miss Crews's.

From *The New York Sun,*
December 21, 1926.

MAXWELL ANDERSON'S *MARY OF SCOTLAND*

By GILBERT W. GABRIEL

MAXWELL ANDERSON is back among the Elizabethans. Last night, in the Alvin, the Theatre Guild presented his *Mary of*

Scotland, a stately and eloquent tragedy, employing none less than Helen Hayes in its title rôle, Philip Merivale and Helen Menken in the generous group around her.

I suspect *Mary of Scotland* of being a beautiful play. I suspect this of it through the mists of a performance which seemed to me to hang occasionally low. I don't care how stiffly the Guild stages it, how content their time-keepers of the conversation are to let the pace die down into too pretty singsong ... I still suspect it with all my senses of being a truly beautiful play.

To Mr. Anderson's *Elizabeth the Queen,* which formerly served the Lunts so well, this *Mary of Scotland* is not so much a companion-piece as a reverse of the medal. That glacial patriot, England's great Bess, retains all of her most forbidding virtues in the new tragedy, takes on the swarthy guile and cruelty of an inflexible fiend, and is now a bilious villainess, jealousy incarnate.

That, of course, is the prerogative, indeed the tradition, of all playwrights who, falling in love with the still warm and enigmatic ghost of Mary Stuart, have treated her to famous tragedy. Elizabeth is their black beast, always Mary is ever their whited martyr. So it is with Schiller, Swinburne, all of them ... and so with Mr. Anderson, now.

Though even the idolizing Swinburne, when he came out of his dramatic swoon and turned to precise biography, had to admit, along with the rest of the historians, that Mary had really been a bit of a chucklehead and waggletail, a true chip of the old Medici, an irresistible nuisance to all the best bedsteads and thronerooms of Europe, almost until the last five minutes before they chopped off her charming head.

You may fight that all out, though, with the fond accounts of Brantome and Company. Mr. Anderson has double license as poet and dramatist to turn completely cavalier and make the tall, impetuous, heedless Mary of history completely over into a pocket-sized saint, England's dupe, Bothwell's faithful wife and posterity's pet. So long as he does—and he quite does!—make her into a heroine of such shining loveliness, such memorable appeal, as, in her own defiantly prophetic words, "will win men's hearts in the end ... though the sifting takes this hundred years ... or a thousand."

More things than this mere wrangle in the royal hennery were entirely Elizabeth's fault, according to Mr. Anderson's story—and we must stick to it. Elizabeth it was who counted on her rival's pique and married her slyly off to the arch-weakling, Darnley. Elizabeth it was who poured golden fat on the fire of John Knox's religious wrath. Elizabeth it was who, from the center of her spider web below the Scottish border, slimed her captive with slander of harlotry, murder and treason. Elizabeth it was who rejoiced with greedy malice against the supposedly innocent bystander at Rizzio's stabbing, at Darnley's strangling, at the midnight smithereens of Kirk O'Fields, on the belated nuptial couch with that gallant bully, Bothwell... and then coldly, slowly ate her up, a limb a year.

Bothwell is the whole hero here in Mr. Anderson's conception: a Bothwell who loves his queen from first meeting when she comes on that oft-celebrated voyage from France, and who continues to love her through blood and gunpowder, calumny, mismarriage, exile and utter ruin thereafter.

Much of all this is immensely touching—in the first and last acts, especially. In the middle act almost as much of it pales away into arctic elocution, seemingly more the stuff of noble literature than galloping drama. Never mind, I'm not retracting. I still suspect that it is a potentially beautiful play.

For I am already certain that Mr. Anderson chose his scenes and his episodes with a genuinely first-rate playwright's instinct for picturesque effect, for passion, excitement and deep sympathy. His play has not only large dimensions, it has the sturdiness of shrewd building, too, and high coloring, heat and surgent feeling. It has—as precious few plays by Americans can claim to have—a true beauty in its writing, a march of splendid word and proud cadence to the theatre's finest heights.

Here, at any rate, is one case in which I do not hesitate to divulge that much of the play is in blank verse. For it is in blank verse so strong and necessitous and vivid, even the dullest listener will forget his prejudice and feel that it could not have been written otherwise. When rough prose is in order, Mr. Anderson knows well what to do about that, too.

In a last, too hasty paragraph I must pay my respects to Miss

Hayes, who returns to the Guild for the first time since she was Shaw's and Caesar's kitten ... and who is, I feel, very heaven-sent from Hollywood to play her queenly part now with great clarity, resourcefulness and gentle majesty. And to Mr. Merivale, too, a Bothwell brilliantly speaking, a gentleman too long wasted on modern-clothes comedy when Shakespeare needs someone of his acting stature. And to Ernest Lawford, Charles Dalton, George Colouris and the full array of them ... to Miss Menken, too, if you insist, though I did not like her Elizabeth any more than I suppose I was expected to.

The Guild's first-nighters rose to the occasion's heights, come the final curtain. There was a romantic ovation for them all. The audience suspected, as I had, that we'd seen a most beautiful play.

From *The New York American,*
November 28, 1933.

THOSE VERY FIRST NIGHTERS

By PERCY HAMMOND

NOTHING, it has been said, is so characteristic of New York as its friendliness to visitors from out of town. Let a guest approach and we open the gates, roll out the red carpet, spread the canopies, and send a band to the depot to meet him. Flags fly; the air is filled with confetti and the loud "halloos" of welcome.

"Place," we say to him, "your little hand in ours, and we shall take you to see the sights. You are not interested in fish? Then we shall omit the Aquarium. But in our zoölogical gardens pleasing elephants swing their lithe proboscides, and the wary wart-hog is at hand, eager to divert you. In case you are a bookworm, repair with us to the libraries; or if you are fond of art and archæology, many museums are available for your edification."

You may, in the event that you are both literary and athletic, take a brisk walk around the Reservoir in Central Park to watch the heroes and heroines of New York fiction pursuing their romantic exercises. If patriotic, Grant's mausoleum is available and the effigies of General Sherman, and Franz Sigel.

If you like, you may look at the Hudson River, that mighty, mystic stream—as ancient as the Nile and much more sophisticated. Fifth Avenue is hard by, and sinister Broadway, of which it has been sung that there is a broken heart for every light upon it. If fond of fisticuffs, the pugilists at Madison Square Garden will engage in gentle gladiations. Commodious omnibuses wait on many street corners to transport you to Chinatown and Coney Island, to the residence of Charles M. Schwab and the birthplace of Theodore Roosevelt.

If you need the relaxing influence of dancing and other insobrieties, we have provided supper clubs wherein, despite the vigilance of a Puritan constabulary, vinous eye may look into vinous eye across the hootch and chicken sandwiches. It may interest you to scrutinize the Pittsburgh banker's son in one of these ruddy rendezvous as he tells the shrewd milliner from Altoona that she is the only woman he ever loved. And to watch her as she yearns for her room at the Ritz, replying, "Be yourself, Big Boy, be yourself."

These are the commonplaces of our hospitality, the habitual deeds of good-fellowship, the fresh log in the fireplace. It is our desire, if not our passion, to be open-armed. If, as our guest, you are robbed, bilked, or assassinated, as you may be in your home town, we provide you with policemen and competent district attorneys to avenge you. Our bootleggers are alert and well bestowed; our magistrates humane and sagacious; our morgues and penitentiaries adequate. As Ed Howe of the Atchison *Globe* said to a traffic policeman who permitted his daughter, Miss Effie, to motor illegally through a one-way street:

> Oh! call it by some other name,
> For friendship sounds too cold.

It is no more than right, then, that so wide-armed an institution should reserve one little pleasure to itself—one chamber in its vast open house whence it may retire occasionally and be alone. This New York retreat to which guests are not bidden and which the keys of the city will not unlock is the First Night at the theatres. There, and there only, are the real New Yorkers unsociable, asking for privacy. Sequestered among themselves in restful seclusion, they find comfort. Now and then, of course, a pushing outlander intrudes in the sanctum, but he meets with small cordiality. The First Night is New York's and New York's alone. As the signboards say in the rural districts, "No Trespassing Allowed on These Premises." The charters and franchises that admit you to the Stock Exchange or Van Cortlandt Park are useless as credentials to one of Mr. Belasco's or Miss Jane Cowl's "openings." To pass these sacred frontiers one must be native or at least naturalized.

It is the belief of New York dramatists, producers, and actors that nobody knows much about a play unless he is a New York first nighter. The "New York verdict" is to them the ultimate decree in dramatic judgments. They may be aware that human beings exist in Harrisburg and Stamford, and that the inhabitants of Chicago, Philadelphia, and Brooklyn are no more ignorant of life and the theatre than are the residents of Manhattan. The people of Denver, and other points West, read H. G. Wells and Miss Edna Ferber; they go to Yale or other universities, and they are as well versed in the sins and the atonements as the New York first night crowd. But to the New York man of the theatre their disapproval of an entertainment is as insignificant as their applause.

I asked an American manager why he was so contemptuous of an opening performance in Brooklyn or Newark and so obsequious about one across the river in New York. "Have not," I inquired, "the Brooklyn first nighters got organs, dimensions, senses, affections, passions? Are they not fed with the same food, interested in the same plots, and cheered by the same songs and dances? A soap-maker regards a soap-user in Fort Wayne with as much respect as he does one in New York. The breakfast foods are contrived to nourish the suburbanite as well as the metropolitan. Velasquez was overjoyed when peasants liked his pictures, and Molière read all his plays to his cook. Successful magazines and periodicals are edited and written as carefully for the Lincoln Avenues as they are for Forty-second Street. The manufacturers of chewing gums will tell you that if the flavour does not last in Zanesville, it will be impermanent also in Times Square. Why, then, should the Drama be so exclusively of New York?"

"Well," this impresario answered, "everybody connected with the theatre lives in New York, from stars to scene painters. If they think of anything else than New York it is in terms of New York. And they think of it in the way they believe the New York first nighters will think of it. They write, produce, and act to please that first night audience, and they are blind to all others. If an author composes a rural play, it is certain that he will want to have a traffic cop standing beside the town pump. By the way," this manager added, "perhaps you can tell me why the New York dramatic critics ignore a play when it is produced in Brooklyn, Atlantic City, or New Rochelle, and get all excited about it when it comes a week later to Broadway?"

Since these New York premieres are so important, let us try to attend one, carefully passported and viséd by a regular New Yorker. The entertainment may be one of the several *Follies* or a more serious effort supervised by Winthrop Ames, Arthur Hopkins, or George Tyler. We shall arrive punctually so that we may stand upon the curbstone and observe the celebrities as they approach. What a spectacle it is! The Mardi Gras, the Field of the Cloth of Gold, Carnival Time in Venice, Old Home Week in Hollywood, all in a night!

Bud Fisher draws up in a limousine, followed a moment later by Bugs Baer and James Montgomery Flagg. Then a Vanderbilt, a couple of Astors, and a Gould or two arrive in taxicabs. Avery Hopwood and William Anthony McGuire saunter along and engage in deep conversation with Dr. Frank Crane and Rube Goldberg. Bernard M. Baruch, Theodore Dreiser, Claire Briggs, Odd McIntyre, Ring Lardner, Harold Ross of *The New Yorker,* Harry Sinclair, Babe Ruth, and Frank Crowninshield. Who, you will ask, is that dejected boy on whose musical visage pale melancholy sits enthroned in gloom? Is he the composer of "Abide With Me"? Whereupon you will be informed that he is Irving Berlin, author of "Alexander's Ragtime Band." With him are the Selwyns, Edgar and Archibald, Martin Hermann, who directs the destinies of the A. H. Woods enterprises, and Gene Buck, the musical revue librettist. The ticket brokers come in swarms to estimate the values of the play.

Ssh! The critics are approaching. Upon their fronts deliberation sits and princely counsel. The carriage man takes Alan Dale's hat and stick amid a reverential silence. A cry "Make way!" is heard, and Alexander Woollcott appears, immersed in meditation. Burns Mantle and Walter Winchell are now seen, arm in arm, discussing, as they walk along, the *Œdipus* and *Abie's Irish Rose.* They frown a little at such cheers as may be raised, and the demonstration is quickly suppressed. The sidewalk teems with distinguished characters—dramatists, *entrepreneurs,* reviewers, executive editors, column conductors, film stars, actors, actresses, some minor poets, and, no doubt, an adventuress or two. There they are—a brilliant entourage for the impending accouchement—bright and voluble courtiers in an anteroom awaiting the birth of another Broadway drama.

The curtain goes up, and there is loud applause for the scenery. An obscure debutante comes on, representing a maidservant, and there is another demonstration. Ovations follow for all the players as they enter, and also as they exeunt. Between the acts there are visiting and exchange of opinion concerning the play. Like professional critics, these laymen have their pet phrases. The auditorium fairly sings with a chorus of "Awfully worth while," and "Isn't it adorable?" In other, less cultured communities, the audience usually describes acting and the drama as "cute" or "cunning."

At the intermissions we are confronted with an embarrassment of pleasures. Shall we remain inside and watch the "aisle actors" as they perform their modest histrionics; or shall we venture to the sidewalk and listen to the line-pullers as they pull their witty lines? Well, after observing for a moment a distinguished reviewer as he illustrated with gestures how Mansfield would have played the leading rôle in Broadway, let us hasten to the foyers and be regaled by the merry entr'acte banter and repartee of the first night humorists. You may see Professor Brander Matthews whispering to Clayton Hamilton, and you can imagine that he is saying, "I'm afraid it's a success." Or Robert Benchley remarking to Professor Wm. Lyon Phelps that he likes Peggy Hopkins Joyce because she has never got a nickel out of him. "Are you with this show?" you may hear Miss Edna Ferber inquire of Franklin P. Adams, as Mr. Adams emerges from the stage alley between the acts. "No," Mr. Adams will respond, "I'm against it."

But we must seek out Mr. Kelcey Allen, the critic of *Women's Wear,* for the jauntiest expressions of opinion. It was Mr. Allen who, on the opening night of Lionel Barrymore's débâcle in *Macbeth,* gave sententious advice to Mr. McBride, the ticket broker. Mr. McBride, sitting next to Mr. Allen, was wondering whether or not he should buy a lot of seats for *Macbeth,* when the line was spoken, "Lay on, Mac-Duff!"

"Lay off, McBride," whispered Mr. Allen, and Mr. McBride did so, greatly to his profit.

"This is Mr. Allen," I say, introducing you and hoping for the best. Whereupon Mr. Allen will remark: "If the guy who wrote this show has a lot of enemies, he's even with them all."

The New York first night audience is the Ku Klux of the drama. Its judgments are not final; but its shallow precepts are the frightening creed of all the playwrights from Sidney Howard to Samuel Shipman. When, if ever, an American dramatist endeavours a serious play, he finds this siren congregation looking over his shoulder and telling him what and what not to write. The Drama Leagues and the Culture Clubs should strive to abolish this nefarious institution, and succour the stage from the influences of a selfish insularity.

From *But—Is It Art?*
(Doubleday, Page, 1927).

THE THEATRE GUILD'S *PORGY*

By PERCY HAMMOND

I T is encouraging in *Porgy* to find that the dissensions between a novel and the stage may be pacified by the exertion of tact and understanding. For years we have stood by and watched the dramatists maltreat our pet works of fiction, and we were beginning to suspect that their differences would never be justly litigated. Savage playwrights have seized their silent victims, dragged them behind the footlights and there subjected them to all sorts of cruel indignities. The novels, resenting this uncongenial treatment, have licked their bruises sullenly and balked when ordered to be entertaining. You may recall the horror with which we averted our faces when the Drama picked its brutal quarrels with *The Green Hat* and *An American Tragedy,* and those abused masterpieces appeared before us so disfigured by amputations and bandages that we suffered almost as much as they did.

The Theatre Guild, as was to be expected, is the reconciling influence, the oil upon the troubled waters, the bearer of the white flag of truce, the efficient undertaker that buries the bloody hatchet. Being the boss of the Drama in these parts, it bids that unruly ruffian to be nice to *Porgy* and to treat it with consideration. Unusually acquiescent, the vandal takes the virgin by the hand and they play together at the Guild Theatre with all the amity of life-long pals. Peace, according to the poets, is the offspring of power, and the union of *Porgy* the novel with *Porgy* the drama is evidence that fruitful harmony may exist between two of the most antagonistic of the arts.

Before *Porgy* became a play doubts were expressed in bookworm circles that the story could be translated into the terms of the theatre. Its principal character is a lame Negro who crawls through the streets of Charleston, S. C., beseeching alms from the philanthropists of that charitable metropolis. His legs are shriveled and he is drawn to and from his business by a goat hitched to a little cart. So odorous is his engine of locomotion that complaints are made and he is frequently asked to move on. This figure, it was feared, was not sufficiently heroic for exhibition upon the stage—interest in crippled Negroes being at a low ebb. Readers of the book knew that Porgy, though black, crippled and a mendicant, was as soulful as many white men, and that he was apt at gambling, romance and murder in their most human aspects. But in spite of these qualifications it was regarded as improbable that the theatre-goers would sanctify his lowly career with their attentions. What excitement, it was inquired, could there be in the activities of a legless Afro-American beggar, living, loving and killing in a city so distant from New York?

Well, the life of Porgy and his associates in Catfish Row, as depicted by Mr. and Mrs. Du Bose Heyward, the Theatre Guild and a company of excellent black and tan actors turns out to be a thrilling bit of mysterious actuality. In it you may see the primitive Negroes of Charleston touched up by the friendly Drama's magic rouge until they become a satisfactory evening's entertainment. Oddly enough, this miracle is wrought by a new stage director, Rouben Mamoulian by name, an importation from the Balkans, they say, a quarter from which you would not expect an understanding of the nature and habits of the South Carolina colored folks. A showman and an esthete, Mr. Mamoulian waves his wand over the proceedings at the Guild Theatre and fools you into believing that the characters and occurrences in *Porgy* are real and significant. He knows the value of little tricks in stage direction, and when among the details of the eerie obsequies over the corpse of the murdered Robbins he causes theatrical shadows to dance upon the walls he is that most successful of combinations—artist and mountebank.

Although it is not in the book, you will not object to that scene wherein, while the hurricane rages and the Negroes are huddled in terror, "Crown," the sardonic assassin, appears and laughingly blasphemes Heaven. Nor will you, I think, complain because Mr. and Mrs. Heyward have changed the ending of the novel so that the curtain falls upon poor Porgy as he directs his goat to take him to New York in pursuit of his Bess, who has been enticed thither by a yaller bootlegger and vender of "happy dust." Altogether the play is more moving than the printed story, even if it isn't as literary. *Porgy* should congratulate itself that it has fallen upon the stage under careful and tender auspices and that its hazardous experiences have improved rather than hurt it.

I hear it whispered that *Porgy* is a series of pictures rather than a play—that it lacks the rhythmic conflict said to be the essence of dramatic wonder works. It seems to me to be full of war, with Porgy, the maimed beggar, Sportin' Life, the sleek dope peddler, and Crown, the handsome black devil, ever at grips over Crown's Bess, the noble Jezebel of Catfish Row. Perhaps it is not drama when the frightened negroes battle the hurricane with prayer and spirituals; nor when Porgy sinks his knife into Crown's heart. But these and other skirmishes are no mean substitute for the real thing; and if it is possible to arouse more than a casual interest in Afro-American affairs, *Porgy* is dramatic enough to do it.

Besides, for those who know the book, there is the combat between it and the Stage. Much of the novel's charm is in the lovely prose in which Mr. Heyward portrays the scene, its people, and their movements. What is the Drama to do with a picture like that wherein Porgy waits for news from the conjuress who is to cure his sweetheart of her miseries?

Far away St. Christopher struck the hour. The mellow bells threw the quarter hours out like a handful of small gold coins to ring down upon the drowsy streets. Then, very deliberately, they dropped ten round, heavy notes into the silence.

Nothing much, but what can be done, is done in that and similar cases by the Guild.

From *The New York Herald-Tribune,*
October 16, 1927.

E. E. CUMMINGS'S *HIM*

By ROBERT LITTELL

MR. E. E. CUMMINGS'S mixed wagonload of gargoyles and refuse, *Him,* which was dumped upon our suffering heads at the Provincetown Playhouse on Wednesday night, was doubly annoying—annoying in the first place simply because it was so hideously tiresome and distasteful, but also annoying because Mr. Cummings, who has shown himself capable of extraordinarily good and original work, seems to prefer playing hari-kari with his brains on our doorstep. Instead of hammering a fine intelligence, a rich command of every shade of language and the keenest perceptions into sense, or even admirable nonsense, he takes delight in committing literary nuisances. He insults himself and us and anything else in sight, not because he chooses to, but from habit.

The tragedy of Mr. Cummings's gifts (*The Enormous Room* is one of the most remarkable American books published since the war) going sour on him with his own connivance wouldn't be so important if he weren't one of a small group of rebellious writers addicted to an addled satiric nonsense for which they have no talent. It is a left-wing literary fashion, and, like most fashions nurtured in backwaters, it is green, stagnant and slightly slimy.

It is a pretty poor age that cannot boast of some rebels—good, healthy, destructive rebels—shouting wild, red songs and throwing real hard stones through comfortable windows. We had them, not so long ago. The old Masses crowd at its best was fearless, hungry, angry, dangerous. When they said things you could hear glass splintering in the distance; you could hear the swish and thud of the nightstick as it descended on their bloody, unbowed heads. Men like Carl Sandburg, John Reed, Max Eastman, knew what they were hitting at, aimed straight, and often left a black eye behind them. They were out in the traffic, they usually were run over, but they stood up in the middle of the road and enjoyed it.

The literary rebels of today keep to the side of the road and stand on their heads in weary mockery. They are anarchists of the most futile type, not philosophic anarchists, or humanitarian anarchists, or pacific anarchists, but just plain organic anarchists; in other words, people who recognize no principle in life but the pleasant indulgence of the language habit.

Their revolt from modern life is a running away from it and a taking shelter from it under the thin roof of their own inverted raillery.

Mr. Cummings is in many ways fairly representative of this group and its intellectual weary-willyism. He revolts from sense, but he doesn't achieve nonsense. He simply has not got the streak of genuine humor which makes the fun that Benchley, Stewart, Sullivan and Ring Lardner extract from the main props of the American scene so wonderfully funny. He doesn't know how to touch advertising and go-gettism with the sure wand of satiric nonsense; all he can manage is to allude to familiar Americana and twist them slightly into a shape which is neither funny nor satiric, but simply peculiar.

For instance: "She married a Holeproof.... Stop, look and listen. ... Beware of a woman called Metope who is in the pay of a Triglyph disguised as either an insurance agent or I forget which.... Look for the union label on every garment.... If it isn't an Eastman it isn't a kodak.... King C. Y. Didn't Gillette Meknow.... Stop, look and listen...."

This sort of stuff means nothing, as satire or nonsense. It is almost exactly what the psychologists mean by free association; allowing memory to pull up one string of verbal recollections after another without any effort or selection by the brain.

Did you ever play a parlor game which requires that every one in turn talk as fast as possible without stopping for a certain number of minutes? One word suggests another, one phrase suggests another, and out tumbles a yard or two of completely meaningless and otherwise unremarkable syllables. Mr. Cummings's play seems to be largely a stenographic report of what was said by one of the winners of this game.

Him, when asked by Me what he is writing, says it is "a little embonpoint to the dearly beloved master of my old prep school at Stonacre Heights, regretting that the undersigned is unable for pressing reasons to be present at the annual grand ball and entertainment to be held forthwith on the thirteenth Friday of next Thursday beginning with last Saturday until further notice to be furnished by——"

And on page 123: Him—"A papyrus from Haroun-al-Raschid inviting us all to petit déjeuner in the most excellent Arabic at twenty-three hours on January thirty-second, seven thousand one hundred and seventeen Columbus crossed the ocean blue."

This is neither nonsense, nor satire, nor deep stuff, nor parody, nor burlesque, nor revolt, nor art, nor dogma, nor entertainment, but simply rather painful evaluation of the contents of a weary, disordered, defeated and uninteresting mind.

From *The New York Evening Post,*
April 21, 1928.

LYNN RIGGS'S SOUTHWEST

Green Grow the Lilacs

By RICHARD LOCKRIDGE

LYNN RIGGS, playwright of the great Southwest, pounded his dramatic bass drum lustily last evening for the Theatre Guild. That generous organization, sensitive as always to its obligations, chimed in with an accompaniment, so creating a theatrical symphony in which the somewhat hollow reverberations of Mr. Riggs's play, called *Green Grow the Lilacs,* after its theme song, was a minor incident. The end product lies somewhere between drama and cowboy vaudeville, with the vaudeville having—and giving—somewhat the best of it.

The Guild, in other words, did precisely what Arthur Hopkins failed to do when, earlier in the season, he also was confronted with a play by Mr. Riggs. The Guild has wrapped about a drama which is sometimes harsh, now and then anxiously poetical, often needlessly pretentious, a production which does much to soften its crudities and to heighten its occasional moments of freshness and challenge. It is a play cushioned in cowboy songs, sustained by good performances in several of the more important roles. It has, because of its producers rather than its author, many happy moments of rollicking liveliness. Yet not even the Guild can altogether disguise the hollowness of the underlying drum.

Mr. Riggs has turned to much the same materials he used in *Roadside*. He has made more of them—a little more. Now and then, in *Green Grow the Lilacs,* he almost attains that freshness, that gustiness, he seeks. From the lips of Franchot Tone those strange, half realistic, half poetical speeches which the dramatist seems to believe represent the spirit of the Southwest in its earlier days—the time of the play is 1900—have sometimes the sound of a new tune. Now and then one may catch in them the wail of the wind across the prairie; feel a little of the gusto of a country where a man has room to stretch his arms.

Tone's Curly McClain is a cowboy—a roistering, laughing youth, bellowing his songs to the open sky and the fenceless plains. He comes courting to the home of Aunt Eller Murphy, looking for Laurey Williams—snatching her from the sinister attentions of a black villain of morbid propensities; a symbol, it is not hard to suspect, of all men who live cramped lives. The villain, a purely theatrical character, storms and threatens, skulks and waves pistols and finally runs about setting fire to haystacks. Curly and Laurey are married, the cowboys give them a shivaree on their wedding night, and the villain is killed by accident at the foot of one of the haystacks. In the end everything looks bright for the cowboy and his girl—the future, a long vista of minor poetry, stretches away before them.

It is no valid objection to Mr. Riggs's play that it is essentially melodrama. The difficulty lies deeper. It lies somewhere in the author's belief that extravagant statements are in themselves poetry; that shy young maidens give a new meaning to life when they gaze out over the audience and report that they cut off their pigtails when they were little girls and that once they saw a farmhouse burn down.

Miss June Walker is put under such a necessity and, for one scene, it floors her completely. She does not believe, I suspect, that young women talked so in the Indian Territory in 1900 nor in any other place at any other time, nor even that such words are the symbolic reflection of some hidden reality. Neither do I.

The dialogue is almost always cursed with this pretentiously literary quality. It never quite rings true; is never inevitable. It is not that the idiom is strange. That is a detail. It is that Mr. Riggs has made it all up out of his own head, arbitrarily. The play is essentially hollow. The Guild manages to make most of it very good fun. The production is not hollow, only the play. The cowboy singing is grand; Miss Helen Westley is grand, thanks largely to her own harsh, uncompromising insistence on talking like an actual person. There is movement and color upon the stage always. And Mr. Riggs seems to me to have had precious little to do with it.

The acting honors go to Miss Westley, with Mr. Tone not far behind. Miss Walker, after one really disastrous scene, rallied nobly, although without ever quite convincing me of Laurey's reality. Richard Hale skulked beautifully in a role primarily designed for skulking and evil glances; Ruth Chorpenning did excellently a caricature sketched on extraordinarily broad lines. The word "shivaree" is carefully explained in the program for the benefit of any whose lives may have been spent on the Atlantic coast, where gunny sacks are burlap bags.

From *The New York Sun,*
January 27, 1931.

ON THE SIDE OF THE ANGELS

Channing Pollock

By RICHARD LOCKRIDGE

I T is both ironical and unfortunate that the defense in the modern world of certain enduring concepts, in themselves neither outmoded nor intrinsically absurd, should ordinarily be left to warriors whose most extravagant efforts serve chiefly to bring new ridicule to the things they support. This is a thought which can hardly fail to strike

one while attending a play of Channing Pollock or, by some mis-
adventure, reading a poem by Edgar Guest. Here are two men, both,
I am sure, sincere and anxious to support the eternal verities in an
excited world and both singularly adept at arousing perverse thoughts
in those to whom they address their sermons.

Mr. Pollock, in *The House Beautiful,* is sincere almost to the
point of tears. He believes so earnestly in home and fireside, in
the romance of fidelity and the gallantry of the commonplace, in the
virtue of sentiment. Why should he arouse, even in one inclined on
the whole to agree with him, a temptation to make sneering sounds,
to punctuate his most aphoristic passages with derisive ejaculations and
to go straight from the theatre to the noisiest of night clubs? Why
should his pretty pictures of modern knights, valorous suburbanites,
suggest so compellingly the duty to seize a volume of Peter Arno's
drawings and leer over those matchless insults to human dignity?

Mr. Pollock, of course, will answer that the fault is ours. He will
nod his head wisely and suggest that it is precisely that tendency he is
writing about; he will contend that our topsy-turvy response to his eloquence merely proves how far we have wandered from devotion to the
"ancient, beautiful things." I can almost hear him now. "That's the
modern for you," Mr. Pollock is saying. "He must turn everything
upside down; he must be superior to every simple human emotion;
he must have his bridge and his cocktails and his superficially sophisticated reading matter." And he will add, truly enough, that he is not
writing for these hard, hopeless people, but for those who weep with
him—who wept, I can assure you, on the opening night of his play
and assured one another that never had they been so touched.

And I suppose, there are some who will insist that the fault is
with Mr. Pollock's ideas. Those ideas are, they will insist, the quaint
superstitions of the pre-Freudians. The merest suggestion that home
and fireside, fidelity and courage amid the commonplace, are concepts
of some significance will bring from them only a slight twisting of the
lip. They will hardly even bother to argue with Mr. Pollock. He is
a childish sentimentalist, fighting for Christmas-card slogans which
never reflected anything but the ingenuousness of the race. It is a
short life and a bitter one, and they will accept no sugar for its

amelioration. Better to get drunk, take what you can grab, leave morals for moralists.

It is lamentable that the free sugar of Mr. Pollock's preachment forces so many of us to the temporary acceptance of this bitter attitude as an antidote. It is really not an attitude any sane man would care to be found dead with; it certainly is not one that any logical man could hope to defend, except against Mr. Pollock.

The sentiments which Mr. Pollock defends undoubtedly will persist, even despite his defense. But it is unfortunate that the good words said for them should, on the whole, be such sophomoric ones. Mr. Pollock is singularly gifted with the ability to make the better seem the worse. His hopeless divagations into grandiloquence, marked in the present play by scenes of allegory nicely contrived to make any reticent man blush for his race; his old-maidish irritation at so many of the harmless aspects of civilized life; his essential prudishness—all of these weigh heavily upon Mr. Pollock, the champion, and bear down crushingly upon the sentiments whose colors he wears.

It is depressing to think no keener sword is drawn on the side of the angels, when their adversaries are represented so ably. Sentiment is in a parlous state with only Channing Pollock, Edgar Guest, et al to defend it.

From *The New York Sun,*
March 16, 1931

REUNION OF WEBER AND FIELDS

By BURNS MANTLE

F R O M the moment that Frankie Bailey, encased in yellow, walked blithely to the center of the Broadway stage, and everybody saw that Frankie was all there—from that moment until William the Wit remarked in the burlesque of "Bunty" that he must be a Scotch Collier, which was four hours later, the Weberfields jubilee was one huge, inspiriting success.

Not a player disappointed. Not a song went wrong. Not a chorus was bungled. Not a joke, new or old, failed to score. If new it was welcomed, if old it had its whiskers neatly plaited and was properly spruced up for the occasion.

And right in the middle of it, just before the first enthusiasm of the noisiest, dressiest, happiest audience that ever paid auction prices and was proud of itself for the money it had spent—before this first wild enthusiasm had passed, in walked David Warfield, with Yiddish whiskers on his chin and the old Levy smile on his face. David came as a happy surprise and, unlike his friend, Peter Grimm, had not the slightest difficulty getting his message across.

Weber, as in the old days, playfully pulled a few hairs from his whiskers; Fields danced joyfully around in his best imitation of a nervous capon; Lillian Russell made a furtive, though affectionate, dab at the putty nose he had hastily adjusted, and Collier, the born kidder, tried to include the incident as a part of the evening's entertainment.

There was much cheering, and then more cheering, and finally Father Belasco, who had come over with David, was dragged reluctantly forward and forced to make a bow. After which the scene that had been interrupted was resumed.

It really was a great jubilee—great in being free from disappointments. The best of the old Weberfields entertainments—the lesson in etiquette, in which Weber tries to make the silk hat serve as a crush hat; the poker game, in which his three friends bet all of Weber's money; the drinking scene, with only the one nickel and Weber's promise not to order anything; the modern drama burlesque of the Colliers—"I have something to say to you, Mary. I'm going away from here"; the best of the Russell songs, the best of the Templeton songs, the best of the chorus evolutions—these all have been revived as a part of the "pot-pourri reminiscences."

It is remarkable how well they stand the test of eight, nine and ten years in time and a legion of bad imitators.

Neither is it a makeshift revival. Handsomer costuming has not been offered in any of the winter's productions. And neither have handsomer girls been found to wear them. It is as though the Weberfields again had their pick of all the markets and had taken only the most shapely and the liveliest of the lot. The stage literally is studded with frankiebaileys.

The comedians themselves were in excellent spirits and perfect trim. Their old scenes went quite as well as though there never had been a separation. Weber seemed especially happy. He wanted to talk to every one in the audience and flirted gayly with the members of his family in a stage box.

That national institution of beauty preserved, Lillian Russell, defied the spotlight men to do their durndest. All lights were alike to her, and she was as glorious under one as under another. Every time she appeared she was done up in a new creation, "smothered with chopped ice," as Collier described the jewels, and if she does marry the Pittsburgh editor next summer, it's a safe wager he will have no wardrobe to buy for her for months to come. She sang well, too, and accepted the whirlwind applause that greeted her with the graciousness that has always been her greatest charm.

Miss Templeton rolled in good-humoredly and remarked that all the old crowd was there—paired off a bit differently, perhaps, but still there. She sang "Rosie" and "Buttercup," burlesqued a Spanish señorita deliciously and seemed in better voice than she was before she retired.

"Bunty Bulls and Strings" didn't get started until near midnight, and seemed a bit heavy after the lively froth that had gone before. It has the groundwork of good travesty, however, and should be a scream within the week. Collier plays Tammas Biggar and smokes the bagpipes. Helena Collier Garrick is his "past." Fay Templeton was the Bunty, with hoops big enough to support her in place of a chair. Ada Lewis, with a remarkably good make-up, plays the female villain, Susie Slimson; Fields is the Weelum, taking lessons from Tammas that he may know how to "cop the shillin's" at the plate; Weber is the boy who beats his "feyther," and Beban his sweetheart, Teenie.

As is usually the case, the best of the lines are yet to be added. Some of those that have found their way in thus far went very well, however. Collier grabbed one from Chicago and described a quartet as "three men and a tenor." Kelly remarked that for a bed that was 400 years old the one he slept on in Paris was the liveliest he ever had known. Miss Russell suggested that it takes an angel to catch an angel, and Fields classified Paris as one of the most unprincipled cities of the world.

From *The New York Evening Mail,*
February, 1912.

JOHN DREW

By BURNS MANTLE

I T is only when one of the older actors dies in harness, as the expression goes, that his passing means much to the current generation of playgoers. The players are so soon forgotten.

The talk this week has been mostly about John Drew and mostly, as is natural, by the older followers of the theatre. And yet so tenaciously did this fine old comedian cling to his profession that there were still many who are young and devoted to the encroaching movies who felt some little sense of personal loss in his passing.

He was a familiar Broadway figure. For the last ten years he has played but few parts, usually in all star revivals and at benefit performances for his beloved Players' club. But such was his interest in the theatre that he frequently was one of the first night crowd.

Usually he came with his daughter, Louise, and her husband, Jack Devereaux. Even with the aid of the thick lensed glasses he wore he found it difficult to find his way about, and one or the other of the younger people led him to and from his seat in the first row.

A pathetic memory I have of him is that of his playing Sir Peter Teazle to the Lady Teazle of Ethel Barrymore three or four years ago. He was having a bad spell with his eyes that season. Sitting where I could note his entrances, I could see one of the players lead him into the wings and indicate by pointing and whispers the location of the chair in which he was to seat himself or the table by which he was to stand on the stage. At his cue he would make his way bravely to that spot and take up the dialogue of his part.

But when it came time for his exit he must make his own way into the wings or toward a door, and once or twice he missed it. My heart ached for him as he bumped into the edge of a set and quickly tried to recover his position and not mar the performance. A hand would then reach out to guide him through the offstage darkness.

And yet, aside from this uncertainness of movement, John Drew never seemed an old man. He bore the burden of his years beautifully, was always most immaculately groomed, stood straight and firm, and talked with the ease and poise of a man of 50. It was only when we remembered back such a little while to the days when he was in very fact the glass of fashion and the mold of form of whom tailors boasted and from whom young men set their sartorial styles that it was hard to think of him as our John Drew.

This matter of clothes was both a blessing and a curse to John Drew. When he swung into the modern repertoire in the early nineties and was a star in his own right he paid particular attention to his wardrobe. Playing gay gallants or handsome leading men's parts, he saw to it that his tailors turned him out perfectly. Usually he was a full season ahead of the styles. His press agents made a point of calling attention to that fact. His tailors, eager to try out something new, often exaggerated the cut of his coats and the flare of his trousers. In those days any review of a John Drew performance that failed to make mention of the actor's grooming was taken as an indication either of the reviewer's carelessness of observation or his lack of experience.

In time the phrase, "a typical John Drew part," made its annual appearance, and the actor was spoken of slightingly as a mere "clothes horse." It was natural for the younger reviewers to doubt the quality of his art and belittle the range of his versatility. During the years that he was prosperous and the leading actor of his day he was content to answer the slights with a shrug and let his past record speak for itself. But as he grew older it hurt him to be catalogued as a one part actor. He delighted then in such plays as *Rosemary,* for instance, in the last act of which he put on a gray wig and hobbled the stage as an octogenarian.

Yet he never really overcame the handicap. Once he passed the day that he could convincingly simulate youth and play the so-called "John Drew parts" convincingly he was practically through. *Rosemary* really saw the beginning of the end of his career. He regained a bit of prestige after he gave up trying to go on being the actor we knew as John Drew and played a middle-aged husband in *The Circle*. But not much. Not many will remember him as Major Pendennis in

Pendennis, or the Marquis of Quex in *The Gay Lord Quex,* or the aging chap in *The Catbird*. He had earned fame and a fortune giving the public what it wanted of him, and he paid the price.

It was fine, I think, that he could die on the road. He had made a last tour in a good part surrounded by pleasant associates. Wherever he played he was the star of a cast of stars, and his were the outstanding receptions. In *Trelawny of the Wells* his entrance was delayed until the second act. Mrs. Whiffen, Mr. Lackaye, Miss Crosman, Miss Shannon, Mr. Heggie and Mr. Kellerd had all been welcomed with enthusiasm. And then Uncle John came on, and the tumult started all over. Just the other day I read the lament of a Los Angeles writer that John Drew should be taken from the cast before "his company" reached southern California.

I like to think, too, of the pleasure he had in being the president of the Players' club for so many years. It was, he used to say, the greatest honor that had been paid him in all his professional career. Here he was loved, honored and respected by those who knew him best, and here he was surrounded by mementos handed down from the days of his grandmother, Mrs. Kinlock, and his mother, Mrs. John Drew. Here the personal belongings of Edwin Booth are preserved in the room in which he died, and as he left them—his smoking things, the old leather jacket he used as a housecoat, flung carelessly over a chair; a volume of William Winter's verse, with an ivory bookmark where he had placed it a short time before he died. And here John Drew's memory will live longest and be most honestly revered.

From *The Sunday News,*
July 17, 1927.

ALFRED LUNT AND LYNN FONTANNE

Reunion in Vienna in Boston

By H. T. PARKER

THE new play at the Plymouth, Mr. Robert Sherwood's *Reunion in Vienna,* is material for acting. What independent life, what intrinsic quality, it possesses, may await leisurely discovery on printed pages.

In cursory reading it soon appears that, as there are words for music, so there are speeches gaining shape and color by the phrasing and intonation of the actors, shaded as well by the immediate play of face or hand, pose or pause. Likewise with the encounters, the turning points, of Mr. Sherwood's comedy. If they are to be salient and pungent, actors must transfuse them into flesh and blood, project them from a stage upon an audience in the theatre.

When it also happened that the principal players were Miss Lynn Fontanne and Mr. Alfred Lunt, the inference is plain. The substance and the show, the interest, merit and pleasure of the evening were primarily of the actors' making. Long since and by just deserts, Miss Fontanne and Mr. Lunt became the chartered libertines of our boards. They have imposed their personal quality upon a grateful public. When the actress quirks a finger and the actor sports a leg, when both cry "Let's pretend," along we spectators go for the pleasure of the game. For pleasure also in the skill of these two comedians, ripened by long association into full maturity. For our two hours in the playhouse, the playwright may go hang—or thank his lucky stars. All of which, as the wiseacres like to tell us, is a return to "pure theatre," to the actors' stage.

Consequently, when Mr. Sherwood sets in contrast the Vienna of the final years of the Hapsburgs and the Vienna of 1930, we do not inquire how large or deep runs his first-hand knowledge of either. Enough for us on the sidelines that he has led Miss Fontanne and Mr. Lunt back to one of their favorite and exhilarating playing fields —the field of the early *Guardsman* and the subsequent *Caprice*. When, again, he invents his Archduke of the old régime and his psychiatrist of the new order to set them in contest over the Elena who was the mistress of the prince and is the wife of the physician, we do not ask how true they may be to type. Enough, again, that he sketches personages for Miss Fontanne, Mr. Lunt and Mr. Watson to enlarge, vitalize and adorn. Mr. Sherwood's Frau Lucher is obviously modeled after the half-factual, half-legendary Frau Sacher whose nineteenth-century hotel was the seat of archducal intrigue and archducal pleasure-seeking. We sit by, content to observe her in the visible, audible, characterizing presence of Miss Westley. In his retrospective *Olympia,* fetched from Budapest as far as New York, Molnar was both humorous and sentimental over the vanished nobility. It better suits Mr. Sherwood's purpose to show us a frowsy parcel thereof re-gathered in decay to celebrate at Frau Lucher's the hundredth anniversary of Emperor Franz Josef's birth. Well and good so long as their rites make an amusing scene and playwright and producer imagine and cast them as half-ridiculous, half-pitiable figures. . . .

Goodbye, then, to Mr. Sherwood, while Miss Fontanne and Mr. Lunt keep, and deserve, the center of the stage, with the secondary and the minor players in complementary circle around them. At the very center Miss Fontanne. As a keen actress should, she may achieve her *Strange Interlude,* her *Elizabeth the Queen.* But to most of us, in the give-and-take of the theatre, she remains the unmatched comédienne of the present American stage. How finely strung are her bodily means, how transparent her fleshly envelope! A flick with her hands, a turn of her head, a glint in her eye—each not too often—and she has sped light banter or happy raillery. A graver thought, a mounting impulse, a warming emotion, traverse her personage. Like light through alabaster it permeates her physical being.

How sensitive, ready and graphic is her technical resource! She sets in a pause and it points a whole sentence. She molds a phrase and the playwright's plain prose becomes a distinguished speech. An intonation and the colored word turns light or dark, warm or chill. Her every stroke is prepared; yet each seems the release, through the character, of the instant in the play. Her tongue is stilled; her face is motionless, her body in repose. By the telepathy of the theatre she and her personage still signify. The moment comes for change. The impetus is clear, the transition instant and irresistible. Imaginatively and technically, she is mistress of light mockery, swift implication, the concentrating, illuminating flash that darts across the theatre.

Follow Miss Fontanne through this present Elena. She counts the wash, and domestic routine becomes a grace. She listens to the earnest fatuities of two of her husband's pupils. Malice of the tongue and malice of the eye twinkle out of her answers. She has not an illusion about Frau Lucher, the party, the guests thereat. Off the radio comes a waltz of old imperial Vienna. Forthwith memories trouble and elate her. She will go to the encounter with the returned Archduke. The Lucher's fiddler stings her again toward the end of the lovers' romp.

From coquetries she leaps into rollicking, upon the broadest of breadths she lays her light comédienne's hand. The Archduke pursues her to her husband's house. In an undercurrent of amusement she listens to their ravings. The ways of rival, angry men. How much more deft is woman's wit and other feminine weapons! The husband, turned magnanimous, departs to save the Archduke from the police. This Rudolf declines in self-pity—and she humors him. Who shall read the actress's enigmatic face in the pause at the door, as she follows him from the living room? The end, next morning, hints—or rather affirms—a happy solution. And ever, like the light upon the alabaster, Miss Fontanne herself is shining through the character.

In turn the Archduke gives Mr. Lunt a part upon which he can wreak himself—in exuberant make-believe, in prodigious swagger, sensual and sentimental, playboy and prince of the blood. Rudolf in his uniform, a little faded and with rents in the lining, receives the Lucher's guests with a remote, placid imperial dignity—all Hapsburg. In his shirt tail and nothing else, he can bow in courtly salutation. Dress him in a Tyrolean disguise and he will rough-house, hand or tongue, with old Lucher. Man, as reminiscent sensual animal, romps and rollicks with the enkindling Elena. A child-mind, extravagant, irritated, goes up against the provoked but still rational husband. Then as extravagant a melancholy of romantical self-pity. The touched Elena, the happy ending of the night into the day, of passion into escape. "Pure theatre" from the first tumultuous entrance to the final exit appeased, a part that meets half way many a Luntian inclination, that invites the actor over a wide range of robust resource. An elder generation used to be told that it went to see Mansfield through the adventures set down for his personage. Its children may behold now an Austrian Archduke in the terms of Alfred Lunt. Perhaps protrusive acting is the word....

From The Boston Evening Transcript,
September 20, 1932.

ALICE IN FOURTEENTH STREET

Eva Le Gallienne's *Alice in Wonderland*

By H. T. PARKER

FIRST, the audience—at a Saturday matinée, which was enough; on the day before Christmas, which was full measure added. Below stairs it filled every chair in the old Fourteenth Street Theatre, now Miss Le Gallienne's playhouse with the long name; as often as it liked set the reverberant walls ringing with cries and chatter. For no one expects, and only a curmudgeon could want, a still audience before *Alice in Wonderland* and *Through the Looking Glass,* transcribed, as the musicians might say, for the stage. As that fortunate pageant of sights, sounds, marvels and mischief unfolds, one must "exclaim" on the instant or perish.

Especially if one is at the right age. That age, of course, is debatable, like everything else in Alice's two books—unless the Queen of Hearts happens to be about, bawling her catchword. Some say, it is adult years, because though the books were written to amuse girl-children in a university town, the grown-ups found them the more diverting, not to say meaningful. Everyone knows that *Peter Pan* is a play about childhood, as adult years fancy they remember it or out of whole cloth like to imagine it. Even so, say the reasoners, with *Alice.* It is not she, in the seventh year of her age, who falls in the well at the bottom of the rabbit-hole or slips through the gauzy looking glass. Rather, it is adult minds bent on one more Carrollian spree.

The adults were there, sufficiently. Some had come of their own motion, being Carrollians from youth upward, the riper for a devotion waxing with the years. Others, when you chanced upon them and they chanced upon you—both surprisedly—professed to be escorting their own, their kinsfolk's or their neighbors' offspring. But it was to be observed that as soon as the curtain rose they forgot their young charges; could be a bit petulant when shrill questioning, not to be denied, distributed their absorption in the transactions of the stage. Unmistakably the children were at the right age. The wrong age, of course, is the middle teens. Then, whether one is sub-sub-deb or only "prep" schoolboy, one knows everything and is quite sure of it; is vastly superior to Alice and all her train; may even prattle in girlish treble or rumble in boyish bass that this is the machine or scientific age. Leave them at home, or send them to Roxy's gilded and electrified braggadocio.

Fortunately none was audibly present last Saturday, which to them, no doubt, was merely December 24. Younger and more guileless children abounded—to see with Alice's eyes, hear with her ears, keep her company through the whole afternoon, wander and wonder —be careful Mr. Compositor—and believe, as she wandered and wondered and believed. Only in one respect did they differ from her. Whereas at many moments she, on the stage, stood rapt and mute, they, in the auditorium, laughed, or chattered, or any old way rattled out their delight. Atmosphere, they say, makes half the fortune of a play. It was not lacking in Fourteenth Street on Christmas Eve.

Second, to the stage—over the heads of the little orchestra for which a Londoner, Richard Addinsell, had written the music. It was light, pleasing and in tune with the play. Out of it came occasional glints of Carrollian fancy and humor—mostly from the songs into which the verses had been transcribed. All of which was something— the more when one remembered that Sir Arthur Sullivan himself once gave up the setting of these rhymes as an impossible job. . . . The curtain rose upon Alice in her bright-red armchair; the black kitten; the ball of worsted; any other indispensable was by this reporter overlooked. Alice speculating in her child's voice about the beyond behind the looking glass. Alice stepping magically and wonderingly through it into a changeful land where no dimension was quite as in reason and nature it should be. . . .

So to the pageant. Turn and turn about the Carrollian troop peopled it. The White Rabbit, apt with his handkerchief, was an early comer. The Crab, by the Pool of Tears, shone bright red. The Duck ogled him, matron-like. The Caterpillar sat on his mushroom plying an acid tongue. The Fish Footman bowed solemnly to the Frog Footman. The Cheshire Cat grinned down from its perch. The March Hare, the talkative Mad Hatter, the sleepy Dormouse shared their tea. The Mock Turtle would have drawn tears to the eye of a needle— tears of joy. The Queen of Hearts stormed about the croquet-ground.

High-enthroned, the King of Hearts conducted one of the most celebrated of trials, though no case-book, they say, except Lewis Carroll's, precisely records it.

So much for Part One which, as long as we went along with Alice—swimming the pool and running beside her—was rather like an unfolding narrative, tied together by the Carrollian logic. (One is not a mathematician for nothing, even when one writes a fantastical book for the children in the Master's house.) Part Two was more desultory, as though Miss Le Gallienne and Miss Friebus, stringing together the play, would make sure that they had omitted nothing expected. Consequently in rather disorderly succession, the two Chess Queens, red or white; Tweedledum and Tweedledee, joyously recognized by oldest and youngest; Humpty Dumpty, explaining from his wall; the White Knight, slipping off, and climbing on, his knowing steed, with Alice and the ladder for help. And, "lest we forget," the Walrus and the Carpenter, colloguing almost as large as life, while the little blue oysters waltzed along the shore. Finally "Alice at Home Again" as the program had it—in the red chair, by the fire, no doubt missing her tea; while we others stumbled out, as dazed as she, into the murk of Fourteenth Street, the grime of Sixth Avenue.

From *The Boston Evening Transcript,*
December 29, 1932.

TALLULAH BANKHEAD IN *FORSAKING ALL OTHERS*

By WALTER WINCHELL

I T ' S about time that Arch Selwyn, the most patient of the showmen, had a hit. How he beamed in the foyer of the Times Square Theatre after Act II last evening, where *Forsaking All Others* brought Tallulah Bankhead back to town.

This is the new comedy which fooled so many of the suburban oracles, who sent out the most aggravating libels on New York's newest comedy delight. It is the New Yorkiest of the amusements, therefore the provincials must have missed an abundance of fun.

Go and have an entire First Actful of rib-aching laughter, and be charmed by Senator Bankhead's gal, Tal. And then spend the following two acts with an excellent troupe of make-believers, who quit fencing with each other to comfort a bride, "who flunked her finals." Her groom, you see, married another woman just as the *Lohengrin* cue was signaled.

Forsaking All Others, in fewer sentences, is the sort of smart talk you could hear a second time, which is exactly what one reviewer intends to do at the next opportunity. That's how funny *Forsaking All Others* really is, and how human and genuine are its people, particularly Miss Bankhead.

You probably can't recall ever witnessing an actress who played her rôle as though she loved every moment of it. Tallulah plays Mary with such abandon and with such energy (she even does a handspring when she is saddest!) that the spectator is tempted to reach across the bulbs and pat her on the cheeks. In admiration, of course. It was Miss Bankhead's triumph last night. And her co-authors, newcomers, merit equal honors. For theirs is a swift and refreshing entertainment, better, perhaps, in its opening act, but tip-top-notcher amusement throughout. Edward Roberts and Frank Cavett wrote it. Mr. Cavett, until he helped prepare *Forsaking All Others,* carried manuscripts in movie studios.

Their sophisticated and big-town clowning snugly fits Tallulah Bankhead. And after enjoying every moment of her talent and charm on Mr. Selwyn's Times Square stage—you are convinced that she didn't fail Hollywood so much as Hollywood must have failed her. She is a star!

The new hit glides along—spraying lusty laughter generously—when, that is, it isn't groaning over the fiasco at the church on Mary's wedding noon. The repartee is sane—for it doesn't risk being brisk—when there are tears to weep—and the authors reveal understanding New Yorkers, who know better than to crack flip—when the near-bride herself confesses—that she never again will laugh at the comedians "when they kick the lady in the fanny." I enjoyed it all. It is grand. It is New York. And about New Yorkers I've known and liked.

Besides the magic of Miss Bankhead, there are excellent performances by such experts as Donald MacDonald, Nancy Ryan, Millicent

Hanley (a masterful actress), Ilka Chase, Anderson Lawlor and Cora Witherspoon. But the huge surprise of the eventful proceedings is the delightful performance of Frederick Keating! You must have enjoyed his bird-cage illusion at the Palace or at Miss Guinan's former addresses.

To Mr. Keating falls an orchard of crisp comments, but he juggles them skillfully and comes in so close to the star for high honors, you suspect she could feel him breathing on her neck. Oh, it can't be the same Keating! Not the former reporter on *The World?* The Keating last night is a clever actor! No keating!

At any rate, mind your Winchell and forsake all the other plays for *Forsaking All Others*—and, of course, Miss Bankhead, my newest valentine among the enchanting Pagliaccis.

From *The Daily Mirror,*
March 2, 1933.

THE CENTURY GIRL

By SIME SILVERMAN

THE CENTURY GIRL is a tremendous show. Charles Dillingham and Florenz Ziegfeld, Jr., co-jointly produced it for the Century Theatre.[1] It opened Monday night at 8:25 and ended that same evening at 12:58. The double effort of Messrs. Ziegfeld and Dillingham seemed to be individual after all, for instead of giving but one show, they piled up two or three in one. It might be some fun to hang around and listen to those two managers discussing what there is to be cut out of the performance. Or they may make it neutral and call in outsiders, to save injured feelings. As there are only about 90 or 100 minutes to be taken out, it doesn't require much of a knife, just a hydraulic dredge.

The Century Girl could throw everything out, retaining only the second act finale and the burlesque ballet and still be certain of two sure draws. The second act finale, to a march song by Victor

[1] The Century Theatre, demolished in 1932, was first known as the New Theatre, and was opened in 1909, under the direction of Winthrop Ames, as a privately financed attempt to create a national theatre in this country. The venture lasted for only two and one half years.

Herbert and Henry Blossom, was staged by Ned Wayburn. It's all Mr. Wayburn did in this show and it's enough. Wayburn can now retire on his laurels if he wishes to, for he has surpassed all of his own efforts as a stager and those of all others by this one thing. The revolving stage is employed. On it are high flights of stairs, and with the background of Urban scenery, the set looks like a steeplechase course. Girls in patriotic dress line the edge of the stage, in single file. Behind them are grouped sailors and soldiers, boys and girls. As the stage commences to revolve, the girls edging the stage do a single side step, to the music, while those behind march and countermarch, in twos, fours and eights alternately, up and over and down the flights of stairs, presenting a spectacle that has a real stir, and a sight that is the only thing in this performance worth going over once to see. The Herbert music of this number stands out beyond the other melodies of the show, especially written by the two composers, Mr. Herbert and Irving Berlin.

Mr. Berlin made a serious mistake and a natural one, in writing lyrics and composing for the Century. He evidently overlooked the bigness of the house. So doing and giving the lyrics of his numbers the customary Berlin attention, the Berlin songs of the show did not get over as they should have done. None of the women principals has a voice capable of sending a "lyric" over in the big auditorium with its poor acoustics, and the chorus fell down the same way. The "Alice in Wonderland" scene had a splendid lyric probably intended to carry the thing along, but few in the house got it. The nearest Berlin's songs and music got to the front was in "They's Got Me Doing It, Too," as sung by Elsie Janis during a "Stage Door" scene with the sixteen English (Bell and Tiller schools) "Sunshine Girls." And at that one couldn't decide between Miss Janis, the song or the dance finish of the number as to which was responsible for its success. Another Berlin song helped by a number was "Hunting for a New Dance" in the "Forest Glade" scene that ended with "The Chicken Walk." This was Leon Errol's staging contribution and also a bright production spot in the performance.

Elsie Janis at 12:30 made the personal hit of the show. What Miss Janis is doing in this performance tells why she is in continual demand on two continents.

Next to Miss Janis in favor was Sam Bernard. Mr. Bernard made them laugh whenever in sight and capped the evening for himself by his vaudeville political speech just before the finale of the second act.

There were other individual scores of greater or less extent. Myles McCarthy made one as "straight" when working with Frank Tinney in the "Street Traffic" scene. Mr. Tinney did not fare as well. There was a lot of Tinney in black and white face, besides Miss Janis's invitation. While Tinney with a remark here or there got a laugh, nobody would deny his material as a rule seemed forced without any brilliancy at any time. Tinney's talk at times was just a trifle rough for the production he was in.

What little talk there is in the show is altogether too "wise." There isn't much, the management seemingly have realized the impossibility of the Century for a musical comedy "story." There is not a bit of "story," "book" or "plot" to The Century Girl, just big scenes and acts in "one" to make the sets. Some of these latter are so heavy it calls oft'times for more than one act in "one" to make the time. Through this perhaps it looks as though all the "one" turns were allowed to do all they could. This in part helped to delay the performance until the late hour. Still Harry Langdon withdrew from the show Monday afternoon and it was reported as the reason Langdon was given one minute in "one" to do his turn (The Langdons).

A hit of no mean proportion scored early was made by Van and Schenk, from vaudeville, with their own songs. While the applause sounded more healthy than one would think warranted under the circumstances, there was no doubt the house liked the boys, who had a novel opening. Two dress-suited young men the audience thought were the principals retired immediately after the piano was set, and the "stage hands" who had moved the piano turned out to be the singers. Van and Schenck nearly did their full act. Tinney did his blackface turn in the second act, aided by Max Hoffmann, the orchestra's conductor.

Miss Dressler did a song specialty in the last act (there are three), and her heavy, rough comedy was well liked all the way.

The show jumped into its finale, "On the Train of a Wedding Gown," with Hazel Dawn in it. The jump skipped the "Procession of

Laces," probably a "parade," that may have been thought unnecessary, as it seemed also were the Barr Sisters, programed, but who did not appear. Miss Dawn looked her prettiest and played the violin once, but kept her voice on the stage almost as much as herself.

The scenic end by Urban guaranteed itself before the show opened, while the costuming is in step with the rest. The Century has been redecorated throughout and looks better. The stage has a second proscenium arch to cut down its size in looks.

Messrs. Dillingham and Ziegfeld have built up opposition to their other musical comedy enterprises in *The Century Girl*. What they will do with this show to competitors will be a pity. It's the biggest thing of its kind New York has ever seen, and no one will sidestep it. No one can afford to.

From *Variety*,
November 10, 1916.

THE BROADWAY BELLES

By JACK CONWAY [1]

OPPENHEIMER and Leavitts' *Broadway Belles* is burlesque goulash, pure and unadulterated, with a perfect average maintained as far as mellowness and age of material are concerned. If the authors spent over thirty minutes putting the book together they loafed on the job. There isn't a piece of business, a line or a situation that isn't familiar to the burlesque patron.

And why not? The biggest laugh getter was a restaurant scene that has seen service since the first Turkey started to play the slabs

---

[1] Jack Conway, who has been listed along with Sime Silverman, H. L. Mencken, "Bugs" Baer, Ring Lardner and George Ade as one of the native authors who have done most to extend the American vocabulary was the first to introduce such phrases as "palooka," "pushover," "clicked," "scram" and "S.A." into theatrical parlance. Explaining his use of slang in an article which was first printed in *Variety* on December 29, 1926, Mr. Conway said, "I think 'guts' has it all over 'courage,' 'clicked' can outpoint 'satisfactory' any time, and 'brodied' can give 'failed' seven in the rack and bank the last ball.... I am proud to be labeled a slangster; to be articulate and understandable to my mob....

"Broadway slang differs from gun talk as much as Bostonese from hog Latin. Broadway chatter is full of theatrical cracks such as 'flopped,' 'clicked,' 'wowed,' 'kayoed 'em,' 'knocked 'em bowlegged,' 'four frolics daily,' 'ten per center,' all of which would be mashed potatoes to the wire who buzzes glibly about 'mouthpieces,' 'big house,'' 'head screw,' etc."

of our forefathers at Hensfoot Corners. It is the bit where the two comics agree to stage an argument as to which will pay the check, one finally inviting the other out in the alley, following which they will run away. It works out with reverse English and is always sure fire at the Columbia of Tomashefsy's National Winter Garden.

Eddie Cole is the featured comedian, assisted by Earl Kern, who does a tramp. Both work cleanly, side-stepping the double entendre and getting over the wheezy lines and bits with deliveries that deserve better material.

Cole does a red-nosed Dutch minus crepe or chin piece with a fractured dialect, while Kern sticks to a crummy looking vag. Both are good low comedians and good showmen, having no trouble with the regulars at the Fourteenth street house where they kept the laughs flowing continuously.

Burton Carr and Bobby Burch both handle straight and minor roles, the former taking the piece as seriously as Dr. Stratton would.

Phil Hart opens in blackface as a loud-voiced bellhop, then shows as half of an ordinary dancing team in which he is partnered by Peggy Hart in a routine of soft and hard shoe dancing that lacked grace and modernity and lastly in an effeminate bit with a college boy make-up and a voice of a padrone. He was as effeminate as Jack Dempsey would be in the same bit.

Of the women, Helen Gibson stood out like an oasis in the Sahara. She flashed a half dozen changes, all in excellent taste, danced with unusual grace and lightness for a big woman and led several numbers exhibiting a pleasing voice and plenty of personality.

Florence Whitford, a heavy soubrette, turned in the usual shimmying peppery performance. Miss Whitford is the stereotyped soube who shouts her numbers, sprinkles hitch kicks at the boxes and reads lines with her mind somewhere in Bronx Park. Myrtle Andrews was the other female principal and held the voice of the production.

The costuming of the regulation sixteen choristers was up to the wheel average. Twelve changes were made, a one-piece bathing suit effect getting most attention led by Helen Gibson who hogged attention with her symmetrical lines. The girls sang and danced acceptably, the back row harboring two or three females who might be parents of some of the down-front steppers.

Despite the program, which credits the first act with four scenes, there are only two. They are full stage affairs with house drops used for the bits in "one" that are sandwiched in between the seats.

Act II is played entirely in a full stage set "Boardwalk at Atlantic City." This set, though not new, takes the honors in that department without much competition.

"Pick up my old hat," won the handicap for age with the "burglar and stick-up" stunt close up.

The rain kept the attendance down Monday night to half a house full but those who were in laughed and commented favorably on the show as they went out. So Oppenheimer and Leavitt have ducked royalty fees, and if the Olympic is a criterion of what they have to please around the American circuit, they have a pleasing show.

From *Variety,*
November 26, 1920.

APPENDIX

ACKNOWLEDGMENTS

W E wish to acknowledge the courtesy of those contemporary critics who have made this book possible by graciously giving us permission to include their writings in this collection and immensely facilitated our preparation of it.

We also wish to thank the editors of *The Atlantic Monthly* for permission to reprint extracts from L. Clark Davis's article on "Jefferson's Rip Van Winkle" and Henry James's "Salvini"; the *Boston Transcript* for the use of H. T. Parker's review of Eva LeGallienne's *Alice in Wonderland* and the Lunts in *Reunion in Vienna; The Commonweal* for R. Dana Skinner's article on *The Green Pastures; The Daily Mirror* for allowing us to include Walter Winchell's review of *Forsaking All Others;* Doubleday, Doran & Co. for Percy Hammond's chapter, "Those Very First Nighters," from *But—Is it Art?;* the Funk and Wagnalls Company for permission to reprint J. Ranken Towse's studies of Clara Morris, Mary Anderson, Augustin Daly's company and Ada Rehan which first appeared in *Sixty Years of the Theatre;* Harper Brothers for Gilbert Seldes's "Tribute to Florenz Ziegfeld" which was published in *The Seven Lively Arts;* the editors of *Harper's Magazine* for allowing us to include William Dean Howells's paragraphs on Edward Harrigan's comedies which first appeared in "The Editor's Study"; Harcourt, Brace and Company for the use of Ludwig Lewisohn's chapter, "A Note on Tragedy," which was reprinted in *The Drama and the Stage;* the *Herald-Tribune* for Heywood Broun's review of *Beyond the Horizon,* Percy Hammond's article on *Porgy* and the final section of Arthur Ruhl's notice of *Ah, Wilderness!;* Henry Holt and Company for the use of "Themes in the Theatre" which is taken from Clayton Hamilton's *The Theory of the Theatre;* Alfred A. Knopf for permission to use "Legend's End: David Belasco" which was a chapter in Mr. Nathan's book, *Mr. George Jean Nathan Presents,* and "Drama as an Art" which appeared in Mr. Nathan's *The Critic and the Drama;* the Life Magazine, Inc., for the use of James Metcalfe's reviews of *The New York Idea* and *Romance,* and the excerpts from Robert Benchley's bulletins on *Abie's Irish Rose;* Little, Brown and Company for permission to include the preface Heywood Broun wrote for George Kelly's *The Show-Off,* and Montrose J. Moses's introduction on Philip Barry which appeared in Mr. Moses's anthology, *Representative American Dramas; The Nation* for allowing us to use Henry James's "Notes on the Theatre," Ludwig Lewisohn's review of Elmer Rice's *The Adding Machine,* Mr. Lewisohn's "A Note on Tragedy" (which was afterwards reprinted in *The Drama and the Stage*), and Joseph Wood Krutch's essay on "The Comic Wisdom of S. N. Behrman"; *The New Republic* for its permission to include Francis Hackett's review of John Barrymore's *Richard III* and Stark Young's review of Susan Glaspell's *The Verge; The New York American* for allowing us to use Alan Dale's review of *The Easiest Way* and Gilbert Gabriel's review of *Mary of Scotland;* the *New York Journal* for permission to reprint John Anderson's reviews of *Street Scene* and *Days Without End; The New York Evening Post* for the inclusion of William Coleman's piece on Kean's *Richard III,* William Leggett's analysis of Charles Kemble's *Hamlet,* J. Ranken Towse's review of John Barrymore's *Hamlet,* Robert Littell's article on E. E. Cummings's *Him,* and John Mason Brown's "Mae West"; *The New York Sun* for the use of Alexander Woollcott's review of *What Price Glory?,* Gilbert W. Gabriel's review of *The Silver Cord,* and Richard Lockridge's "On The Side of the Angels" and his review of *Green Grow the Lilacs; The New York Times* for permission to include E. A. Dithmar's reviews of *Shenandoah* and *Margaret Fleming,* John Corbin's essay entitled "Moscow and Broadway" and his review of *The Great Divide,* and Brooks Atkinson's reviews of *The Green Pastures* and *Of Thee I Sing* and his articles on Katharine Cornell in *The Barretts of Wimpole Street* and "In Praise of Ed Wynn, Comic"; *The New Yorker* for allowing us to reprint Alexander Woollcott's article on Lillian Gish's *Camille* and Robert Benchley's review of *Mourning Becomes Electra; The North American Review* for the use of Montrose J. Moses's "A Plea for Folk Basis in American Drama"; *The New York World-Telegram* for Gilbert Gabriel's review of *Processional* and Robert Garland's review of *As Husbands Go* and his piece on "Mrs. Fiske in a Farce"; W. W. Norton & Company for permission to reprint John Mason Brown's study of "Otis Skinner" which is taken from *Upstage;* The Press Publishing Company which, in behalf of the late *World,* have allowed us to include Nym Crinkle's article on Steele MacKaye's *Paul Kauvar* and Alexander Woollcott's review of *An American Tragedy;* Random House for the use of excerpts from Joseph Wood Krutch's introduction to the *Nine Plays* by Eugene O'Neill it has issued; *The Saturday Evening Post* for permission to reprint William Winter's study of Charlotte Cushman; *The Saturday Review of Literature* for permitting us to reprint parts of J. Ranken Towse's essay on "Edwin Booth: The Last Tragedian of His Era"; Charles Scribner's Sons for permission to include "On Putting Literature Into the Drama" from Brander Matthews's *The Principles of Playmaking,* "Ibsen the Individualist" from James Gibbons Huneker's *Iconoclasts: A Book of Dramatists* and "Mary Garden As An Actress-Singer" from Mr. Huneker's *Bedouins,* "Minor Poet of Broadway—George M. Cohan" from Arthur Ruhl's *Second Nights,* and "Letter to Duse" from Stark Young's *The Flower in Drama; The Sunday News* for the use of Burns Mantle's "Tribute to John Drew"; *Theatre Arts Monthly* for permission to reprint Kenneth Macgowan's review of The Jones-Barrymore-Hopkins *Macbeth; Variety* for the use of Sime Silverman's review of *The Century Girl* and Jack Conway's review of *The Broadway Belles;* Cleveland Rodgers of *The Brooklyn Daily Eagle* for his permission to include Walt Whitman's article on "The Miserable State of the Stage" and Whitman's analysis of Forrest in *The Gladiator* which Mr. Rodgers and Mr. Black reprinted from *The Eagle* in their volume known as *The Gathering of the Forces;* Henry James for graciously allowing us to use excerpts from his uncle's essays on Salvini and

Coquelin, and his article in *The Nation* called "Notes on the Theatre"; Ina Ten Eyck Firkins for enabling us to include her brother's review of Walter Hampden's Shylock; and the Viking Press for letting us include Mr. Woollcott's article on Lillian Gish's Camille which has been reprinted in Mr. Woollcott's *While Rome Burns.*

We also wish to express our indebtedness to Mr. George Freedley and Miss Marion E. Crist of the Theatre Collection of the New York Public Library at Forty-Second Street, and to Miss Julia Gardner of the Fifty-Eighth Street Library for all that they have done to aid us in collecting the materials used in this book. And to Catherine Meredith Brown we wish to express our thanks for the manner in which she has helped us in assembling these materials and in the arduous task of reading proof.

CONTENTS
ARRANGED CHRONOLOGICALLY

BIOGRAPHICAL SKETCHES

I. AMONG THOSE IN THE CAST

MAXWELL ANDERSON. 1888—Playwright. Born at Atlantic City, Pa. Educated at North Dakota and Stanford Universities. Schoolmaster for two years, then drifted into journalism. Contributed to *San Francisco Bulletin, The Chronicle,* and the New York *New Republic* (1914-1918). Was subsequently (1918-1924) on the staff of the *New York Globe* and *The World.* Author of *The White Desert* (1923), *What Price Glory* (with Laurence Stallings, 1924), *Outside Looking In* (1925), *First Flight* and *The Buccaneer* (with Stallings, 1925, 1926), *Saturday's Children* (1927), *Gods of the Lightning* (with Harold Hickerson, 1928), *Gypsy* (1929), *Elizabeth the Queen* (1931), *Night Over Taos* (1932), *Both Your Houses* (1933), *Mary of Scotland* (1933).

MARY ANDERSON. 1859—. Actress. Born in Louisville, Ky. Encouraged by Edwin Booth and Charlotte Cushman, made her way to the top of her profession with remarkable speed. Especially famous as Perdita and Hermione in *The Winter's Tale,* as Julia in *The Hunchback,* as Galatea in *Pygmalion and Galatea,* as Juliet and as Rosalind. Retired in 1889 and since 1890 (when she married Antonio de Navarro) has lived in England.

MARGARET ANGLIN. 1876—. Actress. Appeared with Richard Mansfield in *Cyrano de Bergerac* (1898). Was a member of Charles Frohman's famous Empire Stock Company. Co-starred with Henry Miller in *The Great Divide* (1906). Well known for her performances of Electra and Antigone.

TALLULAH BANKHEAD. 1902—. Actress. Born at Huntsville, Ala. Made her New York debut in *Squab Farm* (1918). After appearing in several plays, including *Nice People,* she went to London in 1923, where she became immensely popular in such productions as *The Dancers, Fallen Angels, The Green Hat, They Knew What They Wanted, The Gold Diggers* and *Her Cardboard Lover.* Then went to Hollywood and returned (1933) to the New York stage in *Forsaking All Others.*

PHILIP BARRY. 1896—. Playwright. Born at Rochester, N. Y. Clerk in the State Department in Washington, with the U. S. Embassy in London. Graduated from Yale and later studied with Professor George Pierce Baker at Harvard. Author of: *You and I* (1923), *The Youngest* (1924), *In a Garden* (1925), *White Wings* (1926), *John* (1927), *Paris Bound* (1927), *Cock Robin* (with Elmer Rice, 1928), *Holiday* (1928), *Hotel Universe* (1930), *Tomorrow and Tomorrow* (1931), *The Animal Kingdom* (1932), *The Joyous Season* (1934).

JOHN BARRYMORE. 1882—. Actor and screen star. Born in Philadelphia, son of Maurice Barrymore and Georgie Drew. Appeared first in such light comedies as *The Dictator* (1904) and *The Fortune Hunter* (1909). Later emerged as a tragic actor of great promise in such productions as Galsworthy's *Justice* (1916), *Peter Ibbetson* (1917), Tolstoi's *Redemption* (1918), Benelli's *The Jest* (1919), *Richard III* (1920) and *Hamlet* (1922). He then deserted Broadway for Hollywood. See his *Confessions of An Actor* (1926).

LIONEL BARRYMORE. 1878—. Actor and screen star. Like his brother, John, and unlike his sister, Ethel, he has deserted the theatre for the motion pictures. First played with his grandmother, Mrs. John Drew; then with his uncle, John Drew. Appeared under the direction of Charles Frohman, and in the plays of Augustus Thomas. Especially remembered for *Peter Ibbetson* (1917), *The Copperhead* (1918) and *The Jest* (1919). In 1921 played Macbeth in Arthur Hopkins's production, for which Robert Edmond Jones designed the settings.

MAURICE BARRYMORE. 1847-1905. Actor. Father of Lionel, John and Ethel Barrymore and husband of Georgie Drew, who was John Drew's sister. A picturesque performer and engaging personality. Supported Booth, Barrett, McCullough and Modjeska. In later years was in Fanny Davenport's and Mrs. Leslie Carter's companies.

S. N. BEHRMAN. 1893—. Playwright. Born at Worcester, Mass. Attended Clark University and took G. P. Baker's English 47 at Harvard. Worked on *The New York Times* for a while and was press agent for Jed Harris's production of *Broadway* (1926). Author of *The Second Man* (1927), *Serena Blandish* (1929), *Meteor* (1929), *Brief Moment* (1931), and *Biography* (1932).

DAVID BELASCO. 1853-1931. Producer and playwright. Identified with the early theatre days of California and with the Madison Square Theatre era of New York (1882). Famous for his realism, his innovations in lighting and his development of such stars as Mrs. Leslie Carter, Frances Starr, David Warfield and Lenore Ulric. First plays written in collaboration with Henry C. DeMille and James A. Herne. Author of such plays as *Madame Butterfly* (1900), and *The Darling of the Gods* (1902) with John Luther Long; *The Auctioneer* (1901), *The Music Master* (1904), *The Girl of the Golden West* (1905), and *The Return of Peter Grimm* (1911). See William Winter's *Life of David Belasco* and *The Theatre Through Its Stage Door* by Belasco and Louis Defoe.

EDWIN BOOTH. 1833-1893. Actor. Son of Junius Brutus Booth (1796-1852). Made his first appearance as Richard III in place of his father in 1851. Established a much talked of record of one hundred consecutive nights as Hamlet, a record recently surpassed by John Barrymore. Owner (1869) for a few seasons of his own theatre. Gave memorable performances of *Julius Cæsar,* playing with his two brothers, Junius Brutus, Jr., and John Wilkes. Appeared with Salvini in a bi-lingual production of *Othello.* Toured for many seasons with Lawrence Barrett (1838-1891). Particularly famous as Hamlet, Richelieu, Lear, Iago and Othello. See Winter's *The Art of Edwin Booth;* also Lockridge's *Darling of Misfortune: Edwin Booth* (1932).

DION BOUCICAULT. 1822-1890. Irish actor, playwright and manager. Wrote and played in such sentimental pieces as *London Assurance* (1841), *Old Heads and Young Hearts* (1843), *The Octoroon* (1859), *Colleen Bawn* (1860), *Arrah-na-Pogue* (1865), a version of *Rip Van Winkle* (1865) and *The Shaugraun* (1874). Several of his melodramas, such as *After Dark* and *The Streets of New York* have recently been given "spoof" revivals. See *The Career of Dion Boucicault* by Townsend Walsh, Series 3, Vol. I, of the Dunlap Society Publications, New York (1915).

BOWERY THEATRE. Once upon a time (1827-1833) the democratic rival of the then aristocratic Park Theatre in New York. Several times destroyed by fire and rebuilt. Boasted such managers as Charles Gilfert, Thomas Hamblin and James H. Hackett. It was identified with the early career of Edwin Forrest.

MRS. LESLIE CARTER. 1862—. Actress. Her career is closely identified with David Belasco's rise as a manager. He wrote for her *The Heart of Maryland* (1895), *Zaza* (1899), *DuBarry* (1901). See her reminiscences.

KATE CLAXTON. 1849-1924. Actress. Identified with romantic melodrama, especially *The Two Orphans*, by d'Ennery and Cormon, which achieved a long run when it was produced in New York, December 21, 1874, at the Union Square Theatre. In the cast were Kitty Blanchard and James O'Neill.

GEORGE M. COHAN. 1878—. Actor, playwright, producer and composer. First appeared on the stage at Haverstraw, R. I., in *Daniel Boone* (1888). Toured (1890) in title rôle of *Peck's Bad Boy*. Appeared with The Four Cohans—his father, mother, and sister. Famous as song and dance man, and composer of such songs as "It's a Grand Old Rag, It's a High-Flying Flag" and "Over There." Author of such plays as *The Governor's Son, Little Johnny Jones, Get-Rich-Quick Wallingford, Forty-five Minutes From Broadway, Seven Keys to Baldpate*. Recently has appeared in a revival of *The Tavern*, a new play of his own writing called *Pigeons and People,* and Eugene O'Neill's *Ah, Wilderness!* (1933).

MARC CONNELLY. 1890—. Playwright. Born at McKeesport, Pa. Collaborated with George S. Kaufman on such comedies as *Dulcy* (1921), *To The Ladies* (1922), *Merton of the Movies* (1922), *Beggar on Horseback* (1924). Wrote *The Wisdom Tooth* (1926) alone. Won the Pulitzer Prize for 1931-32 with *The Green Pastures* which he based upon Roark Bradford's *Ol' Man Adam an' His Chillun.*

THOMAS ABTHORPE COOPER, 1776-1849. Actor. With an English tradition of acting behind him, Cooper was brought to this country by Thomas Wignell (1753-1803), an actor and manager. In 1796 Cooper made his first American appearance as Macbeth. His passion as an actor was generally recognized but his careless charm was the cause of his eventual undoing.

BENOIT CONSTANT COQUELIN. 1840-1909. French actor. Prominent at the Comédie Française. Came to America in 1888, in 1894, and in 1900 with

Sarah Bernhardt. Noted for his characterization of Cyrano de Bergerac. Distinctive as Mascarille in *Les Précieuses Ridicules,* and Tartuffe.

KATHARINE CORNELL. 1898—. Actress. Born at Buffalo, N. Y. Made her first New York appearance in *Bushido* (1916) with the Washington Square Players. In 1918 with Jessie Bonstelle's stock company in Buffalo. Scored a success in *Little Women* (1918) in London. Has acted in such plays as *Nice People* (1921), *A Bill of Divorcement* (1923), *Will Shakespeare* (1923), *The Outsider* (1924), *Candida* (1924), *The Green Hat* (1925), *The Letter* (1927), *The Age of Innocence* (1928), *Dishonored Lady* (1930), *The Barretts of Wimpole Street* (1931), *Lucrece* (1932), *Alien Corn* (1933) and *Romeo and Juliet* (1933).

RACHEL CROTHERS. 1878—. Playwright and director. Most widely known for such plays as *A Man's World* (1910), *Old Lady 31* (1916), *A Little Journey* (1918), *39 East* (1918), *Nice People* (1921), *Mary the Third* (1923), *Expressing Willie* (1924), *Let Us Be Gay* (1929), *As Husbands Go* (1931), and *When Ladies Meet* (1932).

E. E. CUMMINGS. 1894—. Author, painter. Born at Cambridge. A.B. Harvard (1915) M.A. (1916). With Norton Harjes Ambulance, World War. Later as private Camp Devens. Has exhibited paintings with Society of Independent Artists and Salons of America. Author of *The Enormous Room* (1922), *Tulips and Chimneys* (1923), *XLI Poems* (1925), *&(And,* 1925), *Him* (1927), *By E. E. Cummings* (1930), *CI O P W* (1931), *ViVa* (1931).

CHARLOTTE CUSHMAN. 1816-1876. Tragedienne. Made her first appearance on the stage in 1835. Her severest critic was William C. Macready. Played Lady Macbeth at the Bowery Theatre, September 12, 1836. Famous as Meg Merrilies. Created much excitement by appearing as Romeo in *Romeo and Juliet* and as Cardinal Wolsey in *Henry VIII.* Her farewells in Boston and New York were great evidences of the esteem in which she was held. See Emma Stebbins's *Charlotte Cushman: Her Letters and Memoirs of Her Life.* Also Winter's *The Wallet of Time.*

ARNOLD DALY. 1875-1927. Actor. Born in Brooklyn. Made his first appearance in 1892 in *The Jolly Squire.* Toured in *Aristocracy, The Girl I Left Behind Me,* etc. New York début at the Herald Square Theatre in *Pudd'nhead Wilson* (1899); with Julia Marlowe in *Barbara Frietchie.* Famous for his early Shaw productions (see Shaw): *Candida* (1903), *Mrs. Warren's Profession* and *You Never Can Tell* (1904). Toured in 1906 with *The Man of Destiny, Arms and The Man, How He Lied To Her Husband, The Monkey's Paw,* etc. Played *Arms and The Man* in London (1911). Appeared in the Theatre Guild production of *Juarez and Maximilian* (1926).

AUGUSTIN DALY. 1838-1899. Manager and playwright. Manager of a series of playhouses in New York as distinguished in history as the Madison Square Theatre, the Union Square Theatre, and Wallack's Theatre. Wrote or adapted such plays as *Leah the Forsaken* (1862), *Under the Gaslight* (1867), *Divorce* (1884) and *Article 47.* As a manager he was identified with

New York from 1869-1899, also with London. Players under his direction or in his famous company included: Agnes Ethel, Ada Rehan, Mrs. G. H. Gilbert, Fanny Davenport, John Drew, Otis Skinner and James Lewis. See *The Diary of a Daly Debutante.* Also Judge Joseph F. Daly's *The Life of Augustin Daly* (1917).

CHARLES DILLINGHAM. 1868-1934. Producer. Born at Hartford, Conn. After college, a journalist. Dramatic editor of the *New York Evening Sun.* Became a producing manager in 1898. Has managed such stars as Julia Marlowe, Maxine Elliott, Henry Miller, Margaret Anglin, Fritzi Scheff, Elsie Janis, Montgomery and Stone, Nance O'Neil and Kyrle Bellew. Co-producer with Ziegfeld of *The Century Girl.* Has been associated with such varied productions as *The Slim Princess, Chin-Chin, M'lle. Modiste, A Bill of Divorcement, Loyalties, Stepping Stones, These Charming People, The Last of Mrs. Cheyney, The High Road* and *New Faces.*

THEODORE DREISER. 1871—. Author. Began as a journalist and editor. Author of such novels as *Sister Carrie* (1900), *Jennie Gerhardt* (1911), *The Financier* (1912), *The Titan* (1914), *The Genius* (1915), *The Hand of the Potter* (1919). A volume of *Plays of the Natural and the Supernatural* (1916) created much interest. In 1925 he wrote his novel, *An American Tragedy,* which reached the stage as dramatized by Patrick Kearney.

JOHN DREW. 1853-1927. Actor. In his long career chiefly identified with such managers as Augustin Daly and Charles Frohman. In 1879, when Daly opened his famous playhouse at Broadway and 30th Street, Drew came into his own. Thereafter he was leading man to a galaxy of Frohman stars, beginning with Maude Adams. At the time of his death, he was president of the Players' Club. See John Drew, *My Years on the Stage* (1922).

WILLIAM DUNLAP. See biographical notes on the critics.

ELEONORA DUSE. 1859-1924. Italian actress. Came to America in 1893, 1903, and 1923. During her last tour she died at Pittsburgh. Famed for her performances in D'Annunzio's *Francesca da Rimini, La Citta Morta* and *Gioconda.* She also appeared in Ibsen rôles. In her artistic methods she possessed none of the flamboyant theatricality of Sarah Bernhardt (1844-1923), her contemporary and to some degree her rival.

JAMES FENNELL. 1766-1816. Actor. Among Thomas Wignell's players, he was the idol for many years; particularly famed for his Othello. Married a granddaughter of Benjamin Franklin. Appeared at the Park Theatre, N. Y., on May 1, 1799, as Jaffeir with Cooper, his rival.

MINNIE MADDERN FISKE. 1865-1932. Actress. Was a vital force in the American theatre for half a century. First gained fame and stardom as Minnie Maddern in *Fog's Ferry,* etc. Retired after her marriage in 1889. Four years later (1894) she returned to the stage in Harrison Grey Fiske's *Hester Crewe.* Played in *A Doll's House* (1894), *Tess of the D'Urbervilles* (1897). Successfully fought the theatrical trust. Organized the Manhattan

Company. Appeared in such plays as *Leah Kleschna, Salvation Nell, The New York Idea, Becky Sharp,* etc. Played a number of Ibsen heroines, including Hedda Gabler, Rebecca West and Mrs. Alving. Was famous as a comedienne. Last New York appearance was in *Ladies of the Jury.*

CLYDE FITCH. 1865-1909. Playwright. Born at Elmira, N. Y. Attended Amherst. Began his playwriting career when E. A. Dithmar of the *Times* suggested him to Richard Mansfield as the person to write a play on Beau Brummell. Wrote a long list of popular successes; vehicles for such Frohman stars as Julia Marlowe, Ethel Barrymore, Maxine Elliott and Clara Bloodgood. Among his most distinctive dramas were *Barbara Frietchie* (1899), *The Climbers* (1901), *Captain Jinks of the Horse Marines* (1901), *The Girl With The Green Eyes* (1902), *Major André* (1903), *The Truth* (1906), and *The City* (1909). See Montrose J. Moses's and Virginia Gerson's *Clyde Fitch and His Letters* (1924).

LYNN FONTANNE. 1882—. Actress. Born in London. First appeared in a Drury Lane pantomime. After acting in several productions came to America with Weedon Grossmith (1912-1913). In 1916 again came to America and joined Laurette Taylor. In 1920 played Anna in *Chris,* the O'Neill script that was later to be rewritten and recast as *Anna Christie.* Won much praise for her performance of *Dulcy* (1921). Joined the Theatre Guild with *The Guardsman* (1924). Has appeared under its auspices in *Arms and The Man, Goat Song, At Mrs. Beam's, Pygmalion, The Brothers Karamazov, The Second Man, The Doctor's Dilemma, Strange Interlude, Caprice* and *Reunion in Vienna.* Seen in New York (1933) with Alfred Lunt and Noel Coward in *Design for Living.*

EDWIN FORREST. 1806-1872. Actor. Boasted that he was America's first native tragedian. Was influenced by the English style set by Cooper, Cooke and Edmund Kean. Vigorous, animal interpretation in such parts as Damon, Jaffeir, Marc Antony, Richelieu, Metamora, Spartacus, Jack Cade and King Lear. His rivalry with William C. Macready resulted in the famous Astor Place Riot, May 1, 1849. See the lives of Forrest by Alger, Rees, Barrett, and Moses. Under the encouragement of Forrest, most of the Philadelphia dramatists—John Augustus Stone, Richard Penn Smith, Montgomery Bird, Robert T. Conrad and G. H. Miles—started writing their plays.

CHARLES FROHMAN. 1860-1915. Manager. Educated at public schools, New York. Was employed in the office of the *New York Daily Graphic.* Sold tickets at night at Hooley's Theatre, Brooklyn. In 1877 took charge of the company that was sent west to play *Our Boys.* Was with William Haverly (Haverly's Mastodon Minstrels) in the U. S. and Europe (1879-1880). In 1888 saw *Shenandoah* at the Boston Museum; organized a company and bought the rights to the play outside of Boston. In 1890 organized Charles Frohman Stock Company. Became manager of many theatres in London and New York. Believed in the "star system" and managed, or created, such stars as John Drew, Maude Adams, Ethel Barrymore, Julia Marlowe, E. H.

Sothern, Elsie Ferguson, Pauline Chase, Marie Doro, Ann Murdock, Billie Burke, Otis Skinner, etc.

MARY GARDEN. 1877—. Operatic soprano. Born in Aberdeen, Scotland. Came to America with parents when six. At sixteen took part in an amateur production of *Trial by Jury* in Chicago. In 1896 went to Paris to study. In 1908 made a great success at the Opera Comique in *Louise* when sickness forced Mlle. Rioton to abandon the title rôle in the third act. Especially noted for her acting and singing in such operas as *Thaïs, Pélleas and Mélisande, Salome, Carmen,* etc. Long with the Chicago Opera Association.

GEORGE GERSHWIN. 1898—. Composer. Born Brooklyn, N. Y. Educated at public schools. Studied piano with Charles Hambitzer; harmony with Edward Kilenyi and Rubin Goldmark. Has done scores for the following musical comedies: *La, La, Lucille* (1919), *George White's Scandals* (1920-24), *Our Nell* (with William Daly, 1923), *Sweet Little Devil* (1923), *Lady Be Good* (1924), *Primrose* (1924), *Tell Me More, Tip-Toes, Song of the Flame* (with Herbert Stothard, 1925), *Oh, Kay!* (1926), *Strike Up The Band, Shake Your Feet, Funny Face* (1927), *Rosalie* (with Sigmund Romberg), *Treasure Girl* (1928), *Show Girl* (1929), *Girl Crazy* (1930), *Delicious* (Fox film, 1931), *Of Thee I Sing* (1931), and *Let 'Em Eat Cake* (1933). Serious compositions include: "The Rhapsody in Blue" (1923), "Concerto in F" (1926) and "An American in Paris" (1928). Brother of Ira Gershwin.

LILLIAN GISH. 1896—. Actress. Born Dayton, Ohio. Made stage début when five. Has appeared in motion pictures since 1914. Among her best known films were: *The Birth of a Nation, Hearts of the World, Orphans of the Storm, The White Sister, Romola, La Bohême,* and *The Scarlet Letter.* Returned to the stage in *Uncle Vanya* (1930). Since then has been seen in such plays as *Camille* (1932), *Nine Pine Street* (1933) and *The Joyous Season* (1934).

THE GLADIATOR. A play written by Robert Montgomery Bird (1806-1854) for Edwin Forrest, and produced at the Park Theatre, New York, on September 26, 1831. Forrest's rôle was that of Spartacus.

SUSAN GLASPELL. 1882—. Dramatist and novelist. With George Cram Cook was one of the prime movers in the establishment of the Provincetown Playhouse. Author of such plays as: *Trifles* (1917), *Suppressed Desires* (with Cook, 1917), *Inheritors* (1921), *The Verge* (1922), and *Alison's House* (Pulitzer Prize Play, 1931). See Susan Glaspell's *The Road to the Temple* (1926). Also Helen Deutsch's and Stella Hanau's *The Provincetown: A Story of the Theatre* (1931).

WALTER HAMPDEN. 1879—. Actor. Born in Brooklyn, N. Y. Student at Harvard (1896-97), B.A. at Polytechnic Institute, Brooklyn (1900). First appeared on the stage with F. R. Benson's company in classical repertory in England (1901). Leading man at the Adelphi Theatre, London, for three years. Acted *Hamlet* in 1905, succeeding the younger Irving in the part.

Returned to the U. S. in 1907. Supported Madame Nazimova in repertory. Appeared as Manson in *The Servant in the House*. Widely known for his productions of such classics, *Romeo and Juliet, Hamlet, Macbeth, Othello, Richelieu.* Revived *Cyrano de Bergerac* (1923-24), and *An Enemy of the People* (1927-28). Played *Caponsacchi* (1926-27). President of the Players Club.

EDWARD HARRIGAN. 1845-1911. Born in New York. Famous with Tony Hart in the '70's and '80's for his writing and acting of such lively vaudevilles about New York types as *The Mulligan Guards* (1872), *The Blue and the Gray* (1875), *Old Lavender* (1877), *The Doyle Brothers* (1878), *The Mulligan Guard Picnic* (1878), *The Mulligan Guard Christmas* (1879), *Squatter Sovereignty* (1882), *Cordelia's Aspirations* (1883), *The O'Reagans* (1886), and *The Last of the Hogans* (1891).

BRET HARTE. 1839-1902. Author. Famous for such stories as *The Luck of Roaring Camp* (1868), *The Outcasts of Poker Flat* (1869), etc. Tried his luck as playwright with *Two Men From Sandy Bar* (1876), *Ah Sin* (with Mark Twain, 1877), and *Sue* (with T. Edgar Pemberton, 1896).

HELEN HAYES. 1902—. Actress. Born in Washington, D. C. First appearance (1908) at the National Theatre, Washington, in *The Babes in the Wood*. New York debut (1909) in *Old Dutch*. Well-known at the beginning of her career for her playing of flapper parts in such plays as *Penrod* (1918). Among her notable performances have been Margaret in *Dear Brutus* (1918), Elsie in *To The Ladies* (1922), Cleopatra in *Cæsar and Cleopatra* (1925), Maggie Wylie in *What Every Woman Knows* (1926), Norma Besant in *Coquette* (1927), Mary Stuart in *Mary of Scotland* (1933). She has also had great success in the motion pictures.

JAMES A. HERNE. 1839-1901. Playwright and actor. Received much of his initial training as an actor at Baldwin's Theatre, San Francisco. Gained recognition for his interpretation of such Dickens characters as Daniel Peggotty. At this time, collaborated with David Belasco. His importance as a dramatist began with *Margaret Fleming* (1890), when he definitely declared himself on the side of realism as defined by William Dean Howells. Three plays followed to add to his significance: *Shore Acres* (1892), *Griffith Davenport* (1899) and *Sag Harbor* (1899).

DUBOSE HEYWARD. 1885—. Author. Born at Charleston, S. C. Author of *Skylines and Horizons* (1924), *Carolina Chansons* (with Hervey Allen, 1922), *Porgy* (1925), *Angel* (1926), *Mamba's Daughters* (1929), *The Half-Pint Flask* (1929). *Porgy* was dramatized in collaboration with Dorothy Heyward and produced by the Theatre Guild, 1927.

ARTHUR HOPKINS. 1878—. Dramatist and producer. Came to New York in 1912. Has produced such different plays as *Steve, The Poor Little Rich Girl, On Trial, The Deluge, Good Gracious Annabelle, A Successful Calamity, Redemption, The Wild Duck* (with Nazimova), *Hedda Gabler* and *A Doll's House, The Jest, Richard III* and *Hamlet* (with John Barrymore), *Macbeth* (with Lionel Barrymore), *Romeo and Juliet* (with Ethel Barrymore), *Anna Christie, The Hairy Ape, What Price Glory?, In A Garden, Burlesque, Paris Bound, Machinal, The Commodore Marries, Rebound, Roadside, The Passing Present* and *The Joyous Season.* See Mr. Hopkins's *How's Your Second Act?* for a statement of his theory of direction.

BRONSON HOWARD. 1842-1908. Dramatist. Known as the Dean of the American Drama because in a period when managers thought it a disadvantage to present a play by an American, he stood his ground for native work. In his plays, however, he was mostly under the influence of French convention. Author of such dramas as *Saratoga* (1870), *The Banker's Daughter* (1878), *The Young Mrs. Winthrop* (1882), *The Henrietta* (1887), *Shenandoah* (1889), *Aristocracy* (1892). Founded the American Dramatist Club. Gave a lecture at Harvard on "The Autobiography of a Play," revealing the conventions of his era in playwriting. Reprinted by the Dramatic Museum of Columbia University (1914). Also see *In Memoriam* issued by the American Dramatist Club (1910).

SIDNEY HOWARD. 1891—. Born at Oakland, Cal. Graduated from University of California. Studied playwriting under Baker at Harvard (1915-16). In 1919 joined staff of *Life,* became literary editor (1922). Served in France and the Balkans during the war. Among his plays are: *Swords* (1921), *They Knew What They Wanted* (Pulitzer winner for 1924), *Bewitched* (with Edward Sheldon, 1924), *Lucky Sam McCarver* (1925), *Ned McCobb's Daughter* and *The Silver Cord* (1926), *Salvation* (with Charles MacArthur, 1928), *The Late Christopher Bean* (an adaptation, 1932), *Alien Corn* (1933), *Dodsworth* and *Yellow Jack* (1934).

HENRIK IBSEN. 1828-1906. Norwegian dramatist. Though under the influence of Scribe as a stage director, Ibsen founded the modern movement in the theatre of realistic and symbolic characterization. He went through various periods: 1) his saga plays, 2) his poetic and folk drama, 3) his social studies, 4) his feminine studies and 5) symbolical dramas. Among his best plays are *The Pretenders* (1863), *Brand* (1866), *Peer Gynt* (1867), *The Emperor and Galilean* (1873), *A Doll's House* (1879), *Ghosts* (1881), *The Wild Duck* (1884), *Rosmersholm* (1886), *Hedda Gabler* (1890), and *The Master Builder* (1892). See Shaw's *The Quintessence of Ibsenism* for the reviews *Ghosts* received when it was first produced in London.

HENRY IRVING. 1838-1905. English actor and manager. Began his career in 1856. When he first came to America in 1883 he was established at the London Lyceum as a Shakespearean actor and a lavish and meticulous producer. The American audiences of 1883 saw him as Mathias in *The Bells,* Charles I, Louis XI, Shylock, Gloucester, and in *The Lyons Mail* and *The Belle's Stratagem.* They were likewise enchanted by Ellen Terry's beauty and her brilliant gift for comedy. On a return engagement Irving was seen as Benedick (April, 1884), Malvolio (Nov. 19) and Hamlet (Nov. 27). See Bram Stoker's *Personal Reminiscences of Henry Irving,* Gordon Craig's *Henry Irving,* and *Ellen Terry and Bernard Shaw: A Correspondence.*

JOHN STREET THEATRE. One of the most famous of New York's early playhouses. Royall Tyler's *The Contrast* and many of William Dunlap's plays first presented there. Was a wooden building painted red. Four periods: 1) Opened by Douglas, December 7, 1767, closed in 1774 by the resolution of Congress which put a ban on all theatrical activities in the Colonies; 2) Used by Military Actors during New York's occupation by the British, 1777-1783; 3) Used for Lewis Hallam's tentative offerings during the summer of 1784 to the departure of Wignell and Mrs. Morris, 1789, with a subsequent season (1791-92) without the coöperation of these artists; and 4) Most brilliant period (1793-1798), when it was dominated by the personality of John Hodgkinson. See George C. D. Odell's *Annals of the New York Stage*.

JOSEPH JEFFERSON. 1829-1905. Illustrious member of an illustrious family of comedians. Third Joseph Jefferson chiefly known for his Rip Van Winkle. First performance of this play in version made by Dion Boucicault was given at the London Adelphi Theatre, September 4, 1865. His comedy was equally demonstrated by such rôles as Trenchard in *Our American Cousin* and Bob Acres in *The Rivals*. Also played Dr. Pangloss in Coleman's *Heir-at-Law*. See Jefferson's *Autobiography* not only for his own life but for a stirring picture of the pioneer theatre. Also Winter's *The Art and Life of Joseph Jefferson* and Francis Wilson's *Joseph Jefferson* (1906).

ROBERT EDMOND JONES. 1887—. Stage designer. Born at Milton, N. H. A.B. Harvard, 1910. Has done notable settings for such productions as *The Man Who Married a Dumb Wife, The Jest, Richard III, Macbeth, Redemption, The Birthday of the Infanta, Skyscrapers, Mourning Becomes Electra, The Green Pastures, Mary of Scotland* and *The Green Bay Tree*. See his *Drawings for the Theatre* (1925).

GEORGE S. KAUFMAN. 1889—. Playwright. Born at Pittsburgh, Pa. On the staff of the *Washington Times* as humorous writer (1912-13); *New York Evening Mail* (1914-15); was then a member of the dramatic department of the *New York Tribune,* and afterwards served the *New York Times* as its dramatic editor. Author of: *Some One in the House* (with Larry Evans and Walter Percival, 1918). With Marc Connelly author of *Dulcy* (1921), *To The Ladies* (1922), *Merton of the Movies* (1922), *The Deep Tangled Wildwood* (1923), *Beggar on Horseback* (1924). With Edna Ferber wrote *Minick* (1924), *The Royal Family* (1927) and *Dinner at Eight* (1932). Sole author of *The Butter and Egg Man* (1925). Wrote *The Good Fellow* (1926) with H. J. Mankiewicz. With Morris Ryskind wrote *Animal Crackers* (1928), *Strike Up The Band* (1930), *Of Thee I Sing* (with the Gershwins, 1931), and *Let 'Em Eat Cake* (also with the Gershwins, 1933). With Alexander Woollcott wrote *The Channel Road* (1929), and *The Dark Tower* (1934).

EDMUND KEAN. 1787-1833. Great English tragedian. Made his first appearance at the age of two as Cupid. Appeared first as Shylock at Drury Lane, January 26, 1814, followed by Richard III, Hamlet, Othello, Iago. Then came Macbeth (1814), Romeo (1815) and Sir Giles Overreach (1816).

Rival of Junius Brutus Booth. Came to America in 1820, opening in New York, November 29, 1820. Came again to America in 1825. Last appearance on any stage, London, Covent Garden, March 25, 1833, as Othello. An erratic, fiery genius. See Otis Skinner's *Mad Folk of The Theatre* (1926), Harold Newcomb Hillebrand's *Edmund Kean* (1933), and William Hazlitt's extraordinary criticisms in *A Short View of the English Stage*.

DORIS KEANE. 1885—. Actress. Born in Michigan. New York debut (1903) in *Whitewashing Julia*. After many appearances, scored her greatest success in *Romance* (1913). She has toured extensively in the part and played it for many years. Her subsequent performances include *Romeo and Juliet* (1919) in London, *The Czarina* in New York (1922), *Welded* (1924), and *Starlight* (1924).

PATRICK KEARNEY. Playwright. Born Delaware, Ohio. Graduated from Ohio State University in 1915. Newspaper man and contributor to many magazines. Author of: *A Man's Man* (1925), *An American Tragedy* (dramatization of Dreiser's novel, 1926), *Elmer Gantry* (dramatization of Sinclair Lewis's novel, 1928) and *Old Man Murphy* (with Harry Wagstaffe Gribble, 1931).

GEORGE KELLY. 1890—. Playwright. Born in Philadelphia suburb. When twenty-one won distinction as a juvenile actor. Four years later entered vaudeville, writing his own plays. Author of *The Torch-Bearers* (1922), *The Show-Off* (1924), *Craig's Wife* (1925), *Daisy Mayme* (1926), *Behold, the Bridegroom* (1927), *Maggie the Magnificent* (1929) and *Philip Goes Forth* (1931).

CHARLES KEMBLE. 1775-1854. British actor. Brother of John Philip Kemble and Sarah Siddons; father of Frances Anne Kemble. Excelled as Laertes, Macduff, Jaffeir and a most gifted Romeo. He had no rival as Charles Surface, young Marlow, Mercutio and Benedick. In 1827 he played in Paris. In October, 1892, played Mercutio to the Juliet of his daughter. In 1832 the two came to the United States. He appeared as Hamlet at the Park Theatre, N. Y., on September 17, 1832. Leigh Hunt wrote that Kemble "was the nearest approach I ever saw to Shakespeare's gentlemen and heroes of romance."

AUGUST FRIEDERICK FERDINAND VON KOTZEBUE. 1761-1819. A German playwright who was widely popular in Europe and America. Born at Weimar; assassinated at Mannheim. He wrote more than two hundred plays. Among them were *Menschenhass und Reue* (known in English as *The Stranger*) and *The Spaniards in Peru* which R. B. Sheridan adapted as *Pizarro*.

JOHN HOWARD LAWSON. 1895—. Playwright. Graduated from Williams College (1915). Founder of the New Playwrights Theatre (1928-29). Author of *Roger Bloomer* (1923), *Processional* (1925), *Nirvana* (1926), *Loudspeaker* (1927), *The International* (1928), *Success Story* (1932), *The Pure in Heart* (1934) and *Gentlewoman* (1934).

EVA LEGALLIENNE. 1899—. Actress. Born in London, educated at College Sevigne, Paris. First appearance as a page in *Monna Vanna* at the Queen's Theatre, London. Came to New York in 1915, making her American debut in *Mrs. Boltay's Daughters.* Toured with Ethel Barrymore; appeared with *Elsie Janis and Her Gang* (1919). Acted in *Not So Long Ago* (1920), *Liliom* (1921), *The Swan* (1923), *Hannele* (1923), *Jehanne d'Arc* (Paris, 1925), *The Master Builder* (1925). Founder and director of the Civic Repertory Theatre which opened October 25, 1926. She has there produced (among other things) *Saturday Night, The Three Sisters, The Cherry Orchard, Cradle Song, Peter Pan, Hedda Gabler, La Locandiera, The Sea Gull, Romeo and Juliet, Camille* and *Alice in Wonderland.* See Eva LeGallienne's *At 33* (1933).

ALFRED LUNT. 1893—. Actor. Born in Milwaukee. Educated at Harvard. Made his first appearance at the Castle Square Theatre, Boston, in stock company (1913). In 1914 toured with Margaret Anglin in *Beverley's Balance,* appearing with her at Beverley, Cal., in *Iphigenia in Tauris* and *Medea.* Subsequently toured with Mrs. Langtry in vaudeville, and Laura Hope Crews. Established himself in Booth Tarkington's *Clarence* (1919). After several other productions, including *Outward Bound* (1924), joined the Theatre Guild in *The Guardsman* (1924). Since then has appeared in *Arms and the Man, At Mrs. Beam's, Goat Song, Juarez and Maximilian, Ned McCobb's Daughter, The Brothers Karamazov, The Second Man, The Doctor's Dilemma, Marco Millions, Volpone, Caprice* and *Reunion in Vienna.* Seen in New York (1933) with his wife, Lynn Fontanne, and Noel Coward in *Design for Living.*

STEELE MacKAYE. 1844-1894. Playwright, actor and producer. One of our earliest experimenters in stage technique, and an advocate of the acting theories of Delsarte. Appeared as Hamlet in France (1873); played in London; collaborated as a dramatist with Charles Reade and Tom Taylor. Among his popular plays were *Hazel Kirke* (1880) and *Paul Kauvar* (1887). Planned the Spectatorium at the Chicago World's Fair (1893). See Percy MacKaye's *Epoch: The Life of Steele MacKaye* (1927).

RICHARD MANSFIELD. 1857-1907. Actor. Early in his career appeared in D'Oyly Carte's light opera company in the provinces and in London. New York début (1882). Appeared in *A Parisian Romance* (January 10, 1883) at the Union Square Theatre. Played *Prince Karl* (1887), *Dr. Jekyll and Mr. Hyde* (1887), *Richard III* (1889), *Beau Brummell* (1890), *The Merchant of Venice* (1893), *Arms and the Man* (1894), *Cyrano de Bergerac* (1898), *Henry V* (1900), *Alceste* (*The Misanthrope*), *Peer Gynt* (1906). See Paul Wolstach's *Richard Mansfield: The Man and the Actor* (1908), and William Winter's *The Life and Art of Richard Mansfield.*

PHILIP MERIVALE. 1886—. Actor. Born near Manikpur, India. Educated at Oxford. First appearance in London (1905) in the Orestean trilogy of Æschylus. Played with F. R. Benson's Company and Sir Herbert Tree in many Shakespearean productions. Accompanied Mrs. Patrick Campbell to

America in 1914 appearing with her in *Pygmalion*. Among his most successful American appearances have been such productions as *The Swan* (1924), *The Road to Rome* (1927), *Death Takes a Holiday* (1929) and *Mary of Scotland* (1933).

HENRY MILLER. 1860-1925. Actor and producer. Was under the direction of Charles Frohman from September 9, 1889, when Bronson Howard's *Shenandoah* was produced, until January 11, 1897, when he became a member of the Empire Stock Company. In 1902 he and Margaret Anglin acted together. In 1906 they appeared in Moody's *The Great Divide*. Miller had his early experience at Booth's Theatre (1880), Daly's (1882) and the Madison Square Theatre (1882-85). Father of Gilbert Miller (1884—).

MINSKY BROTHERS. Four brothers—Michael, Abraham, Herbert and Morton —who since 1912, when Michael (or Billy) was called in by his father to organize a show for the National Winter Garden at Houston Street and Second Avenue, have figured prominently in New York burlesque. See Bernard Sobel's *Burleycue: An Underground History of Burlesque Days* (1931).

LANGDON MITCHELL, 1862—. Playwright. Son of Dr. S. Weir Mitchell, author of *Hugh Wynne,* etc. Wrote his play, *The New York Idea,* expressly for Mrs. Fiske who presented it at the Lyric Theatre, New York, November 19, 1906. Mrs. Fiske had previously appeared in his dramatization of *Vanity Fair,* which he called *Becky Sharp* (1899). Mr. Mitchell also made a dramatization of *Pendennis,* entitled *Major Pendennis* (1916), in which John Drew acted.

HELENA MODJESKA. 1844-1909. Polish actress. After acting in Poland she appeared first in San Francisco, August 6, 1877, playing Adrienne Lecouvreur in English. She came to New York in the same part, following it with *Romeo and Juliet, Frou-Frou,* and a vast repertory of classic rôles. Her technique, said Winter, was marked by "exquisite refinement and grace, simplicity of manner, and a rich sensuous beauty." See her *Memories and Impressions.*

WILLIAM VAUGHN MOODY. 1869-1910. Playwright and poet. One time professor at the University of Chicago. Wrote *The Great Divide* (first produced in Chicago as *A Sabine Woman* (1906), and *The Faith Healer* (1909). See Daniel Gregory Mason's *Some Letters of William Vaughn Moody* (1913) and *Poems and Plays of William Vaughn Moody* (2 vols.), edited by John M. Manly (1912).

CLARA MORRIS. 1846-1925. Actress. Played in such pieces as *The New Magdalen* and *Article 47.* Made a great success in such emotional rôles as Camille, Denise and Miss Moulton. Was under the management at different times of Augustin Daly and A. M. Palmer at the Union Square Theatre. See her reminiscences entitled *The Life of a Star.*

MOSCOW ART THEATRE. The famous theatre which was founded by Stanislavsky and Nemirovitch-Dantchenko in 1899. Noted for its realism, its perfection of ensemble, the excellence of its actors and its productions of such plays as *Tsar Fyodor, The Lower Depths, The Blue Bird,* and Chekhov's *The Sea Gull, Uncle Vanya, The Three Sisters* and *The Cherry Orchard.* See Oliver Sayler's *The Russian Theatre* and Stanislavsky's *My Life In Art.* The company visited America in 1923 and the Musical Studio came here in 1925.

MRS. ANNA CORA RITCHIE MOWATT. 1819-1870. Playwright and actress. A society woman of the fabulous forties who took to the stage to recover the family fortunes. She made her début, June 13, 1845, at the Park Theatre as Pauline in *The Lady of Lyons.* She visited England in 1847 as a star. Her own play, *Fashion,* was produced at the Park, March 24, 1845, previous to her appearance as an actress. This was revived by the Provincetown Players in 1923-24. Another play, *Armand, or The Peer and The Peasant,* was amended by order of the censor in London because of its democratic tendencies. It was produced at the Park, September 27, 1847. See Mrs. Mowatt's *Autobiography of an Actress* (1854) and her *Mimic Life, or Before and Behind The Curtain.*

ALLA NAZIMOVA. 1879—. Actress. Born at Yalta, in the Crimea. Came to this country with Paul Orleneff's company. Made her English-speaking début in America (1906) as Hedda Gabler. Identified with many early performances of Ibsen in this country. Appeared in such motion pictures as *A Doll's House, War Brides, Salome, The Madonna of the Streets, Camille,* etc. Among her many successes on the stage have been *Bella Donna* (1912), *War Brides* (1915), *The Cherry Orchard* (1929), *A Month in the Country* (1930), and *Mourning Becomes Electra* (1931).

NIBLO'S GARDENS. In 1823 William Niblo took possession of the Columbia Gardens at the northeast corner of Broadway and Prince Street. At first a rather poor building. Not turned into a regular theatre until 1849; then lasted until 1895 when the playhouse was demolished. In 1866 *The Black Crook* brought permanent fame to the place. Lydia Thompson appeared there, as at various times did several famous Kiralfy pieces and many popular tragedians from Edwin Forrest to John McCullough.

ANNE NICHOLS. Playwright and producing manager. Author of *Heart's Desire* (with Adelaide Matthews), *Down Limerick Way, Seven Miles To Arden* and *Linger Longer Letty* (1919), *The Gilded Cage* (1920), *Love Dreams* (1921), *The Happy Cavalier* (1921), *Abie's Irish Rose* (produced at Stamford, Conn., March 6, 1922 and at the Fulton Theatre, New York, May 23, 1922), *The Land of Romance* (1922). *Abie's Irish Rose* played continuously until 1927, achieving a run of 2,532 performances. Miss Nichols has sponsored such productions as Madame Simone's French repertoire in New York (1924) and *Sam Abramovitch* (1927).

JONATHAN OLDSTYLE. See Washington Irving in biographies of critics.

EUGENE O'NEILL. 1888—. Playwright. Born in New York. Desultory education in early years at Catholic and nonsectarian boarding schools. In 1906 matriculated at Princeton but was suspended. Business experience in a mail order job, then went to sea, and in South America worked for the Westinghouse Company, Swift and the Singer Company. Became a columnist and a reporter on the *New London Telegraph* (1912). Published *Thirst and Other One Act Plays* (1914). Studied with Professor Baker at Harvard (1914). The advent of the Provincetown Players (1915) launched O'Neill in the theatre. In 1920 *Beyond the Horizon* was produced on Broadway. Then followed a long line of plays, among the most distinctive of which are *The Emperor Jones* (1920), *Anna Christie* (1921), *The Hairy Ape* (1922), *Desire Under the Elms* (1924), *Strange Interlude* (1928), *Mourning Becomes Electra* (1931), *Ah, Wilderness!* (1933) and *Days Without End* (1934). See Barrett H. Clark's *Eugene O'Neill,* and Sanborn and Clark's *O'Neill Bibliography* (1931).

CHANNING POLLOCK. 1880—. Dramatist. Born at Washington. Graduated from Bethel Military Academy at Warrenton, Va. (1897). Dramatic critic of the *Washington Post* (1898). Press representative for William A. Brady (1900-04) and the Shuberts (1904-06). Dramatic critic of *Ainslee's, The Smart Set* and *The Green Book* (1905-1919). Author of *Stage Stories* (1901) and *The Footlights—Fore and Aft* (1909), and such plays as *The Pit* (a dramatization, 1902), *The Ziegfeld Follies* (1915 and 1921), *The Sign on the Door* (1919), *The Fool* (1924), *The Enemy* (1925), *Mr. Moneypenny* (1928) and *The House Beautiful* (1931).

ADA REHAN. 1860-1916. Actress. Career identified with Daly and his theatre. Made her first appearance under his management, September 19, 1879. For twenty years she was the radiant centre of his companies, appearing in light comedies and romances, but gaining distinction in such of his classic revivals as *The Jealous Wife, The School for Scandal, A Trip to Scarborough, The Belle's Stratagem* and *The Taming of the Shrew.* Her Katharine was particularly admired. See Winter's *Ada Rehan* (privately printed for Augustin Daly, 1891).

ELMER RICE. 1892—. Playwright and producer. First success as a playwright was achieved with *On Trial* (1914). The Theatre Guild produced his expressionistic play, *The Adding Machine,* in 1923. Author of *Close Harmony* (with Dorothy Parker, 1924), *Cock Robin* (with Philip Barry, 1928), *The Subway* (1928), *Street Scene* (1929), *Counsellor-at-law* (1931), *The Left Bank* (1931), *We, The People* (1933), and *Judgment Day* (1934).

LYNN RIGGS. 1898—. Playwright. Was born on a farm near Claremore, then Indian Territory, now Oklahoma. Author of *Sump'n Like Wings* (1925), *Big Lake* (1926), *Rancor* (1928), *The Domino Parlor* (1928), *Roadside* (1930), *The Iron Dish* (poems, 1930), *Green Grow the Lilacs* (1931).

LILLIAN RUSSELL. 1851-1922. Actress and vocalist. Born at Clinton, Ia. Professional début at Tony Pastor's (1881) as Mabel in a parody of *The Pirates of Penzance,* known as *The Pie Rats of Penn Yann.* Next seen in *The Great Mogul* and *Olivette* (1881), *Patience* and *The Sorcerer* (1882); at Tony Pastor's in *Billee Taylor* in the same year. Appeared in London (1883-84) in

Virginia and Paul and *Pocahontas;* in New York at the Casino (1885) in *Polly;* at the Union Square (1886) in *Tepita,* or *The Girl With the Glass Eyes, The Maid and the Moonshine* (1886), *Dorothy* (1887), *The Queen's Mate* (1888); at the Casino (1889-1891) in *Nadgy, The Brigands, The Grand Duchess, Poor Jonathan* and *Apollo;* at the Garden (1891) in *La Cigale, The Mountebanks* and *Giroflé-Girofla; The Princess Nicotine* (1893); *The Queen of Brilliants* (1894); *Erminie* (1896), with Weber and Fields (1900-04) in *Fiddle-dee-dee, Whoop-dee-doo, Twirly-Whirly,* and *The Big Little Princess; Lady Teazle* (1904), *Wildfire* (1907-08), *The Widow's Mite* (1909); with Weber and Fields in *Hokey-Pokey* (1912), and in Chicago in *Hitchy-Koo* (1918).

MORRIE RYSKIND. Playwright. Born in New York. Educated at Columbia. Collaborated with George S. Kaufman on the book of *Strike Up The Band* (1930); with Russell Crouse and Oscar Hammerstein 2nd on *The Gang's All Here* (1931), and with Kaufman and George and Ira Gershwin on *Of Thee I Sing* (1931) and *Let 'Em Eat Cake* (1933). Author of *The Diary of An Ex-President, by John P. Wintergreen* (1932).

TOMMASO SALVINI. 1829-1916. Italian actor. First visited the United States in 1886. Noted for emotional vigor of interpretation. Famous in such plays as *La Morte Civile, The Gladiator, Othello* and *King Lear.* On his last trip to this country he played Othello in Italian to Booth's English-speaking Iago.

GEORGE BERNARD SHAW. 1856—. Born Dublin, July 26, 1856. *Arms and the Man,* which Richard Mansfield presented on September 17, 1894, at the Herald Square Theatre, was the first of Shaw's plays to be acted professionally in the United States. Though Mansfield acquired the rights to *Candida* and imported Janet Achurch (1864-1916) to play in it, he never produced it. On October 1, 1897, at Albany he did, however, give *The Devil's Disciple* its first professional production. In 1898 Anna Morgan produced *Candida* "privately" at the Fine Arts Building in Chicago, and in February, 1899, a single performance of *The Man of Destiny* was given at the Empire Theatre, N. Y., by the American Academy of Dramatic Arts (Franklin Sargent's School of Acting). Arnold Daly produced *Candida* (September 8, 1903) at a trial matinee at the Princess, N. Y. Daly then added *The Man of Destiny* and *How He Lied To Her Husband* (1904) to his repertory. Daly's next Shavian production was *You Never Can Tell* at the Garrick, New York, January 9, 1905. For a detailed account of the storm which broke out after Daly's production of *Mrs. Warren's Profession* (October 30, 1905) and the full story of Shavian productions throughout the world see Archibald Henderson's *Bernard Shaw: Playboy and Prophet* (1932). Of recent years the Theatre Guild has produced the latest Shaw plays and revived many of the earlier ones.

MARY SHAW. 1860-1929. Actress. Born in Boston, Mass. Made her debut at the Boston Museum in 1878. Two years in Boston, then went to New York, appearing as Lady Sneerwell. Supported Modjeska. In 1890 toured with Julia Marlowe in *Pygmalion and Galatea, The Hunchback,* and *As You Like It.* With Mrs. Fiske in *Tess of the D'Urbervilles* (1895), *Sorrows of Satan*

(1898), *Ben Hur* (1899). Then as Mrs. Alving in *Ghosts*. *Hedda Gabler* in Chicago (1904). *Alice Sit-by-the-Fire* (1906), *The Melody of Youth* (1916), revived *Mrs. Warren's Profession* (1917), *The Idle Inn* (1921) and Mrs. Malaprop in *The Rivals* (1923).

EDWARD SHELDON. 1886—. Playwright. Born in Chicago. A.B. Harvard (1907) A.M. (1908). Author of *Salvation Nell* (1908), *The Nigger* (1909), *The Boss* (1911), *The Princess Zim-Zim* (1911), *Egypt* (1912), *The High Road* (1912), *Romance* (1913), *Song of Songs* (1914), *Garden of Paradise* (1915), *The Lonely Heart* (1920), with Dorothy Donnelly, *The Proud Princess* (1924), with Sidney Howard, *Bewitched.* (1924), with Charles Mac-Arthur, *Lulu Belle* (1926), with Margaret Ayer Barnes, *Jenny* (1929) and *Dishonored Lady* (1930).

OTIS SKINNER. 1858—. First appeared on the stage in 1877; supported Booth in 1880, then with Lawrence Barrett. Joined Daly's company (1884-1888). In 1889 was with the Booth-Modjeska combination, later supporting Modjeska (1892-95) in her own company. In 1903 appeared as co-star with Ada Rehan. Among his later plays have been *The Duel* (1906), *The Honor of The Family* (1907), *Kismet* (1911), *Cock o' the Walk* (1915), *Mister Antonio* (1916), *Blood and Sand* (1921), *King Henry IV*, Part 1 (1926), *The Merry Wives of Windsor* with Henrietta Crosman and Mrs. Fiske (1928), *A Hundred Years Old* (1929), *Troilus and Cressida* (1931), and *Uncle Tom's Cabin* (1933). Author of *Madfolk of the Theatre*. See his reminiscences, *Footlights and Spotlights*.

LAURENCE STALLINGS. 1894—. Journalist, novelist and playwright. Born at Macon, Ga. B.A. Lake Forest (N. C.) College (1915). Was a reporter on the *Atlantic Journal* (1915), in the U. S. Army (1917-18), subsequently on the *Washington Times* and *The New York World*. Author of *Plumes* (a novel, 1925), and with Maxwell Anderson, *What Price Glory?* (1924), *The Buccaneer* (1925), and *First Flight* (1925). In 1926 wrote the book for *Deep River* (a native opera). In 1928 wrote *Rainbow* with Oscar Hammerstein, 2nd. Edited *The First World War* (1933). Author of such films as *The Big Parade* and *Old Ironsides*.

HARRIET BEECHER STOWE. 1811-1896. *Uncle Tom's Cabin* was published as a novel on March 20, 1852. By August it had been dramatized without Mrs. Stowe's permission. She always refused to have it made into a play for the stage but there was no copyright to protect her. The George L. Aiken version of the drama was given at Troy, N. Y., on September 27, 1852. It reached New York, July 18, 1853. See Lyman Stowe's life of his grandmother; also Moses's *Representative Plays By American Dramatists*. Vol. II (1925).

FAY TEMPLETON. 1865—. Actress. Born at Little Rock, Ark. Made her début at the Grand Opera House, New York (1869) as Cupid. Appeared with great success in *Giroflé-Girofla, The Mascot, Patience* and *The Chimes of Normandy*. In 1885 appeared as Gabriel in *Evangeline*. Her subsequent performances include *Hendrik Hudson* (1890), *Madame Favart* (1893), *Ex-*

celsior, Jun. (1895), Broadway to Tokio (1900), Fiddle-dee-dee, Onions, The Stickiness of Gelatine, Du Hurry, The Runaways (1903), In Newport (1904), Forty-five Minutes From Broadway (1905), H.M.S. Pinafore (1911), with Weber and Fields (1912). Her most recent appearance has been in Roberta (1933).

THE THEATRE GUILD. An organization which stemmed from the Washington Square Players (1915-1918). Started out on its career by producing Benavente's The Bonds of Interest at the Garrick Theatre, April 14, 1919. Achieved its first success with St. John Ervine's John Ferguson (May 12, 1919). Since then has made a notable contribution to the American theatre by producing such foreign scripts as From Morn To Midnight, He Who Gets Slapped, Liliom, R.U.R., Fata Morgana, The Guardsman, Goat Song, Caprice; many of Shaw's plays, including The Devil's Disciple, Heartbreak House, Back to Methuselah, Saint Joan, Cæsar and Cleopatra, The Apple Cart and Too True to Be Good. It has also produced such native scripts as Elmer Rice's The Adding Machine, John Howard Lawson's Processional, Sidney Howard's The Silver Cord and Ned McCobb's Daughter, S. N. Behrman's The Second Man and Biography, Robert E. Sherwood's Reunion in Vienna, and Eugene O'Neill's Strange Interlude, Marco Millions, Dynamo, Mourning Becomes Electra, Ah, Wilderness!, and Days Without End. The Guild's parent playhouse, the Guild Theatre on West 52nd Street, N. Y., was opened on April 13, 1925 with Cæsar and Cleopatra. The Guild's board of directors is composed of Theresa Helburn, Philip Moeller, Helen Westley, Lee Simonson, Maurice Wertheim and Lawrence Langner. See W. P. Eaton's The Theatre Guild: The First Ten Years and Oliver Sayler's Our American Theatre.

ELLEN TERRY. 1848-1928. One of the most charming comediennes of the Victorian era. She joined Henry Irving's company at the Lyceum in London in 1878 and was associated with it until 1902. Thereafter she was involved in various ventures, such as Gordon Craig's production of Ibsen's The Vikings (1903), and Shaw's Captain Brassbound's Conversion (1906), and gave many special revivals of her Shakespearean rôles. She was made a Dame of the Empire, and honored by England in many ways. Her record is delightfully set forth in her book, The Story of My Life, and in Ellen Terry and Bernard Shaw; A Correspondence.

LYDIA THOMPSON. 1841-1908. Born in London. Made her début in 1853 at her Majesty's Theatre in a Christmas pantomime. At twenty she appeared in the shadow dance, a feature of Peep o'Day; a spectacular burlesque. The Black Crook (1866) had created a vogue in New York for burlesque. Having won a reputation for her beauty and her daring costumes in Europe, Lydia Thompson was brought to New York with a company including Pauline Markham, and made her debut, September 28, 1868, in Ixion, preceded by To Oblige Benson. Troupe transferred to Niblo's Gardens, January 30, 1869. Distinguished as actress and manageress. Made her last appearance with Mrs. Patrick Campbell in A Queen's Romance (1895). See Bernard Sobel's Burleycue: An Underground History of Burlesque Days (1931).

ROYALL TYLER. 1757-1826. A graduate of Harvard (1776). During Shay's Rebellion (1787) went to New York, and for the first time attended the theatre, witnessing Sheridan's *The School for Scandal*. Wrote his first play, *The Contrast,* in imitation of it. It was produced, April 16, 1787, at the John Street Theatre. Mr. Wignell played Jonathan, supposedly our first stage Yankee. Tyler wrote other plays, but is chiefly remembered for *The Contrast*. In Vermont he achieved the distinction of being made Chief Justice.

EUGENE WALTER. 1874—. Born at Cleveland, O. Educated at public schools. Served as a reporter in Cleveland and later on the *New York Sun*. For a time was in the U. S. Cavalry; afterwards was advance agent for various theatrical companies. Among his plays are: *Sergeant James* (1902), *The Undertow* (1907), *Paid in Full* (1907), *The Wolf* (1908), *The Easiest Way* (1909), *The Trail of the Lonesome Pine* (a dramatization of John Fox Jr.'s novel, 1911), *Fine Feathers* (1912), *Just A Woman* (1916), *The Assassin* (1917) and *Jealousy* (from the French, 1928).

WILLIAM WARREN. 1812-1888. Comedian. Born at Philadelphia, died in Boston. Son of William Warren (1767-1832). Made his debut in Philadelphia (1832), in London (1845). From 1847-82 was connected with the Howard Athenæum and Boston Museum in Boston. Especially successful as Sir Peter Teazle, Dr. Pangloss and Touchstone. When his seventieth birthday was celebrated he had given 13,345 performances and had appeared as 577 characters.

WEBER (JOSEPH) AND FIELDS (LEW). In 1877 these famous comics first appeared in a song and dance number at a Bowery Music Hall. In 1885 they became managers of the hall known as Weber and Fields'. In 1895 they were joint managers of the Broadway Music Hall, where they appeared in such burlesques as *Fiddle-dee-dee, Twirly-Whirly, Pousse-Café, The Geezer, Whoop-dee-doo, Hoity-Toity* and *Higgledy-Piggledy*. The partnership was dissolved in 1904, but in 1912 the two men were reunited.

MAE WEST. Actress and authoress. Appeared at the Folies Bergères in New York (1911); in 1912 as La Petite Daffy in *A Winsome Widow*. In 1913 went in vaudeville for some years. In 1918 appeared in *Sometime* and subsequently in Ned Wayburn's *Demi-Tasse*. Author of *Sex* (1926), *The Wicked Age* (1927), *Diamond Lil* (1928), *The Drag* (1927), *Pleasure Man* (1928) and *The Constant Sinner* (1931). Since then has been seen in such motion pictures as *She Done Him Wrong* and *I'm No Angel*.

ED WYNN. 1886—. Comedian. Born at Philadelphia. Educated at Central High School, Philadelphia. For four months attended a business college and for a short time was at the University of Pennsylvania. Ran away from home at sixteen. Was in vaudeville (1902-1914), *The Ziegfeld Follies* (1914-15), The Winter Garden (1916-17), *Ed Wynn's Carnival* (1919), *The Perfect Fool* (1921), *The Grab Bag* (1924), *Manhattan Mary* (1927), *Simple Simon* (1929), and *The Laugh Parade* (1931). Famous on the radio as The Fire Chief.

FLORENZ ZIEGFELD. 1867-1932. Producer. Born in Chicago. First married to Anna Held, then to Billie Burke. Inaugurated the Ziegfeld Follies in 1907 and presented them until 1924. His productions include *A Parlor Match* (1896), *Papa's Wife* (1899), *The Little Duchess* (1901), *Mlle. Napoleon* and *The Parisian Model* (1906), *Miss Innocence* (1908), *The Pink Lady* (1911), *The Century Girl* (with Charles Dillingham, 1916), *Sally* (1920), *Kid Boots* (1923), *Louie the 14th* (1925), *Rio Rita* (1927), *Show Boat* (1927), *The Three Musketeers* (1928), *Whoopee* (1928), *Show Girl* (1929), *Simple Simon* (1929), etc.

II. BIOGRAPHICAL NOTES ON THE CRITICS

JOHN ANDERSON. Born October 18, 1896, in Pensacola, Fla. Educated at private schools in the South, and at the University of Virginia, 1918. Came to New York the same year and joined the staff of the *New York Evening Post,* serving successively as a reporter, a feature writer and a columnist; became dramatic critic of the *Post* in 1924. Since 1928 dramatic critic of the *New York Journal.* Gives a course in dramatic criticism at New York University. Author of: *Box Office* (1929), and *The Book of The White Mountains* (with Stearns Morse, 1930). Adapted Gogol's *The Inspector General* (1930); and *The Fatal Alibi* and *Collision* (1932).

BROOKS ATKINSON. Born in Melrose, Mass., November 28, 1894. A.B. Harvard (1917). Reporter on the *Springfield Daily News* (1917). Instructor in the English Department, Dartmouth College (1917-1918); Infantry, Camp Upton (1918); (1918-1920) reporter on the *Boston Transcript* and assistant to H. T. Parker; Associate editor of the *Harvard Alumni Bulletin* (1920-1922); Literary Editor of *The New York Times* (1922); dramatic critic of the *Times* since 1926. Contributor to the *London Daily Telegraph* on American theatrical topics until 1930. Author of *Skyline Promenades* (1925), *Henry Thoreau* (1927), *East of the Hudson* (1931), *The Cingalese Prince* (1934).

ROBERT C. BENCHLEY. Born in Worcester, Mass., September 15, 1889. A.B. Harvard (1912). With advertising department of the Curtis Publishing Company, Philadelphia (1912-1914). Industrial personnel writer, Boston (1914-1915). Associate editor of the *New York Tribune Sunday Magazine* (1916-1917). Editor of the *New York Tribune Graphic* (1917). Secretary to Aircraft Board, Washington, D. C. (1917-1918). Managing editor of *Vanity Fair* (1919-1920). Contributed "Books and Other Things" column to the *New York World* (1920-1921). Dramatic critic of *Life* (1920-1929), and of *The New Yorker* since 1929. Author of *Of All Things* (1921); *Love Conquers All* (1922); *Pluck and Luck* (1925); *The Early Worm* (1927); *20,000 Leagues Under The Sea, or David Copperfield* (1928).

HEYWOOD BROUN. Born in Brooklyn, December 7, 1888. Harvard (1910). Reporter on *New York Morning Telegraph* (1908-1909, 1910-1912). With the *New York Tribune* (1912-1921); the *New York World* (1921-1928); the *World-Telegram* and Scripps-Howard newspapers since 1928. Author of *A.E.F.—With General Pershing and the American Forces* (1918); *Seeing Things At Night* (1921); *Pieces of Hate* (1922); *The Boy Grew Older* (1923); *Gandle Follows His Nose* (1926); *Anthony Comstock, Roundsman of the Lord* (with Margaret Leech, 1927). Lecturer on the drama at Columbia (1920); at Rand School (1921).

JOHN MASON BROWN. Born in Louisville, Ky., July 3, 1900. Attended local schools and Morristown School, Morristown, N. J. Graduated from Harvard (1923). Wrote for the *Louisville Courier-Journal* and the *Boston Transcript* (1923-1924). Associate editor and dramatic critic of *Theatre Arts Monthly* (1925-1928). Dramatic critic, *New York Evening Post* since 1929. Has given courses in history of the theatre at the American Laboratory Theatre, the Brooklyn Institute, and the University of Montana. Course in History of Dramatic Criticism at Yale (1931-32). Author of *The Modern Theatre in Revolt* (1929), *Upstage: The American Theatre in Performance* (1930), *Letters From Greenroom Ghosts* (1934), and co-editor with Montrose J. Moses of *The American Theatre, 1752-1934, As Seen By Its Critics* (1934).

HENRY AUSTIN CLAPP. Born at Dorchester, Mass., July 17, 1841. Died in Boston, February 19, 1904. Graduated from Harvard (1860). Taught in the Boston Latin School. Studied law. Was a private in the Civil War in Company F, 44th Massachusetts Volunteers. Served for nine months in North Carolina. Then returned to enter the Harvard Law School, from which he graduated in 1864. For forty years he devoted himself to journalism and literature. Was dramatic critic of *The Boston Advertiser;* also wrote for the *Boston Herald*. For many years he was clerk of the Supreme Judicial Court of Massachusetts. Lectured extensively on Shakespeare. Author: *Reminiscences of a Dramatic Critic* (1902).

WILLIAM COLEMAN. Born in Boston, February 14, 1766, died July 14, 1829. Through genuine vigor rose to distinction as political pamphleteer and journalist. Was known to his enemies, of whom he had many, as the "Field Marshal of the Federalist Editors." Entered Andover Academy soon after it opened, and was classmate of Josiah Quincy. Developed a "stately" taste for English literature. Studied law under the revolutionary Robert Treat Paine at Worcester, Mass. In 1786 marched with militia in Shay's Rebellion. 1788-1799 served at the bar in Greenfield, Mass. While there wrote for *The Impartial Intelligencer*. Was always an active campaigner and served in the Massachusetts Legislature (1795-1796). In 1798 was admitted to the New York bar, coming to the city with an honorary degree from Dartmouth, a letter from Paine, and a slight acquaintance with Alexander Hamilton. Law partnership of short duration with Aaron Burr and John Wells. The latter introduced him to the "Friendly Club," where he met William Dunlap, and Charles Brockden Brown (1771-1810). Clerkship in Civil Court through influence of Hamilton. In 1800 at trial of Levi Weeks won distinction for his short-hand notes. In 1801 was removed from office by Democratic victory, and became editor and proprietor of *The New York Evening Post,* which Hamilton had just established. Through its columns, he fought the policies of Jefferson, argued against the War of 1812, and supported all civic improvements. In 1803 provoked into a duel, though disapproving of the custom. In 1810 was the author of a pamphlet attacking Madison. During his declining years William Cullen Bryant was his Junior Editor. Always vigorous and outspoken in his editorial views. Space meant nothing to him in his expression of opinion. He, and later Leggett, were famed for their lengthy theatrical reviews. One of the longest reviews written in America was Coleman's five column attack on a worthless satire on the critics called "The Wheel of Truth" which appeared in the *Post,* December 31, 1803. See Allan Nevins's *The Evening Post: A Century of Journalism* (1922). Coleman edited *A Collection of the Facts and Documents Relative to The Death of Major General Alexander Hamilton* (1804).

JACK CONWAY (John White Conway). Born in 1888. Died near Hamilton, Bermuda, October 2, 1928. Came to New York with his mother when he was five. Brought up in the Bronx, spending a great deal of his time as a boy in the uptown daily newspaper offices at 125th Street. Was a street car conductor for a few days. Played baseball semi-professionally and finally joined the Brooklyn Federals. A vaudeville actor for one performance. Started on *Variety* as Advertising Solicitor. Became one of *Variety's* ace reviewers over the signature of "Con." During the War enlisted in the Navy and was assigned to the "Ohio" as doctor's assistant. Author of *The Push-Over* (a play), and wrote subtitles for many motion pictures in 1927. See *Variety,* October 10, 1928, and an article by Hugh Kent, called "Variety" which appeared in *The American Mercury* for December, 1926.

JOHN CORBIN. Born in Chicago, May 2, 1870. A.B. Harvard (1892); A.M. (1893). Year's residence at Balliol College, Oxford. Assistant editor of *Harper's Magazine* (1897-1900); Dramatic critic of *Harper's Weekly* (1899-1900); Editorial staff of the Encyclopedia Britannica (1900-1902); Dramatic critic, *The New York Times* (1902); Dramatic critic, *New York Sun* (1905-1907); Literary manager of the New Theatre, New York (1908-1910); Secretary of the Drama Society, New York (1913-1916); Produced *The Tempest* on a reconstruction of Shakespeare's stage (1916); Dramatic critic, *The New York Times* (1917-1919); Editorial writer, *The New York Times* (1919-1926). Author: *The Elizabethan Hamlet* (1895); *Schoolboy Life in England—An American View* (1898); *An American at Oxford* (1902); *A New Portrait of Shakespeare* (1903); *The First Loves of Perilla* (1903); *The Cave Man* (1907); *Which College For The Boy* (1908); *Husband and The Forbidden Guests* (1910); *The Edge* (1915); *The Return of The Middle Class* (1922); *The Unknown Washington* (1930).

NYM CRINKLE (see A. C. Wheeler).

ALAN DALE (Alfred J. Cohen). Born, Birmingham, England, May 14, 1861. Died May 21, 1928. Educated King Edward's School. Passed senior and junior "local" examinations, Oxford. Dramatic critic, *New York Evening*

World (1887-1895); then with the *New York Journal;* later with the *New York American.* Wrote for the Cosmopolitan News Service. Author: *Jonathan's Home, A Marriage Below Zero, An Eerie He and She, My Fortnight Husband, Miss Innocence, Familiar Chats With Queens of the Stage, An Old Maid Kindled, A Moral Busybody, Conscience on Ice, His Own Image, A Girl Who Wrote* (1902), *Wanted—A Cook, The Great White Way* (1909), *The Madonna of the Future* (1918), *When a Man Commutes* (1918).

L. CLARKE DAVIS. Born on September 23, 1835, at a place which became Sandusky, Ohio. Died at Philadelphia, December 14, 1904. In his early years his parents moved to Maryland. At sixteen he was left an orphan. Attended boarding school, near Norristown, Pa., and then entered the Episcopal Academy at Philadelphia from which he graduated in 1855. Read law in the office of Thomas Balch and was admitted to the bar. During this period he helped edit *The Legal Intelligence.* In March, 1863, at Wheeling, W. Va., he married Rebecca Harding, a writer. They were the parents of Richard Harding Davis and Charles Belmont Davis. In 1870, he became managing editor of the *Philadelphia Inquirer.* Mr. Davis wrote much on the drama and was an intimate friend of Joseph Jefferson and Edwin Booth. Contributed stories and sketches to leading magazines. In 1893, he assumed control of the *Philadelphia Public Ledger.*

EDWARD AUGUSTUS DITHMAR. Born in New York, May 22, 1854. Died there October 16, 1917. Educated in the grammar schools. At seventeen employed by the *New York Evening Post.* In 1877 went to *The New York Times,* where he remained for forty years. In 1882 was night editor; in 1884 became dramatic critic and held that post until 1901. He then succeeded Harold Frederic as London correspondent of the *Times* (1901-1902). On his return to New York, the *Times* made him editor of the Book Review, where he remained until 1907, when he became an editorial writer. He was among the first to give encouragement to Clyde Fitch and because of him the young playwright wrote *Beau Brummell* for Richard Mansfield. Was the author of *John Drew* (1910) and *Memories of Daly's Theatres* (1897). His scrapbooks containing his reviews are owned by the New York Public Library.

WILLIAM DUNLAP. Born at Perth Amboy, then the seat for the Government of the Province of New Jersey, February 19, 1766. Died in New York, September 28, 1839. His family were Loyalists in sympathy and the boy must have witnessed, during the Revolution, some of the performances in the theatre given by the Red Coats. In 1784-1789 he was in London, studying painting under Benjamin West. On his return from Europe, he was spurred to playwriting by Royall Tyler. He wrote his first drama, *The Modern Soldier, or Love in New York* (1787). Then followed an active career as producer, dramatist and recorder of theatrical events. Among his best known plays are *The Father or American Shandyism,* produced at the John Street Theatre, September 7, 1789; and *Andre,* produced at the Park Theatre,

March 30, 1798. He translated and adapted a host of dramas from the French and German, particularly those by August Kotzebue (1761-1819). His theatre management brought him into active collaboration and disagreement with Hallam, Hodgkinson and Wignell of Philadelphia. He was active as a painter of portraits and a writer. Among his many books are: *Memoirs of the Life of George Frederick Cooke* (1813); *The Life of Charles Brocden Brown* (1815); *A History of the American Theatre* (1832); and *History of the Rise and Progress of the Arts of Design in the United States* (1834). He was also the author of a temperance novel and a school history of the United States. Not content with these activities, he made great efforts in 1813 to establish a magazine, a favorite pastime of the early writers in this country. His voluminous manuscript diaries are preserved. They are gradually being published; three volumes were recently issued (1930) by the New York Historical Society. He was buried at Perth Amboy.

WALTER PRICHARD EATON. Born, Malden, Mass., August 24, 1878. A.B. Harvard (1900). Reporter on *Boston Journal* (1900); drama department of the *New York Tribune* (1902-07); dramatic critic *New York Sun* (1907-08). Dramatic critic, *American Magazine* (1909-1918). Member of the National Institute of Arts and Letters. Author: *The American Stage Today* (1908), *The Runaway Place* (with Elsie Underhill, 1909), *At The New Theatre And Others* (1910), *Boy Scouts of the Berkshires* (1912), *Boy Scouts in Dismal Swamp* (1913), *Barn Doors and Byways* (1913), *The Man Who Found Christmas* (1913), *Boy Scouts in the White Mountains* (1914), *The Idyl of Twin Fires* (1915), *New York* (1915), *Boy Scouts of the Wild Cat Patrol* (1915), *Plays and Players* (1916), *The Bird House Man* (1916), *Peanut, Cub Reporter* (1916), *Green Trails and Upland Pastures* (1917), *Newark* (1917), *Boy Scouts in Glacier Park* (1918), *Echoes and Realities* (verse, 1918), *In Berkshire Fields* (1919), *On The Edge of the Wilderness* (1920), *Boy Scouts At Crater Lake* (1922), *Penguins, Persons and Peppermints* (1922), *Queen Victoria* (a play with David Carb, 1923), *Boy Scouts in Katahdin* (1924), *Skyline Camps* (1924), *The Actor's Heritage* (1924), *A Bucolic Attitude* (1926), *Hawkeye's Room Mate* (1927), *Boy Scouts on The Green Mountain Trail* (1929), *Ten Years of The Theatre Guild* (1929), and *The Drama in English* (1930). Appointed Instructor of Playwriting, Yale University Theatre (1933).

OSCAR W. FIRKINS. Born at Minneapolis, 1864. Died March 7, 1932. Received his B.A. from the University of Minnesota (1884) and his M.A. (1898). Professor of Comparative Literature at the University of Minnesota. Member of the National Institute of Arts and Letters. A contributor to *The Atlantic Monthly, The North American Review,* the *Yale Review.* From 1915 to 1918 reviewed poetry for *The Nation.* From 1919 to 1921 was dramatic critic for *The Weekly Review.* Author of: *Ralph Waldo Emerson* (1915); *William Dean Howells; Jane Austen* (1920); *Cyrus Northrop: A Memoir* (1925); *Two Passengers For Chelsea and Other Plays* (1928); *The Revealing Moment and Other Plays* (1932); and *The Bride of Quietness and Other Plays* (1932).

GILBERT W. GABRIEL. Born in Brooklyn, January 18, 1890. A.B. Williams (1912), reporter on the *New York Evening Sun* (1912), literary editor of the *Sun* (1915); music critic (1917-1924); dramatic critic of the *Telegram* (1924-1925); dramatic critic of the *Sun* (1925-1929); since 1929 dramatic critic of the *New York American* and for the Universal News Service. Author of *The Seven-Branched Candlestick* (1917); *Jiminy* (1922); *Brownstone Front* (1924); *Famous Pianists and Composers* (1928); *Time Was* (1931); *I, James Lewis* (1932); and *Great Fortune* (1933).

ROBERT GARLAND. Born April 29, 1895, at Baltimore, Maryland. Educated at public and private schools in Baltimore and abroad. Feature writer, the *Baltimore News* (1920-22); dramatic editor and critic of the *Baltimore American* (1922-24); dramatic editor, critic and columnist, *Baltimore Daily Post* (1924-26); columnist the *New York World-Telegram* (1928); dramatic critic the *New York World-Telegram* since 1928. Author of the following plays: *The Double Miracle* (1915), *Importance of Being a Roughneck* (1919), *At Night All Cats Are Gray* (1933), etc.

FRANCIS HACKETT. Born Kilkenny, Ireland, January 21, 1883. Educated at Clongowes Wood College, Kildare, Ireland. Came to America in 1900. With a law firm in New York until 1902. Editorial writer on the *Chicago Evening Post* (1906-1909). Editor of the *Friday Literary Review* of the same paper (1909-1911); associate editor of the *New Republic* (1914-1922). Author of *Ireland—A Study in Nationalism* (1918); *Horizons* (1918); *The Invisible Censor* (1920); *The Story of The Irish Nation* (1922); *That Nice Young Couple* (a novel, 1924); *Henry the Eighth—A Personal History* (1929).

CLAYTON HAMILTON. Born, Brooklyn, November 14, 1881. B.A. Polytechnical Institute of Brooklyn (1900); M.A. Columbia (1901). Tutor in English Columbia and Barnard Colleges (1901-1904); extension lecturer at Columbia (1904); since 1900 has lectured throughout the country. Dramatic critic and associate editor of *The Forum* (1907-1909); dramatic critic, *The Bookman* (1910-1918); *Everybody's Magazine* (1911-1913); *Vogue* (1912-1920). Wrote many plays in collaboration with A. A. Thomas and others such as *The Big Idea; Thirty Days* (1916); and *The Better Understanding* (1917). Author: *Materials and Methods of Fiction* (1908), *The Theory of the Theatre* (1910), *Studies in Stagecraft* (1914), *On The Trail of Stevenson* (1915), *Problems of the Playwright* (1917), *A Manual of the Art of Fiction* (1918), *Seen on the Stage* (1920), *Conversations on the Contemporary Drama* (1924), *Wanderings* (1925), *Friend Indeed* (1926). Edited: Stevenson's *Treasure Island,* Pinero's *R. L. Stevenson As a Dramatist* (1914), *The Social Plays of A. W. Pinero,* etc.

PERCY HAMMOND. Born in Cadiz, Ohio, March 7, 1873. Student at Franklin (Ohio) College. Reporter, correspondent, editorial writer and dramatic critic of the *Chicago Evening Post* (1898-1908); dramatic critic of the *Chicago Tribune* (1908-1921). Also served as Paris correspondent. Dramatic critic of the *New York Tribune,* 1920; dramatic critic of the *New York Herald-Tribune* since 1924. Author of *But—Is It Art?* (1927).

NORMAN HAPGOOD. Born in Chicago, March 28, 1868. A.B. Harvard (1890); A.M., L.L.B. (1893). Dramatic critic of the *New York Commercial Advertiser* and *The Bookman* (1897-1902); editor of *Collier's Weekly* (1903-1912); editor *Harper's Weekly* (1913-1916); *Hearst's International Magazine* (1923-25). Author of: *Literary Statesmen* (1897), *Daniel Webster* (1899), *Abraham Lincoln* (1899), *George Washington* (1901), *The Stage in America* (1901), *Industry and Progress* (1911), *The Advancing Hour* (1920), *Up From The City Streets* (with Henry Moskowitz, 1927), *Why Janet Should Read Shakespeare* (1929).

WILLIAM DEAN HOWELLS. Born March 1, 1837, at Martin's Ferry, Ohio. Died April 11, 1920. Contributed youthful poems to *The Atlantic*. In 1860 published with John J. Piatt a book of poems called *The Two Friends*. Wrote a *Life of Lincoln* in the same year. Appointed consul to Venice (1861-1866). Worked on *The Atlantic* (1866-1881), became its editor (1872). In 1886 joined the staff of *Harper's Magazine,* conducting a department known as "The Editor's Study." Left *Harper's* temporarily but returned in 1901 to conduct "The Editor's Easy Chair" until his death. One of the first seven members of the National Institute of Arts and Letters. Later its president. Author of: *Italian Journeys* (1867), *Their Wedding Journey* (1871), *A Chance Acquaintance* (1872), *A Foregone Conclusion* (1875), *A Counterfeit Presentment* (1877), *The Lady of Aroostook* (1879), *The Undiscovered Country* (1880), *A Fearful Responsibility* (1881), *Dr. Breen's Practice* (1881), *A Modern Instance* (1882), *Three Villages* (1884), *The Rise of Silas Lapham* (1885), *The Minister's Charge* (1886), *Indian Summer* (1886), *April Hopes* (1888), *Annie Kilburn* (1889), *A Hazard of New Fortunes* (1890), *The Coast of Bohemia* (1893), *Their Silver Wedding Journey* (1899), *The Kentons* (1902), *The Son of Royal Langbirth* (1904), *Miss Bellard's Inspiration*. Wrote several farces such as *The Sleeping Car, The Elevator, The Mouse Trap,* and *Out of the Question*. Among his non-fictional and critical works are: *Modern Italian Poets* (1887), *Criticism and Fiction* (1891), *A Traveller in Altruria* (1894), *Impressions and Experiences* (1896), *Literary Friends and Acquaintances* (1896), *My Mark Twain: Reminiscences* (1910), *Tuscan Cities* (1885), *A Boy's Town* (1890), *London Films* (1905), and *Familiar Spanish Travels* (1913).

JAMES GIBBONS HUNEKER. Born Philadelphia, Pa., January 31, 1860. Died, February 9, 1921, in Brooklyn. Attended Roth's Military Academy from which he graduated in 1873. Studied law and the pianoforte. Moved to New York in 1886. Pupil of Alfredo Barili and Theodore Ritter. At Sorbonne in Paris; music under Georges Mathias at the Conservatoire. With Rafael Joseffy; taught the piano at the New York National Conservatory. Wrote for the *London Musical Courier* (1890-1895), *The New York Musical Courier* (1887-1902). Was music and dramatic critic of the *New York Recorder* (1891-1895) and occupied the same position on *The Advertiser* (1895-1897). In 1900 was music critic for the *New York Sun,* and on the same paper followed Franklin Fyles as dramatic critic (1902). In 1906-07 wrote constantly for *The Sun.* In 1912 while in Europe wrote for *The New York*

Times, and during the Great War, while Richard Aldrich was absent from his post, wrote as music critic for *The Times* (1918). In 1917 was music critic of the *Philadelphia Press.* In 1919 was musical editor of the *New York World.* His contemporaries in the field of musical criticism were Henry E. Krehbiel, Henry T. Finck, W. J. Henderson, Richard Aldrich, Charles Henry Meltzer, and Pitts Sanborn. Was a member of the Institute of Arts and Letters and an officer of the Legion of Honor. As a writer he was as versatile in criticizing the plastic arts as he was in writing about music and the drama. Among his many books are: *Mezzotints in Modern Music* (1899), *Chopin, The Man and His Music* (1900), *Melomaniacs* (1902), *Overtones* (1904), *Iconoclasts: A Book of Dramatists* (1905), *Visionaries* (1905), *Egotists: A Book of Supermen* (1909), *Promenades of an Impressionist* (1910), *Franz Liszt* (1911), *The Pathos of Distance* (1913), *New Cosmopolis* (1915), *Ivory Apes and Peacocks* (1915), *Unicorns* (1917), *Bedouins* (1920), *Steeplejack* (1920), *Painted Veils,* a novel (1920), *Variations* (1921). See *The Letters of James Gibbons Huneker,* edited by Josephine Huneker (1922); and *Intimate Letters of James Gibbons Huneker,* edited by Josephine Huneker (1924). Also *Essays* by James Huneker, with introduction by H. L. Mencken (1929).

WASHINGTON IRVING. Born in New York City, April 3, 1783. Died at Sunnyside, Irvington, N. Y., November 28, 1859. Poor health kept him from attending Columbia College. In 1804 went to Europe, returning in 1806 to be admitted to the bar. Took part in the trial of Aaron Burr, conducted in Richmond. Gave up all connection with his brother's mercantile ventures to devote himself to literature. In 1807-1809 appeared the *Salmagundi Papers;* in 1809 Dietrich Knickerbocker's *History of New York.* In 1814 Irving saw light military service, and then in 1815 went again to Europe. His literary career was fairly launched, and his friendship included Campbell, Moore and Walter Scott. In 1820 appeared *The Sketch Book* as by Geoffrey Crayon, Gent., followed in 1822 by *Bracebridge Hall.* In 1824, while he was making ready his *Letters of Jonathan Oldstyle* (which had first been published in *The Morning Chronicle* in 1802, when he was writing dramatic columns for this paper that his brother edited) he was also preparing *Tales of a Traveller.* In 1826 again abroad, soon attached to the Legation at Madrid. During this time he wrote and published *The Life and Voyages of Christopher Columbus* (1828); *The Chronicle and Conquest of Granada* (1829); and *The Alhambra* (1833). In 1832 returned to New York, and in 1842 John Tyler appointed him Minister to Spain. In intervening ten years he wrote *A Tour on the Prairies* (1835) and *Astoria* (1836). During the closing years of his career he issued such books as *Oliver Goldsmith* (1849); *Mahomet* (1849), and *The Life of George Washington.* Buried in Sleepy Hollow Cemetery. During 1823-24 Irving advised, and actually wrote several plays, with John Howard Payne (1791-1852). One was called *Richelieu, or The Broken Heart* (1826); another *Charles the Second, or The Merry Monarch* (1824).

HENRY JAMES. Born at New York, April 15, 1843, of Scotch, Irish and English extraction. Died in London, February 28, 1916. His father was a writer;

his brother, William, the famous Harvard psychologist. Early education at private schools. Adolescent period covered by him autobiographically in *A Small Boy* (1913) and *Notes of A Son and Brother* (1914). From 1855-1859 lived abroad with his parents. Studied law at Harvard (1862) and while there began writing. In 1869 he took up his residence abroad, a step which prompted him eventually (July, 1915) to become a naturalized British citizen. In 1916 among King George V's New Year's honors was The Order of Merit for James. Among his most distinctive works are: *The American* (1877), *The Europeans* (1878), *Daisy Miller* (1878), *French Poets and Novelists* (1878), *Roderick Hudson* (1879), *Hawthorne* (1879), *The Portrait of a Lady* (1880), *The Bostonians* (1886), *Essays in London and Elsewhere* (1893), *What Maisie Knew* (1897), *The Awkward Age* (1899), *The Wings of the Dove* (1902), *The Ambassadors* (1903), *The Golden Bowl* (1905), *English Hours* (1905), *The American Scene* (1907), *Italian Hours* (1909), *A Small Boy* (1913), *Notes of A Son and Brother* (1914), *Notes on Novelists* (1914). For a bibliography of James, see Frederic A. King's valuable work. James's interest in the theatre was very keen. From 1875 to 1887 he contributed occasional articles on plays and players to *The Atlantic, The Century, The Galaxy,* and *The Nation.* In 1891 and 1893 he wrote two papers on Ibsen. See his *Essays in London and Elsewhere.* In 1895 he wrote on Alexander Dumas, fils. See *Notes on Novelists.* His theatrical ventures included a dramatization of *Daisy Miller* (1882); a stage version of *The American* (1891), a book of four comedies (*Tenant, Disengaged, Album* and *Reprobate,* 1894); *Guy Donsville* (1895), produced in London by George Alexander; *Covering End* (1898), produced later by Forbes-Robertson as *High Bid.* Other attempts include *Other House* and *Outcry.* See Brander Matthews's "Henry James and the Theatre" in *Playwrights on Playmaking.* Also James's novel, *The Tragic Muse.*

JOSEPH WOOD KRUTCH. Born Knoxville, Tenn., November 25, 1893. B.A. University of Tennessee (1915); M.A. Columbia (1916); Ph.D. Columbia (1923). Instructor in English at Columbia (1917-1918). Associate professor of English at Polytechnic Institute of Brooklyn (1920-1923). Dramatic critic and associate editor of *The Nation* since 1924. Literary editor 1933. Special lecturer with rank of professor at Vassar (1924-1925). Associate Professor at School of Journalism at Columbia since 1925. Member of the editorial board of the Literary Guild of America since 1926. Author of *Comedy and Conscience After The Restoration* (1924); (with others) *Our Changing Morals* (1925); *Edgar Allan Poe—A Study in Genius* (1926); *The Modern Temper* (1929); *Five Masters* (1931); *Experience and Art* (1932).

WILLIAM LEGGETT. Born on April 30, 1801, in New York. Died May 29, 1839. Went to Georgetown College but did not graduate. In 1822 was appointed midshipman. In 1823 on the "Cyana" in the Mediterranean. Court martialed in 1825 for a duel. During this year published his youthful verse, *Leisure Hours At Sea.* Resigned his commission (1826) and published another volume of verse, *Journals of the Ocean.* Launched a magazine, *The Critic,* which lasted ten months. Was the author (1829) of *Tales and*

Sketches of a Country Schoolmaster. In 1829 became part owner and assistant editor with William Cullen Bryant (1794-1878) of the *New York Evening Post,* and from June 1834 to October 1835 served as its editor while Bryant was abroad. Was regarded as the champion of Edwin Forrest in the theatre. (See extracts from his review of Forrest's Jack Cade in Montrose J. Moses's *The Fabulous Forrest.*) Bryant was called home from abroad because of Leggett's severe illness (1835-1836). Leggett resigned from the *Post* in October 1836. From December 1836 until September 1837 he edited *The Plain Dealer;* wrote a daily column for *The Examiner.* In 1839 was sent by Van Buren as a diplomatic agent to Guatemala. Buried in New Rochelle. See *Collection of the Political Writings of William Leggett* (1840). Also Allan Nevins's *The Evening Post: A Century of Journalism* (1922).

LUDWIG LEWISOHN. Born in Berlin, May 30, 1882. Brought to America in 1890. B.A. and M.A. at the College of Charleston, S. C. (1901); M.A. Columbia (1903); Litt.D. (1914). On the editorial staff of Doubleday, Page (1904-1905). Magazine writer (1905-1910). Instructor in German, University of Wisconsin (1910-1911). Associate Professor of German Language and Literature, Ohio State University (1911-1919). Dramatic critic of *The Nation* (1919). Associate editor (1920-1924). Author of *The Broken Square* (1908); *A Night in Alexandria* (dramatic poem, 1909); *German Style* (An introduction to the study of German Prose) (1910); *The Modern Drama* (1915); *The Spirit of German Literature* (1916); *The Poets of Modern France* (1918); *The Drama and the Stage* (1922); *Upstream* (1922); *Don Juan* (1923); *Creative Life* (1924); *Israel* (1925); *Cities and Men* (1927); *Roman Summer* (1927); *The Island Within* (1928); *Adam* (1929); *Mid-Channel* (1929); *Stephen Escott* (1930); *Last Days of Shylock* (1931); *Expression in America* (1932). Edited, with William P. Trent, *The Letters of an American Farmer* (1904) and *A Book of Modern Criticism* (1919). Translated Sudermann's *Indian Lily* (1911); Halbe's *Youth* (1916). Editor and chief translator in English of the works of Hauptmann. Lecturer on drama and poetry.

ROBERT LITTELL. Born Milwaukee, Wis., May 15, 1896. Educated at Groton and Harvard. Assistant editor of *The New Republic* (1922-1927). Dramatic critic of *The New York Evening Post* (1927-1929). Dramatic critic of *The New York World* (1929-1931) and columnist on the same paper (1931). Dramatic critic *Theatre Arts Monthly* (1928-1929). Frequent contributor to *Harper's, The New Republic,* etc. Author of: *Read America First* (1926); *Candles In The Storm* (a novel, 1934).

RICHARD LOCKRIDGE. Born September 26, 1898, St. Joseph, Missouri. Educated at Kansas City schools and the Junior College, Kansas City. Enlisted in the navy. Missouri University (1919); George Washington University (1920). Served on the staff of the *Scrap Metal Reporter* (1920). Returned to Kansas City (1921) and from 1921-1922 reported for the *Kansas City Kansan,* the *Kansas City Journal* and the *Kansas City Star.* Came to New York in the fall of 1922. Joined the staff of the *New York Sun* (1923) as rewrite man. Dramatic critic of the *Sun* since 1928. Author of *Darling of Misfortune: Edwin Booth 1833-1893* (1932). Frequent contributor to *The New Yorker*.

KENNETH MACGOWAN. Born Winthrop, Mass., Nov. 30, 1888. Harvard. Assistant dramatic critic of the *Boston Transcript* (1910-1913). Dramatic and literary editor of the *Philadelphia Evening Ledger* (1914-1917). 1918 on the staff of the *New York Tribune*. Dramatic critic of the *New York Globe* (1919-1923). Dramatic critic of *Vogue* (1920-1924). Dramatic critic and associate editor of *Theatre Arts Magazine* (1919-1925). Director of the Provincetown Players (1924-1925). Also with R. E. Jones and Eugene O'Neill at the Greenwich Village Theatre (1925-1927). Producer for Actor's Theatre (1927). Among productions made under his management were *Fashion, All God's Chillun, The Great God Brown,* and *Desire Under the Elms;* and, with Joseph Verner Reed, *Children of Darkness,* Jane Cowl's *Twelfth Night* and *Springtime for Henry*. Editor, editor-in-chief and associate director for R.K.O., 1932. Author of *The Theatre of Tomorrow* (1921); *Continental Stagecraft* (with R. E. Jones, 1922); *Masks and Demons* (with Herman Rosse, 1923), *What Is Wrong With Marriage?* (with Dr. G. B. Hamilton, 1929); and *Footlights Across America* (1929).

BURNS MANTLE. Born in Watertown, N. Y., December 23, 1873. Educated at public schools and Normal College. Dramatic editor of the *Denver Times* (1898-1900), the *Denver Republican* (1901), the *Chicago Inter-Ocean* (1901-1906), *The Chicago Tribune* (1906-1907), Sunday Editor (1907-1910); dramatic critic of the *New York Evening Mail* (1910-1922), and, since 1922, dramatic critic of the *Daily News*. Editor of *The Best Plays,* an annual compilation which has appeared since 1919; and with Garrison P. Sherwood of *The Best Plays 1909-1919* (1933). Author of *American Playwrights Today* (1929).

(JAMES) BRANDER MATTHEWS. Born in New Orleans, February 21, 1852. Died in New York, March 31, 1929. Educated in private schools in New York. Graduated from Columbia (1871) and from Columbia Law School (1875). Was admitted to the bar. A.M. Columbia (1874). In 1891 was a lecturer in English at Columbia and from 1892 to 1900 was Professor of Literature at the University. From 1900 to 1924 Professor of Dramatic Literature at Columbia. One of the founders of the Authors Club (1882), the Players Club (1889), and the Dunlap Society; and one of the organizers of the American Copyright League. In 1907 was decorated by France with the Legion of Honor. In 1908 elected to the American Academy of Arts and Letters. Chancellor of American Academy (1922-1924). President of the Modern Language Association (1910). President of the National Institute of Arts and Letters (1913-1914). First chairman of Simplified Spelling Board (1906). Officer of the Legion of Honor (1922). Collaborated with G. H. Jessup on several comedies, and with Bronson Howard in the writing of *Peter Stuyvesant* (1899). Wrote several volumes of fiction such as *A Secret of the Sea and Other Stories*. Among his better known works are: *The Theatres* of Paris (1880); *French Dramatists of the Nineteenth Century* (1881); *Actors and Actresses of the United States and Great Britain* (with Laurence Hutton, 1886); *Americanisms and Briticisms* (1892); *Studies of the Stage* (1894); *Vignettes of Manhattan* (1894); *Introduction to the Study of American Literature* (1896); *Studies in Local Color* (1899); *The Action and the Word* (1900); *The Historical Novel and Other Essays* (1901); *Parts of Speech, Essays on English* (1901); *The Philosophy of the Short Story* (1901); *The Development of the Drama* (1903); *The Short Story* (1907); *Americans of the Future and Other Essays* (1909); *Molière: His Life and Works* (1910); *A Study of the Drama* (1910); *Shakespeare as a Playwright* (1913); *On Acting* (1914); *The Oxford Book of American Essays* (1914); *A Book About The Theatre* (1916); *These Many Years* (1917); *Principles of Playmaking* (1919); *Essays on English* (1921); *Playwrights on Playmaking* (1923); *Rip Van Winkle Goes to the Play* (1926). Editor of the Publications of the Dramatic Museum of Columbia University.

JAMES STETSON METCALFE. Born in Buffalo, June 27, 1858. Died, May 26, 1927. A.B. Yale (1879). A.M. Yale (1891). Editor and publisher, *The Modern Age* (1883-4). Editorial writer, *The Buffalo Express* (1884-85). Editor of the *People's Pictorial Press* (1886). Manager of the American Newspaper Publishers' Association (1886-89). Dramatic critic of *Life,* 1889 to 1920. Afterwards on the *Wall Street Journal*. Literary editor of *Life* (1890-1895). Managing editor, *Cosmopolitan Magazine* (1895). Democratic candidate for the Assembly (1913). Chevalier of the Legion of Honor (1919). Author of *Mythology for Moderns* (1900); *The American Slave* (1900); *Another Three Weeks* (1908); *The Diary of a District Messenger* (1909); *Jane Street* (1912).

MONTROSE J. MOSES. Born in New York City, September 2, 1878. Died March 29, 1934. Educated at private schools, Montgomery, Ala., and graduated B.S. College of the City of New York (1899). Editorial staff of *The Literary Digest* (1900-02), dramatic editor of *The Reader's Magazine* (1903-07), dramatic critic of *The Independent* (1908-1918), *The Book News Monthly* (Philadelphia, 1908-1918), *The Bellman* (Minneapolis, 1910-1919). Editor of Drama Department for Collier's National Encyclopedia. Drama articles for the *North American Review*, 1931, seq. Among his many books on the drama and theatre history are: *Famous Actor Families in America* (1906); *Children's Books and Reading* (1907); *Henrik Ibsen, The Man and His Plays* (1908); *The Literature of the South* (1909); *Maurice Maeterlinck* (1911); *The Life of Heinrich Conried* (1916); *The American Dramatist* (1911, 1917); *Clyde Fitch and His Letters* (in collaboration with Virginia Gerson, 1924); and *The Fabulous Forrest, The Record of An American Actor* (1929). Editor: *Everyman, a Morality Play* (annotated with critical introduction 1903, 1908); memorial edition of *The Plays of Clyde Fitch* (1915). American editor, *The Green Room Book and Anglo-American Dramatic Register; Representative British Dramas: Victorian and Modern* (1918); *Representative Plays by American Dramatists* (3 volumes, 1918); *A Treasury of Plays for Children* (1921); *Representative Continental*

Dramas, Revolutionary and Transitional (1924); *Six Plays of David Belasco* (1928); *British Plays From The Restoration to 1820* (1929); *Dramas of Modernism and Their Forerunners* (1931); *Ring Up The Curtain* (1932); *Representative American Dramas: National and Local* (1933); *The American Theatre as Seen By Its Critics, 1752 to 1934* (in collaboration with John Mason Brown, 1934).

GEORGE JEAN NATHAN. Born at Fort Wayne, Ind., February 14, 1882. A.B. Cornell (1904). 1904-1907 on the staff of the *New York Herald.* Subsequently dramatic editor of *The Bohemian.* Contributed articles on the theatre to *Harper's Weekly, Munsey's Magazine, Theatre Magazine* and *The Green Book.* Dramatic critic of the *Burr McIntosh Monthly.* 1912-1919 syndicated newspaper articles on the drama. Dramatic critic of *Puck* (1915). Dramatic critic, and with H. L. Mencken, editor of *The Smart Set* (1908-1923) and of *The American Mercury* (1923-1932). Dramatic critic of *Judge* since 1922 and *Vanity Fair* since 1930. Editor and dramatic critic of *The American Spectator* since 1932. Author of *Europe After 8:15* (with Mencken and Wright, 1914); *Another Book About The Theatre* (1915); *Mr. George Jean Nathan Presents* (1917); *Bottoms Up* (1917); *The Popular Theatre* (1918); *A Book Without a Title* (1919); *Comedians All* (1919); *The American Credo* (with Mencken, 1920); *Heliogabalus* (with Mencken, 1920); *The Theatre, The Drama, The Girls* (1921); *The Critic and The Drama* (1923); *The World in Falseface* (1923); *Materia Critica* (1924); *The Autobiography of An Attitude* (1925); *The House of Satan* (1926); *Land of The Pilgrims' Pride* (1927); *Art of The Night* (1928); *Monks Are Monks* (1929); *Testament of a Critic* (1931); *Intimate Notebooks of George Jean Nathan* (1932); *Since Ibsen* (1933). See Isaac Goldberg's *The Theatre of George Jean Nathan* (1926).

H. T. PARKER. Born in Boston, April 29, 1867. Died March 30, 1934. Harvard (1886-1889). Studied in Europe (1889-1891). New York correspondent of the *Boston Transcript* (1892-1898, 1901-1903). London correspondent for the *Boston Transcript* and *New York Commercial Advertiser* (1898-1900). Dramatic critic (1903-1904) and dramatic and music critic (1904-1905) for the *New York Globe.* Dramatic and music critic for the *Boston Transcript* (1905-1934). Author of *Eight Notes* (essays on music, 1922).

EDGAR ALLAN POE. Born at Boston, Mass., January 19, 1805. Died at Baltimore, Oct. 7, 1849. His family of Irish origin. Both mother and father were on the stage. The parents died, leaving three children. Edgar was adopted by John Allan of Richmond, Va. It was in Richmond that Poe was educated until Allan took him to England when he was sent there in 1815. In 1820 Poe returned to Richmond. Matriculated at the University of Virginia, Charlottesville, February 14, 1826. In May 1827, he enlisted in the United States Army. That year he published *Tamerlane and Other Poems.* After two years' service was honorably discharged with rank of Sergeant Major. *Al Aaraaf and Other Poems* appeared in 1829. In 1830 entered West Point. The next year (1831), he was discharged from the Military Academy for neglect of duty. Allan cut him off from any pecuniary expectations. Published another volume of verse. He now lived (1833) with his aunt, Mrs. Clemm, and was soon married to the youthful Virginia Clemm whose tragic life closed in 1847. Between 1835 and 1847 Poe was associated with *The Southern Literary Messenger, Burton's Gentleman's Magazine,* and *Graham's Magazine.* He also wrote for *The New York Evening Mirror,* in association with N. P. Willis, and for *The Broadway Journal,* and tried to further his own magazine, *The Stylus* (1843). In 1837 appeared *Tales of the Grotesque and Arabesque;* in 1845 *The Raven and Other Poems.* In 1846 was living in his cottage at Fordham where his wife died. He wrote often on the theatre and was so conscientious that he went seven times to see Mrs. Mowatt's *Fashion* before writing his review of it.

ARTHUR RUHL. Born at Rockford, Ill., October 1, 1876. A.B. Harvard (1899). On the *New York Evening Sun* (1899-1904). With *Collier's Weekly* (1904-1913); dramatic critic of the *New York Tribune* (1913-1914); correspondent for *Collier's* in France and Belgium (1914), Central Europe (1915), Russia (1916-1917), Baltic States (1919). Correspondent for the *New York Evening Post* in the Balkan States and Poland (1920). Berlin correspondent of the *New York Herald-Tribune* (1925-1926). Drama department, *New York Herald-Tribune* (1927). Author of *A History of Track Athletics in America* (1905); *A Break in Training* (1906); *The Other Americans* (1908); *Second Nights* (1914); *Antwerp to Gallipoli* (1916); *White Nights* (1917); *New Masters in the Baltic* (1921); *The Central Americans* (1928); *With the American Relief Administration in Russia in 1922-1923.*

GILBERT SELDES. Born in Alliance, N. J., January 3, 1893. Prepared at Central High School, Philadelphia. A.B. Harvard (1914). Music critic of the *Philadelphia Evening Ledger* (1914-1916). Newspaper correspondent abroad during the World War. Sergeant in the United States Army (1918). Political correspondent in Washington for *L'Echo de Paris* (1918). Associate editor of *Collier's* (1919). Associate editor and later managing editor of *The Dial* (1920-1923). Dramatic critic of *The Dial* (1919). Dramatic critic of the *Graphic* (1929-1931). Columnist for the *New York Evening Journal* since 1931. Contributing editor to *The New Republic.* Author of *The United States and the War* (1917); *The Seven Lively Arts* (1924); *The Stammering Century* (1928); *The Movies and the Talkies* (1929); *The Wings of the Eagle* (1929); *The Future of Drinking* (1930); *The Years of the Locust* (1933). Has written two novels, *The Victory Murders* (1927) and *The Square Emerald* (1928), and the following plays—*The Wisecrackers* (1925) *The Orange Comedy* (an adaptation, 1926); and *Lysistrata* (an adaptation, 1930).

SIME SILVERMAN. Born at Cortland, N. Y., May 19, 1872, died September 22, 1933. Educated at grammar schools in Cortland and Syracuse, then went to business school, but came as young man to New York and got his first job on *The Morning Telegraph.* With Al Greason and Epes Winthrop started *Variety* ("The Showman's Bible") in 1905. His now famous magazine gives each week a lively and hard-boiled picture of all phases of "the show business." It is noted for its slang, its box-office slant on productions and its expression of the Broadway attitude.

R. DANA SKINNER. Born in Detroit, Mich., April 21, 1893. Graduated from Harvard (1915). On Editorial Staff of the *Boston Herald* (1915-1917). Went Overseas in 1917. Became Captain in the U. S. Air Service and American Secretary for the Inter-Allied Advisory Committee on Aviation. Received citation from General Pershing, the Legion of Honor from France and the order of Saints Maurizio and Lazzaro from Italy. Banking. Associate Editor and dramatic critic of *The Commonweal* since 1924. Author *Our Changing Theatre* (1931).

J. RANKEN TOWSE. Born at Streatham, Surrey, England, on April 2, 1845. Died at Streatham, April 12, 1933. Went to school at Highgate and studied at Cambridge. In 1869, imbued with the theatre traditions of Old Drury, the Haymarket and Samuel Phelps at Sadler's Wells, he came to the United States. He was never naturalized. From 1870 to 1874 Mr. Towse served as reporter, city editor, assistant editor and foreign editor of the *New York Evening Post*. In 1874 he became dramatic critic of the *Post* and held the position until his retirement on June 24, 1927. During these years he contributed frequently to the columns of *The Nation*. Author of *Sixty Years in The Theatre* (1916).

ANDREW CARPENTER WHEELER (Nym Crinkle). Born in New York, June 4, 1835. Died March 10, 1903, at Monsey, N. Y. Educated at public schools and at the College of the City of New York. In 1857 became a reporter on *The New York Times*. Resigned position to go to Kansas to get taste of frontier life. In 1858 obtained a job on *The Milwaukee Sentinel*. During the Civil War was a correspondent at the front. At the end of the war returned to New York and over the signature of "Trinculo" contributed to *The Weekly Leader*. Became dramatic editor of *The Leader;* soon afterwards was offered the same position on *The World,* where he first signed himself Nym Crinkle. Was dramatic critic of *The Sun* for two years, but returned to *The World*. In 1889 wrote every week a column, known as "Nym Crinkle's Feuilleton" in *The New York Dramatic Mirror*. Author of: *The Chronicles of Milwaukee* (1861); *The Twins* (a comedy); *The Iron Trail* (1876); *The Toltec Cup; The Primrose Path of Dalliance; Easter In A Hospital Bed;* and, with Edgar Mayhew Bacon, *Nation Builders*. After his retirement from journalism he wrote under the pen name of J. P. Mowbray *A Journey To Nature; The Conquering of Kate* and *Tangled Up in Beulah Land*. See *The New York Dramatic Mirror,* March 21, 1903, and Percy MacKaye's *Epoch: The Life of Steele MacKaye*.

RICHARD GRANT WHITE. Born at New York, May 22, 1821. Died in New York, April 8, 1885. Graduated at New York University in 1839. Studied medicine and the law. Contributed musical, art and dramatic criticisms to the *New York Courier and Enquirer,* and was editor of the same paper

(1854-1859). Contributed articles on Shakespeare to *Putnam's Magazine* (1853). From 1860-1861 was on the *New York World*. Became chief clerk of the United States Revenue Marine Bureau for the district of New York, which post he occupied from 1861 to 1878. Contributed a series of "Yankee Letters" from 1863 to 1867 to the *London Spectator*. Wrote: *Shakespeare's Scholar* (1854); edited Shakespeare's plays (1857-1863), preparing in 1883 the popular Riverside Edition of Shakespeare. Author of *Memoirs of the Life of William Shakespeare* (1865) and *Studies in Shakespeare* (1866). Issued many philological studies, such as *Words and Their Uses: Past and Present.*

WALT WHITMAN. Born at West Hills, L. I., May 31, 1819; died at Camden, N. J., March 26, 1892. Educated in Brooklyn and New York at the public schools. Learned carpentry and printing. At seventeen taught school on Long Island. In 1839 edited and published a weekly paper at Huntington, L. I. From 1846 to 1848 edited *The Brooklyn Eagle.* During this time he wrote about the theatre and commented on music and art. In 1848 he went to New Orleans, working on *The New Orleans Crescent.* In 1850 established *The Freeman* in Brooklyn. In 1855 appeared *Leaves of Grass,* afterwards enlarged and revised. During the Civil War he served as an army nurse; the results of his experiences seen in *Drum Taps* (1865) and *Memoranda During the War* (1867), consisting of letters sent to *The New York Times.* From 1865-1873 he held a clerkship in the Treasury Department at Washington. Had been dismissed in 1865 from the Interior Department because of his *Leaves of Grass.* In 1873 he had a slight stroke and resigned his position, moving to Camden, N. J., where he resided until his death. See Emery Holloway's *Whitman: An Interpretation in Narrative* (1926); Horace Traubel's *With Walt Whitman in Camden* (1906-12); Whitman's *Gathering of the Forces,* edited by Cleveland Rodgers and John Black (1920), and *The Uncollected Poetry and Prose of Walt Whitman* (2 vols. 1921), edited by Emery Holloway.

WALTER WINCHELL. Born New York City, April 7, 1897. Left school at thirteen to go on the stage with Gus Edwards in "Newsboys Sextette" of Edwards 1910 *Song Review.* Appeared in one act in vaudeville, 1917. With U. S. Naval Reserve during World War. Returned to vaudeville in song and dance act. Joined the staff of *Vaudeville News* (1922). With *The New York Evening Graphic* (1924-1929) as columnist, dramatic critic and dramatic editor. Columnist on *The New York Mirror* (syndicated) since June 10, 1929. Also dramatic critic. Has appeared in several movie shorts for Warners and Universal. Sold one movie, *Broadway Thru a Keyhole* to Twentieth Century Productions. On the air for several large concerns.

WILLIAM WINTER. Born at Gloucester, Mass., July 15, 1836. Died, June 30, 1917. Early education at Gloucester, Boston and Cambridge schools. LL.B. Harvard Law School (1857). Litt.D. Brown (1895). In 1859 in New York as literary critic of *The Saturday Press.* Dramatic critic of *The Albion,* New York (1861-1865), often signing himself "Mercutio." From July 12, 1865, to

August 14, 1909, was dramatic critic of the *New York Tribune.* Thereafter he wrote for *Harper's Weekly* and other periodicals. In 1916 was given an impressive testimonial by the profession. Among his best known books are: *English Rambles and Other Fugitive Papers* (1884); *Henry Irving* (1885); *The Jeffersons* (1881); *Life and Art of Edwin Booth* (1893); *Shakespeare's England* (1886); *Old Shrines and Ivy* (1892); *Shadows of the Stage* (1892-1895); *Life and Art of Joseph Jefferson* (1894); *Ada Rehan* (1898); *Other Days of the Stage* (1908); *Old Friends* (1909); *Poems* (1909); *Life and Art of Richard Mansfield* (1910); *The Wallet of Time* (1913); *Life of Tyrone Power* (1913); *Vagrant Memories* (1915); *Shakespeare on the Stage* (1911-1915); *Life of David Belasco* (1918). Edited Prompt Copy of Booth's *Richelieu, Ruy Blas, Brutus, Richard III, The Fool's Revenge* and Daly's *As You Like It, The Taming of the Shrew* and *The School for Scandal.*

ALEXANDER WOOLLCOTT. Born, Phalanx, N. J., Jan. 19, 1887. Educated at Central High School, Philadelphia and Hamilton College. 1914-1922 dramatic critic of *The New York Times.* 1922-1925 dramatic critic of the *New York Herald.* 1925-1928 dramatic critic of the *New York World.* Since 1928 conducted "Shouts and Murmurs" page in *The New Yorker.* Acted in *Brief Moment* (1931). Co-author with George S. Kaufman of *The Channel Road* (1928) and *The Dark Tower* (1933). Author of *Mrs. Fiske—Her Views on Acting, Actors and the Problems of the Stage* (1917); *The Command is Foreword* (1919); *Shouts and Murmurs* (1922); *Mr. Dickens Goes To The Play* (1923); *Enchanted Aisles* (1924); *The Story of Irving Berlin* (1925); *Two Gentlemen and a Lady* (1925); *Going To Pieces* (1928); and *While Rome Burns* (1934). Popular on the radio as The Town Crier.

STARK YOUNG. Born Como, Miss., Oct. 11, 1881. B.A. University of Mississippi (1901), M.A. Columbia (1902). Instructor of English, University of Mississippi (1904-1907), instructor of English Literature at the University of Texas (1907-1910), Professor of Literature at the University of Texas (1907-1910), Professor of English, Amherst (1915-1921). Member of the editorial staff of *The New Republic* since 1921; associate editor of *Theatre Arts Monthly* (1921-1924), dramatic critic of *The New York Times* (1924-1925). Since 1925, dramatic critic of *The New Republic.* Author of *The Blind Man at the Window* (verse, 1906); *Guenevere* (play in verse, 1906); *Madretta Addio, The Twilight Saint; The Seven Kings and the Wind; The Queen of Sheba; The Dead Poet; The Star in the Trees* (one act plays in prose and verse, 1911); *Three Plays* (1919); *The Flower in Drama* (1923); *The Three Fountains* (1924); *The Saint* (1924); *Sweet Times and The Blue Policeman; The Colonnade* (a play); *Rose Windows* (one-act play); *Glamour; Heaven Trees* (a novel); *Encaustics* (1926); *The Theatre* (1927); *The Torches Flare* (a novel, 1927); *River House* (a novel, 1929); *The Street of the Islands* (short stories, 1930); *So Red the Rose* (a novel, 1934).